Y0-BWW-996

Elements of Formal Semantics

An Introduction to Logic for
Students of Language

Elements of Formal Semantics

An Introduction to Logic for Students of Language

John N. Martin

Department of Philosophy
University of Cincinnati
Cincinnati, Ohio

1987

ACADEMIC PRESS, INC.
Harcourt Brace Jovanovich, Publishers
Orlando San Diego New York Austin
Boston London Sydney Tokyo Toronto

ACADEMIC PRESS, INC.
Orlando, Florida 32887

United Kingdom Edition published by
ACADEMIC PRESS INC. (LONDON) LTD.
24–28 Oval Road, London NW1 7DX

Library of Congress Cataloging in Publication Data

Martin, John N.
Elements of formal semantics.

Bibliography: p.
Includes index.
1. Semantics (Philosophy) 2. Logic. I. Title.
B840.M34 1987 160 86-17212
ISBN 0–12–474855–4 (hardcover) (alk. paper)
ISBN 0–12–474856–2 (paperback) (alk. paper)

PRINTED IN THE UNITED STATES OF AMERICA

87 88 89 90 9 8 7 6 5 4 3 2 1

To my mother
DOROTHY MARTIN SWIFT

Contents

Preface

This book is an introduction to that part of logic of most interest to linguists and philosophers of language. Quite generally, formal semantics is the study of meaning for formal languages defined and explored by means of set theory. For this reason it is sometimes called set theoretic semantics. Since set theory is a technical idiom, the interesting results of semantics are inaccessible without special training. The purpose of this book is to bring the reader to a point from which he or she may easily read and evaluate ordinary research in formal semantics. The book is also intended to provide a solid introduction to standard logic and to more specialized textbooks on modal logic, Montague grammar, and philosophical logic.

Propositional and first-order logic are treated separately, including for each its syntax, natural deduction proof theory, and formal semantics with Henkin-style completeness proofs. The nine chapters of the book divide into groups of three, each suitable to a quarter-length course. Standard logic is fully covered in the first two parts, and the third part is suitable for a more advanced course in philosophical logic.

Readers are first introduced to proof construction informally, the way logicians and mathematicians have traditionally learned to do proofs, rather than through the artificial means typical of many texts that expect students to work immediately with fully defined and rigorously stated deduction rules. Precise statements come in later chapters, when they can be appreciated and contrasted with practice.

Set theory, the working language of formal semantics, is employed throughout. An early chapter introduces the ideas, and they are used extensively later in definitions, proofs, and exercises. When finished, a reader should have no difficulty understanding and verifying the technical claims found in standard works.

An effort is made to present semantics as a lively field of research. There is extensive discussion of methodology and the criteria used in evaluating rival accounts, both in the abstract and in application to examples of competing theories. Among the nonstandard logics discussed are Aristotle's syllogistic, many-valued logic, intuitionistic logic, supervaluations, free logic, quantified modal logic, intensional logic, and situational semantics.

Logic is made relevant to philosophy students by underlining its link to traditional problems from the history of philosophy, to the ideas of Plato, Aristotle, Ockham, Leibniz, Frege, Russell, Quine, Carnap, and Davidson. Also, philosophical controversies unique to logic are explained, such as the debate between intuitionistic and classical logic, and the metaphysics of possible world semantics.

The subject is made accessible to linguists by special attention to differences between the vocabulary and methodology of linguistics and those of logic. Differences in approach to grammar and in criteria of evaluation are explained at some length, as well as the implications for natural language that logicians see in their work.

Techniques of more advanced metalogic are represented by the book's use throughout of standard distinctions from syntax, proof theory, and semantics. Special emphasis is given to the metatheoretic use of inductive sets and abstract algebra. Diverse examples of grammar and proof theory are presented as special cases of inductive sets, and the substitutional properties of extensional and intensional logics are discussed as congruence relations between algebraic structures.

My experience is that introductory students are perfectly capable of evaluating rival theories. They enjoy seeing the subject as one grounded in traditional issues but still in a state of evolution. It is this vitality that I find interesting in the study of language, and I hope this book helps to convey it to others.

I would like to thank my colleagues William Todd for inspiration and encouragement, John Schlipf for helpful comments on Chapter 6, and Jenefer Robinson, who kindly proofread the entire book. Most of all I would like to thank my students who suffered through various even-less-perfect versions. Word processing support for AcademicFont and Edix/Wordix was graciously provided by Joshua Sommer of University MicroComputers and Susan MacFadden of Emerging Technology. Jong-Boon Moon, Douglas Slaton, and Cheryl Hilton also deserve thanks for help in producing a legible typescript. Funds for part of the research leading to the book and for manuscript preparation were provided by the University of Cincinnati Research Council and Taft Fund.

JOHN MARTIN

1

Informal Reasoning

1.1 LEARNING PROOFS BY IMITATION

Every science has its own method, designed to ensure that the proper sort of knowledge is acquired. Biologists experiment and archeologists do digs. To guarantee that the method is carried out correctly, it is often formalized by a series of almost ritualized conventions. Measurements are made according to agreed-upon scales, with standard devices, and reported in a prescribed style. Semantics too has its method, elaborated in special conventions. The method is partly deductive and partly inductive. It begins by laying down a series of definitions or fundamental assumptions (called *axioms*) dealing with the nature of language that are drawn from logic and mathematics. From these assumptions are then deduced various, more or less obvious, consequences (called *metatheorems*) that make up the corpus of the science, and it is the logical derivation of these results that constitutes the deductive part of the semantic method. The combined package of assumptions together with their consequences (called a *metatheory*) is then compared to the 'facts'. In the case of metatheory the facts are about language and reasoning, because these are the facts that the theory is supposed to explain. If facts, as we observe them, correspond to the assertions of the theory, then the theory provides a neat intellectual structure setting out basic assumptions or *laws*, and from them proofs of the diverse facts of the case. The comparison of the claims of semantic theory with the facts of usage constitutes the inductive or empirical part of the semantic method. In later chapters we shall study in detail the types of linguistic fact semantics endeavors to explain, but we must start by mastering the deductive form of the theory. In particular we must study what it is to perform a deduction or, as logicians say, to give a proof.

One of the distinctive features of semantics is that though it is like any other science in that it states its claims and results in language, it is unlike most sciences in that its subject matter is also language. In this respect semantics is like grammar or linguistics. We make a distinction between the language used for the statement of the semantic results, on the one hand, and the language which is the object of study, on the other. The language of the theory is called the *metalanguage*, and the particular language under investigation is called the *object language*. For example, if we were studying the grammar of French and conducting our study in English, English would be the metalanguage and French the object language. In later chapters we shall use a special mathematical language called set theory as our metalanguage, and various carefully defined symbolic languages as object languages.

The deductive part of semantic method requires doing proofs, which consists of deducing metatheorems from more basic assumptions and definitions. This chapter will explain what doing a proof amounts to. Fortunately, deductions are highly stylized and governed by very clear, fairly straightforward conventions. Mathematics students usually learn how to do proofs without ever receiving any formal instruction on how to do so. They pick up the technique simply by watching their teachers in class or reading enough examples in texts. The pointers they receive from instructors are really quite minimal. However, there *are* rules for constructing proofs, and the precise formulation of these rules is a large part of the discipline called logic.

In this chapter we provide a practical introduction to proof construction. Our account of proofs will not be complete or mathematically precise; we leave a fully adequate theoretical description of a 'proof' to later chapters. But what we shall study at this point is preliminary to more careful formulations later. We shall master the practical skill necessary to construct rough-and-ready, common or 'garden' proofs. The rules are easily stated and are much like the rules of a game. They are harder than those of checkers, but much easier than those of bridge. Each rule explains a particular kind of logical consequence that follows from previous assumptions on the stipulation that the assumptions and the consequence have a required grammatical form. Any combination of premises and conclusion with the right grammar is acceptable. An inference evaluated solely in terms of its grammar is called *formal*, and we may define a *proof* to be a series of sentences each of which is either an assumption or follows from previous sentences in the series by one of the rules of formal inference. In this chapter the rules of formal inference will be stated and explained.

It will not be our goal in this chapter to state these rules with all the full theoretical rigor and completeness that is possible. Complete and mathematically precise versions of the rules will have to wait until later chapters. What is needed at the beginning is a practical knowledge of logic and its rules, and so the versions we will meet first will be designed to that end. We shall call them *rules of thumb*, and they capture the understanding picked up rather informally by mathematics and logic students when they learn to produce proofs by imitating their teachers.

We will be learning, in effect, how to do proofs before mastering a theoretical understanding of what a proof is. It is like learning how to walk before learning the physiology of walking. This order is a natural one. It was only after years of experience at doing proofs that logicians tried to codify in a rigorous manner exactly what they were doing. Even though the rigorous statement of the logical rules is quite complex, it is perfectly possible to learn how to do proofs without first knowing the theory of proofs. Moreover, a critical appreciation of the precise formulations of the rules that we shall meet later presupposes a practical familiarity with doing proofs. These more precise versions that are found in proof theory are supposed to describe the more informal practice. As we shall see, the rules of informal proof are somewhat vague, and when theorists in proof theory attempt to formulate the rules precisely, there is often debate about just what the informal practice is.

We shall turn now to the less rigorous introduction to the logical rules of thumb. In this chapter we shall explain the rules, and in Chapter 2 we will see numerous examples. A rule will state when it is logically acceptable to reach a conclusion from a series of assumptions or hypotheses. For simplicity we introduce the following notation. We shall represent a series of assumptions or hypotheses by the letters $H_1, H_2, \ldots, H_n$, and a single conclusion by the letter C. Thus, the rules will explain when it is possible to reason from $H_1, H_2, \ldots, H_n$ to C.

1.2 SOME SEMANTIC IDEAS AND TRUTH-TABLES

1.2.1 Truth Relative to a Possible World

If there is one idea central to all of logic it is that of a logical leap of reasoning. Some inferences are 'logical' and others are not. If all men are mortal and Socrates is a man it follows 'logically' that Socrates is mortal, and it does not follow from those assumptions that Plato is mortal. The genuinely legitimate inferences can be labeled by various words of praise, for example 'reasonable', 'logical', 'rational'. But the adjective standardly applied by logicians to good steps of reasoning is 'valid'. One of the main objectives of logic as a science is to shed light on just what validity is and on which inferences are valid. This goal of explaining validity is reached by stages and consists first of defining some preliminary ideas. The preliminary concepts needed for the definition of validity are possible world and truth. We shall begin, therefore, with an introduction to these basic notions. With them we shall be able to define validity, and once validity itself is defined we shall then go on to define the important idea of soundness.

We do not really have to know very much about truth, just a few fairly obvious matters. First of all, in logic and philosophy generally, truth is understood to be a property of sentences—sometimes philosophers prefer to say it is a property of propositions. What is crucial is that we use the terms 'true' and 'false' to divide assertions into those that do and those that do not correctly describe a given situation. Situations that might be described in language are called by philosophers possible worlds. There are, for example, the possible worlds in which Pecos Bill dug the Rio Grande, in which cows fly, and in which things are exactly as they are in the actual world. These commonsense intuitions have been recognized in logic from the time of its inception in classical Greece, and have been gathered together into what is known as the correspondence theory of truth. The theory may be variously stated, but common to all versions is the idea that sentences either do or do not match up with a reality that language is designed to describe. The various bits of reality that we talk about may be called situations, facts, or, as logicians of the twentieth century prefer to call them, possible worlds. These insights may be formulated as a definition of truth and falsity: if a sentence correctly describes a given possible world, the sentence is said to be true of or true 'in' that possible world; if a sentence incorrectly describes a possible world, it is said to be not true, or false, relative to that possible world.

Notice here that the concepts of truth and falsity are defined by reference to what must be considered a deeper and more fundamental notion of possible world. Though we cannot here try to give anything like a serious definition of what a possible world would be, we can give a rough characterization.

One way to think of a possible world is as the sort of thing we can imagine or conceive. The world we live in is one such. It is the familiar world we are all acquainted with. This world is called by logicians and philosophers the actual world. We can also let our imagination loose and conceive of things differently. We use the subjunctive mood to talk about situations as they 'might' or 'may' have been. Roughly, a possible world is any situation that is conceivable or imaginable. Thus, we may think of a possible world as any situation describable in a work of fiction. This definition, however, is not quite complete. Unfortunately our imagination is limited by the scope of our creativity, so there are possible situations we have not actually imagined. Moreover, sometimes our imagination leads us astray and leads us to think of something as possible which really could never be. Imagination errs in this way when it posits a situation containing a hidden contradiction or inconsistency. Novels sometimes contain contradictions unintended by their authors, or even in some cases intentional contradictions. But such stories cannot describe even a possible situation because, as we shall see, contradictions could never be true. Thus we can roughly define a *possible world* as any situation that can be described in a consistent story. Assuming that imagination were creative enough and never led us into contradictions, we could say that a possible world was any imaginable situation.

This brief explanation of possible worlds will have to suffice until later in the book. What is important from the perspective of logic is that there are many possible worlds, the actual world among them. Whether a sentence is true (has the *truth-value* T) or false (has the *truth-value* F) will differ from world to world. Thus, the notion of truth is elliptical: one should always say true with respect to, or in, a stated world. The sentence 'Pecos Bill dug the Rio Grande' is false in the actual world but true in the world of the American legend.

1.2.2 Logical Truth and Validity

Thus far we have introduced without a formal definition the notion of possible world, and used it to give in the correspondence theory a definition of the concept of truth-in-a-possible-world. With these ideas we can now proceed to the main goal, the definition of validity. Let us begin by defining the closely related notion of a logical truth. The standard definition of a logical or necessary truth is often attributed to Leibniz but really goes back to his classical and medieval predecessors.

DEFINITION: The statement '*P* is a *logical truth*' means *P* is true in all possible worlds.

Some sentences are always true, and they are so because of their grammatical form. No matter what term is repeated in the subject and predicate position of the following sentence, any sentence with its form will be true, no matter what world is being described.

EXAMPLE All men are men.

The reason such sentences are always true is that the grammar forces the sentence in a sense to repeat itself, to say nothing new, to state a triviality. Such same-sayings are called *tautologies.* In ordinary writing and science tautologies are avoided unless the subject matter is complicated and needs to be expressed in several equivalent ways. But in logic they are very important. Indeed, one of the goals of logic is to discover or otherwise characterize all the grammatical tautologies that exist. These are logical truths since they are true in every world, and may then be assumed by the various sciences as true in our world. Thus logic is at once the most general science, being assumed by all others, and the most trivial.

The second fundamental idea explained by possible worlds is that of an acceptable inference or logical leap of reasoning. These valid inferences are loosely characterized by the following formula using the subjunctive mood: an argument is valid if the conclusion would be true if the premises were true. Logicians explain this subjunctive idea in terms of possible worlds. We imagine all the possible worlds. We then look at all the worlds in which the premises are true; we ignore the worlds in which they are false. All we care about is whether the conclusion happens to be true in those worlds in which the premises are true.

DEFINITION: The argument 'From $H_1, \ldots, H_n$ to C is *valid*' means for any world w, if all of $H_1, \ldots, H_n$ are true in w, then C is true in w.

Below, we separate the premises of the argument from the conclusion by the customary device of drawing a horizontal line. Later we sometimes use a slash mark '/' to separate premises from conclusion when we list them all from left to right on a single line, as in $H_1, , \ldots, H_n/C$. No matter what world you think of, if the premises of the following argument are true in that world, the grammar ensures that the conclusion will also be true in that world.

EXAMPLE All B are C
All A are B
―――――――
All A are C

It is important not to confuse appraising an argument's validity with appraising whether its premises and conclusion happen to be true in the actual world. The following examples all have the same form as the last example and are accordingly valid. After each sentence is its truth-value in the actual world.

EXAMPLES All men are mortal. (T)
All Greeks are men. (T)
―――――――
All Greeks are mortal. (T)

All men have wings. (F)
All donkeys are men. (F)
―――――――
All donkeys have wings. (F)

All men have wings. (F)
All birds are men. (F)
―――――――
All birds have wings. (T)

The actual truth-values of these examples fall into the patterns T,T/T; F,F/F; and F,F/T, respectively, yet they are all valid. Even though some of the premises and the conclusions may be false in the actual world, there is still no possible world in which the premises are true and conclusion is false simultaneously. A valid argument precludes just the pattern T,T/F, and none of the above examples have that pattern.

☐ **EXERCISE**

Which of the following arguments are valid? If invalid sketch the details of a world showing that in that world the premises are true, but the conclusion is false. One way to sketch these details would be to write a short (one paragraph) story describing that world. Another equally good way would be to draw a picture with objects grouped into sets represented by circles and labeled 'cows', 'mice', 'men', 'mortals', 'angels'. The circles would have to overlap and be included in one another in such a way as to make the premises true and the conclusion false. After each premise and conclusion write in its truth-value T or F in the actual world.

Some men are not mice.
All men are cows.

Some mice are cows.

All men are mortal.
Socrates is not mortal.

Socrates is not a man.

Some men are mortal.
Some angels are mortal.

Some men are not angels.

1.2.3 Soundness

If after appraising validity, we want also to appraise the truth-value in the actual world of the premises and conclusion, we do so in terms of the concept of soundness.

DEFINITION: The statement 'An argument from premises $H_1, \ldots, H_n$ to conclusion C is *sound*' means the argument is valid and each premise H_i is true in the actual world.

Given these definitions, it is possible for an argument to be valid but not sound (because its premises are not all true in the actual world). It is also possible for an argument to have all its premises true in the actual world and be neither valid nor sound (because the conclusion does not follow from those premises and because soundness, by definition, presupposes validity). Notice also that if the argument is valid and all its premises are actually true, we need look no further to know that the conclusion is actually true because, by definition, the conclusion of any sound argument must be true in the actual world. Before proceeding to the next exercise the reader should make sure he or she see that all the points of this paragraph do in fact follow given the definitions of validity and soundness.

□ **EXERCISE**

Which of the arguments given in the previous exercise are sound?

1.3 THE SENTENTIAL CONNECTIVES AND TRUTH-TABLES

1.3.1 Negation

Certain inferences follow logically because of the grammatical arrangement of what are called the sentential connectives: 'not' (called *negation*), 'and' (called *conjunction*), 'or' (called *disjunction*), 'if...then' (called the *conditional*), and 'if and only if' (called the *biconditional*). We shall explain the meaning of these connectives and the rules of inference appropriate to them by means of devices called truth-tables.

Let us start with negation. For brevity we shall symbolize the English sentence 'It is not the case that P' or 'Not P' by $\sim P$. Before explaining when arguments using negations are valid, we must first explain the prior notion of the condition under which a negated sentence is true or false in a possible world. Intuitively, a negative assertion is true just when the sentence which it denies is false, and vice versa.

DEFINITION: $\sim P$ is false in w if P is true in w, and $\sim P$ is true in w if P is false in w.

Let us draw a rectangle representing the set of all possible worlds and divide it across the middle into two subsets. Let us put the worlds in which P is true and $\sim P$ is false on top, and those in which P is false and $\sim P$ is true on the bottom.

The Set of All Possible Worlds

Worlds in which P is true and $\sim P$ false.
Worlds in which P is false and $\sim P$ true.

This picture partitions the set of worlds; it divides it into exhaustive, nonoverlapping subsets. We can represent this partition in a convenient table.

Truth-Table for Negation

P	$\sim P$
T	F
F	T

The table must be understood as follows: each line of truth-values from left to right across the page represents one of the mutually exclusive sets of possible worlds. Beneath each sentence, on that line, is its truth-value in any of the worlds contained in the subset of worlds described by that line. Thus each line from left to right in a truth-table represents one of the subsets in a partition of the whole set of possible worlds. Just from inspection of the partition for negation illustrated above or by reading the truth-table for negation which contains the same information as this partition, it is easy to see that the following arguments using negations are valid. Look at each of the subsets of the partition, or equivalently look at each line of the truth-table. In neither of the two types of world represented can the premises of the following arguments be true and the conclusions false.

EXAMPLE $\dfrac{P}{\sim\sim P}$ $\qquad \dfrac{\sim\sim P}{P}$

THEOREM. The argument from P to $\sim\sim P$ is valid.

We shall now give our first example of a proof. Part of the job of the student is to ponder this and later examples carefully so that eventually he or she can imitate this behavior and do his or her own proofs. The important point to see is that the conclusion of the proof (which is the same as the theorem to be 'proven') is supposed to follow in logical steps from the assumptions of the proof, which in this case consist of the definitions of valid argument and negation. Note that all the information contained in the definition for negation is also contained in its truth-table, so that the two are really equivalent ways of saying the same thing.

Proof. An arbitrary possible world w is one of two kinds. Case I: P is T in w. Then by the definition for negation (or equivalently, by the truth-table for negation) $\sim P$ is F in w and $\sim\sim P$ is T in w. Case II: P is F in w. Then by the truth-table for negation $\sim P$ is T in w and $\sim\sim P$ is F in w. By inspection of all the possible cases we can see that in all worlds in which P is T (as in Case I), $\sim\sim P$ is also T. Hence by the definition of validity, the argument is valid. QED.

It is an ancient custom to indicate the point at which a proof ends because, at least on first reading, it is often not clear to the reader what is going on in the proof. He or she may have missed the fact that what was to have been proven has in fact been proven. Later in the text we mark the end of a proof by the words 'End of Proof'. In this chapter we shall use the traditional QED, which stands for the Latin sentence *Quod erat demonstrandum.*

☐ **EXERCISE**

Show that the argument from $\sim\sim P$ to P is valid.

1.3.2 Conjunction

The next grammatical form to discuss is conjunction. Let us abbreviate the English phrase 'P and Q' by $P \wedge Q$. Intuitively a conjunction as a whole is true in a world only when both its parts (called *conjuncts*) are also true.

DEFINITION: $P \wedge Q$ is T in w if both P and Q are T in w, and $P \wedge Q$ is F in w if either P or Q or both is F in w.

The set of possible worlds may again be partitioned according to what truth-values are assigned to P and Q.

Worlds in which P, Q, and $P \wedge Q$ are all T.
Worlds in which P is T, Q is F, and $P \wedge Q$ is F.
Worlds in which P is F, Q is T, and $P \wedge Q$ is F.
Worlds in which P, Q, and $P \wedge Q$ are all F.

This information may be collected in tabular form.

Truth-Table for Conjunction

P	Q	$P \wedge Q$
T	T	T
T	F	F
F	T	F
F	F	F

Again, each line corresponds to one of the mutually exclusive sets of possible worlds from the partition, and listed under each sentence is its truth-value in all the worlds represented by that line. The truth-table is sufficient for determining whether arguments involving conjunction are valid.

EXAMPLE The following are valid:

$$\frac{P \wedge Q}{P} \qquad \frac{P \wedge Q}{Q}$$

But the inferences from P to $P \wedge Q$ and from Q to $P \wedge Q$ are invalid.

THEOREM. The argument from $P \wedge Q$ to P is valid.

Proof. Take any world w. There are four possible cases. Case I: P and Q are both T in w. Case II: P is T and Q is F in w. Case III: P is F and Q is T in w. Case IV: Both P and Q are F in w. It is only in Case I that both premises are T. Then in these worlds the definition of truth for the conjunction (or equivalently, the truth-table for conjunction) ensures that $P \wedge Q$ is T. Hence, by the definition for validity, the argument is valid. QED.

THEOREM. The argument from P to $P \wedge Q$ is invalid.

Proof. Consider the world w in which P is T and Q is F. In this world $P \wedge Q$ would be F according to the truth-table for conjunction. Hence there is some world in which the premise is T but the conclusion F. Thus, by the definition of validity, the argument is not valid. QED.

□ **EXERCISE**

Prove that the argument from $P \wedge Q$ to Q is valid, but that its converse, i.e., the argument from Q to $P \wedge Q$, is invalid.

With negation and conjunction we can formulate quite elaborate sentences, some of which produce logical truths and valid arguments in a manner not straightforwardly visible from the basic truth-tables. But the basic tables do allow for a procedure that will determine the truth-value of a grammatically complex sentence given only the truth-values of its simplest parts. For example, the sentence $\sim(P \wedge \sim P)$ is a logical truth.

THEOREM. $\sim(P \wedge \sim P)$ is a logical truth.

Proof. Case I: P is T in w. Then by the truth-table for negation, $\sim P$ is F in w. Then by the truth-table for conjunction $P \wedge \sim P$ is F in w. Again by the truth-table for negation, $\sim(P \wedge \sim P)$ is T in w. Case II: P is F in w. Then by the truth-table for $\wedge$, $P \wedge \sim P$ is F in w. By the truth-table for $\sim$, $\sim(P \wedge \sim P)$ is T in w. Hence in both possible cases the sentence is T, and it is therefore a logical truth by the definition of that notion. QED.

It would be nice, however, to be able to test such examples automatically. The method we shall employ does so by first assigning all possible combinations of truth-values to the simplest parts of a complex sentence and then truth-values to each larger part according to the truth-tables until the sentence as a whole is assigned a truth-value.

DEFINITION: The *truth-table* for P is defined as follows:

(1) Start by listing all the simplest (called *atomic*) parts of P together with P across the top of a page from left to right.

(2) Possible worlds are then partitioned into categories representing all the possible assignments of T and F to the atomic parts of P. A separate horizontal line beneath the line containing the sentence and its parts is assigned to each of these categories. On each line and directly beneath the atomic parts is then written the truth-value of each atomic part in the worlds represented by that line.

(3) Within a line the truth-values of progressively larger parts of P are calculated from the truth-values of the known smaller parts and the tables for the connectives. These truth-values of larger parts are written directly beneath their connectives.

EXAMPLE

Step 1. $P \mid \sim(P \wedge \sim P)$

Step 2.

P	$\sim(P \wedge \sim P)$
T	
F	

Step 3.

P	$\sim$	$(P$	$\wedge$	$\sim$	$P)$
T		T			T
F		F			F

P	$\sim$	$(P$	$\wedge$	$\sim$	$P)$
T		T		F	T
F		F		T	F

P	$\sim$	$(P$	$\wedge$	$\sim$	$P)$
T		T	F	F	T
F		F	F	T	F

P	$\sim$	$(P$	$\wedge$	$\sim$	$P)$
T	T	T	F	F	T
F	T	F	F	T	F

The truth-table recapitulates the reasoning in the proof of the last metatheorem and shows graphically that in any kind of possible world the sentence as a whole is true. The stages in completing Step 3 indicate the order of calculating the truth-value of the whole from its parts. This technique is the basis of our first important rule of thumb for a practical knowledge of doing proofs.

Within a complex sentence let us identify its *major connective* as that which joins together its two largest parts. Equally we might define it as that connective used last in constructing the sentence from its various parts. Usually, if we ask 'What kind of sentence is it?' we are asking for its major connective. Thus, $(P \wedge \sim Q) \wedge (R \wedge \sim\sim S)$ has as its major connective $\wedge$ and is a conjunction, whereas $\sim((P \wedge \sim Q) \wedge (R \wedge \sim\sim S))$ has as its major connective $\sim$ and is a negation. We now use this idea to formulate the truth-table test for logical truth.

Truth-Table Test for Logical Truth (Rule 1, R1). P is a logical truth if T occurs on every line beneath its major connective.

For further examples we shall introduce more connectives.

1.3.3 Disjunction

Let us abbreviate the English phrase P or Q or both by $P \vee Q$. In English, use of 'or' often precludes the alternative 'or both' as in 'I want coffee or tea'. When I say that, I do not usually want both coffee and tea. Sometimes we *do* want to allow for the possibility that both may hold, as in 'I'll accept either a Monet or a Picasso'. The two senses of 'or' are called, respectively, the *inclusive* and the *exclusive* disjunctions. (Latin has a different word for each: *vel* and *aut*. In logic the sense used is the inclusive and hence the $\vee$ from *vel*.)

DEFINITION: $P \vee Q$ is true in w if either P or Q or both is true in w, and $P \vee Q$ is false in w if both P and Q are false in w.

Truth-Table for Disjunction

P	Q	$P \vee Q$
T	T	T
T	F	T
F	T	T
F	F	F

Again read each line as recording what happens in one subset of a mutually exclusive and exhaustive partitioning of worlds.

□ **EXERCISE**

Show by a truth-table test that $P \vee \sim P$ is a logical truth.

1.3.4 The Conditional

Another connective is that for the conditional. We translate the English phrases 'If P, then Q' and 'P only if Q' by $P \rightarrow Q$. In $P \rightarrow Q$, P is called the *antecedent* of the conditional, and Q the *consequent*.

The truth-table for the conditional, unlike those for negation, conjunction, and disjunction, must be arrived at by indirection. Instead of thinking of when a conditional dependence is true, we think about when it is false. The way to show such a claim to be false, i.e., the way to refute it, is to find a case in which the condition (the antecedent) is satisfied but in which the alleged dependency (the consequent) does not hold. The conditional 'If the apple is red, it is sweet' is false because there are cases in which 'The apple is red' is true, but 'The apple is sweet' is false. In general terms, a conditional is false in a world if the antecedent is true in that world but the consequent is false in that world. In all other cases we say the conditional as a whole is true in that world. That is, it is true if either both antecedent and consequent are true in the world, or the antecedent is false and the consequent is either true or false in the world.

In addition to intuitions about when a conditional is refuted, we have another source of guidance in constructing the truth-table for the conditional. There are a series of quite obvious logical facts that involve the conditional, and it is reasonable to require of any truth-table for the conditional that it be able to explain why these truths hold. Four facts are particularly basic:

(1) $P \rightarrow Q$ is F only in the case $P \wedge \sim Q$ is T.
(2) $P \rightarrow Q$ holds only when $\sim P \vee Q$ does.
(3) The argument from $P \rightarrow Q$ and P to Q is valid. (This argument pattern is called *modus ponens* in traditional logic.)
(4) The argument from $P \rightarrow Q$ and $\sim Q$ to $\sim P$ is valid. (This argument pattern is called *modus tollens*.)

It is well worth pausing to think about points (1) to (4) to see that they do record part of our understanding of 'if...then', and that it is reasonable to require of any adequate theory of the conditional that it explain why they hold. In fact the truth-table which we sketched previously and which we now define more formally yields these results as theorems.

DEFINITION: $P \rightarrow Q$ is T in w if either both P and Q are T or P is F in w, and $P \rightarrow Q$ is F in w if P is T and Q is F in w.

Truth-Table for the Conditional

P	Q	$P \rightarrow Q$
T	T	T
T	F	F
F	T	T
F	F	T

One feature of this table calls for some special comment. Notice that whenever the antecedent of a conditional is F, the conditional as a whole is T regardless of the truth-value of the consequent. It is possible to construct examples which make this feature plausible. For an example of a true conditional with both antecedent and consequent false consider assertions like 'If Jones is an embezzler, I'm a monkey's uncle'. That the speaker asserts the conditional indicates that he thinks of the conditional as a whole as true. But he clearly does not intend to suggest either that he is a monkey's uncle or that Jones is an embezzler. On the contrary, he is using the conditional to assert that Jones is not an embezzler. He is, in fact, using the reasoning pattern called *modus tollens* stated in point (4) above. From the truth of the conditional and the obvious falsity of its consequent, the falsity of the antecedent follows.

It is also possible to construct cases of a true conditional with false antecedent and true consequent. Suppose we reason as follows. P is the case, and hence if condition Q holds, P will remain the case. Thus for any Q, it seems to be the case that when P is true, it is also true to say that if Q, then P. Suppose it is raining, then it follows that if the sea is wet, then it is raining.

It may not be very interesting or useful to make conditional assertions in these cases, but they would nevertheless be true. Such cases are called *degenerate* because though true they are extremes and we would not normally assert them. The student should take away from this discussion the lesson that conditionals in degenerate cases (with false antecedents) are automatically true. This fact about conditionals is admittedly not very intuitive but it turns up repeatedly in formal logic, and it is best to accept it at this point. It will often be the case that a rather complex issue formulated as a conditional will be resolved simply by showing that its antecedent is false.

THEOREM. $P \rightarrow P$ and $(P \wedge Q) \rightarrow P$ are logical truths.

P	$P \rightarrow P$
T	T T T
F	F T F

P	Q	$(P \wedge Q) \rightarrow P$
T	T	T T T T T
T	F	T F F T T
F	T	F F T T F
F	F	F F F T F

□ EXERCISES

1. Let P, Q, and R be three different sentences. There are eight possible assignments of T and F. Show by truth-tables that the following are logical truths:

$(P \wedge Q) \rightarrow Q$

$P \rightarrow (P \vee Q)$

$(((P \vee Q) \wedge (P \rightarrow R)) \wedge (Q \rightarrow R)) \rightarrow R$

$(P \wedge (P \rightarrow Q)) \rightarrow Q$

$(\sim Q \wedge (P \rightarrow Q)) \rightarrow \sim P$

$((P \vee Q) \wedge \sim P) \rightarrow Q$

$P \rightarrow (Q \rightarrow P)$

$(P \rightarrow Q) \rightarrow ((P \wedge R) \rightarrow Q)$

$((P \vee Q) \rightarrow R) \rightarrow (P \rightarrow R)$

Display the eight possibilities on lines as follows:

P	Q	R	(write the full sentence here)
T	T	T	
T	T	F	
T	F	T	
T	F	F	(calculate the truth-values of the
F	T	T	sentence and its parts here)
F	T	F	
F	F	T	
F	F	F	

2. Show by truth-tables that the following are not logical truths:

$P \rightarrow (P \wedge Q)$

$(P \vee Q) \rightarrow P$

$P \rightarrow Q$

$((P \rightarrow Q) \wedge Q) \rightarrow P$

$((P \rightarrow Q) \wedge \sim P) \rightarrow \sim Q$

1.3.5 Testing for Validity and Logical Truth

As the previous exercise may suggest, there is a very close tie between an argument being valid and a corresponding conditional being a logical truth. This tie will enable us to extend our truth-table test so that we can check whether arguments are valid.

THEOREM. The argument form $H_1, \ldots, H_n$ to C is valid if, and only if, the conditional $(H_1 \wedge \cdots \wedge H_n) \rightarrow C$ (which we shall call the *conditional corresponding to the argument*) is a logical truth.

Proof. Case I: Suppose $H_1, \ldots, H_n/C$ is valid. Now consider any world w. Either some H_i is F in w, in which case $H_1 \wedge \cdots \wedge H_n$ is F and $(H_1 \wedge \cdots \wedge H_n) \rightarrow C$ is T, or all H_i are T, in which case $H_1 \wedge \cdots \wedge H_n$ is T in w. But in the latter case C would also be T in w (since the argument by assumption is valid) and therefore $(H_1 \wedge \cdots \wedge H_n) \rightarrow C$ would be T in w in this case too. Thus in either case the conditional is T. Since w is typical of every world, the conditional must be a logical truth. Case II: Suppose the conditional is a logical truth, and suppose further that in a typical world w all of $H_1, \ldots, H_n$ are T. Then clearly C must also be T in w because $(H_2 \wedge \cdots \wedge H_n) \rightarrow C$ is T in w. QED.

This metatheorem justifies the following extension of the truth-table method.

Truth-Table Test for Validity (R2). An argument from $H_1, \ldots, H_n$ to C is valid if T occurs in every line under the connective $\rightarrow$ of its corresponding conditional $(H_1 \wedge \cdots \wedge H_n) \rightarrow C$; i.e., if the corresponding conditional is a logical truth.

We list below the arguments (with their traditional names) corresponding to the conditionals of the previous exercise. We have in effect already shown that these arguments are valid because we demonstrated in the exercise that their corresponding conditionals are logical truths.

Simplification

$$\frac{P \wedge Q}{P}$$

Addition

$$\frac{P}{P \vee Q}$$

Constructive dilemma

$$\frac{P \vee Q,\ P \rightarrow R,\ Q \rightarrow R}{R}$$

Modus ponens

$$\frac{P,\ P \rightarrow Q}{Q}$$

Modus tollens

$$\frac{\sim Q,\ P \rightarrow Q}{\sim P}$$

These inferences are fairly obvious. Addition says that if P is true so must $P \vee Q$ be, as the truth-table for $\vee$ confirms. Constructive dilemma says that to prove something follows from a disjunction, all we need do is show it follows from each disjunct separately. Constructive dilemma is quite useful and we shall return to it a little later when we elevate it to the status of a rule of thumb.

The three examples below record some useful arguments for deriving conclusions that are formulated in terms of the conditional. These, too, we have proven valid since we have shown their corresponding conditionals to be logical truths.

$$\frac{P}{Q \rightarrow P} \qquad \frac{P \rightarrow Q}{(P \wedge R) \rightarrow Q} \qquad \frac{(P \vee Q) \rightarrow R}{P \rightarrow R}$$

Before leaving the conditional we should say a little more clarifying the relation between the conditional and the concept of a valid argument. The core of the relationship between the two ideas is contained in the last metatheorem. It is easy to see that something may be true in the actual world, that is, true in the ordinary sense, yet not be a logical truth, for the simple reason that truth in one world does not ensure truth in every possible world. It is a truth, but not a logical truth, that the Rio Grande was carved by erosion. Likewise a conditional may be true in the actual world yet not be a logical truth. All we need to make a conditional actually true is for its parts to have the right truth-values: either the antecedent must be actually false (regardless of the actual truth-value of the consequent, as in the first two examples below) or both the antecedent and consequent must be actually true (as in the third example).

EXAMPLES If the moon is made of green cheese, the oceans are full of water.

If the moon is made of green cheese, the oceans are made of concrete.

If the moon is not made of green cheese, the oceans are full of water.

An important consequence of the last metatheorem is that it provides a very useful method for constructing proofs of conditionals. It is a fact about science and epistemology generally that many, probably most, of the important principles anybody would be interested in proving are of the 'if...then' form. Thus how to prove such statements is very important indeed. The metatheorem not only allows us to detect valid arguments by means of logically true conditionals; we may also proceed in the reverse direction. If we know an argument is valid, then we know its corresponding conditional is not only true but logically true.

COROLLARY. If the argument from $H_1, \ldots, H_n$ and P to Q is valid, then so is the argument from $H_1, \ldots, H_n$ to $P \to Q$.

Proof. Suppose $H_1, \ldots, H_n, P/Q$ is valid. Then by the previous metatheorem $(H_1 \wedge \cdots \wedge H_n \wedge P) \to Q$ is a logical truth and is true in any world w. Now it is easy to see by truth-tables that the following is a logical truth, $((H_1 \wedge \cdots \wedge H_n \wedge P) \to Q) \to ((H_1 \wedge \cdots \wedge H_n) \to (P \to Q))$. Since this conditional is true in every world and since its antecedent is too, so must its consequent be true. Hence, $(H_1 \wedge \cdots \wedge H_n) \to (P \to Q)$ is a logical truth, and therefore by the last metatheorem $H_1, \ldots, H_n/P \to Q$ is valid. QED.

This corollary justifies the following proof strategy. To prove $P \to Q$ from a set of assumptions, we assume P together with the original assumptions and then reason by steps we know to be logically acceptable to the conclusion Q. The fact that we have reasoned by logically valid steps from the original assumptions together with P to the conclusion Q ensures that the argument as a whole is in fact valid. The metatheorem then guarantees that the conditional $P \rightarrow Q$ follows from the original assumptions alone. This technique for proving conditionals is used constantly and is one of the more important rules of thumb.

Conditional Proof (R3). In order to prove $P \rightarrow Q$ from assumptions $H_1, \ldots, H_n$, assume not only these assumptions but also P and then deduce Q in a series of valid steps.

A particular application of conditional proof is a generalization of the argument form we have previously met called constructive dilemma. Recall that we have shown that the following is a logical truth and that therefore the corresponding argument form (constructive dilemma) is valid:

$$(((P \vee Q) \wedge (P \rightarrow R)) \wedge (Q \rightarrow R)) \rightarrow R$$

Hence we get the following special proof strategy for establishing a conclusion from a premise that is a disjunction.

(Generalized) Constructive Dilemma (R4). To show that R follows from $P \vee Q$ and the assumptions $H_1, \ldots, H_n$ it suffices to show that (Case I) assuming $H_1, \ldots, H_n$, and P we can validly deduce R and that (Case II) assuming $H_1, \ldots, H_n$, and Q we can validly deduce R.

(It is a useful but at this point difficult exercise to give a detailed proof of how this rule follows from conditional proof and the ungeneralized form of constructive dilemma. Try it.)

1.3.6 Relevance and the Material Conditional

Let us look again at the examples of true conditionals:

EXAMPLES If the moon is made of green cheese, the oceans are full of water.

If the moon is made of green cheese, the oceans are made of concrete.

If the moon is not made of green cheese, the oceans are full of water.

The striking feature of these examples is that though true according to the truth-table for the conditional they are all silly. In actual usage we do not bother uttering such inane truths. The first two examples are what we have called degenerate conditions (because their truth derives from the falsity of the antecedents).

But there is more oddness about them than the fact that they are degenerate. The third case, for example, is odd even though it is not degenerate. What is common to these and similar cases of true conditionals is that though true there is no connection or relevance linking what is being talked about in the antecedent with what is being talked about in the consequent. What the moon is made of has no bearing on the composition of the oceans. There are many different sorts of relevance, and it is worthwhile to list the sorts suggested by the use of 'if...then'. One type of dependence is what we may call *natural* or *scientific*. Among the discoveries of science are natural dependencies such as the fact that green cheese is cultured by means of a mold. This dependency accounts for the fact that the following conditional is not only true but, unlike the earlier cases, it is also a reasonable thing to say.

EXAMPLE (*A natural dependency.*) If the moon is made of green cheese, it is cultured by means of a mold.

Some dependencies are not as hard and fast as those fixed by natural law but they nevertheless underlie many of the conditionals we take to be reasonable. Among these are ones determined by social practice (we might call them *conventional*), such as the rules of a game, the legal system, or the standards of polite behavior.

EXAMPLES If that pawn reaches the eight rank, then it will become a queen.

If that computer was not purchased for use on your job, then it is not tax deductible.

If that student doesn't distinguish between 'lay' and 'lie', then we should not admit him to college.

In making these assertions the speaker is presuming that he or she could spell out some linkage between the fact contained in the antecedent and that contained in the consequent. Notice, however, that the truth-table for the conditional does not make the truth of the conditional as a whole dependent on any linkage or relevance joining the antecedent to the consequent. Thus there are many true conditionals that, though true, are odd because they lack this additional feature of relevance. Such bare-boned 'if...then' statements are grouped under the technical term of the *material conditional.* Material conditionals are those whose truth-value is calculated solely by means of the truth-table for the conditional without any additional requirement that the antecedent bear some relevance to the consequent. They are to be contrasted with the conditionals we assert in science, in law, and in the commonsense 'folk' knowledge which we use all the time when we explain how things or people work. Thus within the genus of true conditionals there is an important species, the conditional that in addition to being true as dictated by the truth-table of the material conditional also exhibits some kind of relevance. The truth of the matter is that outside technical discussions of logic and mathematics the bare material conditional is seldom seen.

The material conditional is nevertheless extremely important to logic. In the special case in which a material conditional is not only true but logically true, it marks a valid argument. Thus we can use material conditionals as a device for investigating logical reasoning. If we are curious about an example of reasoning, one way to proceed is to recast it as a conditional using the connective '$\rightarrow$' and then test it by truth-tables to see if it is a logical truth. Most logically true conditionals are in fact a special case of true conditionals that exhibit an especially strong relevance between antecedent and consequent. In these cases the grammar of the antecedent forces the truth of the consequent. In some blatant examples of logically true material conditionals, the antecedent may even contain the consequent as a conjunct, e.g., $(P \wedge Q) \rightarrow P$. In other cases the forcing depends on the meaning of the connectives and may not be obvious, e.g., $\sim P \rightarrow (P \rightarrow Q)$. But in most cases of logically true conditionals, there is a linkage; given the meaning of the connectives, if the antecedent is true in a world w, so is the consequent. We might call this sort of relevance *logical*. (There are, however, a few cases of logically true conditionals that have antecedents which are irrelevant to their conclusions, and we shall study these shortly.)

Let us summarize these remarks. In actual usage when we say 'if...then' we are much more likely to be asserting not just that the conditional is true in the sense of the truth-table, but that there is some sort of linkage as well between the antecedent and the consequent. In logic we are nevertheless interested in the material conditional because in the special case in which it is also a logical truth it corresponds to a logically valid argument. Logicians in fact have a variety of special names they give to material conditionals that are also logical truths. As we have done in this book, they are called logical truths or tautologies. In technical work in logic it is always clear what sense of 'if...then' is meant. It is always presumed to indicate the material conditional, and if something stronger is intended one always explains what is meant and often introduces special technical vocabulary to stand for the stronger idea. Among the terms used for logically true conditionals are *logical truth*, *implication*, *entailment*, and *validity*.

1.3.7 The Paradoxes of the Material Conditional

Another proof strategy, which will work to prove any kind of statement, depends on the truth-table for the conditional and on the fact that degenerate cases (those conditionals with false antecedents) are automatically true. Notice that when the antecedent of a conditional is always false, for example when it is a contradiction, then the conditional must always be true regardless of its consequent. That is, a conditional with what we might call a logically false antecedent is itself a logical truth, and the argument from the logically false antecedent to its consequent, no matter what that consequent is, must be valid. Hence a contradiction validly implies anything.

THEOREM. $(P \wedge \sim P)/Q$ is valid.

Proof. $(P \wedge \sim P) \rightarrow Q$ is a logical truth:

P	Q	$(P \wedge \sim P) \rightarrow Q$
T	T	T F F T T T
T	F	T F F T T F
F	T	F F T F T T
F	F	F F T F T F

QED.

□ **EXERCISE**

Prove that a logical truth such as $(P \vee \sim P)$ validly follows from anything. Do so by showing with a truth-table that the following is a logical truth: $Q \rightarrow (P \vee \sim P)$.

These two truths, that a contradiction implies anything and that anything implies a logical truth, are somewhat nonintuitive and are called the *paradoxes of material implication.*

A closely related fact also depending on the truth-table for the conditional is that anything which implies a contradiction must be false.

THEOREM. If $H_1, \ldots, H_n, \sim P/Q \wedge \sim Q$ is valid, then $H_1, \ldots, H_n/P$ is valid.

Proof. Suppose that in some world w, $H_1, \ldots, H_n$ are all T, and that $(H_1 \wedge \cdots \wedge H_n \wedge \sim P) \rightarrow (Q \wedge \sim Q)$ is a logical truth. Since this sentence is a logical truth it must be T in w. We must show that P is T in w. Suppose for the sake of argument that P is F in w. Then $\sim P$ is T in w, and by the previous logical truth together with the truth in w of $H_1, \ldots, H_n$, we see that $Q \wedge \sim Q$ would be T in w, which cannot happen. Since the assumption that P is F in w has led to an absurdity, we know it must be false. Hence we conclude that P is T in w. QED.

This result justifies a very important proof strategy that can be tried no matter what the grammatical form is of the sentence to be proven.

Reduction to the Absurd (Reductio ad Absurdum, R5). Let us assume some so-called *background* assumptions $H_1, \ldots, H_n$ that are not in dispute. One way to prove P on the basis of assumptions $H_1, \ldots, H_n$ is to assume $\sim P$ together with the assumptions and to show that there is a contradiction $Q \wedge \sim Q$ such that the argument $H_1, \ldots, H_n, \sim P/Q \wedge \sim Q$ is valid. We would then know that the argument $H_1, \ldots, H_n/P$ is valid.

In other words, in order to prove something assume its opposite and argue to a contradiction. This strategy often works when all else fails.

EXAMPLE There is no last positive integer. *Proof.* Suppose the opposite that there is a last positive integer. Call it N. We know by assumption (by an axiom of arithmetic) that for any number X, there exists its successor $X + 1$. Hence $N + 1$ exists. But $N + 1$ is larger than N. Hence N both is and is not the last positive integer, which is absurd. Thus our original assumption must be false, and we may conclude that truly there is no last positive integer. QED.

1.3.8 The Biconditional and Logical Equivalence

The last connective to discuss is called the *biconditional*. Let us abbreviate the English locutions 'P if and only if Q', and 'P holds exactly when Q does' by $P \leftrightarrow Q$. Frequently, 'if and only if' is abbreviated 'iff'. The idea is that a biconditional asserts both that $P \rightarrow Q$ and conversely that $Q \rightarrow P$.

DEFINITION: The statement '$P \leftrightarrow Q$ is T in w' means P and Q are either both T in w or both F in w; $P \leftrightarrow Q$ is F in w if P and Q have different truth-values in w.

Truth-Table for the Biconditional

P	Q	$P \leftrightarrow Q$
T	T	T
T	F	F
F	T	F
F	F	T

The biconditional asserts that in fact its two components have the same truth-value. Like the material conditional it may be *actually* true but not *logically* true. This happens when it is true in the actual world but in some other possible world the components have different truth-values.

☐ **EXERCISE**

Find two examples of biconditionals that are true in the actual world because both halves are true, and two other examples that are true because both halves are false.

Often we would like to assert that not only do two sentences have the same truth-value but also that they must have it in every possible world. To do so we coin a special term: logically equivalent.

DEFINITION: 'P and Q are *logically equivalent*' means that in all possible worlds w, P and Q have the same truth-value or, to put it another way, $P \leftrightarrow Q$ is a logical truth.

There are in fact many useful pairs of logical equivalents (i.e., biconditionals that are logically true). Their use lies in the fact that they guarantee that arguing from one equivalent to the other is valid.

THEOREM. If $P \leftrightarrow Q$ is a logical truth, then P/Q is valid.

Proof. Suppose that $P \leftrightarrow Q$ is true in every world and that P is true in w. We must show Q is true in w. Since $P \leftrightarrow Q$ is T in every world, it is also T in w. Then P and Q must have the same truth-values in w. Hence Q is T in w. QED.

□ **EXERCISE**

Show by truth-tables that the following are logical truths. Traditional names for the equivalences and their corresponding valid arguments are given.

Double negation:	$P \leftrightarrow \sim\sim P$
Commutation:	$(P \wedge Q) \leftrightarrow (Q \wedge P)$
	$(P \vee Q) \leftrightarrow (Q \vee P)$
Association:	$(P \wedge (Q \wedge R)) \leftrightarrow ((P \wedge Q) \wedge R)$
	$(P \vee (Q \vee R)) \leftrightarrow ((P \vee Q) \vee R)$
Distribution:	$(P \wedge (Q \vee R)) \leftrightarrow ((P \wedge Q) \vee (P \wedge R))$
	$(P \vee (Q \wedge R)) \leftrightarrow ((P \vee Q) \wedge (P \vee R))$
DeMorgan's laws:	$(P \wedge Q) \leftrightarrow \sim(\sim P \vee \sim Q)$
	$(P \vee Q) \leftrightarrow \sim(\sim P \wedge \sim Q)$
	$\sim(P \wedge Q) \leftrightarrow (\sim P \vee \sim Q)$
	$\sim(P \vee Q) \leftrightarrow (\sim P \wedge \sim Q)$
Contraposition:	$(P \rightarrow Q) \leftrightarrow (\sim Q \rightarrow \sim P)$
Useful untitled equivalences:	$(P \rightarrow (Q \rightarrow R)) \leftrightarrow ((P \wedge Q) \rightarrow R)$
	$\sim(P \rightarrow Q) \leftrightarrow (P \wedge \sim Q)$
	$(P \rightarrow Q) \leftrightarrow (\sim P \vee Q)$
	$(P \leftrightarrow Q) \leftrightarrow ((P \rightarrow Q) \wedge (Q \rightarrow P))$
	$(P \leftrightarrow Q) \leftrightarrow ((P \wedge Q) \vee (\sim P \wedge \sim Q))$

The laws of association and commutation justify what will be our practice in this book of ignoring parentheses and order within conjunctions and disjunctions. For example, we shall write both $((P \wedge Q) \wedge R)$ and $(P \wedge (Q \wedge R))$ as $(P \wedge Q \wedge R)$, and freely assume that $(P \wedge Q \wedge R)$ is equivalent to $(R \wedge Q \wedge P)$. Given the last theorem and the fact that the biconditionals listed above are all logically true, we know that arguing from the right half of any biconditional on the list to the left half or vice versa is valid.

Two of the equivalences call for special comment. The first explains how to apply the strategy of conditional proof to a biconditional.

Conditional Proof for a Biconditional (R6). To prove $P \leftrightarrow Q$ from assumptions $H_1, \ldots, H_n$ it suffices to prove both $P \rightarrow Q$ and $Q \rightarrow P$ by arguing that

(Case I) you can validly deduce Q from $H_1, \ldots, H_n$ and P, and that (Case II) you can validly deduce P from $H_1, \ldots, H_n$ and Q.

These two cases would establish by conditional proof the two conditionals whose conjunction is logically equivalent to the biconditional.

The last example of the exercise shows how to set up a *reductio* proof (R5) for a conditional.

Reduction to the Absurd for a Conditional (R7). To show $P \rightarrow Q$ follows validly from assumptions $H_1, \ldots, H_n$ it suffices to show that a contradiction $R \wedge \sim R$ follows validly from $H_1, \ldots, H_n$, P, and $\sim Q$.

We have now completed the short introduction to the logic of 'not', 'and', 'or', 'if...then', and 'if and only if'. Since these expressions join sentences to form longer sentences, this logic is known as *sentence logic*. Just as frequently it is called *propositional logic*, in one of the few occasions in the terminology of modern logic in which the English term *proposition* is taken as equivalent to *propositio*, the technical term in medieval logic for sentence.

1.4 SCHEMATIC LETTERS AND VARIABLES

1.4.1 Letters and Form

We must pause now to discuss briefly a feature of logic that we have already used without comment, the abbreviation of parts of expressions by letters. The use of letters for this purpose is as old as logic and is found in Aristotle. Indeed, it is not an exaggeration to say that logic would be impossible without the technique.

The purpose of letters is, above all, to unify in a single symbol what would normally be a longer phrase containing irrelevant and distracting details. Consider the letters P, Q, etc. that we have already used in the discussion of propositional logic. They enabled us to avoid the needless detail of writing out full sentences as they occur as parts of a longer sentence or argument. By eliminating irrelevant detail, they also enable us to see the form of the larger sentence or argument. There is probably no more basic notion in logic than that of form, and to a large extent figuring out the form of a sentence or argument consists of some analysis that replaces phrases by letters and then joins them together in a grammatical matrix to produce longer structures.

Aristotle was able to generalize from linguistic patterns such as the following:

All mortals have wings.
All men are mortal.
____
Therefore all men have wings.

He substituted letters for what he called the subject and predicate terms, and concluded that every argument of the following 'form' is valid:

All M is P.
All S is M.
____
Therefore, all S is P.

We shall discuss some of the details of Aristotle's theory in a later chapter, but by reference to this example it is possible to make some general points about the use of letters in logic. These points may be made (in a style beloved by medieval logicians) by drawing a series of distinctions.

1.4.2 Letters for Descriptive Terms

The first distinction to be drawn is that between expressions which by themselves stand for something in the world and those which alone do not stand for anything. The former are what modern logicians call *referring* or *descriptive* terms and what the medievals called *categorematic* terms. It is these expressions that logicians represent by letters. Distinguished from these are the terms that do not stand for anything in the world but rather serve to draw together smaller referring terms into longer expressions. These nonreferring terms are called *logical signs* in modern discussions or *syncategorematic terms* in medieval logic.

The motivation for the distinction is an assumption about the way language represents the world. In the standard view, descriptive terms point to things in the world. These real 'entities' so picked out may be of various sorts. Singular noun phrases, as we memorized in high school grammar, pick out persons, places, and things. Collective noun phrases refer to groups or classes. Verb phrases stand for actions, adjectives for properties, and adverbial phrases for the manner in which actions are performed. Sentences are said to correspond to facts. Each of these diverse parts of speech—singular noun phrases, collective noun phrases, verb phrases, adjectives, adverbial phrases, and sentences—is a distinct variety of the wider class of referring expressions. Conflicting accounts of the proper way to divide up the referring expressions and of what sort of entity, if any, the diverse groups refer to occupy a large part of traditional logic and metaphysics, and make up one of the more interesting topics we shall discuss later. The point to see now is that this kind of expression has quite a different function from the logical signs which alone do not describe anything. The function of a logical sign is to aid in the construction of longer referring expressions out of shorter ones.

A longer verb phrase may consist of a shorter transitive verb combined with a proper noun serving as direct object, and a simple sentence may be made up of a noun phrase serving as the subject and verb phrase serving as its predicate. In propositional logic a longer conjunction, itself a sentence, is made up of two shorter sentences. The role of the logical signs is to aid in this construction. They signal that a series of referring parts are being joined together to make a longer referring whole. Thus in the English sentence 'All men are mortal', the words 'all' and 'are' count as logical or syncategorematic. The word 'all' is a particle which affixes to the referring collective noun 'men' to yield a longer noun phrase 'all men'. The word 'are' is a form of the verb 'to be', which is called the *copula* in traditional logic. Its role is to join the two referring expressions consisting of the subject noun phrase 'all men' and the adjective 'mortal'. The result is the complex expression 'All men are mortal'. In languages like English in which word order is very important, rules of combination sometimes do not require the explicit addition of a new particle in order to make up longer referring expressions from shorter. Thus 'white' and 'donkey' yield 'white donkey' without adding any further logical sign. In languages in which order is less important, like the inflected languages of Latin and German, case endings and similar symbolic clues are explicitly present. In formal logic it is a rule that there must be a logical sign signaling what sort of whole is being formed from the parts. The role of the connectives is exactly this. The sign '$\wedge$' signals that a conjunction is formed from the parts P and Q in the whole $P \wedge Q$, whereas the sign '$\vee$' signals that a disjunction is formed from the same parts in $P \vee Q$.

The classification of signs into those which are referring expressions and those which are logical signs is not important to us now because its details will differ from language to language, theory to theory, logician to logician. But some such division is always drawn. The distinction is important to understanding the logician's use of letters because letters are always understood to replace or represent referring rather than logical expressions. Relative to a given theory, the referring expressions of the various categories are not usually written out in full but represented by single letters. So that the letters may be easily read and understood, they are usually chosen so that there is a fairly clear orthographic similarity among the letters representing one part of speech and a fairly clear difference among the letters representing different parts of speech. For example, nouns may be represented by A, B, and C and sentences by P, Q, and R.

Thus the first point to make in understanding a logician's use of schematic letters is that the reader must be clear about the grammar of the formal language being used, about which are the categories of referring expressions and which are the logical signs. Letters will always be representatives of some category of referring expression. There will usually be a distinctive variety of letter for each such category. The letters condense to a single perceptual point the needless detail of the orthography internal to referring expressions and leave the eye to scan exactly how these parts go together to form the whole expression. In this way, they exhibit the form of the sentence or argument of which they are part, and for this reason they are frequently called *schematic*, a term which derives from the Greek word *schema* meaning form.

1.4.3 Letters for Simple and Complex Expressions

The second important point about letters depends on the distinction we have already drawn between simple and complex referring expressions. Some referring expressions are short, consisting sometimes of only a single word, and others are long. The long ones (usually called *phrases* in modern grammar) are made up of shorter referring expressions together with logical signs. Thus referring names and adjectives combine with logical signs such as 'all', 'are', and the connectives of propositional logic to produce longer referring sentences—some very long indeed, containing within them shorter sentences. For various purposes, however, we sometimes wish to block out and represent by a single letter a complex referring expression. It often happens that a complex symbol is itself part of an even longer complex expression and that we wish to draw attention to the grammatical position it occupies in the longer matrix. We do so by condensing and representing the part, even though it is complex, by a single letter. Thus though schematic letters themselves are very short, being just single symbols, they may represent any expression of the relevant category, simple or complex. For example, when a logician says any sentence of the form $P \vee \sim P$ is a logical truth, P here may be understood as any sort of (declarative) sentence, simple or complex, short or long. Likewise a logician may use a single letter A for all noun phrases, both short ones like 'men' and long ones like 'men in tall hats', in the generalization that all sentences of the form 'All A are A' are logical truths. In these cases the internal structure of the contained referring expressions, whether they be complex or not, is irrelevant to the point about form that the logician wishes to make. The use of letters to represent any expression of a category, simple or complex, makes it possible to suppress this irrelevant detail.

In sum then, categories of referring expressions are represented by single letters, and sometimes these letters are meant to stand for complex as well as simple expressions of that type. Because these are letters and not actual words, we usually do not know exactly which words they stand for. What is important from the perspective of form, however, is not what they refer to but what part of speech they are. That information is contained in the orthographic conventions governing what kind of letter stands for a particular kind of expression. Their main use is in suppressing irrelevant detail so as to highlight grammatical form and to make generalizations about sentences or arguments of that form. We say, for example, that sentences like $P \vee \sim P$ and 'All A is A' are logical truths, or that the arguments

$$P \wedge Q/P,$$

$$\text{All } M \text{ is } P, \text{ All } S \text{ is } M/\text{All } S \text{ is } P$$

are valid. A feature of schematic letters is that they represent simple as well as complex expressions of the appropriate grammatical type. In the example just cited about logical truths and valid arguments, any expression of the right grammatical type may replace the schematic letters and the result would yield a logical truth or valid argument. Indeed, it is one of the more important rules of logical reasoning that once the form of a logical truth or valid argument is stated in terms of schematic letters, it is legitimate to infer that any sentence or argument of like form is a logical truth or a valid argument. It is legitimate, for example, to erase a letter and replace it by another of the same type so long as every occurrence of the letter is erased and replaced by the same letter. If 'All A is A' is a logical truth, so is 'All B is B'. Since $P \vee \sim P$ is a logical truth so is $Q \vee \sim Q$. This type of uniform replacement of schematic letters by others of the same type is universal and important enough to be highlighted as a rule of thumb.

Alphabetic Variation (R8). The result of replacing every occurrence of a category letter by another letter of the same category is a logical truth or valid argument whenever the original is.

1.4.4 Constants and Variables

The final important distinction to be made is one between two sorts of schematic letters representing a single category of referring expression. Referring expressions of a single category all have in common the fact that they stand for the same sort of thing in the world. But within that category there are two important ways these entities may be picked out. An expression may have a fixed invariant referent, or it may stand indiscriminately for an entity of the relevant sort. The first kind of referring expression is called a *constant* and the second a *variable.* As an example consider the category of noun phrases. These are referring expressions that share the property that they all stand for the same type of entity, namely persons, places, or things. Among noun phrases we may distinguish those constants which have a fixed and determined reference. Among these would be proper names from English such as 'Socrates' and 'Greece', or the numerals from mathematics such as 5 and -8. These are to be distinguished from noun phrases with variable reference. In English, pronouns like 'he', 'she', and 'it' have no fixed invariant referent, but rather stand in different contexts for different things. Demonstratives like 'this' and 'that' function similarly. In mathematics we contrast constants (indicated by either standard numerals or the lowercase letters from the beginning of the alphabet, a, b, c) with variables (usually lowercase letters from the end of the alphabet, x, y, and z) which are understood to stand for unspecified numbers. Exactly how constant terms and variables function in logical arguments is a large subject to which we now turn. What we should take away from the discussion here is the fact about schematic letters that the letters representing a given category of expression will frequently fall into the two subvarieties of constants and variables.

☐ **EXERCISES**

Using the rule of alphabetic variation is tricky because it is hard to keep track of (1) letters standing for different categories, (2) all the occurrences of the letter being replaced, and (3) all the occurrences of the new letter. Here are some exercises to illustrate.

1. First substitute $P \rightarrow Q$ for each occurrence of P and R for the single occurrence of Q in $(P \rightarrow Q) \vee \sim P$. Second, substitute $P \rightarrow Q$ for both occurrences of P in $(P \rightarrow Q) \vee \sim P$, and then substitute in the new sentence R for each occurrence of Q. Are the two final results different? If so, why?
2. Keeping Exercise 1 in mind, reformulate the rule of alphabetic variation so that it remains correct when several category letters are replaced by several other (possibly the same) letters of the same category.
3. Substitute P for both Q and R in $Q \rightarrow R$ and in Q/R. Are these results logically true or valid? If so, explain how this fact is consistent with the rule of alphabetic variation.

1.5 ARGUING WITH QUANTIFIERS

1.5.1 The Quantifiers

Some logical truths and valid arguments are compelled by the grammar of what are called quantifier terms, the English words 'all', 'any', 'every', 'no', 'none', 'some', and 'there exists a...'. Unfortunately these terms are not wholly explicable in terms of truth-tables, but they can be codified informally by four rather intuitive rules. In mathematical jargon all talk of quantification is forced into two sorts of locution that always employ variables:

The Universal Quantifier: For all x, ...
For every x, ...
For any x, ...

The Existential Quantifier: For some x, ...
There exists an x such that...

Here are some common English sentence forms and the corresponding mathematical reformulation.

English	Mathematicalese
All A are B. Any A is B. Every A is B.	For all x, if x is A, then x is B.
Some A are B.	For some x, x is A and x is B. There exists an x such that x is both A and B.
No A are B.	It is not the case that there exists an x such that x is both A and B. For any x, if x is A, then x is not B.

We can use what we already know about truth-tables and propositional logic to explain the logic of the quantifiers if we make two rather idealized assumptions, first that there are only finitely many things in the world and second that each of them has a name. Let $c_1, \ldots, c_n$ be a series of names (mathematicians call them *constants*) such that every object in the universe has at least one name in the series. Let $P(x)$ be a sentence containing occurrences of a variable x. For example, $P(x)$ could stand for any of the following sentences because each contains occurrences of x.

x is red

x loves Socrates

x is red $\rightarrow$ x loves Socrates

Let us call an occurrence of a variable x *free* in a sentence if it does not occur as part of a shorter section of the sentence beginning with 'for all x' or 'for some x', or as we briefly say, 'it is not quantified over'. Thus x is free in 'x is red' but not in 'For all x, x is red'. Likewise in the following complex example both occurrences of x are free, the occurrences of y are not, and the first occurrence of z is free but its second occurrence is not.

For all y ((x loves $y \wedge y$ loves z) $\rightarrow$ (for some z, z knows x))

Occurrences that are not free are called *bound*. Intuitively free variables are like pronouns and demonstratives in English, and when they become bound they pick out everything or something as the grammar indicates. It is bad practice to write sentences in which different instances of the same variable sometimes occur free and sometimes bound, as the previous example shows in its odd, almost equivocal, use of z. Now let us introduce some notation. Let

$P(x)$ represent a sentence containing the variable x at some point or other. It might represent the sentence 'Socrates sees x' or equally the sentence 'For some y, $2y = x$'. Furthermore let c represent a constant term. What we require is a notation to represent the expression we get by erasing all the free occurrences of x in $P(x)$ and replacing them by c. We shall say that $P(c)$ is just like $P(x)$ except that c replaces all free occurrences of x in $P(x)$. (We will explain the importance of the qualification 'free' in a later chapter.) Thus if $P(x)$ is 'x is red' then $P(c)$ is 'c is red'. If $P(x)$ is 'x is red $\rightarrow$ for some x, x loves y' then $P(c)$ is 'c is red $\rightarrow$ for some x, x loves y' because only the first occurrence of x is free. We also allow that we can write quantifiers in front of $P(x)$ in expressions like 'For all x, $P(x)$' and 'For some x, $P(x)$'. For example, let $P(x)$ be 'x is red'. Then, 'For all x, $P(x)$' is 'For all x, x is red'.

1.5.2 Rules for the Universal Quantifier

Our task of explaining the quantifiers can now be formulated in terms of this notation. It is to explain, in what is known as *quantificational logic*, what valid argument patterns depend on the grammatical form of 'For all x, $P(x)$' and 'For some x, $P(x)$'.

In the fourteenth century William of Ockham observed the close tie between universal quantification and conjunction and between existential quantification and disjunction. To say 'Everything is red' is to say 'This is red $\wedge$ that is red $\wedge \cdots$' in a long conjunction naming everything. Likewise to say 'Something is red' is to say 'This is red $\vee$ that is red $\vee \cdots$' in an inclusive disjunction naming everything. This idea leads to the following analyses of the quantifiers:

Quantified sentence	Translation
For all x, $P(x)$	$P(c_1) \wedge \cdots \wedge P(c_n)$
For some x, $P(x)$	$P(c_1) \vee \cdots \vee P(c_n)$

The ellipsis '...' is meant to be filled in by all $P(c_i)$ for $1 \leq i \leq n$, and the analysis is plausible only on the assumption that for anything that exists there is some such constant c_i that names it. Given this translation every argument involving quantifiers could be translated into propositional logic and appraised by truth-tables.

Unfortunately the translation assumes the world is finite and fully named. Since we often wish to discuss subjects with unnamed elements and universes of infinite expanse, logicians do not rely on these translations but explain quantificational logic by a series of rules. These rules are meant to suffice for all valid inferences either to or from quantified sentences. The first rule for the quantifiers records the obvious fact that if something holds for everything it holds for any particular case. In order to state it in a sufficiently general form, we shall allow that we can refer to a particular thing by either a proper name or a pronoun. Proper names are represented by constants and pronouns by variables. What is common to both sorts of expression is that once their meaning is fixed they refer to individual things. Let us use t to stand for any expression that is either a constant or a variable.

Universal Instantiation (R9 or UI). In a proof it is valid to introduce a new line $P(t)$ if there is a previous line 'For all x, $P(x)$'.

If a sentence is introduced into a proof by the application of a rule to a series of previous lines of the proof, the sentence is said to be inferred from them by rule. Thus the rule says that $P(t)$ may be inferred from 'For all x, $P(x)$' by UI.

We cannot at this point 'prove' this rule. It is rather self-evident and we shall return in a later chapter to its formal justification. At this point we can show that the rule holds if we make the idealized but untrue assumption that all worlds have a finite number of things and each of them has a name. The argument then is the same as

$$P(t_1), \ldots, P(t_n)/P(t_i), \text{ for some } i \text{ such that } 1 \leq i \leq n.$$

This argument is formulated in propositional logic and is a special case of the fact that if a conjunction is true, then all of its conjuncts are true.

The rough-and-ready rules used in metatheory are fairly simple and plausible. The rule we have just discussed records the fairly obvious fact that 'all' implies 'some'. Given that everything in the universe has a property, we can infer that any particular we can name must have that property. We often simplify proofs by deleting talk of 'for all x' and just talking about one of them. The reverse argument, however, is completely invalid. You cannot logically generalize to everything from just one case.

It is true that in the empirical sciences, part of the ordinary scientific method is to discover general laws through the study of particular cases. Sometimes these special cases take the form of experiments in a laboratory, sometimes they are carefully recorded observations of particular phenomena found in the world outside the laboratory, but in all such cases the 'data' collected are all merely a representative sample of their type. What the scientist does is to generalize beyond this data to a general law. This logical leap from *some* to *all* is called by philosophers *induction.* The most striking feature of scientific induction is that on the face of it, it is a terribly bad argument form. Just because some things have a property does not mean we are justified in concluding that everything has it. In fact scientific inductions often fail. The hunch is wrong, not confirmed by later experiments or observation. Systematic efforts to minimize the element of failure in induction have led to careful formulations of the scientific method, and a large part of the modern study of the philosophy of science concerns the puzzle of why scientists seem to have had such success at discovering universal laws through what looks like illogical leaps of reasoning. But the important point for our discussion is that unqualified generalizations to *everything* from assumptions concerning only something are logically invalid.

Generalizing from a single case, however, can be rendered logically valid by adding an extra premise to the effect that the special case is 'typical' of everything in the universe. To say that something is perfectly typical, that it is a genuine Everyman, means that we must not assume anything about it that is not known to be true of everything. The only facts we can assume about such a typical case are facts already established as universally true. We can actually be somewhat clearer about what being typical amounts to. For the practical task of proof construction we may use the following definition.

DEFINITION: The occurrence of an expression t in a proof is *typical of everything* in a universe U (t in this case is also called *arbitrary*) iff every sentence in the proof that mentions t either

(1) is inferred from an earlier sentence of the proof of the form 'For all x, $Q(x)$' by UI, or

(2) is inferred by UI from some previously known general truth of the form 'For all x, $Q(x)$' that is appealed to in the proof but perhaps not explicitly stated.

This definition ensures that a typical usage genuinely represents a whole universe and that it would be valid to universally generalize from it.

Universal Generalization (R10 or UG). In a proof it is valid to introduce a new line 'for all x, $P(x)$' if there is a previous line $P(t)$ and if that occurrence of t is typical of everything in the universe in that proof.

In applying this rule it is important to note two cases in which t would not be typical as that notion has been defined. If t occurs within a premise of a proof or if any previous occurrence of t is introduced into the proof by application of a rule other than UI, then that occurrence of t is not typical. If we assume something special about t, i.e., if t occurs in a premise of the proof, it is not typical. Nor is it typical if it is introduced other than by UI; it must not be introduced into a proof on any line which is justified by a logical rule other than UI. If t were to be introduced by UI it would indeed be typical of everything because applying UI consists merely of reasoning from the fact that everything has a property to the fact that this particular t has it. We shall find in a moment, however, that some other rules also allow one to introduce into a proof a line with a constant like t in it, and these rules do not require that t be typical of everything. We shall spell out these cases of nontypical use of t shortly.

1.5.3 Rules for the Existential Quantifier

For each of the two rules for the universal quantifier, there are parallel rules for the existential quantifier. Though universally generalizing from a single case to everything is not valid without a special assumption, it is perfectly valid to infer from just one case that something, at least one thing, has a property.

Existential Generalization (R11 or EG). In a proof it is valid to introduce a line 'For some x, $P(x)$', if there is a previous line $P(t)$.

Once again this rule is obviously legitimate and reduces in the case of finitely named worlds to a propositional equivalent easily verified by truth-tables. Under these assumptions the rule amounts to saying that the following argument is valid:

$$P(t_i)/P(t_1) \vee \cdots \vee P(t_n), \text{ for some } i,\ 1 \leq i \leq n.$$

The converse is not valid except in special situations. Just because we know that something has a property, we have no right to infer that this or that particular individual has it, for it might be some other individual that makes the existential quantification true. That somebody is rich does not imply that I am. Within a proof, however, it is sometimes convenient to give a name to one of the individuals that has a property which we know holds for something even though we really do not know which one. Proofs get rather complicated and wordy. It simplifies matters to name a particular thing rather than to keep repeating 'For some x, x is such that'. We can so baptize the holder of a nonuniversal property so long as we then do not go on to think we know anything else about this individual. All we know is that we are giving one of the holders of the property a name, say t. We may assume nothing else about t except perhaps facts that we already know hold true for absolutely everything in the universe. We make these rather vague conditions more precise in the statement of the rule.

Existential Instantiation (R12 or EI). In a proof it is valid to introduce a line $P(t)$ if

(1) there is a previous line 'For some x, $P(x)$';

(2) all previous occurrences of t, if any, are introduced by UI or are inferred from still earlier lines which are introduced by UI; and

(3) t does not occur in either the premise or conclusion of the proof.

Clause (2) ensures that all we assume about the proxy t is what we already know of everything. Clause (3) ensures that we did not start by making particular assumptions about t and that we rid our conclusion of any mention of t with its temporary meaning.

□ **EXERCISE**

For each of the following examples find a way of filling out the details of a picture so that the example is satisfied. Let the set of all things existing in the world w be represented by a rectangle and let circles within it represent the specific subsets of the existing things such that they are $P(x)$ and $Q(x)$, respectively. To indicate that a region of the rectangle is empty, shade it. To indicate that a region is not empty, draw at least one dot in it representing an existing thing. To indicate that an object is in one of two regions but you do not know which, draw a dot on the border separating them. (Such representations are called *Venn diagrams* after their nineteenth century inventor John Venn.)

a. 'For all x, $P(x) \to Q(x)$' is T in w, but
'For all x, $P(x) \wedge Q(x)$' is F in w.

b. 'For some x, $P(x) \to Q(x)$' is T in w, but
'For some x, $P(x) \wedge Q(x)$' is F in w.

c. '(For all x, $P(x)$) $\to$ (for all x, $Q(x)$)' is T in w, but
'For all x, $P(x) \to Q(x)$' is F in w.

d. '(For some x, $P(x)$) $\wedge$ (for some x, $Q(x)$)' is T in w, but
'For some x, $P(x) \wedge (x)$' is F in w.

Figure 1.1 is an example of a Venn diagram with its interpretation. In this diagram, the universe contains four things (dots): one in both $P(x)$ and $Q(x)$, one in just $Q(x)$, and two in neither. In this world the following are true:

For all x, $P(x) \to Q(x)$.

For some x, $P(x) \wedge Q(x)$.

$\sim$(For all x, $P(x) \vee Q(x)$).

For some x, $Q(x) \wedge \sim P(x)$.

1.5.4 Converting between Quantifiers

We conclude our discussion of the quantifiers by showing how it is possible to reformulate statements containing one quantifier in terms of expressions mentioning only the other.

Rule of Quantifier Conversion (R13). Each of the following pairs are logical equivalents and one member of a pair can be introduced as a line in a proof if the other occurs as a previous line:

For all x, $P(x)$	$\sim$(For some x, $\sim P(x)$)
For all x, $\sim P(x)$	$\sim$(For some x, $P(x)$)
$\sim$(For all x, $P(x)$)	For some x, $\sim P(x)$
$\sim$(For all x, $\sim P(x)$)	For some x, $P(x)$

The truth of these conversions is obvious enough if one thinks about what they say, but they are easily proved on the assumption that everything is finite

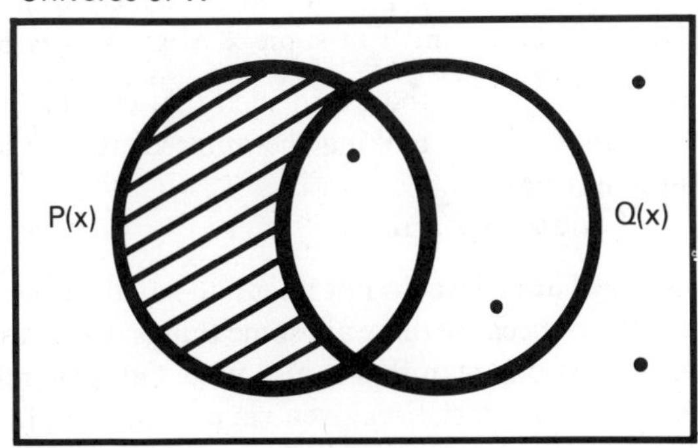

Fig. 1.1

and named. To prove that the first left-hand sentence follows logically from that on the right, here are a series of logical equivalents and the reason why each line can be seen to be an equivalent of its predecessor.

Proof of the first conversion (from left to right)

(1)	For all x, $P(x)$	Assumption
(2)	$P(t_1) \wedge \cdots \wedge P(t_n)$	Follows from line (1) by translation into conjunction
(3)	$\sim(\sim P(t_1) \vee \cdots \vee \sim P(t_n))$	Follows from line (2) by DeMorgan's laws
(4)	$\sim$(For some x, $\sim P(x)$)	Follows from line (3) by translation from disjunction

The proof that the right-hand sentence follows logically from that on the left consists of this argument in the reverse direction, and the proof of the other conversions in both directions can be established similarly.

We can now see why 'All A are B' is rendered mathematically as 'For all x, x is $A \rightarrow x$ is B', and why 'Some A are B' is translated as 'For some x, x is $A \wedge x$ is B'. The mathematical use of the universal quantifier is accompanied by the conditional, but the existential quantifier is accompanied by conjunction. To see why this is so, consider what universal quantification with conjunction and existential quantification with the conditional would mean. Suppose the universalized conjunction below is true.

For all x, x is $A \wedge x$ is B.

This proposition may be expressed in English as follows:

Everything in the world is both A and B.

Now surely all men can be mortal without everything in the world being both a man and a mortal. All we mean to assert is that those things which are men are also mortal, which the usual translation by the conditional admirably captures. Likewise, the statement 'For some x, x is $A \rightarrow x$ is B' means

There is at least one thing in the world such that either
(1) it is not an A (hence making the antecedent false and the whole conditional true), or
(2) it is an A and also is a B.

But in saying 'Some A are B' we do not intend to say the first possibility; we assert 'Some A is B' not because there are some things which are not men, but because there is at least one man that is also wise. Our true intention is well captured by the standard translation given via conjunction. In practice what we will have to prove will already be written in mathematicalese, so there will not be much need to translate difficult English idioms that use 'all' and 'some' into the quantifiers. When we actually start studying natural language quantification in later chapters we shall see that both codifying its rules for valid argument and formulating its grammar in mathematical language are deep theoretical problems.

☐ **EXERCISES**

1. By translating into long conjunctions and disjunctions, as in the proof of the first conversion from left to right, show that the remaining three conversions going from left to right would likewise be valid if all worlds were finite and named.
2. By appeal to quantifier conversions and simple logical equivalences, show that in the following pairs, the expression on the left is logically equivalent to that on the right. Follow these steps: first transform the quantified expression on the left into a long conjunction or disjunction in the manner of Ockham. (We are assuming in doing so the idealization that the world is finite and named.) Second, transform the conjunction or disjunction by appeal to DeMorgan's laws and the fact that $P \rightarrow Q$ is logically equivalent to $\sim P \vee Q$. You should arrive at a disjunction or conjunction that (given our idealization) is logically equivalent to the quantified formula on the right.
   a. Show that 'For all x, $F(x) \rightarrow G(x)$' is equivalent to '$\sim$(For some x, $F(x) \wedge \sim G(x)$)'.
   b. Show that 'For some x, $F(x) \wedge G(x)$' is equivalent to '$\sim$(For all x, $F(x) \rightarrow \sim G(x)$)'.

Here $F(x)$ and $G(x)$ are possibly different sentences containing the variable x.

1.6 TWO USEFUL RULES

1.6.1 Replacement 'by Definition'

A common and important way to advance a proof is by appeal to definitions. Once our metatheory starts unfolding we shall have occasion to state definitions. Indeed we have done so already. A definition always take the form of abbreviating a long expression which we already understand (called the *definiens*, Latin for 'that which is doing the defining') by a new short expression (called the *definiendum*, 'that which is being defined'). Thus the role of definitions is to make the theory manageable by replacing central but complex formulations, often requiring many words to state, with single key ideas. If the idea used to abbreviate the complex phrase has previously been poorly understood, having only obscure or muddled explanations, then the new definition in the context of a well-defined theory amounts to a conceptual clarification and scientific advance.

Definitions often play a crucial role within proofs. Proofs proceed by drawing consequences from previous lines in virtue of their grammatical form. Often this form is only revealed after key ideas have been expanded (colloquially, 'cashed out') or translated into the longer formulations to which they are equivalent by definition. A typical pattern in a proof is to start with assumptions that are simple in grammar but rich in theoretical vocabulary. The theoretical ideas are replaced in subsequent steps of the proof by their longer definitional equivalents, thereby transforming the assumptions into grammatically complex sentences. The more elaborate grammar logically implies other complex sentences in virtue of its form, and these occupy the next lines of the proof. Finally, it is often possible to reapply theoretical definitions to the intermediate results by abbreviating some of their complex phrases by key words. The final line of the proof is then usually in the same condensed and informative form as the original assumptions. We explicitly recognize this use of definitions in the following rule of thumb.

Inference by Definition (R14). If P is just like Q except that some part of one contains the definitional abbreviation of some part of the other, then Q follows logically from P and may legitimately be introduced into a proof containing P as a previous line.

1.6.2 Judicious Hand-Waving

Ideally, in some Platonic Heaven where there is an infinity of time and leisure for clarity and logical thinking, absolutely every step of every proof would be fully stated and documented. Such is a philosophical ideal. In practice such proofs are tedious, and the novelty of a new proof is often lost in the forest of detail. Thus, in practice logicians usually conflate (combine) whole series of fairly obvious steps to a single line of a proof. For example, nobody bothers to justify explicitly the reordering or regrouping of conjunctions. The question accordingly arises of when it is all right to conflate steps and when is it not. The honest answer is that it depends on your mathematical sophistication and that of your audience. In this text we shall use the rule of thumb that you may conflate steps whose logic depends on something studied in a previous chapter.

Conflation (R15). Intermediate steps between P and Q may be omitted from a proof without citation if they depend on definitions or logical rules that are well known and not at the moment the subject of study.

We are now ready to try constructing proofs for the first time. Our practice material will be what is called *naive set theory*. Proving theorems in set theory not only teaches how to do proofs, but has the additional benefit of providing us with a mathematical language that we can later use as a theoretical metalanguage for the study of the semantics of particular object languages.

2

Naive Set Theory

2.1 LOGIC AND IDENTITY

2.1.1 The Axiomatic Method

The purpose of this chapter is to give practice constructing proofs according to the rules presented previously and at the same time to introduce set theory, which will provide the theoretical ideas needed later when we turn to the study of language. The form set theory takes is that of an axiom system. We shall lay down its basic axioms and then prove what follows from them.

As we shall see in detail in later chapters, set theory has some general features that recommend it as a metatheory for studying language. Above all, because set theory is a branch of mathematics, it allows assertions about language to be formulated in a precise vocabulary and then rigorously proven. Laws written in set theory can be clearly stated and their consequences clearly demonstrated, in the manner of any mature science. Choosing set theory as a metalanguage also has the unfortunate consequence of making linguistics as done by logicians rather esoteric. Since logicians write about language in set theory and since set theory itself is rather symbolic and technical, only the initiated can read what is said. Fortunately set theory in the simple form used is easy to learn. Some of it is even taught in elementary schools as part of the 'new math', but sometimes in a form that leaves both students and teachers unclear about its motivation. In this chapter we present and prove basic facts about sets. In later chapters we shall see its utility in talking about language. For the present we shall be talking in English, our metalanguage, about set theory, our object language.

The theory employs all the logical terms we have already encountered and a few new ones of its own. It uses the logical connectives for negation, conjunction, disjunction, the conditional and biconditional, as well as variables and the universal and existential quantifiers. We learned in Chapter 1 that these logical terms function grammatically as a glue that binds together simpler expressions to make more complex ones. They presuppose that there are some basic, simple assertions to which they may be attached. The way in which set theory goes beyond the logic we have studied is that it provides a repertory of elementary or basic sentences that may then be combined with the logical signs we have already met to form a large body of sentences, both simple and complex. As in any group of sentences some of these will be true and others false. Our goal will be to explain in a careful and clear manner exactly which of these sentences are true. For this purpose we shall use what is called the axiomatic method. First we shall lay down as given a small number of basic truths or axioms. We shall also state from time to time various definitions. From the axioms and the definitions we shall then derive various consequences which are called theorems. The theorems together with the axioms and definitions on which they are based constitute the truths of set theory. One of the goals of the chapter is to introduce these truths. Since there are rather a lot of truths about sets, indeed an infinite number, we organize our knowledge by concentrating on those which are fundamental, mainly the axioms, the definitions, and a small number of key theorems.

Equally important will be the method used for the derivation of the theorems. This method is that of proof construction, and one of our main goals in proving theorems about sets is to provide numerous examples of what a proof is. The technique of constructing proofs is not limited to set theory but is widely applicable to diverse branches of mathematics and science. Each step in a proof will generally consist of the application of one of the rules of thumb from Chapter 1; the many examples of their use are meant to familiarize the student with how the rules are used in practice. The instructional method employed in the chapter is based on the assumption that students learn how to do proofs largely through imitation. First, a theorem is stated. Then an informal analysis is given of a reasonable strategy for attempting to prove it. This analysis is given in English and is designed to reproduce the logician's reasoning in creating the proof. Finally, the proof itself is stated. It is a formal step-by-step statement of the steps sketched more informally in the proof analysis. After each theorem and its proof, one or more exercise is given. These consist of proving theorems very similar to the example proven in the text. Only slight alterations in the example are necessary, so that in general it is possible to imitate quite closely the reasoning used in proving the example. Here the goal is to be a careful mimic.

2.1.2 Truths of Logic

The first axiom of set theory is essentially the first axiom of any science whatever. It concerns what set theory has in common with every other science, its obedience to logic.

Axiom of Logical Truth (A1). Any truth of logic is a truth of set theory.

This axiom may seem trivial, but it is very useful in constructing proofs. It allows us to introduce any truth of logic anywhere in a proof. These truths often provide reformulations, in equivalent but slightly different grammar, of propositions previously established in the proof. The new grammatical form may be open to the application of a logical rule that the original formulation was not, hence making it possible to advance the proof by applying the rule. Frequently we shall begin a proof by deriving some fairly obvious consequences from our assumptions, in a manner sometimes called 'working forward'. It is a good idea to get into the habit of viewing a single sentence as really the representative of a wider group of logical equivalents, any one of which may be appropriate for advancing the proof at hand. Which equivalent is wanted can often be determined by looking at the conclusion. In a process often called 'working backward', we note various reformulations of the conclusion or other propositions from which it would obviously follow. Sometimes working forward and working backward have the result that one of the obvious consequences of the assumptions is a sentence that obviously implies the conclusion. If the process of working forward and backward does not meet at a common point, then the proof requires some extra thinking. In major metatheoretic results, the gap is bridged by creativity or appeal to facts in other branches of logic or mathematics. But the proofs in this chapter are really quite trivial in the sense that all we need do to fill in the middle part of the proof is appeal to fairly obvious logical truths. We shall find that the reformulations of the premises together with simple truths of logic do imply the conclusion or some equivalent of it. To introduce these required logical truths into a proof we shall use the first axiom.

2.1.3 Identity

We begin the statement of the basic truths of set theory by introducing two undefined notions. These are *set membership* indicated by the symbol '$\in$' and *identity* or *equality* indicated by '$=$'.

Symbols in set theory	Translations into English
$x = y$	x is identical or equal to y
$x \in y$	x is a member or element of y

These translations are not really adequate as explanations of membership or identity because we do not really know what the translations themselves mean. Moreover, the concepts are so fundamental that it is difficult to think of anything much to say about them that would be couched in terms more basic or clearer than these. One method of illuminating very basic concepts, and the one we shall employ here, is merely to lay down as given some basic truths or axioms. These are not really definitions because they do not have the form 'This concept is defined as ...' in the manner of dictionaries or formal definitions in mathematics. Rather, they are simple fundamental truths which seem logically to lie beneath all the other truths of the subject. (Sometimes the axioms are said to provide *implicit* definitions of their undefined terms, because though they do not define them in any explicit way we nevertheless gather some understanding of them from the fact that the axioms state some truth involving them.)

Identity is a notion that is not peculiar to set theory. After all, all things, not just sets, are self-identical. Because it is such a general notion it is usually classified as part of logic itself. Within logic two axioms are usually used to explain the idea.

Axiom of Self-Identity (A2). For any x, $x = x$.

Everything is the same as itself, a paradigm of both a truth and a triviality. Sometimes, however, even this truth is useful. More important is what this axiom fails to include among those things identical to x. No matter how similar y is to x, no matter how many properties x and y have in common, if they are two different things, if, as philosophers say, they are 'numerically different', then they are not identical. Thus identity, as it is used in logic, is sometimes called *numerical identity* and is narrower than the ordinary language concept of sameness. If two things are different, no matter how similar, they are not identical, and strictly speaking there is only one thing identical with anything, and that thing is itself.

Even though a thing is identical to itself and nothing else, we sometimes have two different names for the same thing. The second axiom of identity allows us to substitute different names for the same thing in a proposition already proven. In order to state the axiom we need some new notation. Let us use $P(x)$ to stand for a sentence containing the variable x, and let $P(y)$ be the sentence just like $P(x)$ except that y occurs in some place (not necessarily every place) that x does in $P(x)$. When we use a variable without a quantifier (a *free variable*, as it is called), it should be thought of as a pronoun or demonstrative having the function of standing for a particular individual even though which individual that is may not have been specified.

Axiom of Substitutivity of Identity (A3). For any x and y, $(x = y \wedge P(x)) \rightarrow P(y)$.

In practical terms, this axiom allows us to rewrite what we already know substituting one name for another if they stand for the same thing.

THEOREM. For any x and y, $x = y \rightarrow y = x$.

Analysis of proof. Since this holds for any x and y whatever, we must be careful to 'be general in x and y', i.e., not to assume anything about them except perhaps facts which we know hold for anything whatever. Also the theorem is a conditional and therefore should be proven, if it can, by conditional proof (R3 in Chapter 1). We will assume $x = y$ and deduce $y = x$. To bridge the gap we will appeal to the previous axiom.

Proof. Let x and y be arbitrary, and assume $x = y$. Now, by the axiom of identity we know $x = x$. Combining these facts, we know $x = y \wedge x = x$. One instance of the substitutivity axiom is $(x = y \wedge x = x) \rightarrow y = x$. We obtain this instance by understanding $P(x)$ to be $x = x$ and replacing just one occurrence of x by y in $P(x)$. Then by *modus ponens*, we know $y = x$. Hence by conditional proof, $x = y \rightarrow y = x$. QED.

☐ **EXERCISE**

By appeal to the axioms of identity and the laws of logic in the last chapter, prove the following theorem. Precede your proof with an analysis explaining your strategy.

THEOREM. $(x = y \wedge y = z) \rightarrow x = z$.

2.2 AXIOMS OF NAIVE SET THEORY

2.2.1. Extensionality

The previous identity axioms hold for everything, but there is a special ruie of identity that holds only for sets. It says that the only way two sets can differ is by having different members. To put it another way, if two sets have the same members, they are really one and the same set.

Axiom of Extensionality (A4). For any x and y, $x = y$ iff (for any z, $z \in x \leftrightarrow z \in y$).

Let us call the list of the elements of a set its *extension*. Then, this axiom says that two sets are identical if their extensions are the same. (Hence the name of the axiom.) What is important about this rule is that it provides for a very common strategy for proving two sets, say x and y, to be the same. First show for any z, $z \in x \leftrightarrow z \in y$. We show this by choosing an arbitrary z and showing $z \in x \leftrightarrow z \in y$. We show this latter by showing first $z \in x \rightarrow z \in y$ and then showing $z \in y \rightarrow z \in x$. Each of these we show in turn by conditional proof, first assuming $z \in x$ and deducing on that assumption that $z \in y$, and then assuming conversely that $z \in y$ and then deducing on that assumption that $z \in x$. If we have done so and z is truly arbitrary, we can universally generalize (the UG rule) and establish the identity of x and y by appeal to this axiom. Because this line of argument is used over and over again, the student should pause to master it at this point. Keep rehearsing it until its reasoning makes clear sense.

Proof strategy to show two sets are identical. To show $x = y$, first lay down the assumption that z is arbitrary. Then proceed by distinguishing two cases. Case I; Assume $z \in x$. On this assumption then deduce $z \in y$. If you can make this deduction it follows by conditional proof that $z \in x \rightarrow z \in y$. Case II: Assume $z \in y$. On this assumption then deduce $z \in x$. If you can make this deduction, it then follows that $z \in y \rightarrow z \in x$. If both conditionals hold, then by propositional logic (truth-tables) the biconditional $z \in x \leftrightarrow z \in y$ must be true. If z is arbitrary and we have assumed nothing particular about z, it is legitimate to apply UG to the biconditional and thus derive the theorem in its generalized form.

2.2.2 Abstraction

Only one other axiom is needed for the simple version of set theory we shall employ. Put simply it says two things: (1) if you can define a set it exists, and (2) an object has the property which characterizes members of a set if, and only if, it is in that set. To state the axiom formally, we introduce a special form for naming sets called a *set abstract*. Let $P(x)$ be an open sentence. Then, we use the set abstract $\{x | x \in P(x)\}$ to refer to the set of all x such that $P(x)$.

EXAMPLES

Set theory	English translation
$\{x \mid P(x)\}$	The set of all x such that $P(x)$
$\{x \mid 0 < x\}$	The set of things greater than 0
$\{x \mid x \text{ is red}\}$	The collection of red things
$\{x \mid x \text{ is a noun}\}$	The set of nouns

The axiom explaining this notation has two parts. It says first that the set in question exists and second that the things in the set are just those things having its defining property. Both these principles are rather obvious from the choice of notation and its translation into English, but for rigor and clarity it is important to spell them out explicitly.

Axiom of Abstraction (A5).

(1) $\{x | P(x)\}$ exists and there is only one of them.

(2) Let $P(y)$ be the result of replacing every free occurrence of x in $P(x)$. Then, for any y, $y \in \{x | P(x)\} \leftrightarrow P(y)$.

Philosophers and scientists are always concerned about what exists—scientists because they hope to unfold the marvels of the universe and philosophers because in metaphysics they probe the ultimate constituents of reality. Part (1) makes explicit the basic scientific and metaphysical assumption of set theory that sets exist. We shall see later that this assumption has been seriously questioned by some philosophers.

Part (2) is famous because it is both obvious and paradoxical. It is obvious because it seems to capture exactly what we intend by the notation. If sets exist at all then they must be composed of exactly those things that have the property defining the set, and furthermore if we can think up a property, then there seems to be no reason whatever why we should not be able to draw the entities having that property together into a set. On the other hand, part (2) seems to lead to a contradiction. For simplicity in the derivations below we use the slash notation $\notin$ for the negation of set membership: instead of $\sim(x \in y)$ we write $x \notin y$.

THEOREM. *Russell's paradox.* The set of all things which are not members of themselves (called *Russell's set* and written $\{x|x \notin x\}$) both is and is not a member of itself:

$$\{x|x \notin x\} \in \{x|x \notin x\} \wedge \{x|x \notin x\} \notin \{x|x \notin x\}.$$

Proof analysis. Suppose, on the one hand, that Russell's set is a member of itself. Then it must have the property which characterizes all members of that set, namely that it is not a member of itself. Suppose, on the other hand, that it is not a member of itself. It therefore has the property which qualifies it for admission into Russell's set, and hence it is a member of itself.

Proof. An instance of part (2) would be the following, taking $x \notin x$ for $P(x)$:

$$\text{For any } y,\ y \in \{x|x \notin x\} \leftrightarrow y \notin y.$$

Since this holds for any y, by universal instantiation (UI) it must hold as well for the particular set $\{x|x \notin x\}$ which, as a set, exists. It must be one of the entities included in the universe and embraced by the universal quantifier. Hence, by UI,

$$\{x|x \notin x\} \in \{x|x \notin x\} \leftrightarrow \{x|x \notin x\} \notin \{x|x \notin x\}.$$

But since $(P \leftrightarrow \sim P) \rightarrow (P \wedge \sim P)$ is a logical truth (by truth-tables), the line above logically implies the theorem. QED.

The controversy among philosophers and mathematicians surrounding the existence of sets derives in large part from this and similar paradoxes. Some conclude that this contradiction just shows by a *reductio ad absurdum* proof that sets do not exist. The majority think it shows we have not stated part (2) quite right. The field of logic known as *axiomatic set theory* consists of technical attempts to reformulate part (2) in weaker forms so as to avoid paradox. Doing so in a thorough manner has been one of the greatest challenges to mathematics in the twentieth century.[1] For the purposes of applying mathematics to the study of language in formal semantics, however, we ignore these refinements and adopt parts (1) and (2) as they stand in what is called *naive set theory*.[2]

The principle of abstraction provides the basis for the remaining concepts of set theory that we shall meet in this introduction. All follow a common pattern. In each case a special set is introduced by means of a defining property. The axiom ensures that the set exists. The axiom also provides the framework for showing whether something is in the set. We merely show that it does or does not have the property definitive of the set. Below is given the list of the simple sets we shall meet. First is the symbolic abbreviation of the set, second is its fully explicit name given in the form of a set abstract, and last is the English reading of the name.

$A \cup B$	$\{x \mid x \in A \vee x \in B\}$	Union of A and B
$A \cap B$	$\{x \mid x \in A \wedge x \in B\}$	Intersection of A and B
$-A$	$\{x \mid x \notin A\}$	Complement of A
$A - B$	$\{x \mid x \in A \wedge x \notin B\}$	Complement of B in A
$\varnothing$	$\{x \mid x \text{ does not exist}\}$	Empty set
$\mathbf{V}$	$\{x \mid x \text{ exists}\}$	Universal set
$\{x_1, \ldots, x_n\}$	$\{y \mid y = x_1 \vee \cdots \vee y = x_n\}$	Set containing $x_1, \ldots, x_n$

Since the language of set theory is new it is important to be clear about its grammar, about which symbols are names, and about which longer strings of symbols form sentences. Notice that in each case the new symbol is the name of a set and thus assumes the grammatical role of name. Each is an expression standing for an entity in the world, an unusual and 'abstract' entity but a thing in the world nevertheless. With these names we form longer sentences making assertions about the abstract entities so named. Below are examples of sentences asserting that something is in each of these sets. Following each sentence is another asserting that the entity contained in the set has the

[1] On the paradoxes of set theory, see W. V. O. Quine, 'Paradoxes' (1962). For an informal introduction to axiomatic set theory, see Raymond L. Wilder, *Introduction to the Foundations of Mathematics* (1965).

[2] For more practice in or greater detail about naive set theory, see Seymour Lipschutz, *Schaum's Outline of Theory and Problems of Set Theory and Related Topics* (1964), Paul Halmos, *Naive Set Theory* (1960), and D. van Dalen, *Sets: Naive, Axiomatic, and Applied* (1978).

property definitive of the set. The principle of abstraction assures us that each of these pairs says the same thing. They are logically equivalent in the sense that one is true if and only if the other is.

$x \in A \cup B$	$x \in A \vee x \in B$
$x \in A \cap B$	$x \in A \wedge x \in B$
$x \in -A$	$x \notin A$
$x \in A - B$	$x \in A \wedge x \notin B$
$x \in \varnothing$	x does not exist
$x \in \mathbf{V}$	x exists
$x \in \{y_1, \ldots, y_n\}$	$x = y_1 \vee \cdots \vee x = y_n$

The device of replacing one of these equivalents by the other is fundamental to proofs about sets, and we shall take up the details in a moment. But before introducing in more detail the special sets we have just named, we state two theorems linking the notions of set abstraction and identity. They appeal in their proofs to both the axioms of extensionality and abstraction.

THEOREM. $\{x|P(x)\} = \{y|Q(y)\} \to$ (for any z, $P(z) \leftrightarrow Q(x)$).

Analysis of proof. Note that the main connective of the theorem is a conditional. Hence we use a proof strategy appropriate to it: conditional proof. We will assume the antecedent, $\{x|P(x)\} = \{y|Q(y)\}$, and attempt to deduce the consequent, for any z, $P(z) \leftrightarrow Q(z)$. Now notice that this antecedent is an identity between two sets and that the axiom of extensionality allows you to reformulate such an identity in longer terms. In doing so, we will use a new variable so as not to get confused with the old. Since z is the variable in the consequent let us try it. Thus by extensionality the antecedent can be rewritten in the following equivalent form:

For any z, $z \in \{x|P(x)\} \leftrightarrow z \in \{y|Q(y)\}$.

By universal instantiation we simplify and get rid of the complicating initial quantifier 'for any z':

(1) $z \in \{x|P(x)\} \leftrightarrow z \in \{y|Q(y)\}$.

The challenge is to reformulate this biconditional in longer terms to see if we can then find a simple logical step to the consequent to be proved. Notice that each half of the biconditional asserts that z is in a set denoted by abstraction. By the axiom of abstraction, then, we get the following equivalences, one for each half:

(2) $z \in \{x|P(x)\} \leftrightarrow P(z)$,

(3) $z \in \{y|Q(y)\} \leftrightarrow Q(z)$.

We have now expanded our original information enough to jump to what we want by a step of simple logic, for steps (1)–(3) logically imply

(4) $P(z) \leftrightarrow Q(z)$.

To see why, represent step (1) by $R \leftrightarrow S$, step (2) by $R \leftrightarrow T$, and step (3) by $S \leftrightarrow U$. Then step (4) would be $T \leftrightarrow U$. It is a simple matter to check by truth-tables that the equivalents may be substituted, i.e., that

(5) $((R \leftrightarrow S) \wedge (R \leftrightarrow T) \wedge (S \leftrightarrow U)) \rightarrow (T \leftrightarrow U)$

is a logical truth. From step (5) the theorem follows directly by universal generalization and from the fact that we have not appealed to any truth about z that is not also true of everything. We can now formulate this informal thinking into a more formal proof.

Proof. Assume for conditional proof $\{x|P(x)\} = \{y|Q(y)\}$. By extensionality this means for any z, $z \in \{x|P(x)\} \leftrightarrow z \in \{y|Q(y)\}$, which may be universally instantiated as $z \in \{x|P(x)\} \leftrightarrow z \in \{y|Q(y)\}$. But by abstraction each of these halves of the biconditional is equivalent respectively to $P(z)$ and $Q(z)$. By substituting equivalents we get $P(z) \leftrightarrow Q(z)$. Since we *are general in z* (i.e., z is genuinely arbitrary) we may generalize to the consequent of the theorem to be proved. QED.

□ **EXERCISE**

Prove the following theorem.

THEOREM. (For any z, $P(z) \leftrightarrow Q(z)) \leftrightarrow \{x|P(x)\} = \{y|Q(y)\}$.

2.3 OPERATIONS AND RELATIONS ON SETS

2.3.1 Set Union

We are now ready to do set theory in earnest by introducing the standard operations (union, intersection, and complementation), a new relation 'on' sets (the subset relation), and two special classes (the empty and universal sets). For each we provide as definition a longer sentence stated in purely logical vocabulary. Following each definition, we prove a special theorem which states in simple terms the conditions under which something is an element of that set.

Proofs of the theorems are all roughly the same. We figure out what we are able to assume and what we must prove. Both what is given and what needs to be proven are written in set theoretic vocabulary. To bridge the gap from assumption to conclusion, the strategy is always to translate out of set theory by appeal to the definitions and then find a logical bridge from the longer

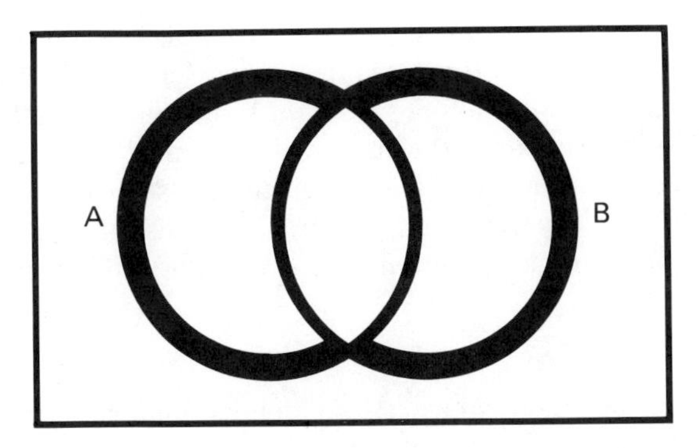

Fig. 2.1

reformulated assumption to the longer reformulated conclusion. The logical bridge will usually be some logical truth we have already proven.

DEFINITION: $A \cup B$ (read *the union of A and B*) is defined as

$$\{x | x \in A \vee x \in B\}.$$

In Fig. 2.1, the heavy line is the boundary of $A \cup B$.

The first consequence we shall prove follows directly from the definition and the axiom of abstraction. It is very useful because it lets us rewrite any assertion of membership in a union as a disjunction. Any rewriting justified on the basis of this trivial theorem is usually just said to follow 'by definition'.

THEOREM. *Abstraction applied to set union.* For any x, $x \in A \cup B \leftrightarrow (x \in A \vee x \in B)$.

Analysis of proof. The theorem is a biconditional, so we break it down into two conditionals and prove each. The obvious way to prove each conditional is by conditional proof, if it works. Notice before we start that $A \cup B$ may be translated into longer logical vocabulary by means of its definition, and that $x \in A \vee x \in B$ is also given an equivalent by the axiom of abstraction. This definition and this equivalent prove in fact to be the same.

Proof. For an arbitrary x. Case I: Assume $x \in A \cup B$. By definition, $x \in \{y | y \in A \vee y \in B\}$. (We use the new variable y because we are already using x and do not want to get confused.) But this by the axiom of abstraction is equivalent to $x \in A \vee x \in B$. Hence by conditional proof, $x \in A \cup B \rightarrow (x \in A \vee x \in B)$. Case II: Assume $x \in A \vee x \in B$. By abstraction $x \in \{y | y \in A \vee y \in B\}$, and by definition of union, $x \in A \cup B$. Thus, by conditional proof, $(x \in A \vee x \in B) \rightarrow x \in A \cup B$. By the two cases, $x \in A \cup B \leftrightarrow (x \in A \vee x \in B)$, and since we have assumed nothing special about x that is not true of everything, we may universally generalize to the theorem. QED.

This theorem justifies the immediate shift from disjunctions asserting that something is in either of two sets to statements asserting it is in the union of the two sets, and these two ways of saying the same thing are so common that often we shall shift from one to the other without explicitly citing the theorem or justifying the step. If a justification is given, it is sufficient to say that the replacement follows 'by definition of union', because the theorem follows directly from the definition of union by a straightforward application of the abstraction axiom.

THEOREM. $A \cup A = A$.

Proof analysis. The theorem asserts an identity, and we try to prove it by appeal to the axiom of extensionality which provides a longer equivalent of every identity. Accordingly, we must show $x \in A \cup A \leftrightarrow x \in A$. This biconditional will be proved by proving both conditionals, each by conditional proof. Going from $x \in A$ to $x \in A \cup A$ is easy because $P \rightarrow (P \vee P)$ is a logical truth and by definition $x \in A \cup A$ means $x \in A \vee x \in A$. The other direction is equally simple: $x \in A \vee x \in A$ also implies $x \in A$, since $(P \vee P) \rightarrow P$ is also a logical truth.

Proof. Let x be arbitrary. Case I: Assume $x \in A$. Then by truth-tables $x \in A \vee x \in A$. Thus by definition of union (and applying to it the definition of the abstraction axiom as in the last theorem) $x \in A \cup A$. Hence by conditional proof, $x \in A \rightarrow x \in A \cup A$. Case II: Assume $x \in A \cup A$. Then by definition $x \in A \vee x \in A$ and by truth-tables $x \in A$. Hence by conditional proof, $x \in A \cup A \rightarrow x \in A$. By both cases, $x \in A \cup A \leftrightarrow x \in A$ and since we are general in x, the theorem follows. QED.

THEOREM. $A \cup B = B \cup A$.

Proof analysis. Like the last theorem, this is an identity and will be proven by two conditional proofs: assume x is in one half and then show it is in the other, and vice versa. Consider just one direction. Assume $x \in A \cup B$. We want to show $x \in B \cup A$. Now, both what we know and what we want to prove are expandable by definition into longer logical vocabulary, into $x \in A \vee x \in B$ and $x \in B \vee x \in A$, respectively. These two are easy to bridge by a simple logical leap: $(P \vee Q) \leftrightarrow (Q \vee P)$ is a logical truth.

Proof. Case I: Let $x \in A \cup B$. By definition $x \in A \vee x \in B$. Then by truth-tables $x \in B \vee x \in A$, and by definition $x \in B \cup A$. Case II: Let $x \in B \cup A$. Then by definition, $x \in B \vee x \in A$, and thus by logic $x \in A \vee x \in B$, and by definition $x \in A \cup B$. By the two cases, $x \in A \cup B \leftrightarrow x \in B \cup A$, and since we are general in x, for any x, $x \in A \cup B \leftrightarrow x \in B \cup A$. And this by extensionality is equivalent to the theorem. QED.

Notice that in both these proofs we translate from statements about sets to longer sentences in logical vocabulary that are universally quantified. The presence of the universal quantifier suggests that the statement starting with it should be proved by universal generalization, and that any series of inferences following from it should begin by an application of universal instantiation. The last two theorems, for example, when translated into logical vocabulary by use of the axiom of extensionality, proved to be universally quantified biconditionals. Thus to prove them we used universal generalization, applied to conditional facts established in turn by conditional proof and use of genuinely 'arbitrary' variables. We ensured that the variables were indeed arbitrary by only proving facts about them that we could in fact have proven about anything.

☐ **EXERCISE**

Prove the following theorem, after first writing a more thorough and chatty proof analysis outlining your strategy.

THEOREM *Associativity.* $A \cup (B \cup C) = (A \cup B) \cup C$.

2.3.2 Set Intersection

Another operation on sets that is much like union is set intersection. This is the operation which forms from two sets that set which consists of the elements they share.

DEFINITION: $A \cap B$ (read *the intersection of A and B*) is defined as

$$\{x | x \in A \wedge x \in B\}.$$

In Fig. 2.2, the heavy line is the boundary of (bounds) $A \cap B$.

The first very useful and obvious theorem for intersection is a direct consequence of the definition of intersection and the axiom of abstraction. As

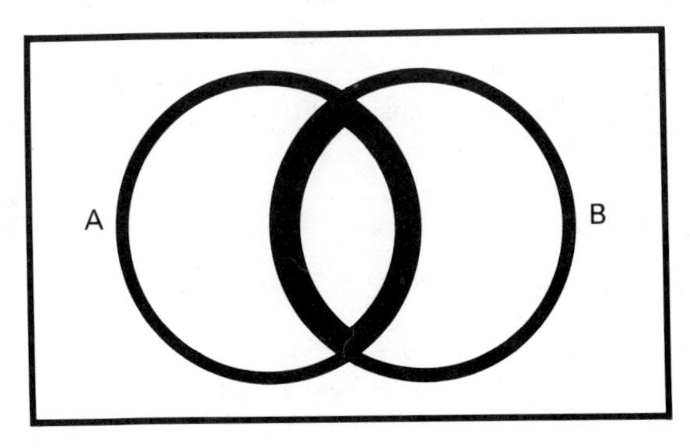

Fig. 2.2

in the case of the first theorem about union, we shall make use of this theorem so frequently that we shall not refer back to it explicitly but merely say that the step in question follows 'by definition of intersection'. This and later theorems are proved just like corresponding theorems for union.

THEOREM. *Abstraction applied to intersection.* For any x, $x \in A \cap B \leftrightarrow (x \in A \wedge x \in B)$.

Proof. For an arbitrary x assume first that $x \in A \cap B$. Then by definition, $x \in \{y \mid y \in A \wedge y \in B\}$, but this by the principle of abstraction is equivalent to $x \in A \wedge x \in B$. Hence by conditional proof $x \in A \cap B \rightarrow (x \in A \wedge x \in B)$. Conversely, assume $x \in A \wedge x \in B$. Then by abstraction $x \in \{y \mid y \in A \wedge y \in B\}$, and thus by definition, $x \in A \cap B$. Hence by conditional proof, $(x \in A \wedge x \in B) \leftrightarrow x \in A \cap B$. Since we have shown both halves of the biconditional, then $x \in A \cap B \leftrightarrow (x \in A \wedge x \in B)$, and by universal generalization we get the theorem. QED.

THEOREM. $A \cap A = A$.

Proof analysis. Since the theorem asserts an identity we will prove it by appeal to extensionality. That is, for an arbitrary x we must show by conditional proof first, on the assumption that $x \in A$, that $x \in A \cap A$, and second, on the assumption that $x \in A \cap A$, that $x \in A$. Consider the first case. Is there anything in either the assumption $x \in A$ or the conclusion $x \in A \cap A$ that can be reformulated into longer logical vocabulary by appeal to definitions? Yes $A \cap A$. Hence what we want to show may be recast by the definition of union as $x \in A \wedge x \in A$. Then there is a simple logical step from assumption $x \in A$ to conclusion $x \in A \wedge x \in A$, for by truth-tables the two are equivalent: $P \leftrightarrow (P \wedge P)$ is a logical truth.

Proof. Case I: Assume $x \in A$. By truth-tables $x \in A \wedge x \in A$. Hence by definition of intersection, $x \in A \cap A$. Thus if $x \in A$, then $x \in A \cap A$ by conditional proof. Case II: Assume $x \in A \cap A$. By definition, $x \in A \wedge x \in A$. Then, by truth-tables $x \in A$. By conditional proof if $x \in A \cap A$, then $x \in A$. Since we have shown both directions of the conditional, we may conclude $x \in A \leftrightarrow x \in A \cap A$. Since we are general in x, we universally generalize, for any x, $x \in A \leftrightarrow x \in A \cap A$. This by extensionality is equivalent to the theorem. QED.

□ EXERCISE

Prove the following theorems. Precede each with a short proof analysis explaining your strategy.

THEOREM. *Commutativity.* $A \cap B = B \cap A$.

THEOREM. *Associativity.* $A \cap (B \cap C) = (A \cap B) \cap C$.

THEOREM. *Distribution.* $A \cup (B \cap C) = (A \cup B) \cap (A \cup C)$ and $A \cap (B \cup C) = (A \cap B) \cup (A \cap C)$.

2.3.3 Set Complementation

Just as union corresponds to and is defined by the connective $\vee$ in propositional logic, and intersection corresponds to and is defined by $\wedge$, there is a set theoretic version of negation, called complementation. It has both a simple and a complex version, both of which will be given definitions here. As we shall see, each version may be fully characterized in terms of the other.

DEFINITION: $-A$ (read *the complement of A*) is defined as $\{x \mid x \notin A\}$.

DEFINITION: $A - B$ (read *the relative complement of B in A*) is defined as

$$\{x \mid x \in A \wedge x \notin B\}.$$

In Fig. 2.3 everything outside of A is included in $-A$, and the heavy line bounds $A - B$.

There follows now a list of theorems that explain complementation and relate it to union and intersection. Like previous theorems the identities are proven by appeal to extensionality: assume something is in one set and deduce that it is in the other, and conversely. Each of these deductions consists of expanding the assumption and desired conclusion by the set theoretic definitions and then finding a simple logical truth to bridge the gap. They differ from earlier proofs only in that here there are sometimes two set theoretic ideas, e.g., both complementation and union, that must be translated within the same set abstract. For example, $x \in A \cup -B$ translates first into $x \in A \vee x \in -B$, by definition of union, and second into $x \in A \vee x \notin B$, by definition of complementation.

THEOREM. For any x, $x \in -A \leftrightarrow x \notin A$.

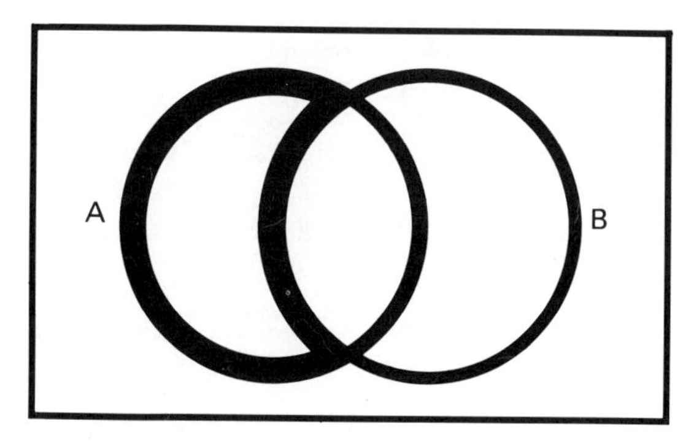

Fig. 2.3

Proof. Let x be arbitrary. Case I: Let $x \in -A$. Then by definition of $-A$, $x \in \{y | y \notin A\}$, and by abstraction, $x \notin A$. Case II: Let $x \notin A$. Then by abstraction $x \in \{y | y \notin A\}$, and by definition of $-A$, $x \in -A$. Hence by conditional proof, $x \in -A \leftrightarrow x \notin A$. Since we are general in x, the theorem follows. QED.

THEOREM. For any x, $x \in A \leftrightarrow x \notin -A$.
THEOREM. For any x, $x \in A - B \leftrightarrow x \in A \wedge x \notin B$.
THEOREM. $A - B = A \cap -B$.

We might have used this theorem to define $A - B$ in terms of simple complementation and union. The following theorems state DeMorgan's laws for sets.

THEOREM. $A \cup B = -(-A \cap -B)$.

Proof analysis. Let us consider just one direction; the other is similar. Let an arbitrary x be in $A \cup B$. Translating, we get $x \in A \vee x \in B$. Now let us look at what we want to prove, namely $x \in -(-A \cap -B)$. This by definition becomes $x \notin -A \cap -B$. But we know that $x \in -A \cap -B \leftrightarrow (x \in -A \wedge x \in -B)$, hence by *modus tollens* $\sim(x \in -A \wedge x \in -B)$, and by DeMorgan's law $x \notin -A \vee x \notin -B$. But we know from a previous theorem that $x \notin -A \leftrightarrow x \in A$, and likewise $x \notin -B \leftrightarrow x \in B$. Thus by truth-tables, $x \in A \vee x \in B$. Look at what has happened. The conclusion we want has been transformed into exactly what we assumed, namely $x \in A \vee x \in B$. All the work of this theorem consists in applying definitions and simplifying, by applying double negation and DeMorgan's laws.

THEOREM. $A \cap B = -(-A \cup -B)$.
THEOREM. $-(A \cup B) = -A \cap -B$.
THEOREM. $-(A \cap B) = -A \cup -B$.

□ **EXERCISE**

Analyze, when necessary, and prove the previous seven theorems.

2.4 THE EMPTY AND UNIVERSAL SETS

We now introduce two important sets, the set with nothing in it and the set that includes everything.

DEFINITION: $\varnothing$ (the *empty set*) is defined as $\{x | x \text{ does not exist}\}$.
DEFINITION: **V** (the *universal set*) is defined as $\{x | x \text{ exists}\}$.

To understand these definitions we must understand how to write in logical notation that something 'exists'. Since logic lacks an intransitive verb 'exists', we manage to say the same thing by means of the existential quantifier and the identity relation. To say something exists is merely another way of saying that there is something which it is identical to, namely itself.

DEFINITION: 'x exists' is defined to mean 'For some y, $y = x$'.

By applying these definitions we get the following trivial theorems. Here we introduce the abbreviated notation for negated identity statements. Instead of $\sim(x = y)$ we write $x \neq y$.

THEOREM. $\varnothing = \{x | \text{for every } y, y \neq x\}$.
THEOREM. $\mathbf{V} = \{x | \text{for some } y, y = x\}$.

Though the definitions just given are the best ones for conveying the intended meaning of the empty and universal sets, they are not the ones usually given. To understand the usual definitions and how they are equivalent to those above, we must see that 'For some y, $y = x$' is a logical truth. That something exists is, of course, no surprise. What is somewhat nonintuitive, however, is that the existence of something should be a fact of logic and not a contingent truth. Isn't it possible, one might argue, that nothing whatever existed? Why should that possibility be precluded by logic alone? That is a good question, and we shall return in a later chapter to versions of logic (called *existence-free logic*) that reject this part of traditional logical theory. But standard logic does assume that there is at least one thing in the world. This assumption is really hidden in the notation, and in particular in the use of free variables. It is assumed that any free variable acts like a pronoun or a demonstrative (words like 'this' or 'that') and picks out something or other in the world. If there were nothing there for it to pick out, it could not function in this way. The proof of the following theorem shows how to transform a referring use of a free variable into an explicit theorem asserting that there is at least one thing.

THEOREM. For some y, $y = x$.

Proof. Consider any arbitrary x. We know $x = x$ by the law of identity. Letting $P(x)$ be $x = x$ and substituting y for one occurrence of x in $P(x)$ we can therefore existentially generalize, for some x, $y = x$. QED.

The last theorem established that the defining condition for the universal set is a logical truth. It holds for any value of the free variable x, no matter what other facts happen to be true. Moreover, the property holds only for the things which exist because only existing things can have properties. Thus, the logically true defining property of the set applies to all and only the existing things, and can legitimately be said to define the "universal" set. An interesting fact to note, however, is that it does not really matter what defining property is used so long as the property chosen is logically true of everything, and there are as many acceptable choices as there are logically true properties of everything. One might, for example, talk about the set of everything that is either red or not red. Since everything is either red or not, this set would also exhaust the universe, and would be identical to **V** as defined above. The logically true property of everything that is usually used to define **V** is self-identity. We first show that, indeed, identity to one's self is a logical truth, and then that the set of self-identical things is the same as the universal set as we have defined it above.

THEOREM. $x = x$.

Proof. By the first axiom of identity, for all x, $x = x$. Hence by UI, $x = x$.

This proposition is a direct universal instantiation of the law of identity and is clearly always true. Since both the previous theorems are logical truths, they are logically equivalent, and when one is true (namely always) so is the other. Hence one can be substituted for the other. In particular the second can be substituted for the first in the definition of the universal set:

THEOREM. (For some y, $y = x) \leftrightarrow x = x$.

Proof. If we know P and we know Q, it then follows from propositional logic that we know $P \leftrightarrow Q$. Thus the theorem follows directly from the previous two. QED.

THEOREM. $\mathbf{V} = \{x | x = x\}$.

Proof. Let y be arbitrary. Case I: Let $y \in \mathbf{V}$. We must show that $y \in \{x | x = x\}$. But that means by abstraction that all we must show is $y = y$. Now this follows directly from the law of identity. Thus we have shown the conditional $y \in \mathbf{V} \rightarrow y \in \{x | x = x\}$ by the trivial method of showing that it is degenerate: its consequent is always true. Case II: Let $y \in \{x | x = x\}$. We must show that $y \in \mathbf{V}$. As in Case I, it is trivially true that $y \in \mathbf{V}$. Hence the conditional $y \in \{x | x = x\} \rightarrow y \in \mathbf{V}$ is likewise degenerate and hence true. Since both directions of the conditional hold, so does the biconditional. Since we are general in y, the theorem follows by UG and extensionality. QED.

THEOREM. $x \in \mathbf{V} \leftrightarrow x = x$.

Likewise the negations of each of the logical truths above must be themselves logically equivalent. They are both always false.

THEOREM. $\sim$(For every y, $y \neq x$).
THEOREM. $\sim(x \neq x)$.
THEOREM. (For every y, $y \neq x) \leftrightarrow (x \neq x)$.
THEOREM. $\varnothing = \{x | x \neq x\}$.
THEOREM. $x \in \varnothing \leftrightarrow x \neq x$.

☐ **EXERCISE**

Give proofs of the previous six unproven theorems.

2.4.1 The Subset Relation

The last basic concept to introduce is the rather intuitive notion of subset.

DEFINITION: $A \subseteq B$ (read *A is a subset of B*) is defined as 'For any x, $x \in A \rightarrow x \in B$'. Both examples in Fig. 2.4 show that $A \subseteq B$. The Venn diagram on the right employs the common convention that a shaded area is understood as empty.

It is important to notice that the string of symbols '$A \subseteq B$' is a sentence rather than a name. It does not name or point to a single entity the way a name does. Rather in the fashion typical of sentences it makes an assertion. It makes a claim that is either true or false. We may pause to note that we have now three ways to make simple assertions about sets. Each is characterized by its own symbol: $=$, $\in$, and $\subseteq$. The reader can easily verify that each of the following (with its English translation) is a sentence.

Set theory	English
$A = B$	A is identical to B
$A \in B$	A is a member of B
$A \subseteq B$	A is a subset of B

Because in each of these two names are yoked by a mediating notion, the intervening ideas of identity, membership, and subset are called *relations on* sets. Of course, the names of the sets on either side may themselves be

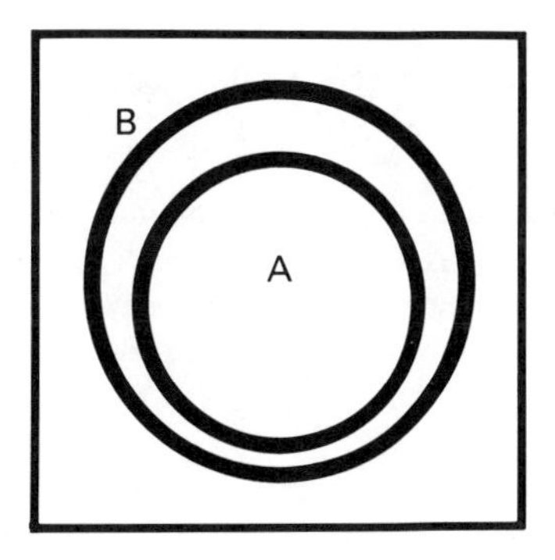

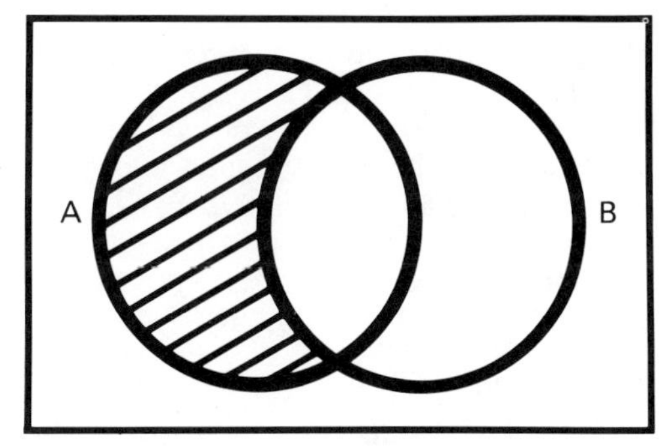

Fig. 2.4

grammatically complex, either abstracts or abbreviations of abstracts, as in the following examples.

$$x \in \{y \mid y = z\}$$
$$A - B = \{x \mid x \in C\}$$
$$\{y \mid y \in A\} \subseteq \{z \mid z = B\}$$
$$A \cap B \subseteq C - A$$

As the definition of subset indicates proof that one set is included in another really amounts to showing a conditional. More often than not such proofs use the strategy of conditional proof. Assume an arbitrary x is in the smaller set and then deduce it is in the larger. The next three theorems state some basic properties of the relation, and each depends on corresponding logical truths about conditionals.

THEOREM. $(A \subseteq B \wedge B \subseteq A) \leftrightarrow A = B$.

Proof. Case I: Assume that $A \subseteq B \wedge B \subseteq A$. Then for any x, $x \in A \rightarrow x \in B$, and for any x, $x \in B \rightarrow x \in A$. Instantiating for x and drawing together the two conditionals into a biconditional, we get $x \in A \leftrightarrow x \in B$. Since we have assumed only truths about x that hold for everything, we can universally generalize, for any x, $x \in A \leftrightarrow x \in B$. Hence by extensionality, $A = B$. Conversely, assume $A = B$. Then by extensionality, for any x, $x \in A \leftrightarrow x \in B$. Instantiating and separating the biconditional into two conditionals we get

(1) $x \in A \rightarrow x \in B$, and

(2) $x \in B \rightarrow x \in A$.

We are general in x, so generalizing clause (1) we get

(3) For any x, $x \in A \rightarrow x \in B$,

and generalizing clause (2) we get

(4) For any x, $x \in B \rightarrow x \in A$.

But these are equivalent by definition to $A \subseteq B$ and $B \subseteq A$, respectively. From the two cases we have shown that from each half of the theorem we can deduce the other, and the theorem's biconditional is therefore established by conditional proof. QED.

The preceding theorem provides a very easy way to think about what set identity means and an intuitive way to go about proving it.

THEOREM. $A \subseteq A$.

THEOREM. $(A \subseteq B \wedge B \subseteq C) \rightarrow A \subseteq C$.

THEOREM. $\varnothing \subseteq$ A.

Proof. For an arbitrary x, we must show $x \in \varnothing \rightarrow x \in A$. We show this conditional is true by showing that its antecedent is false. That is, we shall show $x \notin \varnothing$. Suppose the contrary (for a reduction to the absurd) that $x \in \varnothing$. Then by a previous theorem, $x \neq x$, which contradicts the law of identity. Since $x \in \varnothing$ leads to a contradiction, it must be false. Since the antecedent of the theorem is false, the conditional as a whole must be true. QED.

THEOREM. $A \subseteq \mathbf{V}$.

THEOREM. $A \cap B \subseteq A$.

Proof. Let $x \in A \cap B$. Then $x \in A$ by definition of intersection. Hence by conditional proof, $x \in A \cap B \rightarrow x \in A$. Since we are general in x, it follows by definition of subset that $A \cap B \subseteq A$. QED.

THEOREM. $A - B \subseteq A$.
THEOREM. $A \subseteq A \cup B$.

Last, we provide notation for the idea that a set is a subset of another set but not identical to it.

DEFINITION: $A \subset B$ (read *A is a proper subset of B*) is defined as '$A \subseteq B$ but $A \neq B$'.

Let us conclude this introduction to sets by defining a way to name a set by listing its elements. By this notation, $\{a, b, c\}$ will be the set containing only the elements a, b, and c.

DEFINITION: $\{x_1, \ldots, x_n\} = \{y | y = x_1 \vee \cdots \vee y = x_n\}$.

THEOREM. $\{x, y\} = \{y, x\}$.

☐ **EXERCISE**

Prove the previous six unproven theorems.

2.5 RELATIONS AND FUNCTIONS

2.5.1 Relations as Sets of *n*-Tuples

When a variable, say x, occurs in a sentence or a part of a sentence that begins with a quantifier, either 'for all x' or 'for some x', then the variable is said to be *bound*. When it is not governed in this way by a quantifier it is said to be *free*. We have used sentences with just one free variable, as in 'x is red' or 'x is an even number', to define sets, as in $\{x | x \text{ is red}\}$ and $\{x | x \text{ is an even number}\}$. Such open sentences are said to state the defining property or characteristic of the set. We can extend these ideas by observing that open sentences may have more than one free variable, as in 'x is taller than y' or '$x < y$'. The question we pose is how do we use such defining features to draw together entities into sets? The answer is that we may use such sentences to define sets, made up not of individuals alone, but of pairs of individuals. We use 'x is taller than y' to define the set of all pairs of individuals x and y such that x is taller than y, and we use '$x < y$' to define the set of all pairs of individuals x and y such that $x < y$. In traditional philosophical vocabulary groups of words that bind pairs of individuals are said to stand for relations. In set theory we use open sentences with two free variables to draw together into sets pairs of individuals, and borrowing from philosophy we call these *relations.*

Relational phrases in English have a wide variety of grammars; what they have in common is that when completed by the addition of proper names, they become a complete sentence. The following are some grammatical types that would traditionally be said to describe relations.

(1) Transitive verbs
EXAMPLES x loves y
x discovered y

(2) Verb 'to be' plus a comparative adjective
EXAMPLES x is greater than y
x is taller than y

(3) Verb plus preposition
EXAMPLES x ran into y
x is kept under y

(4) Verb plus common noun plus preposition
EXAMPLES x is a brother of y
x is ruler of y

(5) Passive form of transitive verbs
EXAMPLES x is loved by y
x was discovered by y

Common to all these examples is the feature that if x and y are understood to be replaced by names of individuals, then complete sentences result.

Generalizing from these cases we can see that there is a perfectly clear sense in which we can go backward from any sentence containing two names to an expression that picks out a relation. We merely delete the two names.

EXAMPLES Under the x there slept y.
x is to y like those Nicene barks of yore.
As x walks through y, x fears no ill.

Any such sentence with two free variables can be used in set theory to define a set of pairs.

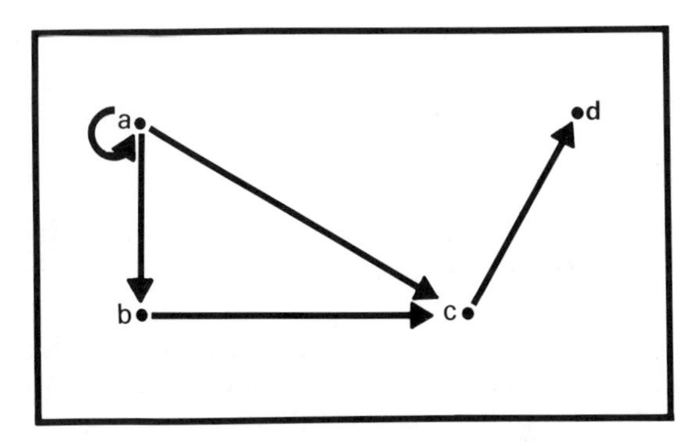

Fig. 2.5

One way to actually picture relations is by means of arrow diagrams. In Fig. 2.5 x bears the relation R to y if there is an arrow from x to y.

Let us introduce the notation $\langle x, y\rangle$ to stand for the ordered pair composed of elements x and y. We may then construct the set theoretic version of R:

$$R = \{\langle a, a\rangle, \langle a, b\rangle, \langle b, c\rangle, \langle c, d\rangle, \langle a, c\rangle\}$$

Notice that just because x bears R to y, it does not follow that y bears R to x. For example, when x is greater than y, y cannot be greater than x. Life would be much duller, for example, if the lover-of relation was genuinely symmetric in this sense.

In addition to picking out a relation by just listing the pairs contained in it, as we did for R, we may use open sentences to define a set of pairs by abstraction. Let $P(x, y)$ stand for a sentence with only two free variables x and y. Then we use the set abstract $\{\langle x, y\rangle | P(x, y)\}$ to refer to the set of all ordered pairs $\langle x, y\rangle$ such that $P(x, y)$.

Notation	Translation
$\{\langle x, y\rangle \| x > y\}$	The set of pairs $\langle x, y\rangle$ such that x is greater than y
$\{\langle x, y\rangle \| x \text{ loves } y\}$	The set of pairs $\langle x, y\rangle$ such that x loves y
$\{\langle x, y\rangle \| {\sim}(x \subseteq y)\}$	The set of pairs $\langle x, y\rangle$ such that ${\sim}(x \subseteq y)$

To really understand this notation, we need more than translations into vocabulary that is itself not very clear. The way we shall proceed is to lay down axioms explaining both the pair notation $\langle x, y\rangle$ and the abstract $\{\langle x, y\rangle | P(x, y)\}$.

All we really need to say about the first of these notions is that a pair $\langle x, y\rangle$ is different from the pair $\langle y, x\rangle$ (i.e., their order makes a difference) unless x

happens to be identical to y. Notice that if $\langle x, y\rangle$ was the same as $\langle y, x\rangle$, then just because $\langle x, y\rangle$ was in a relation R it would follow that $\langle y, x\rangle$ was also in R, and all relations would be symmetric, which they are not.

Ordered Pair Axiom (A6). For any x and y, $\langle x, y\rangle = \langle y, x\rangle \leftrightarrow x = y$.

Similarly we may explain the abstraction notation for relations by an axiom. All we need do is extend the axiom of abstraction so as to cover sets of pairs. We must be able to construct a set of pairs from any open sentence $P(x, y)$ containing free variables x and y. A given pair will be in that set if, and only if, the open sentence is true of it.

Principle of Abstraction for Binary Relations (A7). (1) $\{\langle x, y\rangle | P(x, y)\}$ exists and is unique. (2) Let v replace every free occurrence of x and w every free occurrence of y in $P(x, y)$. Then,

$$\text{For any } v \text{ and } w, \langle v, w\rangle \in \{\langle x, y\rangle | P(x, y)\} \leftrightarrow P(v, w).$$

These two rules fully explain relations understood as sets of pairs. Reasoning in this way, we can also see that a sentence $P(x, y, z)$ with three free variables, e.g., 'x is between y and z' or 'x is taller than y but shorter than z', might equally well be used to make up sets of triples. Sentences with four free variables may be used to make up sets of quadruples, etc. Indeed it is a straightforward matter to generalize these ideas to the case when the defining sentence $P(x_1, \ldots, x_n)$ contains n free variables $x_1, \ldots, x_n$. The generalized notion of a pair is $\langle x_1, \ldots, x_n\rangle$, called an *n-tuple*. The order in any n-tuple must make a difference, as the generalized pair axiom states.

Ordered n-Tuple Axiom (A8). For any $x_1, \ldots, x_n$, and any $y_1, \ldots, y_n$,

$$\langle x_1, \ldots, x_n\rangle = \langle y_1, \ldots, y_n\rangle \leftrightarrow (x_1 = y_1 \wedge \cdots \wedge x_n = y_n).$$

Likewise the open sentence $P(x_1, \ldots, x_n)$ defines a set of n-tuples.

Principle of Abstraction for n-Placed Relations (A9).

(1) $\{\langle x_1, \ldots, x_n\rangle | P(x_1, \ldots, x_n)\}$ exists uniquely.

(2) Let $P(z_1, \ldots, z_n)$ be like $P(y_1, \ldots, y_n)$ except that each z_i replaces each free occurrence of y_i in the original. Then, for any x,

$$x \in \{\langle y_1, \ldots, y_n\rangle | P(y_1, \ldots, y_n)\}$$
$$\leftrightarrow (\text{for some } z_1, \ldots, z_n, x = \langle z_1, \ldots, z_n\rangle \wedge P(z_1, \ldots, z_n)).$$

Clause (1) makes explicit an ontological assumption that sets of n-tuples if definable must exist. Clause (2) records the relational version of the idea that elements stand in a relation if, and only if, they possess the property definitive of the relation. A more convenient form of clause (2) follows directly from it.

THEOREM. For any $y_1, \ldots, y_n$, if y_i replaces every free occurrence of x_i in $P(x_1, \ldots, x_n)$, then

$$\langle y_1, \ldots, y_n \rangle \in \{\langle x_1, \ldots, x_n \rangle \mid P(x_1, \ldots, x_n)\} \leftrightarrow P(y_1, \ldots, y_n).$$

When R is a set of n-tuples we say R is a *relation of degree n*.[3]

☐ **EXERCISE**

Prove the following theorem. Assume $x < y \leftrightarrow y > x$.

THEOREM. $\{\langle x, y \rangle \mid x < y\} = \{\langle x, y \rangle \mid y > x\}$.

2.5.2 Cartesian Product

In talking about relations it often helps to be able to say what kind of things are being related; e.g., the husband-of relation pairs men and women. To do so in the most general way, we should allow for the possibility that objects in one place of the relation may be quite different in kind from objects in another place, just as men occupy the left-hand place of the husband-of relation and women the right-hand. To talk this way, we define a notion $A_1 \times \cdots \times A_n$, which is the set of all n-tuples such that the elements in the first position come from A_1, those in the nth position from A_n, and elements in between come from corresponding A_i's.

DEFINITION: $A_1 \times \cdots \times A_n$ (read *the Cartesian product of* $A_1, \ldots, A_n$) means

$$\{\langle x_1, \ldots, x_n \rangle \mid x_1 \in A_1 \wedge \cdots \wedge x_n \in A_n\}$$

[3] Historically, an important simplification of set theory was the discovery that these two axioms could in fact be proven as theorems of the earlier axioms governing only sets. This simplification is not important for our use of set theory in metalinguistics, but its details may be briefly sketched at this point. The trick of the simplification is to give a definition of ordered pair and then of ordered n-tuples so that the ordered pair and ordered n-tuple axioms simply follow from the definition and the earlier statement of the axioms.

DEFINITIONS: $\langle x, y \rangle$ means $\{\{x\}, \{x, y\}\}$, and $\langle x_1, \ldots, x_n \rangle$ means $\langle \langle x_1, \ldots, x_{n-1} \rangle, x_n \rangle$.

These definitions are not intended to capture any of the intuitive meaning of the idea of a pair. What they do is imply the pair and n-tuple axioms, as readers may check for themselves. Similarly, the relational versions of the abstraction axiom then follow, given the following definition of relational abstraction in terms of abstraction for sets.

DEFINITION: $\{\langle x_1, \ldots, x_n \rangle \mid P(x_1, \ldots, x_n)\}$ means

$$\{y \mid \text{for some } x_1, \ldots, x_n,\ y = \langle x_1, \ldots, x_n \rangle \wedge P(x_1, \ldots, x_n)\}.$$

For our purposes, however, this simplification is a matter of theoretical interest that we will not directly employ. We will merely appeal to the relational axioms in our proofs.

DEFINITION: If $A_1 = \cdots = A_n$, we write A^n (read *the nth Cartesian power of A*) for $A_1 \times \cdots \times A_n$. (*Equivalently*, $A^n = \{\langle x_1, \ldots, x_n \rangle | x_1 \in A \wedge \cdots \wedge x_n \in A\}$.)

THEOREM. $A_1 \times \cdots \times A_n \subseteq \mathbf{V}^n$.

THEOREM. Let $P(x, y)$ be any sentence with free variables x and y. Then

$$\{\langle x, y \rangle | P(x, y)\} \subseteq \mathbf{V}^2.$$

THEOREM. $R \subseteq \mathbf{V}^n \leftrightarrow$ (for some $A_1, \ldots, A_n$, $R \subseteq A_1 \times \cdots \times A_n$).

THEOREM. If $R \subseteq \mathbf{V}^n \wedge S \subseteq \mathbf{V}^n$, then

$$R = S \leftrightarrow (\text{for any } x_1, \ldots, x_n, \langle x_1, \ldots, x_n \rangle \in R \leftrightarrow \langle x_1, \ldots, x_n \rangle \in S).$$

This last theorem means that the extensionality axiom also holds for relations: relations are identical if, and only if, they contain the same n-tuples.

We note last some common variants in notation. If R is a binary relation, $\langle x, y \rangle \in R$ is sometimes written xRy or Rxy. For example, it is customary to write $x = y$ and $x < y$ rather than $\langle x, y \rangle \in =$ or $\langle x, y \rangle \in <$.

☐ **EXERCISE**

Prove the preceding four theorems.

2.5.3 Functions

One way to find a good restaurant on the highway, they say, is to find a truck driver and see where he or she eats. The restaurant y is that entity which the truck driver x bears the eating-at relation to. A binary (two-place) relation is in a sense a matching up of one list with members of a second list. In useful cases this matching has the special property of assigning to each member of the first list a single member of the second list. If, for example, a relation matches dogs with their masters, then one way to find a master is to find one of his dogs and then he will be found paired up at its side on the list. Ronald Reagan may be specified in terms of a given country and the is-president-of relation. Such are the rudiments of the mathematician's idea of a function. A function is a relation that pairs with each x a unique y. Such relations are extremely useful in that they allow us to locate a given y indirectly by specifying it as the object paired with a given x under the relation R.

Such a binary relation is called a *function*, and its defining condition intuitively is that it assigns to each item in one set a unique element in a second set. In a polygamous society, for example, the is-husband-of relation would not be a function, but in our society it is. In general an $n + 1$ place relation is called a function if all sequences of n individuals are paired by the relation with at most one individual in the $n + 1$ place. In the general case, an object occupying some $n + 1$ place may be indirectly specified by naming the appropriate series of n individuals and the relation in question.

DEFINITION: To say R is an *n-place function* means

(1) R is an $n + 1$ place relation and
(2) if $\langle x_1, \ldots, x_n, y\rangle \in R \wedge \langle x_1, \ldots, x_n, z\rangle \in R$, then $y = z$.

To say in slightly different and clearer terms what this definition amounts to, we need the concepts of the argument or 'input' of a function and that of its value or 'output'.

DEFINITION: '$\langle x_1, \ldots, x_n\rangle$ is an *argument for the relation R*' means

$$\text{For some } y, \langle x_1, \ldots, x_n, y\rangle \in R.$$

DEFINITION: 'y is a *value for the relation R*' means

$$\text{For some } x_1, \ldots, x_n, \langle x_1, \ldots, x_n, y\rangle \in R.$$

THEOREM. R is a function iff R is a relation that pairs with each argument at most one value.

Proof. We show both directions of the 'iff' by two conditional proofs. Case I: Assume that R has two values y and z paired with the same argument $\langle x_1, \ldots, x_n\rangle$. Then by the definition of function $y = z$, and the two values are identical. Case II: Assume that each argument of R is paired with at most one value but that what we want to prove is false. We then will find a contradiction. Suppose that it is false that R is a function. Then there exists some $x_1, \ldots, x_n$, y, and z such that $\langle x_1, \ldots, x_n, y\rangle$ and $\langle x_1, \ldots, x_n, z\rangle$ are in R, and $y \neq z$. But then $\langle x_1, \ldots, x_n\rangle$ is an argument for R and is paired with more than one thing, which contradicts our original assumption. Hence our assumption leads to a contradiction and must be false. QED.

If we actually display in a vertical column the pairs contained in a functional binary relation, we can see how to locate elements of the second list by those of the first.

$$\begin{aligned} F = \{&\langle 0, 0\rangle, \\ &\langle 1, 1\rangle, \\ &\langle 2, 4\rangle, \\ &\langle 3, 9\rangle, \\ &\langle 4, 16\rangle, \\ &\langle 5, 25\rangle\} \end{aligned}$$

This relation pairs each natural number from 0 to 5 with its square. We can locate 9 since it is the square of 3. We call the set of items listed to the left the domain of the function, and we call the set of those to the right its range.

DEFINITION: By the *domain* of an n-place function F, briefly $D(F)$, we mean

$$\{\langle x_1,\dots,x_n\rangle \mid \text{for some } y, \langle x_1,\dots,x_n, y\rangle \in F\}.$$

THEOREM. $D(F) = \{x \mid x \text{ is an argument of } F\}$.

DEFINITION: By the *range* of an n-place function F, briefly $R(F)$, we mean

$$\{y \mid \text{for some } x_1,\dots,x_n, \langle x_1,\dots,x_n, y\rangle \in F\}.$$

THEOREM. $R(F) = \{x \mid x \text{ is a value of } F\}$.

Thus far, functions have been explained as relations that match elements from a first list (the function's domain) to unique elements in a second list (the function's range). But there are two other intuitive ways to explain functions, as production rules and as input–output machines. A production rule tells you how to make up new things from old; a recipe would be an example, and so would a blueprint for a house. A recipe tells you how to combine (pair) a given assembly of initial ingredients (the argument) so as to obtain the finished dish (the value). Likewise a blueprint explains how to organize (pair) a given list of materials (the argument) so as to produce a building (the value). An input–output machine is a physical mechanism that actually constructs a product from certain raw materials. A factory would be an example on a large scale and a sausage machine would be one on a smaller scale. They both pair inputs (arguments) with outputs (values).

The mathematical idea of function is an abstraction of what is common to both production rules and input–output machines. In their most abstract form both devices are merely uniquely valued pairings, matching any given argument with at most one value.

The main point of singling out functions as a type of relation of special interest is to use them to identify values indirectly by specifying an argument and a function. A special notation exists to do just this task. If x is an argument for a function F, then the notation $F(x)$ is a name that picks out the value for F given argument x. More generally, if $\langle x_1,\dots,x_n\rangle$ is an argument for F, then $F(x_1,\dots,x_n)$ is a name for that value paired with $\langle x_1,\dots,x_n\rangle$ in F.

DEFINITION: For any $\langle x_1,\dots,x_n\rangle$ in $D(F)$, $F(x_1,\dots,x_n)$ is a name for that (unique) y such that $\langle x_1,\dots,x_n, y\rangle \in F$.

THEOREM. For any function F, $F(x) = y \leftrightarrow \langle x, y\rangle \in F$.

Proof. Assume F is a function. Case I: Assume $F(x) = y$. Then by the last definition, $F(x)$ is that z such that $\langle x, z\rangle \in F$. That is, $\langle x, z\rangle \in F$ and $F(x) = z$. But since $F(x) = y$ and $F(x) = z$, then $y = z$. Moreover, since $\langle x, z\rangle \in F$ and $y = z$ then $\langle x, y\rangle \in F$. Case II: Let $\langle x, y\rangle \in F$. Since F is a function by hypothesis, y must be the unique x such that $\langle x, y\rangle \in F$. Hence by the previous definition, $F(x) = y$. QED.

The functional notation $F(x)$ has counterparts in both ordinary English and familiar arithmetic which, once pointed out, show that the idea is really quite common. For an example, in English we may take any relational expression, i.e., any assertion with names deleted and replaced by variables. We then add to it the phrase 'the x who' or 'the x such that'. The result is a name for the value picked out under the relation for given arguments.

EXAMPLES

Relational open sentences	Noun phrases naming an object in their ranges
x is the wife of y	The x who is the wife of Marc Antony
x corrupted y	The x who corrupted Hadleyburg
x is the captain of y	The x who is the captain of H.M.S. Victory

In arithmetical notation the familiar operations of addition, subtraction, multiplication, and division are all really two-place functions. Indeed, mathematicians use the term *operation* to mean function. For example, the addition function could with infinite resources actually be listed as a set of triples:

$$+ = \{\ldots, \langle 2, 4, 6\rangle, \langle 7, 98, 104\rangle, \langle 34, 81, 115\rangle, \ldots\}$$

The following, then, are all notational variants of the same relational assertion. They all say that a given pair taken as argument yields under the + function a given value:

$$\langle 2, 4, 6\rangle \in + \qquad +(2, 4) = 6 \qquad 2 + 4 = 6$$

Likewise for the other arithmetic operations:

$$\langle 2, 5, 10\rangle \in \times \qquad \times(2, 5) = 10 \qquad 2 \times 5 = 10$$
$$\langle 78, 22, 56\rangle \in - \qquad -(78, 22) = 56 \qquad 78 - 22 = 56$$

When we later turn to the study of particular languages, we shall make much use of functions. Occasionally we will refer to the arithmetic functions, but more often we will refer to functional relations that hold among expressions and between expressions and their interpretations. For example, the rules of grammar may be viewed themselves as functions. They are really production rules that take shorter expressions as inputs and yield longer expressions as outputs. Every grammar then consists of two parts: a short dictionary of ungenerated basic expressions and a list of grammatical functions that make up longer expressions from shorter ones. The generative grammars of modern linguistics are all basically of this sort. Similarly, the idea of an expression's meaning, which is studied in semantics, is investigated by functions. To assign an expression a meaning is to pair it with something it stands for in the world. Such pairings of expressions with meanings are called interpretation functions. Among the interpretations assigned to expressions are truth-values. (These are the semantic interpretations of sentences.) Relations among truth-values are another phenomenon that is studied by means of functions. Indeed the conjunction truth-table defines a function which we may call $f_\wedge$. It pairs $\langle$T, T$\rangle$ with T, but pairs $\langle$T, F$\rangle$, $\langle$F, T$\rangle$, and $\langle$F, F$\rangle$ all with F:

P	Q	$P \wedge Q$
T	T	T
T	F	F
F	T	F
F	F	F

$$f_\wedge = \{\langle \text{T, T, T}\rangle, \langle \text{T, F, F}\rangle, \langle \text{F, T, F}\rangle, \langle \text{F, F, F}\rangle\}$$

□ **EXERCISES**

1. State as sets of triples consisting of truth-values T and F the functions defined by the truth-tables for disjunction, the conditional, and the biconditional. What kind of function, if any, is determined by the truth-table for negation? Explain.
2. Prove the previous unproven theorems of this section.
3. Assuming ordinary facts of arithmetic, prove that F defined below is a function, but that R is not.

$$F = \{\langle x, y, z\rangle \mid (x + y < 0 \rightarrow z = x) \wedge (x + y \geq 0 \rightarrow z = y)\}$$

$$R = \{\langle x, y\rangle \mid y^2 = x\}$$

Functions can pair members of one set with members of another in various ways. Some of the possibilities are important enough to merit special names.

DEFINITION: F is said to be a *function on a set A* and A is said to be *closed under the operation F* iff

(1) $D(F) = A$ and
(2) $R(F) \subseteq A$.

Thus, if both the arguments and values of F are the same sort of thing in the sense that they are all in A, then F is on A and A is closed under F. The square function, for example, is on the real numbers and the real numbers are closed under it. Sometimes, however, the arguments and values of functions are different sorts of things.

DEFINITION: F is a function *from A into B*, briefly $F(A \underset{\text{into}}{\longrightarrow} B)$, iff

(1) $D(F) = A$ and
(2) $R(F) \subseteq B$.

Thus, F may be from A into B yet not exhaust B in the sense that $R(F)$ need not be identical to B: there may be some y such that $y \in B$ and yet no x in A such that $F(x) = y$. When the range does exhaust B the function is said to be 'onto'.

DEFINITION: F is a function *from A onto B*, briefly $F(A \xrightarrow[\text{onto}]{} B)$, iff

(1) $D(F) = A$ and
(2) $R(F) = B$.

☐ EXERCISES

1. Show that F as defined below is a function from I (the set of positive integers) and that it is into but not onto I.

$$F = \{\langle x, y\rangle | x \in I \wedge y \in I \wedge y = 2x\}$$

Analysis of the exercise. Show each of the following:

a. F is a function. Assume that $\langle x, y\rangle$ and $\langle x, z\rangle$ are in F, and then show that $y = z$.

b. $D(F) = I$. Show $x \in D(F) \leftrightarrow x \in I$. Use two conditional proofs and the definition of F.

c. $R(F) \subseteq I$. Assume $x \in R(F)$, and deduce that $x \in I$.

d. $R(F) \neq I$. Find some n in I such that there is no x in $D(F)$ such that $F(x) = n$.

2. Provide an analysis of the steps that would be needed to prove that the inverse, F^{-1}, of F defined below is a function from the set of even integers onto I.

$$F^{-1} = \{\langle y, x\rangle | x \in I \wedge y \in I \wedge y = 2x\}.$$

'Into' and 'onto' functions are frequently pictured as in Fig. 2.6. Notice that in neither case is something in A paired with or 'mapped onto' more than one thing in B; any pairing that does so, as in Fig. 2.7, is a relation but not a function.

If every member of the domain is assigned to one and only one member of the range, then the function is said to be 1 to 1, or 1–1.

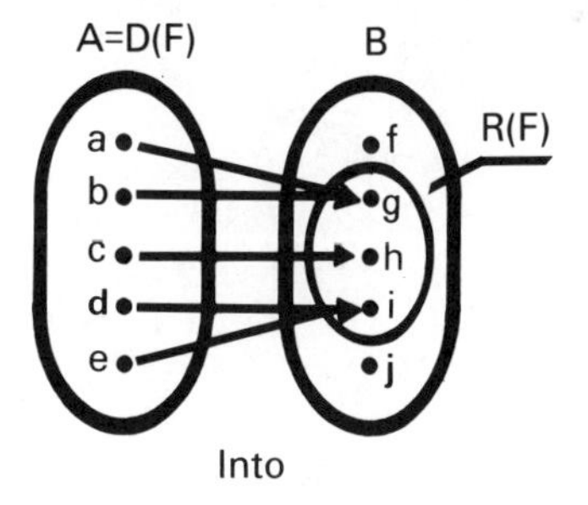

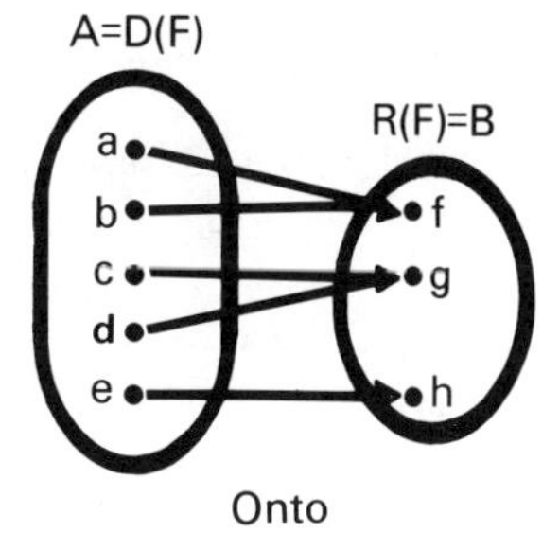

Fig. 2.6

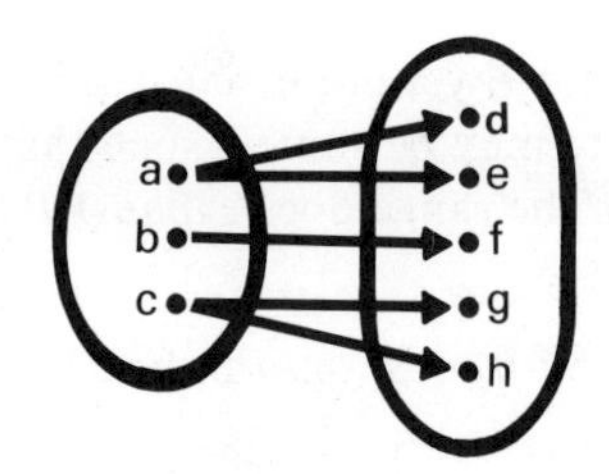

Fig. 2.7. A nonfunctional pairing.

DEFINITION: F is a *1–1 function from A into B*, briefly $F(A \xrightarrow[1-1]{} B)$, iff

(1) F is a function from A into B, and
(2) $(F(x) = y \wedge F(z) = y) \rightarrow x = z$.

□ EXERCISES

1. Suppose $F(A \xrightarrow[\text{into}]{} B)$ and $G(B \xrightarrow[\text{into}]{} C)$. Define $G \cdot F$ (called the *composition function of F and G*) as follows:

$$G \cdot F = \{\langle x, y\rangle | G(F(x)) = y\}.$$

Prove the following three theorems.

THEOREM. $G(F(x)) = z \leftrightarrow$(for some y, $F(x) = y \wedge G(y) = z$).

[*Hint*: To go from left to right, assume the left and observe that $F(x) = F(x)$. Then existentially generalize over some but not all occurrences of $F(x)$. Notice that since '$F(x)$' is a name it can be replaced by a variable and such inferences as '$F(x)$ is red/ Therefore, for some y, y is red' are valid. The theorem in the other direction makes use of the substitutivity of identity.]

THEOREM. $\langle x, z\rangle \in G \cdot F \leftrightarrow$(for some y, $F(x) = y \wedge G(y) = z$).

THEOREM. $G \cdot F(A \xrightarrow[\text{into}]{} C)$.

Analysis of the exercise. There are two assumptions, that $F(A \xrightarrow[\text{into}]{} B)$ and $G(B \xrightarrow[\text{into}]{} C)$. These in turn break down into six useful facts:

(i) $D(F) = A$, or in other words, (for some y, $F(x) = y) \leftrightarrow x \in A$.
(ii) $R(F) \subseteq B$ or in other words, (for some x, $F(x) = y) \rightarrow y \in B$.
(iii) F is a function, or in other words, $(\langle x, y\rangle \in F \wedge \langle x, y'\rangle \in F) \rightarrow y = y'$.
(iv) $D(G) = B$, or in other words, (for some z, $G(y) = z) \leftrightarrow y \in B$.
(v) $R(G) \subseteq C$, or in other words, (for some y, $G(y) = z) \rightarrow z \in C$.
(vi) G is a function, or in other words, $(\langle y, z\rangle \in G \wedge \langle y, z'\rangle \in G) \rightarrow z = z'$.

You must prove that $G \cdot F(A \xrightarrow[\text{into}]{} C)$. That is, you must prove three things:

(vii) $D(G \cdot F) = A$, or in other words, (for some z, $G \cdot F(x) = z) \leftrightarrow x \in A$.
(viii) $R(G \cdot F) \subseteq C$, or in other words, (for some x, $G \cdot F(x) = z) \rightarrow z \in C$.
(ix) $(\langle x, z\rangle \in G \cdot F \wedge \langle x, z'\rangle \in G \cdot F) \rightarrow z = z'$.

Notice that in the analysis x and x' are used as arbitrary elements of A, y and y' as arbitrary elements of B, and z and z' as arbitrary elements of C.

2. Suppose $F(A \xrightarrow[\text{into}]{} B)$. Define the inverse F^{-1} of F as follows:

$$F^{-1} = \{\langle y, x\rangle | \langle x, y\rangle \in F\}.$$

Show that if F is a 1–1 function from A onto B, then F^{-1} is a 1–1 function from B onto A.

2.6 BASIC CONCEPTS FROM ABSTRACT ALGEBRA

2.6.1 Structures and Congruence Relations

In this section we state for later reference some of the basic ideas used to discuss combinations of sets and relations on sets that are called structures or algebras. The material is presented at this point because it is a continuation of set theory, but it is not necessary for understanding most of the first five chapters of this book.[4] Rather than working through this section in its entirety at this point, the reader may prefer to refer back to it from time to time as directed in later sections.

DEFINITION: A *logical structure* is any $\langle A_1, \ldots, A_i, R_1, \ldots, R_j, f_1, \ldots, f_k, o_1, \ldots, o_l\rangle$ such that $i > 0$ and j, k, $l \geq 0$; $A_1, \ldots, A_i$ are sets; $R_1, \ldots, R_j$ are relations on $A_1 \cup \cdots \cup A_i$; $f_1, \ldots, f_k$ are functional relations (often called *operations*) on the same union of the various A_i's; and $o_1, \ldots, o_l$ are elements (members) of that same union.

By a *family* of sets we shall mean a set of sets. The union of a family F of sets, written $\bigcup F$, is the result of taking the union of all its members and is defined as follows:

$$\bigcup F = \{x | \text{for some } A, A \in F \wedge x \in A\}.$$

For example, if $F = \{C, D, E\}$, then $\bigcup F = C \cup D \cup E$, and if F is a family of sets of numbers, then $\bigcup F$ is a set of numbers.

DEFINITION: A *partition* of a set A is any family F of nonoverlapping subsets of A that jointly exhaust all members of A, i.e.,

(1) $\bigcup F = A$ and
(2) if D and E are both in F and $D \neq E$, then $D \cap E = \varnothing$.

DEFINITION: $\equiv$ is an *equivalence relation on* a set A iff $\equiv$ is a relation on A and for any x, y, and z in A

(1) $x \equiv x$ (reflexivity),
(2) if $x \equiv y$, then $y \equiv x$ (symmetry),
(3) if $x \equiv y$ and $y \equiv z$, then $x \equiv z$ (transitivity).

[4] For greater detail on abstract algebra the reader should refer to any standard text on the subject, such as that by James C. Abbott, *Sets, Lattices, and Boolean Algebras* (1960).

If G is a function and $P(x)$ a sentence mentioning the variable x then by $\{G(x)|P(x)\}$ we shall mean the set of all $G(x)$ such that $P(x)$. Strictly, $\{G(x)|P(x)\}$ is $\{x|(\text{for some } y, y = G(x)) \text{ and } P(x)\}$. If $\equiv$ is an equivalence relation on C, then by the equivalence class of x, we shall mean the set of elements of C that bear $\equiv$ to x, and we designate this class by $[x]$:

DEFINITION: $[x]$ means $\{y|y \equiv x\}$.

THEOREM. If $\equiv$ is an equivalence relation on C, then $F = \{[x]|x \in C\}$ is a partition of C.

Proof. Assume the 'if' part. We must show that both clauses (1) and (2) of the definition of partition is met by the set in question. (1) We show $x \in \bigcup F$ iff $x \in C$. The identity would then hold by extensionality. Assume first that $x \in \bigcup F$. Then for some y, $x \in [y]$, and $x \equiv y$. Since $\equiv$ is a relation on C, it follows that $x \in C$. Conversely, assume that $x \in C$. Then $x \equiv x$ and $x \in [x]$. Further since $x \in C$, $[x] \in F$, and it follows that $x \in \bigcup F$. (2) Assume the 'if' part in clause (2) of the definition of partition; i.e., let $[x]$ and $[y]$ be elements of C, and $[x] \neq [y]$. Suppose further for a *reductio* proof that the 'then' part of clause (2) is false, namely that for some z, $z \in [x]$, $z \in [y]$. Then $x \equiv z$ and $y \equiv z$. Hence $x \equiv y$. We now argue that $[x] = [y]$, i.e., that $w \in [x] \leftrightarrow w \in [y]$. Suppose first $w \in [x]$. Then $w \equiv x$, $w \equiv y$, and $w \in [y]$. Suppose conversely that $w \in [y]$. Then $w \equiv y$, $w \equiv x$, and $w \in [x]$. Hence $[x] = [y]$, which is absurd. Thus there is no z in both $[x]$ and $[y]$. QED.

□ **EXERCISES**

1. Give examples of relations on a set C which are
   a. reflexive but not symmetric or transitive.
   b. symmetric but not reflexive or transitive.
   c. transitive but not reflexive or symmetric.
   d. reflexive and symmetric but not transitive.
   e. reflexive and transitive but not symmetric.
   f. symmetric and transitive but not reflexive.
2. Prove that a relation R which is reflexive is an equivalence relation iff, xRy and xRz only if yRz.
3. Show that if R is a relation which is symmetric and transitive in C, then R is an equivalence relation if for every $x \in C$, there is a $y \in C$ such that xRy.

2.6.2 Morphisms

DEFINITION: If $S_1 = \langle C, f_1, \ldots, f_n \rangle$ and $S_2 = \langle D, g_1, \ldots, g_n \rangle$ are structures such that f_i and g_i of the same subscript are both functions of the same number of places on their respective sets (in that case we say that the two structures are of the same *type*), then the function h is called a *homomorphism* from S_1 into S_2 iff

(1) h is a function from C into D,

(2) $h(f_i(x_1, \ldots, x_m)) = g_i(h(x_1), \ldots, h(x_m))$, where f_i and g_i are m-place functions.

Usually homomorphisms are 'onto' functions, and sometimes they are 1–1 and 'onto', in which case they are called *isomorphisms.*

DEFINITION: $\equiv$ is a congruence relation on $S = \langle C, f_1, \ldots, f_n\rangle$ iff

(1) $\equiv$ is an equivalence relation on C, and

(2) $\equiv$ has the *substitution property* for each operation f_i of S: if $x_1 \equiv y_1, \ldots, x_m \equiv y_m$, then $f_i(x_1, \ldots, x_m) \equiv f_i(y_1, \ldots, y_m)$, where f_i and g_i are m-placed.

THEOREM. Every homomorphism determines a congruence relation.

Proof. Let h be a homomorphism from $S_1 = \langle C, f_1, \ldots, f_n\rangle$ into $S_2 = \langle D, g_1, \ldots, g_n\rangle$. Define $\equiv$ on C: $x \equiv y$ iff $h(x) = h(y)$. Clearly $\equiv$ meets condition (1) for being a congruence relation: $\equiv$ must be an equivalence relation on C because $=$ is one on D. For condition (2), suppose $x_1 \equiv y_1, \ldots, x_m \equiv y_m$. Then $h(x_1) = h(y_1), \ldots, h(x_m) = h(y_m)$. Thus,

$$\begin{aligned} h(f_i(x_1, \ldots, x_m)) &= g(h(x_1), \ldots, h(x_m)) \\ &= g(h(y_1), \ldots, h(y_m)) \\ &= h(f_i(y_1, \ldots, y_m)). \end{aligned}$$

Hence $f_i(x_1, \ldots, x_m) = f_i(y_1, \ldots, y_m)$. QED.

□ EXERCISES

1. Show that if h is an isomorphism, then its inverse function h^{-1}, namely $\{\langle y, x\rangle | \langle x, y\rangle \in h\}$, is also an isomorphism.
2. Prove the converse of the above theorem that every congruence relation determines a homomorphism on some structure of like type. *Hint*: Given $S_1 = \langle A, f_1, \ldots, f_n\rangle$ with congruence relation $\equiv$, define $S_2 = \langle B, g_1, \ldots, g_n\rangle$ such that $B = \{[x] | x \in A\}$ and $g_i([x_1], \ldots, [x_m]) = [f_i(x_1, \ldots, x_m)]$. Show then that h defined as $h(x) = [x]$ is a homomorphism from S_1 to S_2.
3. Let h be a homomorphism from S_1 to S_2 and let $h*$ be $\{\langle y, x\rangle | \langle x, y\rangle \in h\}$, the converse of h. Further let $\equiv_1$ be a congruence relation on S_1 and let $\equiv_h$ be the congruence relation on S_1 defined as follows: $x \equiv_h y$ iff $h(x) = h(y)$. Assume further that $x \equiv_1 y$ implies $h(x) = h(y)$. Show then that the relation $\equiv_2$ defined as follows is a congruence relation on S_2: $x \equiv_2 y$ iff $h*(x) \equiv_1 h*(y)$.

3

Metatheory and Its Criteria of Adequacy

3.1 METATHEORY

We are now ready to embark on the study of language. Since our study is to be genuinely scientific, our endeavor will be to formulate theories about language. It is necessary first of all to be clear about what a *theory* is. A very broad definition of theory would be a set of sentences that explains a given subject matter. Explanations are as many and various as the ways people satisfy their curiosity. Even a creation myth is, in a sense, a kind of theoretical account of how the world came to be. In rigorous science, however, theories have a more definite structure. They remain stories in that they are indeed sets of sentences, but these sets are organized as axiom systems. A special subset of sentences, called the axioms or *laws* of the theory, is selected as the premises from which all the other sentences of the theory, called theorems or *predictions*, are proven in a strictly logical manner. The theory as a whole is said to be *confirmed* or *verified* if its theorems or predictions correspond to observed facts. In this simple and rather naive view of science, the process of scientific explanation consists of noting what the facts are, describing them in sentences, and then producing a neat set of axioms or laws that logically imply the reports of observation. When the axioms imply a prediction that does not conform to observation, or when observation provides a fact that is not described by any theorem of the theory, then the theory is imperfect. Progress consists in finding new theories that match the data better. Formal semantics, as a budding science of language, is intended by its practitioners to conform fairly well to this model. Alfred Tarski, who provided many of the basic concepts of semantics, was a mathematician and formulated his ideas in precise ways amenable to treatment in rigorous axiomatizations. Rudolf Carnap, who developed Tarski's ideas into the form we know them today, was a logician and a proponent of this view of science, and there is no doubt that he intended his own scientific studies of language to follow it closely. A fair summary of his view of semantics as a science would be as follows.

In any scientific study of language, language is simultaneously the object of study and the vehicle of explanation. Usually one particular language or group of languages is singled out for study. We might, for example, investigate natural languages such as English or the Indo-European language group, or formal languages such as those of propositional logic. A language considered as the subject matter of a theory is called an object language. The theory itself, however, consists of a set of sentences and must itself be written in a language, which is called the *metalanguage*; and the theory formulated in the metalanguage is called a *metatheory*. To meet the Carnapian ideal, the theory must be axiomatized and produce consequences that match observation. In the case of formal semantics, theory construction is guided in addition by a group of methodological principles commonly accepted by researchers.

Axioms in metatheory are generally of a certain sort. Like any scientific theory they include the laws of logic, but characteristically in formal semantics they also include the axioms of set theory. Occasionally additional assumptions are also made. Sometimes these list some basic properties of things other than sets which students of language must take into account. Such entities are broadly called *syntactic* and are rather abstract representatives of the sounds (morphemes) of ordinary speech. Sometimes special assumptions are made about the world. Such metaphysical or ontological assumptions are especially common in discussions of how various parts of speech match up with various entities in reality. Though such extra assumptions are sometimes needed, it is a striking feature of formal semantics that appeals beyond set theory are rather rare. For the most part it is possible to introduce into set theory by stipulative definition all the terms necessary for the study of a given language and then to deduce from the axioms of set theory and these definitions the predictions in terms of which the theory will be tested. An important feature of metatheory, then, is that like the mathematical sciences (for example, physics and navigation), formal semantics can be rigorously stated and its consequences carefully demonstrated. Its assertions are actually written in the syntax of set theory, and its theorems are proven from the axioms of set theory by logically valid steps. It is now possible to see the point of the two previous chapters. Important aspects of the semantic method were being introduced: first, the very syntax in which semantic theories would be written, and second, the proof procedures for establishing predictions within metatheory. It is characteristic of metatheory that once the basic definitions are laid down, the various assertions or predictions of the theory (the metatheorems) can be proven as consequences of their formulation within set theory. This mathematical aspect of semantics gives its books and papers a technical look somewhat daunting to the uninitiated. It even prevents some researchers in collateral fields like linguistics and philosophy from reading work in formal semantics. But as we shall see here, the idiom is not that hard to understand, and the precision of the method makes it well worth the trouble.

3.2 SYNTAX

3.2.1 Generative Grammar

The particular features of language that metatheory tries to explain are characteristically limited. There are roughly three kinds of 'data' that a theory tries to predict. The first sort is grammatical. In any given object language, some expressions are grammatical or 'well-formed' and others are not. The metatheory attempts to define well-formedness in language L so as to yield predictions of well-formedness that correspond to the data. The data here are usually the unreflective judgments (called *intuitions*) of native speakers of the object language. As competent speakers of L, informants provide the researcher with reports (the data) about what is and what is not grammatical in L. Most often the native informant is the theorist himself (or herself), so his job is to use set theory to design an axiom system that will predict his preanalytic intuitions about what is and what is not grammatical in the language under study.

In his famous systematic divisions of linguistic metatheory, Charles Morris divided what he called the theory of signs (or *semiotics*) into three parts: syntax, semantics, and pragmatics.[1] Each of these in turn is defined by its subject matter, and in particular by what properties of signs it studies. *Syntax* is the study of the relations of signs to one another, *semantics* is the study of the relations of signs to the world, and *pragmatics* is the study of the relations holding among signs, the world, and people. Pragmatics includes much of what today would be called sociolinguistics and psycholinguistics, as well as much of what philosophers call the study of speech acts, and is not discussed in this book.[2] Semantics studies the way signs relate to the world in the

[1] Charles W. Morris, 'Foundations of the Theory of Signs' (1939).

[2] For a comprehensive overview of the subject, see Stephen C. Levinson, *Pragmatics* (1983).

broadest possible sense—it is intended, for example, to embrace how signs acquire meaning—and we shall describe it in detail shortly. Let us first talk in more detail about syntax.

Typically, the syntactic study of a given language consists of two parts: first, the compiling or listing of the basic vocabulary of the language (what is sometimes called its *lexicon*) and, second, the formulation of the language's grammar. A grammar in this sense consists of a series of syntactical rules that explain how to construct all the well-formed expressions of the language from the basic vocabulary. The rules are applied to the basic lexicon to produce longer expressions, and these outputs are themselves taken as inputs to the rules to produce yet longer expressions, and so on.

The motivation for the generative form of syntax is that some such process seems to be at work in human speech. In the earlier parts of this century linguists working in the tradition of structuralism attempted to define the grammatical expressions of a language by directly correlating them with sequences of sounds observed under field observation. The idea was that there should be an empirically rigorous vocabulary for describing sounds and their regularities, and that among these regularities would be found the patterns of grammatical rules. But though this research enterprise yielded many interesting findings about the sound patterns of speech, it did not explain much in the way of grammar. In the 1950s the linguist Noam Chomsky observed that the researchers had misdefined the problem. The phenomenon to be explained, Chomsky reasoned, was not the set of grammatical forms an observer happened to find during field observation. Rather what is more striking about language is the fact that an observer could never identify in a limited finite time all the grammatical forms of a language. What Chomsky calls a speaker's *competence* always outruns, in principle if not in fact, what he called the speaker's *performance*. We can, it seems, recognize as grammatical a potentially infinite number of expressions, many of which have never in fact been uttered by any speaker. At the same time, Chomsky observed, the resources we have to employ underlying this infinite competence are themselves finite. We have only a quite limited period of time in which to learn language, and only the finite resources of our brains with which to produce it. Hence he speculated that grammar must have a generative form. It must begin with elementary building blocks, from which we construct by a finite number of grammar rules the potentially infinite set of well-formed expressions of our language. A striking feature of his program for understanding the grammar of natural languages, however, is that it was anticipated by logicians in their formulations of the rules for the grammar of formal languages. In the 1920s Rudolf Carnap first formulated grammar rules of this sort for the languages of symbolic logic, and the form has been standard in logic ever since. In Chapter 6 we shall investigate more precisely the forms of grammar used by Carnap, which differ in only minor ways from the constituent structure grammars found in linguistics.[3]

The success of any purported lexicon and rules as a grammatical theory is measured by how well their outputs match the utterances accepted by a speaker of the natural language under study, by how good a job the theory does at generating all and only the expressions acceptable as grammatical by a native speaker.

In logic and formal semantics particularly, the languages we shall study are poor approximations of real languages. In propositional logic, for example, we analyze only the English words 'not', 'and', 'or', and 'if...then', and even these are given idealized accounts that suppress some of their properties. But even though the so-called formal languages of logic are simplifications of small parts of real languages, it must be stressed that they are nevertheless intended to approximate parts or 'fragments' of real languages: the well-formed expressions of the formal language should ideally also be grammatically acceptable forms of a natural language. Thus linguistic intuitions about the proper grammar of the English words for the connectives are legitimate measures of how well the grammar rules for propositional logic approximate English syntax.

The reason that our formal languages are seen as approximations of natural languages is that so viewed they may be used as tools to do research into the properties of natural languages. As such, formal languages offer a relatively new method for linguists. But there is another reason that formal languages must be understood as real, and this reason is as old as logic. One of the major points of logic—and in this it differs from linguistics—is to study reasoning. Reasoning is conducted in languages, and though we could invent an entirely new formal language and explain its grammar and meaning, such a language would have little bearing on evaluating the reasoning we are familiar with. It is by abstracting the key words and grammatical patterns found in natural language reasoning, simplifying and if necessary clarifying what we find, that we develop a theory for evaluating reasoning as we find it in daily life or in more sophisticated contexts such as science and philosophy.

3.2.2 Concatenation and Inductive Definitions

The particular form given to syntactic theory in formal semantics is designed to make it clear and mathematically precise. Thus, grammar rules are stated in set theory, and are construed quite literally as set theoretic functions. These functions take input expressions as arguments and yield

[3] Detailed references to the issues discussed here may be found in Chapter 6, but an excellent introductory account is found in Frederick J. Newmeyer, *Linguistic Theory in America* (1980).

output expressions as values. The various parts of speech are treated as sets of expressions.

Sometimes in syntactic metatheory we use concepts that strictly speaking are not found in set theory. These supplementary ideas are usually straightforward concepts about the arrangements of sounds in time or of marks on a page. One of these ideas is *concatenation*. Concatenation is, strictly speaking, a two-place function defined on pairs of expressions or, more generally, on pairs of 'signs'. It takes any two expressions x and y and produces their concatenation, written $x^\frown y$, meaning the result you get when the symbol x is produced first and immediately after it the symbol y. To concatenate two sounds is to utter one immediately after the other. To concatenate two written symbols in European languages is to write first one symbol and then the other immediately to its right. If x and y are such written symbols, then $x^\frown y = xy$. Clearly there are few ideas as simple as concatenation, and it would probably be silly to look for even simpler ideas in terms of which we might define it. Thus, we take the concatenation operation as an undefined primitive term of syntax, along with the other undefined primitives of set theory like membership and set. If we need to appeal to any obvious truth about concatenations in the course of proving syntactic metatheorems, we will simply do so. It is in appealing to such facts, which are not really truths of set theory alone, that syntax has among its assumptions some nonmathematical truths. In Chapter 6 we shall discuss these assumptions in more detail.

Rules of grammar defined in terms of concatenation are used to give a formal definition of the set of grammatical symbol strings, or as logicians prefer to call them, the *well-formed expressions* of the language. Such definitions have a special form that we have not met before in this text. So far we have defined sets in two ways, either by listing their elements (as in the set $\{1, 2, 3\}$) or by grouping together all elements that have a defining property (as in the set $\{x | x \text{ is an integer and } 1 < x < 10\}$). But in grammar the set of acceptable expressions is defined in a third way, by the construction of complex elements from simple ones. First a set of basic building blocks is stipulated by giving a list. These elements from which more complex items will be generated are called atomic expressions by logicians and are roughly synonymous to what linguists call lexical items in generative grammar. Second, a series of grammar rules is defined that explains how to construct longer expressions from shorter ones. The set of well-formed expressions is then defined as the 'closure' of the atomic elements under the rules of grammar. That is, the set as a whole is the set obtained by first putting in the atomic elements, then applying the rules to these elements and putting the results into it, and then applying the rules to these new elements and putting in the results, and so on. Constructive sets of this sort are said to be inductive, an idea that may be defined for the purposes of this chapter as follows.

DEFINITION: A set A is said to be *inductive* iff there is a (possibly infinite) set $x_1, \ldots, x_n, \ldots$ (of *basic* or *atomic* expressions) and series a (again possibly infinite) of functions $f_1, \ldots, f_m$ (called *formation rules*) such that A is the smallest set such that

(1) $\{x_1, \ldots, x_n, \ldots\} \subseteq A$; and
(2) for any f_i and any $y_1, \ldots, y_k$, if $y_1, \ldots, y_k \in A$, then $f_i(y_1, \ldots, y_k) \in A$.

Let us consider as an example a simple language from elementary logic.

EXAMPLE We construct the syntax for a very simple propositional language in two steps. First, we list a basic lexicon of three ungenerated simple sentences, which we call P, Q, and R. Second, we state a series of grammar rules that generate longer sentences from shorter ones. For simplicity both lists are kept short. Complex sentences in this language will consist of only conjunctions and negations.

(1) The category of simple sentences consists of the set BS $= \{P, Q, R\}$.
(2) There are two rules of grammar:
If x is a sentence then the result of prefixing $\sim$ to x is also a sentence.
If x and y are sentences, the result of inserting $\wedge$ between x and y and closing the whole in parentheses is also a sentence.
(3) Nothing beside the simple sentences and those generated by these rules is considered a sentence.

We now state the definition more formally. The two rules may be defined as functions; we call them respectively $f_\sim$ and $f_\wedge$ and we define them by means of the concatenation operation $^\frown$:

$$f_\sim = \{\langle x, y\rangle \mid y = \sim{}^\frown x\}$$

$$f_\wedge = \{\langle x, y, z\rangle \mid z = ({}^\frown x^\frown \wedge {}^\frown y^\frown)\}.$$

The set S of sentences is then defined as the smallest set X such that

(1′) BS $\subseteq X$, and
(2′) If y and z are in X, then both $f_\sim(y)$ and $f_\wedge(y,z)$ are in X.

☐ **EXERCISE**

Formulate grammar rules in English [as in rules (1) and (2) of the example] for generating disjunctions, conditionals, and biconditionals. Then state these rules more formally by defining for each a function on pairs of sentences, call them $f_\vee$, $f_\rightarrow$, and $f_\leftrightarrow$, by means of concatenating sentences with the symbols (,), $\vee$, $\rightarrow$, and $\leftrightarrow$. Finally, give a formal definition of the new set of sentences $S+$ obtained by using all *five* formation functions and the set BS of basic sentences.

If a set is defined by a list or by abstraction, we know how to show that every member of the set has a certain property, say Q. In the former case we show that everything in the list has Q, and in the latter we show that everything that has the defining property of the set has Q. But if the set is defined by induction the situation is more complicated. We prove first (in what is called the *basis step*) that all the atomic elements have Q. Then we prove (in what is called the *inductive step*) the conditional that if all the arguments of a formation rule have Q, then the value produced by applying the rule to those arguments also has Q. The 'if' clause of the conditional is called the *hypothesis of induction* because the conditional as a whole is usually proved by assuming the antecedent and then arguing to the consequent. A proof that induction is a valid argument is postponed to a later point, but a metatheorem suitable for our use may now be stated and its proof sketched. In the following theorem we use a notation that we shall often find convenient. When a series of elements $x_1, \ldots, x_n$ are all in X, instead of writing $x_1 \in X \wedge \cdots \wedge x_n \in X$, we write $x_1, \ldots, x_n \in X$.

THEOREM. Suppose the following three propositions have been established:

(1) A is a set defined inductively relative to B and $f_1, \ldots, f_n$, or more precisely, A is the smallest set X such that $B \subseteq X$ and for any f_i of $f_1, \ldots, f_n$ if $x_1, \ldots, x_m \in X$, then $f_i(x_1, \ldots, x_m) \in X$.

(2) (*Basis step*) $B \subseteq \{x \mid Q(x)\}$.

(3) (*Inductive step*) For any f_i, and $x_1, \ldots, x_m$, if (*induction hypothesis*) $x_1, \ldots, x_m$ are all in $\{x \mid Q(x)\}$, then $f_i(x_1, \ldots, x_m) \in \{x \mid Q(x)\}$.

We may then conclude that $A \subseteq \{x \mid Q(x)\}$.

Sketch of proof. Assume the clauses (1)–(3) but assume that there is some subset C of A of all elements x such that the condition $Q(x)$ does not hold. Clearly none of these are in B. Among these there is at least one element y that is the value of some f_i for arguments $y_1, \ldots, y_m$ that are not in C. For if every element of C is the value of rules only for arguments containing some other elements of C, the set C could not be generated from the atomic elements in B. (Our demonstration here is called a sketch because a rigorous proof of this last claim is beyond us at this point, though its truth is evident enough.) But we know by the inductive step that since each y_j is in $A - C$ (which is the same as $\{x \mid Q(x)\}$) and is such that $Q(y_j)$, y must be such that the condition $Q(y)$ holds, which contradicts our assumption that y is in C. End of proof sketch.

For an example of an inductive proof we prove the following fact about all sentences. Though the fact is true and even obvious, an adequate proof requires induction.

THEOREM. Every element of S contains either 0 or an even number of parentheses.

Analysis of proof. First we reformulate the theorem so as to exhibit what property it is that we are concerned to show holds for all sentences. The theorem says

$$S \subseteq \{x \mid x \text{ contains either 0 or an even number of parentheses}\}$$

and the inductive property $Q(x)$ is in this case captured by the open sentence,

x contains either 0 or an even number of parentheses.

The proof will therefore consist of two steps. First, the basis step will show that all the atomic sentences have the property, i.e., that $\{P, Q, R\} \subseteq \{x \mid x$ contains 0 or an even number of parentheses$\}$. Second, the inductive step will consist of proving the conditional assertion that if all the arguments of a formation rule have the property, then the value of the rule for those arguments also has the property. That is, assume an arbitrary f_i, and arbitrary $x_1, \ldots, x_m$, and assume the induction hypothesis,

(1) each x_j of $x_1, \ldots, x_m$ has either 0 or an even number of parentheses. We must then show on this hypothesis that $f_i(x_1, \ldots, x_m)$ has the property, i.e., that it has either 0 or an even number of parentheses. We would then have established by conditional proof the conditional statement,

(2) if $\{x_1, \ldots, x_m\} \subseteq \{x \mid x$ has either 0 or an even number of parentheses$\}$, then $f_i(x_1, \ldots, x_m) \in \{x \mid x$ has either 0 or an even number of parentheses$\}$.

From statements (1), (2), and the definition of S, the theorem follows by induction.

Proof. *Basis step.* Clearly, each of P, Q, and R contain 0 parentheses, and hence contain either 0 or an even number of parentheses. Thus $\{P, Q, R\} \subseteq \{x \mid x$ contains either 0 or an even number of parentheses$\}$.

Inductive step. Assume for an arbitrary f_i, and arbitrary $x_1, \ldots, x_m$ the induction hypothesis:

$$\{x_1, \ldots, x_m\} \subseteq \{x \mid x \text{ has either 0 or an even number of parentheses}\}.$$

Consider the total number m of parentheses in $f_i(x_1, \ldots, x_m)$. First note that the total number n of parentheses in the group $x_i, \ldots, x_m$ is either 0 or even because we know by the induction hypothesis that the number in each individual x_i of the group is even or 0, and the finite sum of any numbers that are 0 or even is itself 0 or even. Now the total number m of parentheses in $f_i(x_1, \ldots, x_m)$ will either be the same as n or equal to $n + 2$. It is n, the same as the number occurring in the group $x_i, \ldots, x_m$, if f_i is $f_{\sim}$, or it is $n + 2$ if f_i is $f_{\wedge}$. Since the total number of parentheses in $f_i(x_1, \ldots, x_m)$ is either n or $n + 2$, it too is either 0 or even. The inductive step is therefore established. Given the inductive form of the definition of S, the basis step and the inductive step, the theorem follows by the argument form for inductive arguments. QED.

We may summarize this discussion of syntax by laying down a principle requiring that the theories of syntax we shall study be generative.

Principle of an Inductive Syntax. The set of well-formed expressions of a language must have an inductive definition.

It will follow then that we shall have to prove claims about the set of well-formed expressions by inductive proofs.

☐ **EXERCISE**

Let a *string* be defined as any result of concatenating a finite number of symbols. Given this definition, reformulate, analyze, and prove the following metatheorem.

Every element in S consists of a symbol or a string.

3.3 SEMANTICS

3.3.1 Truth-in-a-World and Compositionality

In addition to intuitions about grammaticality, there is a second kind of data that metatheory tries to explain. These are facts about meaning and the way expressions relate to the world. Just as native speakers have intuitions about what expressions are well-formed, they have intuitions also about what inferences in English are logically valid. It is part of daily life to reason, and we all naturally make inferences constantly. Indeed if we were not good at reasoning, our species would not have survived long. Here comes a bus. If I step out in front of a bus, I'll get smashed. It is to our credit, in a weak way, that we stay on the curb. All of us have fairly clear intuitions about the validity of a large number of simple argument patterns like this one, and it is one of the major goals of semantics to explain these intuitions. While most theories of language written by linguists attempt to predict intuitions about grammaticalness, they usually differ from theories of language written in formal semantics in that they tend to ignore or to set to one side the goal of explaining so-called logical intuitions. Formal semantics typically tries to explain more than linguistics in the sense that it tries to explain both logic and grammar while linguistics tends to concentrate on grammar alone. (Linguists would point out quite fairly that concentration on grammar is perfectly legitimate and that the grammar of the formal languages of logicians is a pale reflection of the complex grammars found in natural languages.)

Semantic theories in this narrow sense now tend to assume a standard form pioneered by Alfred Tarski and Rudolf Carnap. Tarski provided a model for defining, relative to a previously defined syntax, a concept of truth-relative-to-a-possible-world, and Carnap showed how to apply Tarski's definition of truth to the definition of valid argument.

Tarski's goal was to provide a rigorous definition of truth for a given formal language (his original example was the language of a first-order theory of classes). Notice first of all that truth here is treated as a property of expressions. We can divide sentences into two groups, those that are true and those that are false. We set aside any informal or ordinary language uses of 'true' other than as a discriminator among sentences. We eschew suggestive but imprecise locutions such as 'Truth is beauty' and 'He saw the truth'.

In the history of philosophy there have been two prevalent sorts of definitions of truth, the so-called coherence and correspondence theories. The coherence theory holds that a total body of sentences as a group is true if it coheres together in the right way. This theory has always had trouble explaining what this coherence amounts to. A minimal condition that is usually required for coherence is that the set of sentences forming the group be internally consistent, and another condition that is often imposed in some form is that the group of sentences be comprehensive or global, comprising an entire world view. Examples of such comprehensive systems might be Thomistic philosophy or Marxism, though there is some question of whether they are internally consistent. Philosophers who favor this theory, such as the German Idealists, are proponents of comprehensive systems, which on the whole have been rejected by philosophers because of their obscurity. A recent and much more persuasive version of something like a coherence theory is the so-called antirealism of Michael Dummett.[4] In our introduction to the topic of truth in this book, however, we shall concern ourselves mostly with the alternative correspondence theory, which is on the whole more commonsensical and has been the one favored by most philosophers of language.

A sentence is true in the standard theory if it corresponds to the world. As Aristotle puts it: to say of what is that it is, is the true, to say of what is that it is not, is the false. A common medieval formula is, a sentence is true if howsoever it signifies so it is. Philosophers today informally explain truth as a kind of correspondence between sentences and facts, or between sentences and 'the way the world is'. These formulas, however, are really not very

[4] For a general discussion of coherence see Nicholas Rescher, *The Coherence Theory of Truth* (1973). For a discussion of Rescher's views and of coherence within the theory of knowledge see Laurence Bonjour, 'The Coherence Theory of Empirical Knowledge' (1976). For Michael Dummett's views see his papers 'Truth' (1959), 'The Reality of the Past' (1969), and 'The Philosophical Basis of Intuitionistic Logic' (1973).

illuminating. Tarski's success was that he provided a detailed account of what correspondence amounts to.

According to the theory, expressions pick out things in the world. This relation of 'picking out' is akin to pointing and is a basic semantic relation named in various ways at different periods in the history of philosophy. Medieval logicians speak of an expression standing in the place of (*supponere*) something in the world and of the phenomenon they call supposition (*suppositio*), that feature of language in which words stand for things in the world. Modern theorists usually speak of *reference*, and of an expression *referring to* or *denoting* an entity in the worlds. What an expression stands for (its *referent* or *denotation*) is certainly part of its meaning, and the theory of meaning limited to the concept of reference is now commonly called, following a suggestion by Quine, the theory of reference.[5] Tarski's theory is a theory of meaning as reference in this sense.[6]

The theory may be divided into two parts according to the difference in grammar between basic and complex expressions. The first part of the theory defines by stipulation what entities the basic or atomic expressions refer to. Usually a given class of expressions, which may be called a *grammatical type* or *part of speech*, is matched up with a characteristic type or class of entities in the world, and this class is called an *ontological category*. Parts of speech are explained this way in traditional school grammar. For example, we learn that the class of nouns stands for 'persons, places, or things', that verbs stand for members of the category of actions, and that sentences are those expressions that stand for 'thoughts'. Philosophers will not be satisfied with the uncritical division of reality found in these categories, but we shall find that even on a more sophisticated level what is called ontology in philosophy consists largely of dividing reality into basic ontological categories that match up with the corresponding parts of speech given in the classification of grammar.

The second part of the theory consists of stating rules that determine the referent of longer expressions from the referents of their parts. Such rules are often called *semantic rules*, and there are just as many semantic rules as there are rules of grammar. Recall that each rule of grammar explains a particular way of generating new expressions from old. Each new type of expression accordingly requires some explanation about how its referent is to be determined. In Tarski's theory, any such semantic rule will have a special

[5] See W. V. O. Quine, 'Notes on the Theory of Reference' (1953).

[6] For a discussion of this semantics in the words of its inventor, see Alfred Tarski, 'The Semantic Conception of Truth' (1944). For descriptions of the standard form the theory now assumed see Donald Kalish, 'Semantics' (1967); John Lyons, 'Logical Semantics' (1977); and W. V. O. Quine, *Philosophy of Logic* (1970).

form. It will define what the referent of a whole expression is by means of a *definiens* (i.e., a defining clause) that mentions only a relevant property of the referents of the parts of the expression:

Principle of the Compositionality of Reference. The referent in a world w of an expression is determined in a rulelike manner from the referents in w of its parts.

The role of a semantic rule then is to correlate two sets of semantic phenomena. First, there is a series of alternative semantic facts about the referents of the parts of an expression. Second, there is a series of possible referents of the whole expression. The rule explains which fact about the referents of the parts is paired with which referent of the whole.

Let us consider the special case of sentences as an example. Sentences in a typical Tarskian theory all have as their referents truth-values. It might at first sound strange to say that a sentence 'refers' to the truth-value T or F, and so it should. In ordinary speech if we say sentences stand for anything, we would say they stand for facts, or states of affairs, or possibly events. But truth-values are technical ideas not found in common sense. What, then, does it mean to say a sentence stands for a truth-value? The easiest answer is to say that T represents reality as a whole and F what is unreal. Then a true sentence stands for what is real and a false sentence for what is unreal, and this state is reflected in the truth-values assigned to them. We shall see in Chapter 9 that it is possible to break up reality into facts and events and to use these as the referents of sentences. The reason we do not do so now is simplicity. We shall find that we can explain a good deal of the behavior of language by the use of truth-values without the additional complication of facts or events, and we shall shortly explain why this sort of simplicity is important. Thus, in a typical Tarski-style semantics, the semantic rule for a particular kind of sentence explains what the truth-value of the sentence is in terms of the referents of its parts. This unique determination of the truth-value of the whole by those of its parts is a special case of the principle of compositionality of reference and is important enough to have a name of its own.

Principle of Truth-Functionality. The truth-value of a sentence that has other sentences as its immediate parts is determined in a rulelike way by the truth-values of its immediate parts.

We shall see that this principle does indeed hold for propositional logic and that the semantic rules needed are none other than the truth-tables for the connectives. But not all sentences are complex structures made up of other sentences; some are simple sentences made up of other parts of speech like noun and verb phrases. In due course we shall have to apply the principle of compositionality to these sorts of sentences and explain how the truth-value of simple sentences is determined by facts about the referents of noun and verb phrases. We shall also find that there are varieties of complex sentence made up of other sentences as immediate parts which do not conform to the principle of truth-functionality. For these we shall have to depart from the simple model of Tarski's semantics outlined here.

Before actually stating the semantic rules for propositional logic, we must make clear one further ground rule of the theory. As in syntax these various metatheoretic ideas are explained, where possible, in the terms of set theory. Thus, the various categories of entities corresponding to the parts of speech are grouped into sets, and the semantic rules explaining referents of wholes in terms of referents of parts are treated as functions which take a certain series of referents as inputs (those of the parts of an expression) and yield a characteristic referent (that of the whole expression) as output. So also is the reference relation itself treated set theoretically as a function that pairs with each expression its referent. The motivation for using set theory is the same as that for using it in syntax; it allows for the rigorous evaluation of the theory. First of all, it allows for unambiguous proof of what follows from the basic principles and definitions of the semantic theory. These theorems constitute the predictions of the theory that are matched against the various semantic data the theory attempts to explain. Some of the phenomena explained are logical, namely the logical inferences deemed logically acceptable by ordinary language speakers, and some are conceptual and concern the adequacy of the definitions found in the theory. But before discussing these predictions and how they are evaluated, we should first summarize the various features of the theory's form and discuss some examples.

The semantics of a formal language in Tarski's model has the following form. The reference relation is defined set theoretically by first stipulating the referents of expressions from the basic parts of speech and then fixing the referent of each complex expression by stating for each grammar rule a corresponding semantic rule which explains how the referent of its outputs is determined by those of its inputs.

EXAMPLE Let us assume the minimal syntax of conjunctions and negations built up from the three basic simple sentences of the previous example. We shall state for the two grammatical rules of negation and conjunction the corresponding semantical rules that explain how the referent of the whole sentence is determined by the referents of its immediate parts. We shall assume that the referents of sentences are the truth-values T and F.

If a sentence refers to T, then its negation refers to F, and if a sentence refers to F, then its negation refers to T.

If two sentences each refer to T, then their conjunction refers to T also, but if either sentence or both refer to F, then their conjunction refers to F.

Just as the rules of grammar could be recast more formally as functions on sentences, so can these be restated as functions on truth-tables:

$$g_{\sim} = \{\langle T, F\rangle, \langle F, T\rangle\} \quad \text{and}$$

$$g_{\wedge} = \{\langle T, T, T\rangle, \langle T, F, F\rangle, \langle F, T, F\rangle, \langle F, F, F\rangle\}.$$

Both these sets are relations, the first a set of pairs and the second a set of triples. They are also functions in that no argument occurs more than once in each relation. It is these functions that are usually displayed in truth-tables. We can now give an example of a particular reference relation, call it R_1, capturing the idea of a particular possible world. The definition of R_1 proceeds in two stages. First, R_1 is required to assign a truth-value to each basic sentence. We do not care what truth-value R_1 assigns to any particular atomic sentence, but we do require that it assign some value to each. Second, R_1 assigns a truth-value to each molecular sentence made up of formation function f_i. It does so by applying the corresponding semantic rule g_i to the truth-values of its parts.

(I) *Assignment of truth-values to basic sentences.* Let $R_1(P) = T$, $R_1(Q) = F$, and $R_1(R) = F$.

(II) *Assignment of truth-values to complex sentences.* If $R_1(A) = T$, then $R_1(\sim A) = F$, and if $R_1(A) = F$, then $R_1(\sim A) = T$.
If $R_1(A) = T$ and $R_1(B) = T$, then $R_1(A \wedge B) = T$, and if $R_1(A) = F$ or $R_1(B) = F$ or both, then $R_1(A \wedge B) = F$.

Clause (II) may be restated more formally using the set theoretic forms of both grammatical and semantical rules:

(II′) $R_1(f(\sim A)) = g_{\sim}(R_1(A))$ and

$$R_1(f_{\wedge}(A, B)) = g_{\wedge}(R_1(A), R_1(B)).$$

Given clause (I) and either clause (II) or (II′), it is clear that every sentence in this restricted language gets a truth-value, and that a story describing a possible world has been completely specified.

□ EXERCISE

Extend the semantic theory of the example so that it applies to the extended syntax of the previous exercise.

a. Add to the two informal semantic rules of negation and conjunction three more rules, one each for disjunction, the conditional, and the biconditional.

b. Recast these rules as functions on truth-values, naming them respectively $g_{\vee}$, $g_{\rightarrow}$, and $g_{\leftrightarrow}$ and making each the appropriate sort of set of triples of truth-values. Each of these relations should be a function.

c. Extend the definition of R_1 to cover disjunctions, conditionals, and biconditionals by adding three clauses to clause (II) stating how R_1 assigns truth-values to $(A \vee B)$, $(A \rightarrow B)$, and $(A \leftrightarrow B)$ given the truth-values R_1 assigns to A and B.
d. Extend the definition of R_1 to the three additional types of sentence as is done in clause (II′). That is, give three additional clauses saying what truth-value R_1 assigns respectively to $f_{\vee}(A, B)$, $f_{\rightarrow}(A, B)$, and $f_{\leftrightarrow}(A, B)$ in terms of $R_1(A)$, $R_1(B)$, and the functions $g_{\vee}$, $g_{\rightarrow}$, and $g_{\leftrightarrow}$.

3.3.2 Tarski's Material Adequacy Condition

That his theory has the right to be called a correspondence theory was shown by Tarski in the following way. Let an expression E be made by formation rule F from other expressions $E_1, \ldots, E_n$, i.e., $E = F(E_1, \ldots, E_n)$. Furthermore, let R be the reference function assigning a referent to every expression. Suppose E is a sentence and that therefore its referent $R(E)$ is a truth-value. Tarski argued that a minimal requirement of any genuine correspondence theory of truth is that there be some sentence in the metalanguage, call it $E*$, that means the same as E and that directly describes the world in a manner equivalent to E. Thus, $E*$ describes in the metalanguage the same facts that make E true. Further Tarski required that we be able to prove in the theory the metatheorem

$$\text{(T)} \quad R(E) = \text{T iff } E*.$$

Here $E*$ is said to state the *truth conditions* of E, those circumstances under which $R(E) = \text{T}$, and the (T) formula as a whole then states necessary and sufficient conditions for the truth of E in equivalent metalinguistic terms that specify some state of affairs in the world. Any correspondence theory of truth worthy of the name, Tarski argued, must yield a (T) formula for each sentence of the language, and he held his own theory to this minimal criterion of adequacy:

Material Adequacy Condition for a Correspondence Theory. A minimal condition for a correspondence theory of truth is that it entail, for any sentence E of the language, a (T) formula stating the necessary and sufficient conditions under which E is true in equivalent metalinguistic terms.

EXAMPLE If E is the expression 'Snow is white', Tarski claimed that his definition of reference will yield a metatheorem of the form: 'Snow is white' is true (in a world w) iff (Snow is white)*. Here, (Snow is white)* states some rule fixing the truth-value of 'Snow is white' (in the world w) in terms of the referents (in w) of 'snow', 'is', and 'white'. Tarski sometimes talked of expressions like (Snow is white)* as 'translations into the metalanguage' of 'Snow is white'.

Let us consider exactly what a (T) formula says. Its first half deals with the sentence, saying that it is true, and the second half deals with the world, stating the facts that must hold in order for the sentence to be true. It is the bridge between sentences and the world that is the essence of correspondence. As such it is part of any genuine correspondence theory.

The theory Tarski actually developed, however, managed to entail all the (T) formulas by conforming at the same time to the principle of compositionality. The way he achieved both at once is by formulating the truth-conditions for a sentence E in terms of the referents of the immediate parts of E. That is, suppose E has as its immediate parts $E_1, \ldots, E_n$. Then the truth-conditions $E*$ of E are formulated by specifying conditions holding in the world among the entities $R(E_1), \ldots, R(E_n)$. In the above example, he would formulate (Snow is white)* in terms of R(snow) and R(white), and some condition on these entities that determines uniquely when R(Snow is white) = T. In the next chapter we shall see in detail how to develop such a theory for simple subject–predicate sentences like 'Snow is white'. We are now, however, in a position to see in detail how (T) sentences conforming to the principle of truth-functionality may be developed for the language of propositional logic.

EXAMPLE Let us adopt the set theoretic grammar and semantic rules $f_{\sim}$, $f_{\wedge}$, $g_{\sim}$, and $g_{\wedge}$ of the earlier exercise, and the definition of the possible world R_1. Then the statement 'A is true in the world R_1' may be formulated neatly as '$R_1(A) = \text{T}$'. Likewise there is a neat way to formulate a rule for a 'translation' operation $*$ on complex sentences that fixes for any sentence A a translation $A*$ of the desired sort. First, let us define $({\sim}A)*$ and $(A \wedge B)*$:

(1) $({\sim}A)*$ is $g_{\sim}(R_1(A)) = \text{T}$ and

(2) $(A \wedge B)*$ is $g_{\wedge}(R_1(A), R_1(B)) = \text{T}$.

Here $g_{\sim}(R_1(A)) = \text{T}$ is a set theoretic way of saying that the result of applying the truth-function $g_{\sim}$ to the truth-value in R_1 of A is T, and $g_{\wedge}(R_1(A), R_1(B)) = \text{T}$ is the precise way of saying that the result of applying the truth-function $g_{\wedge}$ for conjunction to the truth-values in R_1 of A and B is T. Given these and the earlier definitions, it is now easy to establish metatheorems of the form (T) that Tarski desired in a correspondence theory.

THEOREM. $R_1({\sim}A) = \text{T}$ iff $({\sim}A)*$.

Proof. All we need note is that $({\sim}A)*$ means $g_{\sim}(R_1(A)) = \text{T}$ and that by clause (II′), $R_1({\sim}A) = g_{\sim}(R_1(A))$. Clearly given this identity, if we assumed $R_1(A) = \text{T}$ for conditional proof we could deduce $g_{\sim}(R_1(A)) = \text{T}$, i.e., $({\sim}A)*$, and conversely if we assumed $g_{\sim}(R_1(A)) = \text{T}$ we could then deduce $R_1(A) = \text{T}$. QED.

Stop to translate the metatheorem. It says that a negation is true if, and only if, the result of applying the truth-function for negation to the immediate parts of the sentence yields the value true. Both halves of the biconditional are stated in the metalanguage. The left side is a semantic statement saying the negation is true. The right is a sentence equivalent to that on the left and thus qualifies as the left side of a genuine (T) formula. Moreover, the truth-conditions formulated on the left side conform to the principle of truth-functionality because they record how the truth-value of the whole depends on that of its immediate parts.

☐ **EXERCISES**

1. Prove the following, given the definition of $(A \wedge B)*$ and clause (II′).

THEOREM. $R_1(A \wedge B) = \text{T}$ iff $(A \wedge B)*$.

2. For the extended syntax of the previous exercises, define $(A \vee B)*$, $(A \rightarrow B)*$, and $(A \leftrightarrow B)*$ and then prove the following metatheorems:

THEOREM. $R_1(A \vee B) = \text{T}$ iff $(A \vee B)*$.
THEOREM. $R_1(A \rightarrow B) = \text{T}$ iff $(A \rightarrow B)*$.
THEOREM. $R_1(A \leftrightarrow B) = \text{T}$ iff $(A \leftrightarrow B)*$.

3.3.3 Carnap's Analysis of Logical Truth and Validity

Carnap used Tarski's concept of reference to give a definition of valid argument. His insight was essentially that there are as many reference relations as there are possible worlds.[7] Indeed, we may as well consider a possible world to be a reference relation, for consider what a reference relation is. It is one of the many possible permutations of ways to pair atomic expressions with the entities they refer to. Once the interpretations of the atomic items are fixed, the semantic rules then determine the referents of the complex expressions. The name 'Socrates' may stand for any sort of thing and the adjective 'white' for any sort of property. Depending on what they stand for in a given world (in a given reference relation), the sentence 'Socrates is white' will either be true or false according to whether the referents of the parts behave appropriately. If the semantic rule for that type of sentence yields T when applied to the referents of its parts in that world then the sentence is T; otherwise it is not. The sentences true under a given reference relation constitute the story that defines the world, and the referents themselves standing in their various relations constitute the world the story describes. Thus, to the intuitive notion of world, considered as either a story or as the entities described by the story, there corresponds a reference relation and vice versa. Indeed, Carnap suggested, we may consider them to be the same. Carnap's definitions of logical truth and valid argument combine the

[7] The more rigorous statement of this idea is found in Rudolf Carnap, *Introduction to Semantics* (1942), and *Meaning and Necessity* (1947). But more readable is the account by the author in 'Carnap's Intellectual Autobiography' (1963).

traditional definitions of these notions, which we repeat below, with the idea that a possible world may be understood as a reference relation. The traditional definitions read as follows.

DEFINITION: P is a *logical truth* iff for any possible world w, P is true in w.
DEFINITION: The argument from $H_1, \ldots, H_n$ to C is *valid* iff, for any possible world w, if all $H_1, \ldots, H_n$ are true in w, then C is true in w.

Carnap's definitions merely replace the undefined idea of possible world with its set theoretic version:

DEFINITION: P is a *logical truth* iff for any reference relation R, $R(P) = \mathrm{T}$.
DEFINITION: The argument from $H_1, \ldots, H_n$ to C is *valid* iff for any reference relation R, if $R(H_1), \ldots, R(H_n)$ are all T, then $R(C) = \mathrm{T}$.

Given precisely defined reference relations, these definitions of logical truth and validity are in their turn precisely defined. The virtue of these definitions lies not only in their clarity, which is quite important in itself, but also in their theoretical utility. Once the constraints on the acceptable form of the reference relations are defined, it is often possible to prove that a given sentence is a logical truth or that a given argument is valid. That is, we can know in a rigorous way what the predictions of the theory are concerning what is logically acceptable. We may then turn to the data and test the theory. We can consult the logical intuitions of native speakers to see whether the predictions match the evidence.

EXAMPLE We have previously given in detail the definition of a particular reference relation R_1. Tarski, too, in his early work illustrated his ideas with reference to a particular world. But Carnap's extension of Tarski's work required that we be able to talk of all possible worlds. Hence we need a rigorous definition of the set of all possible reference relations for the limited language of negation and conjunction. Simply put, an acceptable reference relation is any relation that assigns T or F to the simple sentences and then assigns T or F to the complex sentences according to the semantic rules.

DEFINITION: The set $[R]$ of *all possible reference relations* (or *possible worlds*) for the syntax of negation and conjunction is
$\{R \mid R(S \xrightarrow[\text{onto}]{} \{\mathrm{T}, \mathrm{F}\})$ such that

(1) if $A \in \mathrm{BS}$, then $R(A) \in \{T, F\}$,
(2) for any sentence $f_{\sim}(A)$, $R(f_{\sim}(A)) = g_{\sim}(R(A))$, and
for any sentence $f_{\wedge}(A, B)$, $R(A \wedge B) = g_{\wedge}(R(A), R(B))\}$.

Study this definition. It uses only ideas previously introduced. Its novelty lies in its formal statement, and the format of the definition is typical of the many notions of possible world we shall encounter later in the book. Given this definition it is possible to prove rigorously, given Carnap's definitions, that certain sentences are logical truths and that certain arguments are valid.

THEOREM. $\sim(Q \wedge \sim Q)$ is a logical truth in the restricted syntax.

Proof. Let R be arbitrary. By clause (1) and the fact that Q is a simple sentence, we know there are two cases. Case I: $R(Q) = \mathrm{T}$. Then by clause (2) and the definition of $g_{\sim}$, $R(\sim Q) = \mathrm{F}$ and by $g_{\wedge}$, $R(Q \wedge \sim Q) = \mathrm{F}$, and by $g_{\sim}$, $R(\sim(Q \wedge \sim Q)) = \mathrm{T}$. Case II: $R(Q) = \mathrm{F}$. Then by the definition of $g_{\wedge}$, $R(Q \wedge \sim Q) = \mathrm{F}$, and as in Case I, $R(\sim(Q \wedge \sim Q)) = \mathrm{T}$. Hence in either case the sentence is T in R. Since R is typical of all members in $[R]$ we know that for any R in $[R]$, $R(\sim(Q \wedge \sim Q)) = \mathrm{T}$. QED.

□ **EXERCISES**

1. By reference to Carnap's definition of validity and the definition of $[R]$, prove the following theorem.
THEOREM. The argument from $(Q \wedge S)$ to S is valid in the restricted syntax.
2. Extend the definition of $[R]$ to include assignments R of truth-values to disjunctions, conditionals, and biconditionals as well as to negations and conjunctions. That is, add appropriate clauses to clause (2) of the definition, one for each of the additional sentence types. Then prove the following metatheorem.
THEOREM. (1) $Q \leftrightarrow Q$ is a logical truth, and (2) the argument from Q and $Q \rightarrow S$ to S is valid.

3.4 PROOF THEORY

A good deal of metatheory consists of laying down the rules of well-formedness in syntax and then defining the corresponding semantic rules so as to produce a Tarski-style definition of reference and the resulting notion of valid argument. In addition, the metatheory can go one step further in a way that is of particular interest, especially historically, to logicians. It has been known since Euclid that the truths of a subject matter may be characterized by axioms. We have used axioms to characterize the truths of set theory, and we have spoken of the idealized theory in science as an axiom system. Indeed, one of the most obvious ways to try to 'characterize' or 'explain' logical truths and valid arguments is to try to axiomatize them. In the nineteenth and early twentieth centuries logic was pursued almost solely in terms of axiom systems. Explaining logical truth consisted for the most part of formulating axiom systems (a set of basic axioms and accompanying inference rules). A particular axiomatization was successful if the theorems following from it corresponded closely to the desired result.

In later chapters we shall investigate some attempts to axiomatize logic, but we may note here that two developments in particular moved logic beyond the concern for axiom systems. The first was the development of semantics as a framework within which axiom systems might be rigorously evaluated. If a given axiom system was supposed to prove exactly the logical truths, a rigorous appraisal of success would presuppose some independent, prior analysis of 'logical truth'. If we could rigorously define logical truth then we could actually demonstrate mathematically that the theorems of a system coincided with the logical truths. The subject matter that developed around the independent analysis of logical truth and valid argument was Tarski-style formal semantics. It is now a standard requirement for an axiom system that it be provided with a rigorous proof (what is called a *completeness* proof) showing that the set of theorems of the axiom system and the deductions it sanctions coincide respectively with the set of logical truths and with the logically valid arguments, as these notions are defined in semantics. We will see examples of such completeness proofs in later chapters. The deep mathematical investigation of the semantics of formal languages is called *model theory*, and it has proven a fruitful and important branch of mathematics during the last 30 years.

A second frontier that has opened in logic which has drawn attention away from axiom systems is the broader understanding of the kind of thing an axiom system is. It turns out that what is particularly interesting about axiom systems is that they allow us to tell by certain simple syntactic manipulations whether a series of sentences is in fact a proof. This ability to evaluate a proof by inspection of its syntax and the more general phenomenon of being able to characterize a set by finite mechanical manipulations has given rise to proof theory and recursive function theory. It has been discovered that there are ways other than axiom systems for the mechanical characterization of logical truth and valid argument. Various types of syntactic algorithms and rules of 'natural' deduction which do not require an initial set of axioms are the most important, and these too we shall meet in later chapters.

3.5 METHODOLOGICAL CONSTRAINTS ON METATHEORY

3.5.1 Conceptual Adequacy

In addition to grammatical and logical data there is another category of pretheoretical intuitions that are important to the appraisal of metatheory, and these concern the proper usage of the theoretical concepts that are defined within the semantic theory itself. Semantics in large part consists of a series of definitions and the consequences that follow from them. Many of the key ideas defined, moreover, are abstract and difficult, having a long history of philosophical controversy connected with them. Concepts of this sort that we have already met are 'possible world', 'truth', 'logical truth', and 'validity'. Later we shall meet semantic categories like 'object', 'property', and 'event'. A good deal of the history of philosophy centers on the proper analysis of just these ideas, and their proper definition is a major theoretical objective.

One of the most interesting features of semantic theory is that many of these ideas receive definition in the course of stating the theory. But how should proposed definitions of these ideas be evaluated? The answer is that they should be evaluated in the same way other definitions are evaluated. If these terms were not scientific or philosophical, if they were words from everyday speech (e.g., 'house', 'dance', 'tall'), their definitions could be evaluated in the same way that dictionary entries of noncontroversial terms are evaluated. For ordinary words we usually appraise a proposed definition by how well its *definiens* provides a paraphrase that could be substituted for it in all contexts of use. We look for synonymous equivalent phrases. Moreover, we can tell whether a proposed analysis is equivalent by asking a native speaker of the language. Competent speakers of the language know how they use words and what word groups can be used interchangeably. This knowledge of 'equivalence classes' of phrases constitutes an important kind of semantic data in terms of which proposed definitions can be evaluated. A proposed definition is acceptable if, and only if, it conforms to the intuitions of native speakers. This is roughly the method used by lexicographers in writing dictionaries and by the Anglo-American tradition of analytic philosophers in the analysis of philosophically relevant terms from ordinary speech. Unfortunately, we shall find that ordinary usage is not a totally successful measure of philosophically obscure theoretical concepts. Ordinary speakers do use the semantic concepts listed above. We do use the words 'true' and 'possible', and thus we do have some intuitions about how they should be used. But as we shall see, these intuitions are often not sharp enough to decide among various alternative attempts to give them precise mathematical definitions. Semantic intuitions in these cases are insufficient for deciding among competing theories, and other criteria of evaluation must be brought to bear.

3.5.2 Ontological Parsimony

One last constraint on good science generally also applies to metatheory. This is the requirement of simplicity. Exactly what simplicity amounts to in general is hard to say, and is a topic properly analyzed in the philosophy of science, but one variety that is often called for in formal semantics is ontological parsimony. Its most famous formulation is due to William of

Ockham who, as we shall see in the next chapter, was at the center of a famous dispute in the Middle Ages about simplifying semantic theory. The philosophic rule called Ockham's razor states, Do not multiply entities beyond necessity. A more accurate formulation of the basic idea would prohibit the postulation of unnecessary *kinds* of entities. The fewer distinctions among types of things the better. Modern metatheory, for example, postulates the existence of sets, and this assumption has on occasion been challenged by theorists who think it unnecessary. Another disputed category that is often posited is that of possible world. In older semantic theories one finds categories like that of substances and properties. We shall see that the famous medieval dispute between realists and nominalists over the existence of properties is in part an issue in the semantic analysis of subject–predicate sentences. Indeed, one of the most interesting aspects of semantics is seeing how these and other traditional metaphysical ideas find their way into philosophy as categories that are ordinarily postulated as part of semantic theories. Their ultimate acceptance or rejection then becomes, at least in part, an evaluation of the semantic theories of which they are a part.

3.6 METHODOLOGY SUMMARIZED

We are now in a position to summarize, first of all, the standard form we shall require for the metatheoretic study of language:

Standard Form of Metatheory. Syntax should ideally define the categories of well-formed expression inductively, and these should likewise be interpreted in the semantics in a manner that conforms to the principle of the compositionality of reference and the material adequacy condition for a correspondence theory of truth.

We may also summarize the main ways in which semantic theories meeting this form will be appraised in our discussion:

1. *Grammatical adequacy.* A proposed set of grammar rules for well-formed expressions for a formal language should ideally generate a set of expressions that is part of some ordinary language as confirmed by a speaker of that language.
2. *Logical adequacy.* A proposed definition for valid argument or logical truth should ideally embrace only arguments and sentences that are part of some natural language and that are recognizable as valid or logically true by a native speaker.
3. *Conceptual adequacy.* Definitions within semantic theory of theoretical ideas should, as much as possible, conform to ordinary usage and to the uncontroversial part of past scientific or philosophical usage.

4. *Mathematical adequacy.* The definitions of both syntax and semantics should ideally be formulated within set theory and their metatheorems established by standard set theoretic proofs.
5. *Ontological adequacy.* The ontological categories posited by the theory should be the minimal number necessary for explaining the phenomena at issue.

Few theories can be expected to score highly on all counts. In general, evaluation usually consists of contrasting how well rival theories do according to the various criteria.

4

Simple Sentences

4.1 SUBJECT-PREDICATE SENTENCES

4.1.1 The Copula

It is natural to start metatheory by a study of the shortest sentences possible. The grammar of sentences as a whole will after all have to explain first what simple sentences are before it can meaningfully explain how to generate longer sentences from shorter ones. Likewise in semantics the referents of simple sentences will be presupposed in explaining the referents of longer sentences because referents of wholes are always explained in terms of referents of their parts. There are actually various kinds of simple sentences, but the one that logicians were almost exclusively concerned with for 2000 years is what is called the subject-predicate sentence. The traditional definition assumes that we know which terms may be subjects and predicates and then defines a subject-predicate sentence as one that yokes a subject to a predicate by inserting an expression called the *copula* between them. The copula, either expressed or implied, is represented in English by the verb 'to be' used in its common or ordinary sense. Explaining just what subjects and predicates are and just what is meant by this ordinary sense of 'to be' are questions that will concern us for some time, but it is possible to give examples of such sentences now.

EXAMPLES Socrates is pious.
Socrates is a man.
Socrates runs.

Aristotelian logic also allows for common nouns like 'mankind', 'horses', 'all men', and 'some men' to serve as subject terms in addition to proper names like 'Socrates'. But let us now restrict attention to the sort of subject–predicate sentence like those of the examples which take proper names as subjects. We can use categories from traditional grammar to attempt a first approximation of a grammatical definition for this class of sentences.

DEFINITION: By a *simple subject–predicate sentence* let us mean the result of concatenating a proper name with either (1) the verb 'to be' and an adjective, (2) the verb 'to be' and a common noun, or (3) an intransitive verb.

A linguist might characterize these sentences schematically as follows. Let PN be the category of proper nouns, Adj that of adjectives, CN that of common nouns, and ITV that of intransitive verbs:

$$\text{PN} + \begin{cases} \text{to be} + \begin{cases} \text{Adj} \\ \text{CN} \end{cases} \\ \text{ITV} \end{cases}$$

In this notation, the 'parts of speech' may be viewed as sets of expressions, and $A + B + C$ as the result of concatenating some symbol x from A with some symbol y from B to some symbol z from C so as to get the string of symbols $x^\frown y^\frown z$. Even this traditional sort of definition appeals to grammatical concepts we have not defined, namely the various traditional parts of speech.

It is interesting to notice that the traditional definitions of the parts of speech are semantic rather than syntactic. A syntactic definition would define concepts solely in terms of other syntactic ideas, talking only about signs and their concatenation. But the traditional categories are defined semantically in terms of how they link up to the world, by what category of entity in the world expressions from that part of speech stand for. A proper noun is said to be a term that stands for a person, place, or thing; a verb is a word that stands for an action; and a sentence is a series of words that 'expresses a complete thought'. It has been an assumption of modern grammar as done both by logicians and linguists that it would be better to define these categories syntactically, solely in terms of syntactic ideas like the arrangements of symbols and the construction rules that make new symbols out of old. Defining the ideas semantically obscures what is the most striking feature of parts of speech, namely that viewed in isolation they form a little universe governed by the laws of grammar. Some parts of speech serve as basic or elementary building blocks, and these are called 'atomic' expressions. From these are constructed longer and more complex parts of speech that are called 'molecular' expressions. The construction, moreover, is predictable and regular, and lends itself to lawlike description solely in terms of symbolic arrangements. In the simplest cases the set of basic expressions is defined by a list. Then, rules of construction are defined that explain how to form longer strings of symbols that incorporate shorter ones. In the last chapter we discussed these ideas in general and saw them applied to the example of the language for propositional logic. We are now going to explain how they may be used to explain the grammar of simple subject–predicate sentences.

EXAMPLE We can construct a very simple subject–predicate syntax by stipulating a set Sbj of subjects and Prd of predicates, both by lists, and by defining in terms of concatenation a rule f_{SP} for generating from these categories the members of a set we shall call S of simple sentences. Traditional English grammar would form sentences by placing the subject first and then following it with the predicate, perhaps with the verb 'to be' in between. The rule we give, however, follows the rather perverse word order of modern logic in which the subject immediately follows the predicate with no explicit copula at all.

(1) $\text{Sbj} = \{a, b, c\}$,

(2) $\text{Prd} = \{F, G, H\}$,

(3) $f_{SP} = \{\langle x, y, z\rangle | z = y^\frown x\}$. (Thus, the function takes two arguments and concatenates them in reverse order.)

(4) S is the range of f_{SP} restricted to the arguments consisting of subject–predicate pairs:

$$S = \{x | \text{for some } y \text{ and } z,\ y \in \text{Sbj} \wedge z \in \text{Prd} \wedge x = f_{SP}(y, z)\}.$$

In such syntaxes the sets of expressions defined by stipulation are considered to be defined syntactically. What is assumed without deeper explanation is that listing some basic syntactic entities is unproblematic, and surely it seems an acceptable assumption that we can list or find names for short series of basic expressions. For scientific purposes it does not matter much what these entities are, so long as they are syntactic and short enough to be useful. They can be any distinct marks or sounds. It is these lists that approximate what a linguist would call the *lexicon* of the language—the basic syntactic entities which the user must master in order to construct by grammatical rules the longer expressions of the language. It is usually assumed in the study of natural languages that the list of lexical items is finite, because it seems that it is both a factual truth and a matter of psychological necessity that human speakers must work with a distinctly limited set of basic elements. (This assumption that the syntax must be 'learnable' as well as more precise mathematical formulations of the basic ideas of syntax will be discussed more fully in Chapter 6.)

□ **EXERCISE**

Write a concatenation function that more accurately generates the subclass of the present tense subject–predicate sentences of English that employs

a. singular subjects in either the first, second, or third person falling into the following subcategories:
   (i) the set of singular first person pronouns: {I}
   (ii) the set of singular second person pronouns: {you}
   (iii) the set of singular third person pronouns: {he, she, it}
   (iv) the set of singular proper names {John, Mary}

b. the set of intransitive verbs: {dance, run}.

4.1.2 Realism and the Problem of Universals

In semantics perhaps no expression is of as much philosophical interest as the simple subject–predicate sentence. Both what categories subjects and predicates stand for and how their doing so determines the truth of simple sentences amount to the core of traditional metaphysics. But discussions of metaphysics are often stated, in both traditional and modern philosophy, in a manner that obscures their close ties to semantic theory. Instead of asking what kind of thing proper names stand for, what kind of thing predicates stand for, and how the referents of subject and predicate determine the truth-value of the whole, slightly different questions are put that talk about the way the world is. Many of these questions about reality are, however, equivalent to questions in semantics.

For example, Plato, Aristotle, and many philosophers since have taken stands on the metaphysical issue called the *problem of universals.* In its simplest form the problem is an inquiry into how two things can be the same and yet different. How can both Socrates and Plato be the same in that they are both men and yet different in that they are distinct individuals? The traditional answer, called *realism,* maintains that existence is divided into two basic sorts of things called *particulars* and *universals.* Particulars are something like localized points in space–time that one could point to, and universals are properties or qualities. It is part of the fundamental nature of reality and a basic fact of metaphysics, according to realism, that universals may 'inhere' or be 'exemplified' in more than one particular at a time. Thus the phenomenon of joint sameness and difference is given a sort of explanation: two things are different inasmuch as they are distinct particulars and the same inasmuch as the same universal inheres in both.[1]

Variations on this basic theory are manifold. The entities serving the role of universals in Plato's cosmos are the perfect Ideas or Forms which never change. Bits of matter work as particulars. Distinct bits of matter, in his

[1] A good introduction to these issues is Michael Loux, 'The Problem of Universals' (1970). A more sophisticated yet still quite readable account is D. W. Hamlyn, 'Particular and General', Chapter 5 of *Metaphysics* (1984).

theory, are distinct but may endeavor to imitate the same perfect Form and thus be similar. The view is somewhat primitive and may have been rejected by Plato later in his career.

Aristotle's view was more plausible and provided the elements of realistic theories that persist today. An undifferentiated stuff, called *prime matter*, provides the ontological medium that serves the role of particulars. A second category of entities which serve the role of universals is postulated, and these *properties* have the fundamental feature that they may be multiply exemplified in various bits of prime matter. An individual object or person (called a *primary substance*) is then explained to be a combination of matter and properties. The differences among primary substances that are qualitatively different is explained by the fact that their different bits of matter exemplify different properties. In a similar way sameness may be explained. The usual sense of sameness is one in which two 'things' are the same in some respects but different in others. In Aristotle's view such cases of sameness may be explained as consisting of distinct primary substances whose properties fall into two groups. There is one group of shared properties that simultaneously inheres in both substances, and another group that is not shared inasmuch as each property from this group inheres in one but not both the substances. In the unusual case in which two 'things' are qualitatively the same in every respect yet numerically different (a possibility that is allowed for in the theory), the difference can be explained by the fact that their collections of properties, although the same, are exemplified by distinct bits of matter.

Such are the bare bones of an 'Aristotelian' metaphysics, but Aristotle's own theory and its developments in the Middle Ages become more complicated because of a secondary explanation Aristotle supplied for the phenomenon of difference. Some universals instantiated in a thing, he thought, are essential to it if it is to remain truly that thing; these defining properties are called its *form* or *essence*. Given the idea of form it becomes possible to explain that two things are different by pointing out that they have different forms, without mentioning matter at all. (Whether two distinct primary substances could have exactly the same form and hence require an appeal to their distinct matter for their individuation is just the sort of problem that Aristotelians debate about.[2]) On the whole, modern philosophers are doubtful about the notion of essential properties and the idea of form. But properties (called 'universals') and individuating points (sometimes called

[2] The details of Aristotle's own theory, both in the exact interpretation of the Greek text and in its philosophical interpretation, are a good deal more complex than the schematic account given here. An excellent summary account is J. L. Ackrill, 'Metaphysics', Chapter 9, *Aristotle the Philosopher* (1981). The best known argument that the Aristotelian ontological divisions should be understood as projections onto reality of semantic distinctions is given by Gilbert Ryle in his paper 'Categories' (1966).

'bare particulars') at which the same property may be exemplified more than once are still very much alive, both in the explanation of similarity and difference and, in what amounts to the same thing, in the semantics of simple predication. As we shall see, logicians usually employ sets to serve the role of universals and the elements of sets to serve the role of bare particulars.

To show how the semantics of simple predication and the solution to the problem of universals really amount to the same thing, we recast the problem of sameness. Instead of asking how two things can be the same, we ask how two subject–predicate sentences with different subjects and the same predicate can both be true. Instead of asking how Socrates and Plato can both be human, we ask in what circumstances would 'Socrates is human' and 'Plato is human' both be true. If we have a general theory explaining when subject–predicate sentences are true, then we should be able to apply it to this special case.

But any sort of general theory about how subject–predicates sentences are true or false would itself presuppose answers to a series of basic ontological questions. What sorts of things, if anything, do subjects stand for? What do predicates stand for? How do these two parts of reality relate to each other? Realism as an ontological theory provides the traditional answers to these questions. One accepts as fundamental the existence of two basic ontological categories, particulars and universals, and posits the basic ontological relation of inherence. Subject terms are then said to stand for particulars and predicates for universals. A subject–predicate sentence 'S is P' is true in a world if in that world the universal that P stands for inheres in the particular that S stands for.

EXAMPLE We can illustrate a realistic semantic theory for the simple subject–predicate syntax previously defined in two stages. First, we list the ontological categories corresponding to the basic sets of the lexicon, and then state a semantic rule that explains how the referent (truth-value) of the subject–predicate sentence is determined in terms of the referents of its parts.

(1) A set of particulars Prt (corresponding to Sbj).
(2) A set of properties Prop (corresponding to Prd).
(3) If the property (paired with the predicate) inheres in the individual (paired with the subject) the two determine the truth-value T (paired with the sentence); if not, they determine the value F.

As in traditional metaphysics, we assume that the sets Prt and Prop and the relation of inherence are ideas too fundamental to admit of definition.

We can cast this semantics in a more modern form by formulating rule (3) in set theory. First we define a semantic rule g_{SP} that will be used to interpret subject–predicate sentences produced by the syntactic formation rule f_{SP}. This semantic rule takes as inputs a particular and a property and as output a truth-value. If the property inheres in the particular, the rule assigns the truth-value T, and if it does not, it assigns the truth-value F:

$$g_{SP} = \{\langle x, y, z\rangle | x \in \text{Prt} \wedge y \in \text{Prop} \wedge z \in \{\text{T}, \text{F}\} \wedge ((y \text{ inheres in } x) \rightarrow z = \text{T}) \wedge ((y \text{ does not inhere in } x) \rightarrow z = \text{F})\}.$$

If we also assume a function R that assigns a referent to each expression of the syntax, then what rule (3) tells us is the condition under which an arbitrary subject–predicate sentence, call it $f_{SP}(x, y)$, is paired with T or F under R. That is, it explains when $R(f_{SP}(x, y)) = \text{T}$. What it says is that this happens when the referents of the parts, namely $R(x)$ and $R(y)$, when taken as inputs of the rule g_{SP}, yield the output T. Given the definition of g_{SP}, then, to say R assigns the value T to arguments x and y is merely another way of saying that the property $R(y)$ inheres in the particular $R(x)$. Thus we may reformulate rule (3) as

(3′) $R(f_{SP}(x, y)) = \text{T}$ iff $g_{SP}(R(x), R(y)) = \text{T}$.

Second, we define a possible world or reference relation for the syntax as any function R that assigns particulars to subjects, properties to predicates, and truth-values to sentences according to the rule (3′). We group all such worlds into a set of all possible worlds called $[R]$:

$$[R] = \{R | R(\text{Sbj} \cup \text{Prd} \cup S \xrightarrow[\text{into}]{} \text{Prt} \cup \text{Prop} \cup \{\text{T}, \text{F}\}) \text{ such that}$$

$$\text{for any } x, x \in \text{Sbj} \rightarrow R(x) \in \text{Prt},$$

$$\text{for any } x, x \in \text{Prd} \rightarrow R(x) \in \text{Prop, and}$$

$$\text{for any } x \text{ and } y, f_{SP}(x, y) \in S \rightarrow R(f_{SP}(x, y)) = g_{SP}(R(x), R(y))\}.$$

(In this example we omit the usual step of defining the notions of valid argument or logical truth, because the syntax of this language is too simple to contain the redundancies typical of these logical ideas. No valid arguments or logical truths can be formulated within its syntax.)

One objection to a semantic theory of this sort is that it appeals to the undefined ontological concepts of particular, property, and inherence, all obscure notions at best. One proposal is to substitute concepts from the relatively clear theory of sets for the obscure ideas of metaphysics, replacing properties and particulars by sets and their members, and inherence by membership. Philosophers actually divide on whether sets or properties are ontologically preferable. In the early part of this century Bertrand Russell argued for the preferability of properties over sets because he thought we are directly acquainted with properties in a way we are not with sets. Later, W. V. O. Quine argued for sets over properties because though it would be better to do without both, mathematics as we know it depends on the existence of sets.[3] Indeed, it is customary in logic, as in much of mathematics, to assume the truths of set theory as the underlying foundation of any particular investigation. Thus in the metatheoretic study of language we employ the vocabulary and assumptions of set theory.

An alternative way to describe the replacement of properties by sets is available if we make use of the concept of the extension of a property. It is customary to distinguish between, on the one hand, a property, which as a basic ontological category is an idea incapable of definition and, on the other hand, the set of objects which have that property. This set is called the *extension* of the property. In this view, then, it is preferable to replace all talk of properties by sets understood as the extensions of the properties.

The virtue of extensions over properties is thought to be their greater clarity. The main way in which the extension of a property differs from the property itself is that it is a set and therefore obeys the axioms of set theory in a way that properties do not. In particular, since extensions are sets, they obey the axiom of extensionality and are identical if they have all the same members. On the other hand, even though properties are not very well understood, we do know some basic things about them, and one of their intuitive features is that two properties can hold for exactly the same individuals yet still be distinct properties. It makes sense, for example, to imagine a world in which everything is both red and square. In this world redness and squareness would still be distinct properties yet the extensions of the two properties would be identical. The preference of some philosophers for sets over properties can now be expressed more precisely in terms of this distinction. Those who think that sets are clearer than properties or who think that for the purposes of science and mathematics it is adequate to talk just about sets would reformulate traditional views about properties as views about sets. For example, instead of talking about an individual having the property of redness, we should, in this view, talk about it falling into the set of red things, and instead of talking about all the properties an individual has, we talk about all the sets the individual falls into.

This use of sets is an example of the technique common in formal semantics of replacing obscure and ill-defined entities from traditional philosophy by set theoretic ideas occupying the same theoretical roles. We have already met the example of replacing the traditional notion of possible world by the function R which pairs expressions with the sorts of things they stand for. The replacement of properties by sets is another nice example of the technique.

[3] For a good discussion of Russell's views see W. V. O. Quine, 'Russell's Ontological Development' (1966), and for Quine's most complete statement of his views on the ontological status of sets see *Set Theory and Its Logic* (1963).

Because the technique is common and because an important part of the scientific strength of metatheory is thought to arise from it, it is worthwhile to dwell for a moment on how such replacements should be evaluated, and on whether this particular replacement of properties by sets makes for a better theory.

The main advantage of the 'extensionalist' reformulation is that it permits semantic claims to be clearly formulated, and once formulated in the mathematically precise idiom of set theory they may then be clearly proven or refuted by standard methods of proof. Thus, the replacement of properties by sets has the effect of replacing something not explained at all by concepts that are axiomatized and well understood within mathematics. Such advances in clarity are rare in philosophy, and the increased precision in this case is the primary virtue of the replacement.

Those like Russell who have philosophical doubts about set theory will not be impressed by a semantics that replaces properties by sets. One of the disadvantages of set theory is that in its naive formulations the axiomatization is inconsistent. Even more careful formulations of axiomatic set theory that manage to avoid any known contradiction contain some counterintuitive assumptions. We shall not discuss the strengths and weaknesses of axiomatic set theory in this book, but it is important to note that the issue of the ultimate success of axiomatic set theory bears directly on the appraisal of semantic theories that use set theoretic ideas. In later chapters on intuitionistic logic and constructive sets, we shall discuss some of the concepts that the critics of set theory would use in place of the unrestricted notion of set.

One quirk of the use of sets in place of properties is that while to each property there is a corresponding set, namely its extension, it is not true that to every set there corresponds some property. We may join together elements in sets in a number of ways. We may define a set by giving a list of its members, which need have no further property in common than that they are on the list. We may also define a set by abstraction, using as defining conditions on membership any set of conditions we like without regard to whether these conditions go 'naturally' together. Sets of this sort do not seem to be the extensions of any intuitively recognizable property. There is, for example, no intuitive property of which the sets {Socrates, 35, Africa, $C^{\#}$} and $\{x|x$ is a bird $\wedge\ x < 2 \wedge x$ is soluble in $H_2O\}$ are extensions, i.e., there are no intuitive properties corresponding to these sets. Thus, sets cannot be understood as 1–1 proxies for properties.

These disadvantages notwithstanding, we shall in our discussions here continue to present metatheory in its common form with full reliance on sets. The replacement of properties by sets in the previous example yields a typically neat and elegant semantics. In the following examples arbitrary elements in the universal set **V** will serve as particulars, and arbitrary sets of these individuals will serve as universals. We group all these sets themselves into a set. To make this grouping, we make use of a new bit of notation from set theory which we introduce first.

DEFINITION: By the *power set of* A, briefly $P(A)$, we mean the set of all subsets of A; i.e., $P(A) = \{B \mid B \subseteq A\}$.

THEOREM. For any x, $x \in P(A) \leftrightarrow x \subseteq A$.

Thus, $B \in P(A)$ is the way we say in set theory that B is a set made up of elements of a given set A. Accordingly, $B \in P(\mathbf{V})$, or equivalently $B \subseteq \mathbf{V}$, is the set theoretic way of saying that B is a set, and the whole set $P(\mathbf{V})$ draws together within itself all the sets that will serve as the referents of predicates. Last, in order to avoid the cumbersome English locution of a 'set of sets', logicians usually use the term *family* to refer to a set which has as its members other sets. In this vocabulary then, the power set of A is the family of all sets made up of elements from A.

EXAMPLE We define what we shall call a *set theoretic semantics for simple subject-predicate sentences.* We stipulate the following.

(1) Corresponding to Sbj is $\mathbf{V}$, the universal set. (This set will contain all 'objects' or 'individuals', the modern equivalent of particulars.)

(2) Corresponding to Prd is $P(\mathbf{V})$, the power set of $\mathbf{V}$. (Note that this set, defined as $\{A \mid A \subseteq \mathbf{V}\}$, is just the family of all sets.)

(3) $g'_{SP} = \{\langle x, y, z\rangle \mid x \in \mathbf{V} \wedge y \in P(\mathbf{V}) \wedge x \in (\mathrm{T}, \mathrm{F}\} \wedge (x \in y \rightarrow z = \mathrm{T}) \wedge (x \notin y \rightarrow z = \mathrm{F})\}$.

(4) $[R] = \{R \mid R(\mathrm{Sbj} \cup \mathrm{Prd} \cup S \xrightarrow[\text{into}]{} \mathbf{V} \cup P(\mathbf{V}) \cup \{\mathrm{T}, \mathrm{F}\})$ and

for any x, $x \in \mathrm{Sbj} \rightarrow R(x) \in \mathbf{V}$, and

for any x, $x \in \mathrm{Prd} \rightarrow R(x) \in P(\mathbf{V})$, and

for any x and y, $f_{SP}(x, y) \in S \rightarrow R(f_{SP}(x, y)) = g'_{SP}(R(x), R(y))\}$.

An alternative to this theory was proposed by Russell himself later in his career.[4] Exploiting something like Aristotle's notion of form, he proposed identifying a person with his or her properties. We shall assume like Aristotle that within a world an individual has his own characteristic set of properties and that for the purposes of the theory we may identify the individual with this set. However, let us drop Aristotle's assumption that the individual has the same set in every possible world. Thus we allow that an individual's property set may change from world to world without conforming to any single set of 'essential properties'. In the semantic theory, then, we let subject terms stand in a world for the set of properties characteristic of or 'true of' that object in that world. Though Russell speaks of properties, let us carry his

[4] See Bertrand Russell, *An Inquiry into Meaning and Truth* (1940).

idea a step further and replace properties in turn by sets, i.e., by their extensions. An individual then consists of a family of sets, intuitively of the set of all the extensions of the properties he has. Subject terms then stand for families of sets, for sets of the extensions of properties. For example, 'Socrates' will stand in w for the family of sets each of which is the extension of one of Socrates' properties in w. Predicates will continue to refer to sets as in the earlier theory. Thus 'human' will continue to stand relative to a world for the set of humans in that world. The truth of a subject–predicate sentence 'S is P' can, as before, be expressed in terms of set theory, but this time predicates refer to entities that are inside sets referred to by subjects: 'S is P' is T in w iff the referent of P is an element of the referent of S in w. Here S stands for all the sets characteristic of the individual and P for the extension of the property predicated in the sentence.

In the course of stating these ideas precisely, we wish below to express the fact that the referent of a predicate is a set. We do so in set theory by saying that it is in $P(\mathbf{V})$, the set of all sets. Thus to say A is a set we write $A \in P(\mathbf{V})$. (We could equally have said $A \subseteq \mathbf{V}$, which says the same thing.) We also wish to say that the subject refers to a family of sets. In set theory we say that it is in $P(P(\mathbf{V}))$, the set of all families of sets. Thus, to say A is a family of sets, we say $A \in P(P(\mathbf{V}))$. (Here too we could have expressed the idea in an equivalent manner using the subset relation, $A \subseteq P(\mathbf{V})$.)

DEFINITION: Let us define what we shall call a *second-order set theoretic semantics of simple subject–predicate sentences*:

(1) Corresponding to the Sbj is $P(P(\mathbf{V}))$, the set of all sets each of which is in turn a set.

(2) Corresponding to Prd is $P(\mathbf{V})$, the set of sets.

(3) $g''_{SP} = \{\langle x, y, z\rangle \mid x \in P(P(\mathbf{V})) \wedge y \in P(\mathbf{V}) \wedge z \in (\mathrm{T}, \mathrm{F})$
$\qquad \wedge (y \in x \rightarrow z = \mathrm{T}) \wedge (y \notin x \rightarrow z = \mathrm{F})\}$.

(4) $[R] = \{R \mid R(\mathrm{Sbj} \cup \mathrm{Prd} \cup S \xrightarrow[\text{into}]{} P(P(\mathbf{V})) \cup P(\mathbf{V}) \cup \{\mathrm{T}, \mathrm{F}\}),$

for any x, $x \in \mathrm{Sbj} \rightarrow R(x) \in P(P(\mathbf{V}))$,

for any x, $x \in \mathrm{Prd} \rightarrow R(x) \in P(\mathbf{V})$, and

for any x and y, $f_{SP}(x, y) \in S \rightarrow R(f_{SP}(x, y)) = g''_{SP}(R(x), R(y))\}$.

In the history of logic it has proven to be rather a difficult task to define both syntactic rules and corresponding semantic rules embracing just the stylized subject–predicate sentences of Aristotle's theory, not to mention the much wider set of subject–predicate sentences sanctioned as grammatical by ordinary languages such as English. Both Aristotle and English accept common nouns with and without modifiers like 'all' and 'some' in subject positions. But it has proven difficult to simultaneously admit these sentence types and to define uniform semantic rules governing the truth of all simple predications. One of the most interesting solutions to this problem has been proposed by Richard Montague who uses what is essentially the semantics just defined.[5] For a long period philosophers rejected such semantic accounts either because they felt that they must employ properties as in Russell's original version or because they thought such theories were committed to essentialism, i.e., to the view that some predications would be necessarily true of some subjects. In Aristotle's original conception both properties and essences are employed, but the semantics just given avoids both. It clearly avoids properties by talking, instead, of sets. That it avoids essentialism is shown by the following result.

THEOREM. In a second-order semantics, no simple subject–predicate sentence is a logical truth.

□ EXERCISES

1. Prove the metatheorem. All you need to do is find at least one possible world, i.e., at least one R in $[R]$, that makes a subject–predicate sentence false. The way to find such a world is to define it or, as is usually said, to 'construct' it. Assume an arbitrary sentence, say $f_{SP}(x, y)$ and call it P for simplicity. Then define a relation R by abstraction and show first that R is a member of $[R]$ (i.e., R meets all the defining conditions for membership in $[R]$; if you define R right this is not hard to prove). Second, show $R(P) = \mathrm{F}$. In order to ensure $R(P) = \mathrm{F}$, you must define in an appropriate way what $R(x)$ and $R(y)$ are and then show, given the definition of g''_{SP} and your stipulations of $R(x)$ and $R(y)$, that $R(P)$ [which is the same as $R(f_{SP}(x, y))$] is F.
2. Let us augment the syntax by adding two formation rules: f_{all} and f_{some} that generate complex common nouns:

   $f_{\text{all}}(x) = \text{all}^\frown x$, and
   $f_{\text{some}}(x) = \text{some}^\frown x$.

   We now redefine the set Sbj so that it includes not only the original proper nouns but also the results of applying the new rules to the common nouns in Prd:

   $$\text{Sbj} = \{a, b, c\} \cup \{x \mid \text{for some } y,\ y \in \text{Prd and either } f_{\text{all}}(y) = x \text{ or } f_{\text{some}}(y) = x\}.$$

   We continue to let the names in $\{a, b, c\}$ stand for sets of sets. The exercise is to define two semantic rules g_{all} and g_{some} which take sets as their inputs (the referents of common nouns in Prd) and yield as their outputs families of sets. The rules must be defined in set theory. Here is Montague's idea: 'all men' will refer to the family consisting of exactly those sets of which the class of men is a subset; 'some men' will refer to that family of sets consisting exactly of those sets that contain any element from the set of men. Explain how on this view proper names as well as modified

[5] The best introduction to Montague's semantics, which is heavily set theoretic and quite a job to read, is David R. Dowty *et al.*, *Introduction to Montague Semantics* (1981).

common nouns all stand for the same sort of thing, and why if $R(Fa) = \mathrm{T}$, then $R(\mathrm{all}F) \subseteq R(a) \subseteq R(\mathrm{some}F)$. Show also that there are now some logical truths by proving that for any R, $R(F\mathrm{all}F) = \mathrm{T}$. (Note that here $F\mathrm{all}F$ is the inverted form of what in English we would write as 'All F are F'.)

3. In the nineteenth century Gottlob Frege proposed the idea that subjects stand for individuals but predicates stand for functions from individuals to the truth-values T and F. His idea was that each predicate constituted a sort of rule that allows a speaker to go through the world passing judgment on each object saying either 'Yes, it falls under the predicate', or 'No, it does not fall under the predicate'. A predicate stands for a given function of this sort, call it h, from individuals to truth-values if, and only if, the predicate is 'true of' any individual x such that $h(x) = \mathrm{T}$ and 'false of' any individual x such that $h(x) = \mathrm{F}$.[6] Define appropriate clauses (1)–(4) as in the previous examples for a functional semantics for simple subject–predicate sentences that captures Frege's idea.

4.1.3 Ockham's Nominalistic Semantics

All of these examples of semantics for simple sentences have assumed that there really exists an entity to serve as the referent of a predicate. It has been a property, or a set, or a function. Some philosophers deeply committed to ontological parsimony object to any such view. It is true that the catalog of existing things does include the referents of subjects, but it is a philosophical invention of a very misleading kind, they hold, to say that there exists more than the things in the world which happen to have properties. There is no additional category of properties, sets, or functions. W. V. O. Quine and Nelson Goodman are proponents of this view in the twentieth century, and their concerns about sets in semantics are well known. It is far from clear, however, whether they have met the challenge of producing an adequate semantic theory without postulating predicates that truly refer. There is one instance in the history of philosophy of such an attempt, and it is proposed by one of the medieval founders of nominalism, William of Ockham.[7] As a champion of common sense and parsimony, Ockham doubted the existence of properties, but as a careful theorist he saw that it was his burden to propose an alternative account. His approach was the sound logical one of offering an alternative theory of the truth conditions for subject–predicate sentences in general. His task was harder than that we have attempted

[6] Frege's fullest statement of his semantic theory is found in his explanations of the notation for his axiomatization of arithmetic, in *Grundgesetze der Arithmetik* (1893, 1903). A very readable introduction to Frege's ideas on semantics, logic, and philosophy is Gregory Currie, *Frege: An Introduction to His Philosophy* (1981).

[7] For fuller accounts of Ockham's semantics see Robert G. Turnbull, 'Ockham's Nominalistic Logic' (1962), and Michael J. Loux, 'The Ontology of William of Ockham' (1974).

because he was working with the wider Aristotelian notion of a subject–predicate sentence. As grammatical subjects and predicates he accepted proper names, common nouns modified by 'all', and common nouns modified by 'some'. Acceptable sentences of the sort he discussed may be schematized as follows:

$$\left.\begin{matrix}\text{PN}\\ \text{all} + \text{CN}\\ \text{some} + \text{CN}\end{matrix}\right\} + \text{copula} + \left\{\begin{matrix}\text{PN}\\ \text{all} + \text{CN}\\ \text{some} + \text{CN}\end{matrix}\right.$$

More formally, we define a set PN of proper nouns and a set CN of common nouns by stipulation:

$$\text{PN} = \{a, b, c, d, \ldots, n\} \quad \text{and}$$

$$\text{CN} = \{F, G, H\}.$$

The set Tm of terms is then defined in three clauses:

(1) $\text{PN} \subseteq \text{Tm}$,
(2) for any x, $\{x \in \text{CN} \wedge y \in (\text{some, all}\}) \rightarrow y^\frown x \in \text{Tm}$, and
(3) nothing else is in Tm.

(That is, $\text{Tm} = \text{PN} \cup \{x | \text{for some } y \text{ and some } z,\ y \in \text{CN} \wedge z \in \{\text{all, some}\} \wedge x = z^\frown y\}$.) The set of sentences S is then defined as the yoking of any two terms by the copula:

(4) $S = \{x | \text{for some } y \text{ and some } z,\ y \in \text{Tm} \wedge z \in \text{Tm} \wedge x = y^\frown \text{is}^\frown z\}$.

Ockham's idea was to interpret these predications not by postulating properties or sets for common nouns to 'stand for' but rather by reformulating each predication as a complex sentence made up of atomic units which are identity sentences. He was then able to interpret these atomic identity statements and the complex sentences made up from them without positing anything in the universe beyond ordinary things.

To see how he managed to do this, let us first review some facts about identity statements. The 'is' of identity differs from the copula of ordinary predication in that it must always link a subject and object that stand for individuals, as in the use of the proper names 'Cicero' and 'Tully' in the identity sentence 'Cicero is Tully'. Semantically both names stand for particular things, and the sentence is true if the terms literally stand for one and the same particular thing. It is false otherwise. In evaluating identity claims, there is no need to talk about properties or other such mysterious entities. Saying $a = b$ is really a kind of semantic stuttering. If it is a genuine stuttering, the assertion is true, and if not, it is false.

Further, identity statements may themselves be joined together in conjunctions and disjunctions, and these too can be understood without talk of properties. All we need are the semantic rules that record how the truth-values of parts determine those of wholes as stated in the truth-tables for $\wedge$ and $\vee$. Ockham's strategy was to translate assertions in the subject–predicate language, which we shall call L, into another language of conjunctions and disjunctions of identity statements, which we shall call L'. This translation, however, presupposes a rigorously defined syntax for both L and L'. For L' we make use of the same set of proper nouns previously defined for L. It must include a name for everything we ever want to talk about, indeed for everything that exists. In particular it includes names for all the entities that we think of as falling under common nouns. Thus, there will be individual names like 'Bossie' and 'Elsie' for all the individuals that we think of as falling under the common noun 'cow'. To avoid confusion let us use the symbol '$=$' to refer to the identity sign in the language L'. In the metalanguage we will use 'is' to say two things are identical. For the 'is' of predication in the metalanguage, as opposed to the metalinguistic 'is' of identity, we use the relation '$\in$' of set theory. We now define the syntax of L'.

(1′) $\mathrm{PN} = \{a, b, c, d, \ldots, n\}$ (as before).

Basic sentences are constructed from proper nouns by means of the identity symbol '$=$':

(2′) $f_=$ is $\{\langle x, y, z\rangle | z \text{ is } x^\frown = {}^\frown z\}$.
(3′) BS' is $\{x | \text{for some } y \text{ and for some } z, y \in \mathrm{PN} \wedge z \in \mathrm{PN} \wedge x \text{ is } f_=(y, z)\}$.

The set S' of sentences of this new syntax is constructed from the basic sentences in BS′ by means of the conjunction and disjunction rules $f_\wedge$ and $f_\vee$ of the last chapter. S' is defined inductively as follows:

(4′) (a) $\mathrm{BS}' \subseteq S'$;
(b) for any x and y, $(x \in S' \wedge y \in S') \rightarrow (f_\wedge(x, y) \in S'$ and $f_\vee(x, y) \in S')$;
(c) nothing else is in S'.

We can now state a semantics for this syntax that makes no mention of anything like properties. We will appeal to the semantic rules $g_\wedge$ and $g_\vee$ of the last chapter (the truth-functions for conjunction and disjunction), and we must define a new semantic rule $g_=$ explaining how the referents of the parts of an identity assertion determine the truth-value of the whole:

(5′) $g_=$ is $\{\langle x, y, z\rangle | (x \text{ is the same as } y \rightarrow z \text{ is T}) \wedge (x \text{ is not the same as } y \rightarrow z \text{ is F})\}$.

(6′) $[R] = \{R \mid R(\mathrm{PN} \cup S' \xrightarrow[\text{into}]{} \mathbf{V} \cup \{\mathrm{T}, \mathrm{F}\})$ such that

(a) for any x, $x \in \mathrm{PN} \rightarrow R(x) \in \mathbf{V}$;
(b) for any x and y,
$f_{=}(x, y) \in S' \rightarrow R(f_{=}(x, y))$ is $g_{=}(R(x), R(y))$;
(c) for any x and y,
$f_{\wedge}(x, y) \in S' \rightarrow R(f_{\wedge}(x, y))$ is $g_{\wedge}(R(x), R(y))$; and
(d) for any x and y,
$f_{\vee}(x, y) \in S' \rightarrow R(f_{\vee}(x, y))$ is $g_{\vee}(R(x), R(y))\}$.

In sum, then, this semantics says that identity sentences are true if both terms stand for the same thing, and that the truth-values of complex conjunctions and disjunctions are calculated according to the appropriate truth-tables. No mention is made of properties.

The next step in Ockham's theory is to provide a clear translation from the syntax of L to that of L', showing how to reformulate predications which appear to talk of properties into complex identity sentences that do not. The basic idea is that to say something about members of a kind is merely to say it distributively about each of its elements. If what you say is to hold for all elements, the distribution is captured by saying it holds for each of the elements conjunctively; if it is to hold only for some elements, it holds for each of the elements disjunctively. To say P holds for all elements of a kind K that we can name by the proper names $a_1, \ldots, a_n$ is merely to assert the long conjunction that P holds for a_1 and P holds for a_2 and $\cdots$ and P holds for a_n. Likewise to say P holds for some of the elements is to assert that P holds for either a_1 or a_2 or $\cdots$ or a_n.

To state this idea precisely, we must define a way of translating those subject–predicate sentences containing a common noun modified by 'all' into conjunctions, and those modified by 'some' into disjunctions. The translation procedure Ockham proposes is essentially the following.

DEFINITION: An acceptable translation from L into L' is a relation $*$ from S into S' defined as follows. If 'x is y' is an arbitrary sentence of S, then there are several possible cases. We define a *translation* (x is y)$*$ of 'x is y' in each case. First for any N in CN of L we stipulate a set, call it $N+$, of proper names; i.e., we stipulate that there is an $N+$ such that $N+ \subseteq \mathrm{PN}$. (Intuitively, $N+$ contains all the names of entities embraced by the common noun N.) We now define (x is y)$*$ by cases.

Case 1: Both x and y are in PN. Then (x is y)$*$ is '$x = y$'.

Case 2: Let $x+$ be $a_1, \ldots, a_n$. Then (All x is y)$*$ is (a_1 is y)$* \wedge \cdots \wedge$ (a_n is y)$*$.

Case 3: Let $x+$ be $a_1, \ldots, a_n$. Then (Some x is y)$*$ is (a_1 is y)$*$ $\vee \cdots \vee$ (a_n is y)$*$.

Case 4: Let $y+$ be $a_1, \ldots, a_n$. Then (x is all y)$*$ is (x is a_1)$*$ $\wedge \cdots \wedge$ (x is a_n)$*$.

Case 5: Let $y+$ be $a_1, \ldots, a_n$. Then (x is some y)$*$ is (x is a_1)$*$ $\vee \cdots \vee$ (x is a_n)$*$.

Cases 2 through 5 define $*$ for a longer sentence in terms of $*$ for shorter sentences. The $*$-translation for these shorter sentences is defined again in terms of $*$ for yet shorter sentences, until finally the sentence appearing in the *definiens* has proper names in both subject and object position, and its $*$-value is defined by case 1 as a simple identity assertion.

EXAMPLES (1) (All F is b)$*$ is (a_1 is b)$*$ $\wedge \cdots \wedge$ (a_n is b)$*$ by case 2, where $F+$ is $a_1, \ldots, a_n$. Furthermore, each of these (a_i is b)$*$ is just $a_i = b$ by case 1. Thus, (All F is b)$*$ is $a_1 = b \wedge \cdots \wedge a_n = b$.

(2) Let $F+$ be $a_1, \ldots, a_n$ and $G+$ be $b_1, \ldots, b_n$. Then by case 2, (All F are some G)$*$ is (a_1 is some G)$*$ $\wedge \cdots \wedge$ (a_n is some G)$*$. But by case 5, each (a_i is some G)$*$ is (a_i is b_1)$*$ $\vee \cdots \vee$ (a_i is b_n)$*$, and by case 1, each (a_i is b_j)$*$ is $a_i = b_j$. Hence (All F are some G)$*$ is $((a_1 = b_1 \vee \cdots \vee a_1 = b_n) \wedge \cdots \wedge (a_n = b_1 \vee \cdots \vee a_n = b_n))$.

One virtue of the resulting theory is that we can use it to explain certain logical intuitions. Let us define logical truth as follows: P of L is a *logical truth* iff (P)$*$ of L' is true in every R of [R]. Likewise we define validity as follows: the argument from $H_1, \ldots, H_n$ to C in L is *valid* iff for any R of [R], if $H_1*, \ldots, H_n*$ are all true under R, then so is $C*$.

THEOREM. 'All F is some F' is a logical truth.

Proof. Clearly the R value of (All F is some F)$*$ is T under any R, because (All F is some F)$*$ is $(a_1 = a_1 \vee \cdots \vee a_1 = a_n) \wedge \cdots \wedge (a_n = a_1 \vee \cdots \vee a_n = a_n)$, each conjunct of which is true because it contains a true disjunct.

THEOREM. The argument from 'All F is all G' to 'All G is all F' is valid.

Proof. Clearly (All F are all G)$*$ and (All G are all F)$*$, given below, are T in exactly the same reference relations, by associativity and commutativity of $\wedge$:

$$((a_1 = b_1 \wedge \cdots \wedge a_1 = b_n) \wedge \cdots \wedge (a_n = b_1 \wedge \cdots \wedge a_n = b_n));$$

$$((b_1 = a_1 \wedge \cdots \wedge b_1 = a_n) \wedge \cdots \wedge (b_n = a_1 \wedge \cdots \wedge b_n = a_n)).$$

☐ **EXERCISES**

1. Derive in steps, citing which case applies, (Some F are all G)$*$ where $F+$ and $G+$ are as in Example (2).

2. Establish whether 'All F is some F' and 'Some F is all F' are logical truths. If so, prove so. If not, prove that too.
2. Establish whether the following arguments are valid or invalid and prove your conclusion:
   a. from 'All F is some G' to 'Some F is some G'.
   b. from 'All G is some F' to 'Some G is all F'.

4.1.4 Syntactic Ambiguity

As the reader may have noticed in doing the previous exercises, the translation rules do not determine a genuine function; it is not the case that there is a unique translation into L' for every sentence in L. For example, (All F is all G)$*$ may be either

$$((a_1 = b_1 \wedge \cdots \wedge a_1 = b_n) \wedge \cdots \wedge (a_n = b_1 \wedge \cdots a_n = b_n))$$

or

$$((a_1 = b_1 \wedge \cdots \wedge a_n = b_1) \wedge \cdots \wedge (a_1 = b_n \wedge \cdots \wedge a_n = b_n)).$$

For the first translation the sentence is viewed as falling under case 2 and its parts as falling under case 4. The second translation is obtained by viewing the sentence as falling under case 4 and its parts as under case 2. But since conjunction is associative and commutative both translations are equivalent. Some cases, however, yield nonequivalent translations. For example, (All F are some G)$*$ is either

$$((a_1 = b_1 \wedge \cdots \wedge a_n = b_1) \vee \cdots \vee (a_1 = b_n \wedge \cdots \wedge a_n = b_n))$$

or

$$((a_1 = b_1 \vee \cdots \vee a_1 = b_n) \wedge \cdots \wedge (a_n = b_1 \vee \cdots \vee a_n = b_n)).$$

In modern terms we might call L the *surface structure* of natural language and L' its *deep structure* (to use terminology from linguistics), or we might say L' captures the *logical form* of the sentences translated into it from L (to use another common terminology). When a natural language sentence has two versions of deep structure, or two logical forms, it is said to be *syntactically ambiguous*. For example, 'Five boys ate four apples' is said to be syntactically ambiguous between 'Five boys divided up four apples among them and ate their portions' and 'Five boys ate four apples apiece'. The ambiguity is said to be syntactic because it is produced by the word order itself and cannot be traced to any double meaning of the lexical terms 'five', 'boy', 'each', 'ate', 'four', and 'apples'. Ockham's theory, then, may be said to embody the claim that some sentences of natural language are syntactically ambiguous. Our intuitions actually condone the ambiguities allowed for, though Ockham himself did not draw attention to the fact that his translation procedure produces multiple translations for the same sentence. Indeed he might not have welcomed that fact. In any case, $*$ as defined is properly understood as a many–many relation rather than as a many–one function. Sentences and arguments of L should, therefore, be said to be logical truths and valid arguments only relative to a given translation.

☐ **EXERCISE**

Find two other sentences of L that have more than one translation into L', and explain why.

There is, however, one major defect in Ockham's semantic theory. It does not do as well as one might want at capturing the grammatical intuitions of native speakers. In asserting sentence forms of the type 'All F are some G' in English, as in 'All men are mortal', we do not normally think of ourselves as really asserting a complex sentence made up of conjunctions and disjunctions. It would be better if possible to give a semantics directly for L without the theoretical intermediary of L' that uses forms of speech that are highly contrived.

The overall appraisal of Ockham's theory is typical of the appraisal of semantic theories generally. By some criteria it does very well. In syntax it manages to go beyond the very simple subject–predicate sentences defined earlier to embrace a wider variety of forms. Ontologically it has the advantage of not positing properties. It also has the virtue of being able to explain certain logical inferences and syntactic ambiguities. Against these advantages must be set the need to posit the intervening language L' with its somewhat contrived syntax. As we shall discuss in detail in Chapter 5, it is also quite implausible to suppose that we can name by finite lists all the objects in every set we wish to talk about. Methodologically we decide the issue by balancing this mixed collection of strengths and weaknesses against those of competing theories.

Let us move on now to discuss Aristotle's own theory of subject–predicate syntax and its logic. We shall discuss a syntax that is actually more limited than that which Aristotle allowed for in his writings. Though he did have views about the semantics of subject–predicate sentences employing proper names and even for sentences containing sentence adverbs like 'necessarily' and 'possibly', we shall focus on the limited syntax of the theory of the syllogism (i.e., the *syllogistic*). What is remarkable about the syllogistic is that it permits subject–predicate sentences which employ common nouns both as subjects and as predicates, a feat it has proven difficult to match in modern logic. His theory has both a clear semantic theory and, something that we shall meet for the first time, a rudimentary proof theory.

4.2 THE SYLLOGISTIC

4.2.1 Semantics

Aristotle's original theory of the syllogism admits subject–predicate sentences of a wide variety of forms.[8] Both proper and common nouns may be subjects, these common nouns may be modified by 'all' or 'some' or by a negative modifier like 'not', predicates may consist of intransitive verbs or of the copula plus a common noun or adjective, and the predicates may be modifed by 'all' or 'some' or a negation or even by the sentence adverbs 'necessarily' and 'possibly'. This wide variety can be schematized as follows. Expressions in parentheses are optional.

$$\left.\begin{matrix}\text{proper noun}\\ (\text{not}) + \left\{\begin{matrix}(\text{all})\\(\text{some})\end{matrix}\right\} + \text{common noun}\end{matrix}\right\} + \left\{\begin{matrix}(\text{possibly})\\(\text{necessarily})\end{matrix}\right\} + \text{copula} + (\text{not})$$

$$+ \left\{\begin{matrix}\text{adjective}\\ \left.\begin{matrix}(\text{all})\\(\text{some})\end{matrix}\right\} + \text{common noun}\\ \text{intransitive verb}\end{matrix}\right.$$

The following examples vary from this scheme only in providing the inflections demanded by English grammar:

(1) Men are rational.
(2) All men are animals.
(3) Some men are possibly not rational.
(4) No men do not run.
(5) Not all men necessarily are rational.
(6) Socrates possibly is not rational.
(7) Socrates necessarily is not a human being.

In the traditional theory of the syllogism, however, this variety is regimented into simpler standard forms. We shall not discuss in this chapter the modifiers 'necessarily' and 'possibly'; they will be covered under the topic of modal logic. Likewise we shall ignore for the moment sentences with proper names

[8] Aristotle's theory of the syllogism is contained in his *Prior* and *Posterior Analytics*. The version we develop here takes great liberties with the actual text and imposes rather anachronistically the modern framework of inductive grammar and set theoretic semantics. Though the presentation is much in the spirit of Aristotle's original version, the main purpose here is not historical accuracy but rather the development of a simple but extended example of a metatheory exhibiting many of the ideas introduced in the previous chapter.

as subjects. The remaining sentence forms are all understood as falling into one of four basic types. Let S and P stand for common nouns.

Type	English sentences	Symbolic notation
A	All S are P	SAP
E	*No* S are P	SEP
I	*Some* S are P	SIP
O	*Some* S are not P	SOP

We will also allow for the negations of these four types. A rigorously defined syntax generating just these sentences proceeds first by stipulating a lexicon of common nouns and then by defining the set of sentences:

DEFINITION: We stipulate a set of *common nouns* CN = $\{F, G, H\}$ and a set of *logical signs* $\{\mathrm{A, E, I, O}, \sim\}$.

The set of *basic sentences* BS is defined as the result of writing one of the first four logical signs between two common nouns:

$$\mathrm{BS} = \{w \mid \text{for some } x, \text{ some } y, \text{ and some } z, x \in \mathrm{CN} \wedge y \in \{\mathrm{A, E, I, O}\} \wedge z \in \mathrm{CN} \wedge w = x^\frown y^\frown z\}.$$

These sentences are said to be of *types* A, E, I, and O respectively, and the common noun on the left is said to be the *subject* and that on the left the *predicate*.

The set of *sentences* Sen is defined inductively:

(1) BS $\subseteq$ Sen,
(2) if $x \in$ Sen, then $\sim^\frown x \in$ Sen, and
(3) nothing else is in Sen.

Aristotle's own semantics for these subjects, predicates, and the sentences formed from them are a matter of difficult scholarly interpretation. Subject terms are said to stand for substances. If the subject is a proper name the substance is called *primary* and is usually, but not always, said to be a combination of matter and essential properties. If the subject is a common noun, the substance is called *secondary* and is a genus or species, something like a set. Predicates that are adjectives seem to stand for properties, and those that are common nouns stand for genera and species. But the texts supporting these interpretations are scattered, obscure, and even contradictory. Medieval accounts are sometimes more consistent and clearer, but they still make explanations largely in terms of properties, genera, species, and substances. In the Middle Ages moreover, an alternative tradition began in which the terms are understood as standing for mental concepts or ideas. The semantics we shall discuss here is modernized.[9] We shall understand terms to

[9] For a discussion of the semantics of the syllogistic see Günter Pazig, *Aristotle's Theory of the Syllogism* (1968).

stand for sets, and the conditions of truth for the various sentence types will all be stated in terms of elementary set theoretic operations.

The account remains Aristotelian in spirit in at least two ways. First of all, the subjects and predicates understood as common nouns stand for sets which are latter-day versions of genera and species. Certainly every genus and species found in natural science, both ancient and modern, constitutes a set. The reverse, however, is probably not true. Any arbitrary grouping forms a genuine set, but such a grouping may not constitute a scientifically interesting classificatory genus or species. Whereas sets are well understood, as the axioms of set theory ensure, genera and species and indeed the whole process of classification in science are rather difficult to explain. Thus, it is in the interest of clarity that we replace the Aristotelian notions by sets.

A second Aristotelian feature of our semantic treatment will be the assumption that every common noun stands for a nonempty grouping. Aristotle's metaphysics does not provide for the extinction of whole classes of natural objects. Species, he thought, are eternal. Individual members come into and pass out of existence, but the type as a whole persists. Accordingly we shall require that common nouns stand only for nonempty sets.

The truth conditions for the four types of sentence are approximately the same as those of the quantified sentences we used to translate them in Chapter 1.

DEFINITION: The set $[R]$ of possible worlds is defined as $\{R \mid R(\mathrm{CN} \cup \mathrm{Sen} \xrightarrow[\text{into}]{} P(\mathbf{V}) \cup \{\mathrm{T}, \mathrm{F}\}$ such that

(1) for any S in CN, $R(S) \in P(\mathbf{V})$ and $R(S) \neq \varnothing$ and

(2) R assigns to each element X of Sen a value in $\{\mathrm{T}, \mathrm{F}\}$ as follows. If X is a basic sentence in BS, then X must be of one of the four types. That is, there are some common nouns S and P from CN such that X is either SAP or SEP or SIP or SOP. In each of these cases R assigns a truth-value to X as follows:

(a) $R(SAP) = \mathrm{T}$ iff $R(S) \subseteq R(P)$;
(b) $R(SEP) = \mathrm{T}$ iff $R(S) \cap R(P) = \varnothing$;
(c) $R(SIP) = \mathrm{T}$ iff $R(S) \cap R(P) \neq \varnothing$;
(d) $R(SOP) = \mathrm{T}$ iff $R(S) - R(P) \neq \varnothing$.

If X is not a basic sentence in BS, then it is a negation. That is, there is some sentence Y such that X is $\sim Y$. In this case R assigns a truth-value to X as follows:

(e) $R(\sim Y) = \mathrm{T}$ iff $R(Y) = \mathrm{F}\}$.

Given this set of possible worlds, the usual Leibnizian definitions of valid argument and logical truth are applicable.

DEFINITION: A sentence X in Sen is a *logical truth* iff for any R in $[R]$, $R(X) = \mathrm{T}$.

The argument from sentences $Y_1, \ldots, Y_n$ in Sen to X in Sen is *valid* (which we abbreviate as $Y_1, \ldots, Y_n \models X$) iff for any R in $[R]$, if $R(Y_1) = \cdots = R(Y_n) =$ T, then $R(X) =$ T.

We can read '$Y_1, \ldots, Y_n \models X$' as asserting in the metalanguage that the relation of logical implication holds between the sentences $Y_1, \ldots, Y_n$ and the sentence X. Though many different arguments are valid in this syntax, attention has traditionally focused on a limited set of arguments called *syllogisms*. Syllogisms have two premises and a conclusion, none of which are negated. They use only three common nouns, each term of the conclusion occurs in one and only one premise, and the remaining term occurs once in each of the two premises.

DEFINITION: A *syllogism* is any $\langle X, Y, Z\rangle$ such that

(1) X, Y, and Z are all in Sen,

(2) none of X, Y, or Z is negated,

(3) the common nouns from CN in X, Y, and Z are such that

(a) Z (called the *conclusion*) has a predicate (represented by P and called the *major term*) that also occurs in X (called the *major premise*),

(b) Z has a subject (represented by S and called the *minor term*) that occurs in Y (called the *minor premise*),

(c) there is a common noun (called the *middle term* and represented by M) that occurs in both X and Y, and these occurrences are in addition to those of the middle and minor terms mentioned in parts (a) and (b).

It is customary to describe syllogisms in terms of certain syntactic features called mood and figure. The mood of a syllogism is a triple of three sentence types: that of the major premise, that of the minor premise, and that of the conclusion in that order.

DEFINITION: A syllogism $\langle X, Y, Z\rangle$ is of *mood* JKL iff X is of type J, Y is of type K, and Z is of type L.

The moods are, therefore, any triple of the four sentence types A, E, I, and O, and hence there are 81 of them ($3^4 = 81$). The figure of the syllogism consists of the order of the subjects and predicates of the premises relative to that of the conclusion.

DEFINITION: A syllogism $\langle X, Y, Z\rangle$ is said to be

(1) in the *first figure* iff the middle term M is the subject and the major term P is the predicate of X, and the minor term S is the subject and M is the predicate of Y;

(2) in the *second figure* iff P is the subject and M is the predicate of X, and S is the subject and M is the predicate of Y;

(3) in the *third figure* iff M is the subject and P is the predicate of X, and M is the subject and S is the predicate of Y;

(4) in the *fourth figure* iff P is the subject and M is the predicate of X, and M is the subject and S is the predicate of Y.

Schematically, the four figures can be represented as follows:

Figure:	First	Second	Third	Fourth
Premises:				
Major	M, P	P, M	M, P	P, M
Minor	S, M	S, M	M, S	M, S
Conclusion:	S, P	S, P	S, P	S, P

The form of a syllogism is fully specified by giving its mood and figure.

EXAMPLE The syllogism of the first figure in the mood AEO is

MAP	All M is P
SEM	No S is M
SOP	Some S is not P

This syllogism happens to be invalid, as we now prove.

THEOREM. The syllogism AEO in the first figure is invalid.

Proof analysis. To show the syllogism is invalid we find or construct by definition some world R such that the premises are true but the conclusion is false; that is, R must both be a world and assign values such that $R(MAP) =$ T and $R(SEM) =$ T, but $R(SOP) =$ F. The strategy is first to define a function R from the expressions of the syntax to various referents. We create R by definition because we know by the principle of abstraction that if a relation is definable, then it exists. But we must then show R is a possible world by proving that it satisfies the five conditions for membership in R. We make sure that we are able to do so by being careful how we define R. We define it in such a way that we make sure it meets the conditions for membership in $[R]$. In particular, we require it to be a function on terms and sentences of the syllogistic that assigns nonempty sets to the terms and truth-values to the sentences in accordance with the rules for membership in $[R]$. Last we show that $R(MAP) = R(SEM) =$ T and $R(SOP) =$ F, again we are able to do so because we define R in a way that ensures these conditions are met. In particular we define sets I, J, and K of objects that overlap in the right way (we do so by appeal to abstraction) and then stipulate that R assign these sets to the terms S, M, and P, respectively. In order to obtain the right truth-values, the sets I, J, and K (the referents of S, M, and P) must stand in the pattern depicted in Fig. 4.1.

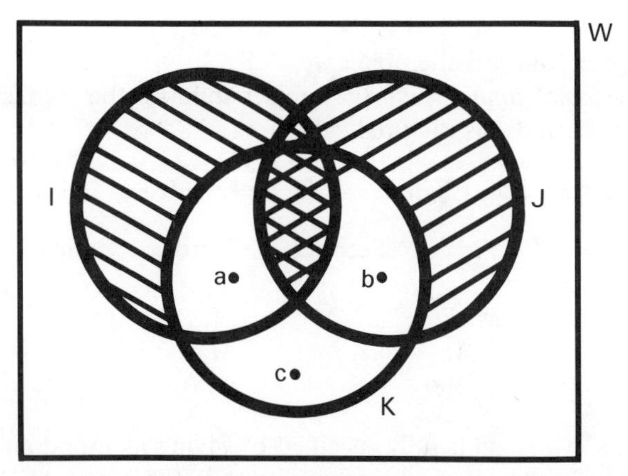

Fig. 4.1

By appeal to the principle of abstraction we may stipulate three such sets and be assured that they exist. We let the universe of a world contain at least the three objects a, b, and c, and let $I = \{a\}$, $J = \{b\}$, and $K = \{a, b, c\}$.

Proof. Let the universe of a world and the sets I, J, and K be as defined above. We now define a relation R as any function with domain CN $\cup$Sen and range $P(\mathbf{V}) \cup \{\mathrm{T}, \mathrm{F}\}$ such that R assigns to every common noun a particular subset of $\mathbf{V}$ and moreover R assigns values of the particular terms S, M, and P as follows: $R(S) = I$, $R(M) = J$, and $R(P) = K$. In addition we stipulate that R assigns truth-values to elements of Sen in the manner required in clause (2) of the definition of $[R]$. Clearly $R \in [R]$, because R is defined so as to conform with clauses (1) and (2) of the definition of $[R]$. Further given $J \subseteq K$, by the substitutivity of identity, $R(M) \subseteq R(P)$. Then by clause (2a) of the definition of $[R]$, $R(MAP) = \mathrm{T}$. Likewise, since $I \cap J = \varnothing$, we know by the substitutivity of identity that $R(S) \cap R(M) = \varnothing$, and hence by clause (2b) of the definiton of $[R]$, $R(SEM) = \mathrm{T}$. But $I - K = \varnothing$, and this by the substitutivity of identity entails $R(S) - R(P) = \varnothing$. Hence by clause (2d) of the definition of $[R]$, $R(SOP) \neq \mathrm{T}$, i.e., $R(SOP) = \mathrm{F}$. Thus by construction we have found the possible world satisfying the premises and falsifying the conclusion. Hence the argument is invalid. QED.

This proof exhibits the most common pattern for demonstrating that an argument is invalid. By ingenuity one defines a relation that both meets the conditions for counting as a genuine world and at the same time assigns values to the basic parts of speech that, given the semantic rules of the language, ensure that in that world the premises are all true but the conclusion false. From language to language the syntax and definitions of possible world will differ, but this proof strategy will remain constant.

Some syllogisms, however, are valid, and these are given traditional names, in the following order.[10]

First figure

M, P	*AAA	Barbara
$\underline{S, M}$	EAE	Celarent
S, P	AII	Darii
	EIO	Ferio
	EAO*	Celaront
	AAI*	Barbari

Third figure

M, P	AAI*	Darapti
$\underline{M, S}$	EAO*	Felapton
S, P	IAI	Disamis
	AII	Datisi
	*OAO	Bocardo
	EIO	Feriso

Second figure

P, M	EAE	Cesare
$\underline{S, M}$	AEE	Camestres
S, P	EIO	Festino
	*AOO	Baroco
	AEO	Camestrop
	EAO*	Cesaro

Fourth figure

P, M	EIO	Ferison
$\underline{M, S}$	EAO*	Fesapo
S, P	IAI	Diamaris
	AAI*	Bramantip (Bramalip)
	AEE	Camenes
	AEO*	Camelop

(Moods suffixed with * all depend for their validity in the figure cited on the assumption that the extensions of terms are nonempty. Those prefixed with * are all interdeducible by the *Reductio ad Impossibile* rule, as explained in the next section on proof theory.)

THEOREM. Barbara is valid.

Proof analysis. A claim of validity is a disguised universally quantified formula about all possible worlds. Thus, a proof of validity generally starts by assuming an arbitrary possible world R and showing that if the premises are true in that world, then the conclusion is true in that world. To show this conditional, one assumes the antecedent clause that R assigns T to the premises and then deduces the consequent clause that R assigns T to the conclusion. The deduction will generally depend not only on the fact that R assigns T to the various premises, but also on the details of the semantic rules in the definition of $[R]$. The fact that these rules apply to R is not a feature peculiar to R but a condition on all members of $[R]$. If nothing peculiar to R is exploited then the universal generalization follows to the effect that all worlds are like R and that the argument is valid.

[10] These names have a long history, and hidden in them are codes. The vowels record the syllogism's mood, and the consonants correspond to certain logical manipulations (some of which we shall see in the discussion of proof theory) used to 'derive' the syllogism from Barbara and Celarent. From the end of the Middle Ages until the mid-nineteenth century, logic of this sort was about all the logic that was remembered. It employed, moreover, a vast body of technical terms and mnemonic devices that are now largely arcane. For a good text in this sort of Aristotelian logic see H. W. B. Joseph, *An Introduction to Logic* (1916).

Proof. For an arbitrary R, assume $R(MAP) = \text{T}$ and $R(SAM) = \text{T}$. Then by the definition of R, $R(M) \subseteq R(P)$ and $R(S) \subseteq R(M)$. Hence by the transitivity of $\subseteq$ in set theory, $R(S) \subseteq R(P)$ and since $R \in [R]$, $R(SAP) = \text{T}$. Since R is arbitrary we can generalize to the conclusion that whenever the premises are T so is the conclusion, and the syllogism is valid. QED.

Since there are 81 moods and 4 figures there are 324 syllogisms. It is easy but tedious to consider each of these and show that all the valid syllogisms are contained on the list above and that no syllogism on the list is invalid. It will suffice for our purposes to do a small sample.

□ EXERCISES

1. Prove Cesare is valid.
2. Prove Bramantip is valid. Would it still be valid if terms could refer to the empty set? Explain your answer.
3. Prove that the syllogism of mood III in the first figure is invalid. (Note that 'I' here refers to sentence type.)

Aristotle introduces some further important semantic ideas to expain in greater detail the logical relations between sentences. Two sentences are said to be contrary if they cannot both be true together, to be subcontrary if they cannot both be false, and to be contradictory if the truth of one implies the falsity of the other and vice versa.

DEFINITION: P and Q are *contraries* iff for any R in $[R]$, it is not the case that both $R(P) = \text{T}$ and $R(Q) = \text{T}$.

P and Q are *subcontraries* iff for any R in $[R]$, it is not the case that both $R(P) = \text{F}$ and $R(Q) = \text{F}$.

P and Q are *contradictories* iff for any R in $[R]$, if $R(P) = \text{T}$ then $R(Q) = \text{F}$, and if $R(Q) = \text{T}$ then $R(P) = \text{F}$.

We will also say for brevity that P *implies* Q iff the argument from P to Q is valid. Then in terms of these four logical notions it is possible to state the logical relations between the four types of statement A, E, I, and O. They are traditionally displayed in the so-called Square of Opposition (Fig. 4.2). S and P stand for arbitrary common nouns.

THEOREM. SAP and SEP are contraries.

Proof. Assume for a *reductio* proof that they are not contraries, i.e., that there is an R in $[R]$ such that $R(SAP) = \text{T}$ and $R(SEP) = \text{T}$. Then since $R \in [R]$, $R(S) \subseteq R(P)$ and $R(S) - R(P) = \varnothing$. But then by set theory

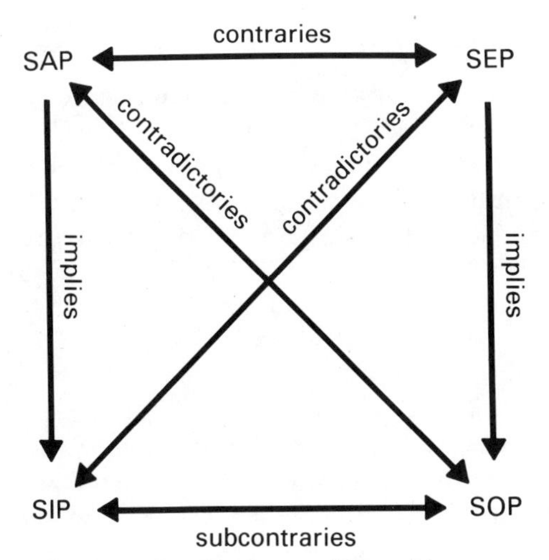

Fig. 4.2. The Square of Opposition.

$R(S) = \varnothing$, which contradicts the fact from the membership of R in $[R]$ that $R(S) \neq \varnothing$. Since we have a contradiction, the assumption is false. QED.

THEOREM. SAP implies SIP.

Proof. For an arbitrary R assume $R \in [R]$ and $R(SAP) = \text{T}$. Then $R(S) \subseteq R(P)$. Since $R(S) \neq \varnothing$, we know by set theory that $R(S) \cap R(P) \neq \varnothing$, and hence, since $R \in [R]$, that $R(SIP) = \text{T}$. Since for an arbitrary R, when SAP is T so is SIP, we conclude that the argument from the first to the second is valid. QED.

THEOREM. SAP and SOP are contradictories.

Proof. Since $\sim(P \leftrightarrow Q)$ is logically equivalent to $P \leftrightarrow \sim Q$, it will suffice to show that for any R, $R(SAP) = \text{T}$ iff $R(SOP) = \text{F}$. Now, $R(SAP) = \text{T}$ iff $R(S) \subseteq R(P)$, since $R \in [R]$. Moreover, $R(S) \subseteq R(P)$ iff $R(S) - R(P) = \varnothing$, by set theory. Also, $R(S) - R(P) = \varnothing$ iff $R(SOP) = \text{F}$, since $R \in [R]$. Hence by transitivity of 'iff', $R(SAP) = \text{T}$ iff $R(SOP) = \text{F}$. QED.

☐ **EXERCISE**

Prove the following:

a. SIP and SOP are subcontraries.
b. SEP implies SOP.
c. SEP and SIP are contradictories.
d. SEP would fail to imply SOP if $R(S)$ could be $\varnothing$.

4.2.2 The Syllogistic: Proof Theory

We have so far defined the syntax and semantics of the theory of the syllogism. It is also possible to develop what is called a proof theory, a characterization in totally syntactic terms of the valid syllogisms. Such syntactic characterizations have come to take a standard form, and in this section we shall introduce its basic ideas by reference to the relatively simple case of a proof theory for the syllogistic.[11] Technically, the proof theory is not difficult nor very interesting, but it will serve to illustrate the basic idea of a proof without the distracting details found in the more complex formal languages we shall study later.

Let us consider the set of valid syllogistic arguments, and recall the notation in terms of the so-called double turnstile symbol '$\vDash$' for a valid syllogism: $P, Q \vDash R$ means that in any world in which P and Q are T so is R. Thus, we may think of the relation $\vDash$ for syllogisms as a set of triples consisting of sentences. Then, $P, Q \vDash R$ is another way of writing $\langle P, Q, R \rangle \in \vDash$. So far we have merely established a notation for discussing the relation $\vDash$ holding among the triples of a valid syllogism. In terms of this notation we can now make some interesting conceptual points. The first is that the relation $\vDash$ is defined in semantic terms. In particular it is defined in terms of the notion of truth relative to a possible world. In general semantic ideas are more problematic than ones defined solely in syntactic terms. Syntactic ideas must all be defined only by reference to marks on a page and the arrangements of these marks. Basic facts about symbols and their arrangements are often easy to establish merely by a finite inspection. Thus it is easy to tell by a finite inspection that $(P \vee \sim Q)$ meets the conditions for membership in the set of sentences of propositional logic, but that $(P \sim \wedge Q)$ does not. What is interesting about the set $\vDash$ of valid arguments is that often it is possible to state necessary and sufficient conditions for membership in $\vDash$ by using only syntactic ideas. Since in general the set $\vDash$ of valid arguments for a language is infinite, the usual form of the syntactic definition is inductive. We first specify some 'basic' arguments as falling in the set, and then explain how to construct new members of the set from old. Moreover, in specifying both

[11] The theory of proof for the syllogistic is inspired by remarks of Aristotle that all the valid syllogisms can be transformed from Barbara and Celarent. For a discussion of exactly what Aristotle might have meant in his 'derivations' for the valid syllogisms see Günter Patzig (1968). The modern version we present here is similar to the approach developed first by Jan Łukasiewicz, *Aristotle's Syllogistic* (1943). We differ from Łukasiewicz, however, not only in points of detail but also in using natural deduction rules instead of an axiom system. Technically, characterizing the valid syllogisms by either axioms or natural deduction rules is uninteresting because they could all be merely listed quite briefly. The point here is rather to introduce, for a simple language, proof theoretic ideas we shall use later. This section is not presupposed by anything later in the book.

the basic elements and the methods of construction we are constrained by the requirement that our definitions must use only syntactic ideas: they must talk only about symbols and their arrangements.

The usual order of development of such a theory is first to define in the syntax the set of sentences for the language. Second, a semantic theory for the language is defined including a definition of the set of possible worlds for the language. In terms of these, a definition of the relation $\vDash$ of valid argument in the language is given. It is only after a specification of the syntax and semantics that a 'proof theory' makes sense, and it proceeds by stating an inductive syntactic definition of a relation that is intended to coincide exactly with $\vDash$. Because at this stage it still remains an open question whether this proposed syntactic definition succeeds in defining exactly the same set as $\vDash$, the new syntactic relation is usually given another name, often the single turnstile $\vdash$. Some contrived way of reading $\vdash$ must also be introduced. It should be emphasized that $\vdash$ is a relation on sentences, just as $\vDash$. In the case of the syllogistic we shall read the assertion $\langle P, Q, R\rangle \in \vdash$ as saying 'the argument from P and Q to R is syntactically acceptable'. Analogously with $\vDash$, we shall write $P, Q \vdash R$ as a more convenient way of writing $\langle P, Q, R\rangle \in \vdash$.

The syntax and semantics have in fact been defined in the last section, including the definition of the semantic relation $\vDash$. We are ready then for the first stage of proof theory, which is to give an inductive definition of a relation $\vdash$ using ideas from syntax. This relation is intended to coincide exactly with $\vDash$. The final stage of the theory will be to prove this coincidence, i.e., to demonstrate that $\vDash$ is identical to $\vdash$. It is first proved that $\vdash$ is a subset of $\vDash$, or that every syntactically acceptable argument is semantically valid. This part of the proof is often called the *soundness result* because it shows that the syntactic construction is sound in the sense of yielding only valid arguments. It is next proved that $\vDash$ is a subset of $\vdash$, or that every valid argument is contained in the syntactic construction. This part of the proof is often called the *completeness result* because it shows that no valid argument is left out of the syntactically defined construction.

In the case of the syllogistic, specifying the set of valid arguments, though tedious, is not hard in principle. We just test all the possible syllogisms by reference to the definition of possible world, and it is a simple matter to establish which are valid and which not. Thus there is no compelling need to find an alternative syntactic definition for this set. Also, since the number of valid syllogisms is finite and really quite small, there is no special need to give a constructive or inductive definition for the set. Other languages are not so simple, and it will be useful to illustrate in the context of this simple syntax and semantics the general method of defining an alternative syntactic inductive definition for a relation $\vdash$ that is probably identical to the semantic relation $\vDash$.

The method we shall use is also of some historical interest because it is based on remarks of Aristotle, to the effect that all the valid syllogisms can be shown to follow in a prescribed way from the two syllogisms Barbara and Celarent. Thus we shall use these two syllogisms, or more accurately, the set of all syllogisms of the form of Barbara and Celarent, as basic elements in our construction of the relation $\vdash$. In addition to Barbara and Celarent, Aristotle also assumed as basic elements some arguments permitted from the Square of Opposition. We shall also need the argument from a sentence to its double negation and vice versa.

DEFINITION: The set of *basic acceptable syntactic arguments* or, what we shall call more briefly the *basic deductions*, is defined as any pair of sentences $\langle P, Q\rangle$ or triple of sentences $\langle P, Q, R\rangle$ meeting one of the following forms (let P be an arbitrary sentence, and X, Y, and Z arbitrary common nouns):

(1)	Barbara		$\langle YAZ, XAY, XAZ\rangle$
(2)	Celarent		$\langle YEZ, XAY, XEZ\rangle$
(3)	Conversions,	CV1	$\langle XEY, YEX\rangle$
		CV2	$\langle XIY, YIX\rangle$
(4)	Implications,	I1	$\langle XAY, XIY\rangle$
		I2	$\langle XEY, XOY\rangle$
(5)	Contradictions,	CD1	$\langle XAY, \sim XOY\rangle$
			$\langle \sim XOY, XAY\rangle$
		CD2	$\langle XOY, \sim XAY\rangle$
			$\langle \sim XAY, XOY\rangle$
		CD3	$\langle XEY, \sim XIY\rangle$
			$\langle \sim XIY, XEY\rangle$
		CD4	$\langle XIY, \sim XEY\rangle$
			$\langle \sim XEY, XIY\rangle$
(6)	Double negation,	DN	$\langle P, \sim\sim P\rangle$
			$\langle \sim\sim P, P\rangle$

In addition to these basic arguments, we also specify some 'rules' or construction functions which explain how to construct new elements in $\vdash$ from ones already in $\vdash$. The first of these is the rule that Aristotle cites as necessary for the construction of the acceptable syllogisms from Barbara and Celarent. This is the rule called *Reductio ad Impossibile*, which is one of the few principles from propositional logic that Aristotle made explicit use of : if it is acceptable to argue from P and $\sim R$ to $\sim Q$, then it is acceptable to argue from P and Q to R. If the triple $\langle P, \sim R, \sim Q\rangle$ is in $\vdash$, then the triple $\langle P, Q, R\rangle$ is also in $\vdash$. In our new notation the rule reads, if $P, \sim R \vdash \sim Q$, then $P, Q \vdash R$. The traditional way to write this is as follows:

Reductio ad Impossibile (RAI)

$$\frac{P, \sim R \vdash \sim Q}{P, Q \vdash R}$$

We can define the set theoretic function that takes as inputs one such triple and yields as output the corresponding triple:

$h_{\mathrm{RAI}} = \{\langle x, y\rangle \mid \text{for some } P, Q, \text{ and } R, x = \langle P, \sim \mathrm{R}, \sim \mathrm{Q}\rangle \text{ and } y = \langle P, Q, R\rangle\}$.

Since our proofs will actually be more rigorous in the modern sense than Aristotle's we shall appeal to two necessary rules which he did not use explicitly. The first, called Cut, is really a principle of transitivity. If a second proposition is provable from a first, and a third from the second, then the third is provable from the first; the second proposition can in this sense be 'cut' out or bypassed. From the point of view of constructing the set $\vdash$, what the rule means is that if two elements are already in $\vdash$ and have the form such that the conclusion of one is a premise of the other, then we add to $\vdash$ a new element that cuts out the redundant sentence. Due to our notation, we shall actually state three versions of this rule, but they all state essentially the same idea. In the notation below, if elements of the form above the line are already in $\vdash$, we add to $\vdash$ the element having the form below the line:

Cut

$$\frac{P \vdash Q,\ Q \vdash R}{P \vdash R} \qquad \frac{P \vdash Q,\ Q,R \vdash S}{P,R \vdash S} \qquad \frac{P,Q \vdash R,\ R \vdash S}{P,Q \vdash S}$$

The corresponding construction function may be formally defined as follows:

$h_{\mathrm{Cut}} = \{\langle x, y, z\rangle \mid \text{for some } P, Q, \text{ and } R \text{ either}$

(1) $x = \langle P, Q\rangle$, $y = \langle Q, R\rangle$, and $z = \langle P, R\rangle$; or

(2) $x = \langle P, Q\rangle$, $y = \langle Q, R, S\rangle$, and $z = \langle P, R, S\rangle$; or

(3) $x = \langle P, Q, R\rangle$, $y = \langle R, S\rangle$, and $z = \langle P, Q, S\rangle\}$.

In addition to *Reductio ad Impossibile* and Cut we will also appeal to an obvious reordering rule which says that the order of assumptions does not matter.

Reordering (RO)

$$\frac{P,Q \vdash R}{Q,P \vdash R}$$

$h_{\mathrm{RO}} = \{\langle x, y\rangle \mid \text{for some } P, Q, \text{ and } R, x = \langle P, Q, R\rangle \text{ and } y = \langle Q, P, R\rangle\}$

We may now inductively define the relation $\vdash$ containing the syntactically acceptable arguments by constructing it from the basic deductions using the rules for *Reductio ad Impossibile*, Cut, and Reordering.

DEFINITION: The relation $\vdash$ (of *syntactically acceptable arguments*) is such that

(1) *Basis clause.* Any basic deduction is in $\vdash$. That is, $\vdash$ contains any triple that conforms to one of the following below. Let P be a sentence in Sen, and let X, Y, and Z be common nouns in CN:

Barbara		$YAZ, XAY \vdash XAZ$
Celarent		$YEZ, XAY \vdash XEZ$
Conversions,	CV1	$XEY \vdash YEX$
	CV2	$XIY \vdash YIX$
Implications,	I1	$XAY \vdash XIY$
	I2	$XEY \vdash XOY$
Contradictions,	CD1	$XAY \vdash \sim XOY$
		$\sim XOY \vdash XAY$
	CD2	$XOY \vdash \sim XAY$
		$\sim XAY \vdash XOY$
	CD3	$XEY \vdash \sim XIY$
		$\sim XIY \vdash XEY$
	CD4	$XIY \vdash \sim XEY$
		$\sim XEY \vdash XIY$
Double negation,	DN	$P \vdash \sim\sim P$
		$\sim\sim P \vdash P$

(2) *Inductive clause.* If x and y are in $\vdash$, then $h_{\mathrm{RAI}}(x)$, $h_{\mathrm{Cut}}(x, y)$, and $h_{\mathrm{RO}}(x)$ are in $\vdash$.

(3) Nothing else is in $\vdash$.

In practice we shall exhibit step by step how a particular element of $\vdash$ is constructed by a device known as a *proof tree.* A tree may be thought of as a graph of connected points (called *nodes*) such that each point in the tree either is the bottom point of the tree (called the *root*) or is right above another lower point of the tree to which it is connected. A series of points starting with the root and continuing upward along a path of connected points is called a *branch.* In the trees we shall be using, each branch eventually terminates at a highest point (sometimes called a *leaf*). The way we use such trees to exhibit the construction of an acceptable syntactic argument A is by pinning to the nodes of a tree the various steps in the construction of the argument. First to each leaf of the tree we assign the basic deductions used to construct A. Then beneath these nodes we assign various elements of $\vdash$ that may be produced directly by the construction rules from the elements on the nodes above. We proceed down the tree in this fashion until we ultimately arrive at inputs that yield A as an output, and we let the node assigned to A be the root of the tree. If an argument $\langle P, Q, R \rangle$ occurs at the root of some proof tree, then we have shown that it is in $\vdash$, or in other words that $P, Q \vdash R$. Likewise if the argument $\langle P, Q \rangle$ is the root of some proof tree, it too is in $\vdash$ and $P \vdash Q$. We say that an argument that is the root of some proof tree is *provable*.

There are a number of conventions customarily used in drawing such trees. If we wish to indicate that an argument $\langle P, Q, R \rangle$ occupies a particular node, we write $P, Q \vdash R$ at that node. Likewise to indicate that the argument $\langle P, Q \rangle$ occupies a node we write $P \vdash Q$ at that node. Instead of literally drawing lines connecting nodes above with those below, it is customary in proof theory to draw a horizontal line with the higher nodes along the top of the horizontal line and with the node they branch from centered beneath the line. To the left of the line we write the abbreviation of the construction rule used to generate the argument assigned to the node written below the line from those arguments assigned to the nodes above the line. The left-to-right order of the nodes above the line indicates the proper order in which the arguments above the line are fed into the construction rule in order to yield the argument assigned to the node below the line. Last, next to the basic deductions occupying the leaves of the tree we write in parentheses what sort of basic deduction it is. Marking the names of the basic deductions and construction rules used is called *annotating* the tree. Some examples will help. We let S, M, and P represent arbitrary common nouns.

THEOREM. Celaront is provable: $MEP, SAM \vdash SOP$.

Proof.

$$\frac{MEP, SAM \vdash SEP \text{ (Celarent)} \qquad SEP \vdash SOP \text{ (I2)}}{MEP, SAM \vdash SOP \text{ (Celaront)}} \text{ (Cut)}$$

This tree has just three points, a root and two leaves. Each leaf is occupied by a basic deduction, and the single descent marked by the horizontal line is justified by the rule Cut. Here are two trees with more luxuriant growth.

THEOREM. Darii is provable.

Proof.

$$\dfrac{\dfrac{SEM \vdash {\sim}SIM \atop \text{(CD3)} \qquad \dfrac{MES \vdash SEM \atop \text{(CV1)} \qquad \dfrac{PES,MAP \vdash MES \atop \text{(Celarent)} \qquad \dfrac{{\sim}SIP \vdash SEP \atop \text{(CD3)} \qquad SEP \vdash PES \atop \text{(CV1)}}{{\sim}SIP \vdash PES}\,\text{(Cut)}}{{\sim}SIP,MAP \vdash MES}\,\text{(Cut)}}{{\sim}SIP,MAP \vdash SEM}\,\text{(Cut)}}{\dfrac{{\sim}SIP,MAP \vdash {\sim}SIM}{MAP,{\sim}SIP \vdash {\sim}SIM}\,\text{(RO)}}\,\text{(Cut)}}{MAP,SIM \vdash SIP \text{ (Darii)}}\,\text{(RAI)}$$

THEOREM. Ferio is provable.

Proof.

$$\dfrac{\dfrac{SEM \vdash {\sim}SIM \text{ (CD3)} \qquad \dfrac{\dfrac{\dfrac{MEP \vdash PEM \atop \text{(CV1)} \qquad PEM,SAP \vdash SEM \atop \text{(Celarent)}}{MEP,SAP \vdash SEM}\,\text{(Cut)}}{SAP,MEP \vdash SEM}\,\text{(RO)} \qquad {\sim}SOP \vdash SAP \atop \text{(CD1)}}{{\sim}SOP,MEP \vdash SEM}\,\text{(Cut)}}{\dfrac{{\sim}SOP,MEP \vdash {\sim}SIM}{MEP,{\sim}SOP \vdash {\sim}SIM}\,\text{(RO)}}\,\text{(Cut)}}{MEP,SIM \vdash SOP \text{ (Ferio)}}\,\text{(RAI)}$$

It is frequently very useful in constructing trees to use some argument that we already know is provable. In that case we need only write down the argument (with a note as annotation that it is previously proven) on the leaf of the new tree, because in principle we could 'graft' the previously constructed tree of the leaf argument onto the new tree at that place. Thus in practice leaves will be occupied by both basic deductions and previously proven arguments.

□ EXERCISES

1. Produce annotated proof trees showing that all the other valid syllogisms are provable.
2. The deductions Barbara, Baroco, and Bocardo may each be proven from one another (i.e., by trees taking each other as leaves) by use of *Reductio ad Impossibile*, among other rules. Prove Baroco from Barbara, and Bocardo from Baroco.

What is philosophically interesting about such proof trees is that one can tell by finite inspection whether a structure is in fact a proof tree of a given argument. First, one checks the leaves to see whether they are all occupied by a basic or previously proven argument. Then one checks the base to see whether it is occupied by the argument to be proved. Last one checks each descent to see whether it conforms to one of the three sorts of construction rules. Each such check consists of comparing two rather short lists to see whether items in the proof match up correctly with the required forms. There is very, very little scope for error. Indeed, one might even say that it is possible to know with certainty whether a given arrangement of symbols is a proof tree for a given argument. Examples of certain knowledge are very rare indeed, and one of the few places they are found, or at least closely approximated, is in proof theory. It is characteristic of proof theory that it defines sets in such a way that we can know with virtual certainty whether a syntactic structure is a proof tree for that argument.

Though such sets are genuinely interesting because they allow us to know with certainty whether something is a construction tree for them, they may be in every other way totally uninteresting. Consider the set C defined as follows. Let A be the first letter of the alphabet.

(1) $A \in C$;
(2) if $x \in C$, then $A^\frown x \in C$;
(3) nothing else is in C.

Thus C is the set of all finite strings of A's, and we can tell by finite inspection whether a string of symbols would count as an element of C. But strings of A's are extremely boring. What is interesting about proof theory is that the sets it defines syntactically coincide with other sets that we have previous reason to be interested in. In particular, proof theory attempts to give syntactic definitions to important sets and relations previously defined in semantics.

Actually, as we noted before, proof theoretic notions for the syllogistic are not very crucial. Since there are only 24 valid syllogisms and 324 syllogisms all together, there is an easy finite procedure for seeing whether any syllogism is valid. We just see whether it is in the list of 24. In richer languages there are literally an infinite number of both arguments and valid arguments. For these languages the notion of a syntactically provable set is very useful. We can define a notion of proof such that we can know in a finite number of steps whether a purported proof tree really is one. For such a language we would then be in a position to accept an argument if we somehow could create a proof tree for it. For some languages we can go one step further and actually provide a finite test procedure for showing whether a proof construction exists. For these languages we need not depend on the vicissitudes of human creativity in order to come up with a proof tree. We can actually manufacture one mechanically by a finite process. But these syntactic tools are interesting only if the set of provable arguments is semantically interesting, and showing so is a major goal of the theory. The coincidence of syntactic and semantic sets is reported in what are called the soundness and completeness theorems. We will limit ourselves here to showing that the set of valid syllogisms coincides with the set of provable syllogisms.

THEOREM. If $\langle P, Q, R\rangle$ is a syllogism, then $P, Q \vDash R$ iff $P, Q \vdash R$.

Proof analysis. In the text and in the exercises we have already shown the completeness theorem, that every valid syllogism is provable. We did so by actually constructing proofs for them. The converse, known as the soundness theorem, requires that we show that every provable syllogism is valid. Thus we must show that every element of the inductively defined set has the property of being valid. Accordingly, we use an inductive proof. We show in the basis step that all the basic elements of $\vdash$, namely the basic deductions, are valid. In the inductive step we show that if the arguments in $\vdash$ which are then taken as inputs for the construction rules are valid, then so are those yielded as outputs. If all the basic deductions are valid and if the rules take valid arguments to valid arguments, then anything provable must be valid.

Proof of the Basis Step. It is a straightforward matter to check that the conversion arguments of the form CV1 and CV2 are valid. Moreover, we have already established in previous exercises the validity of Barbara, Celarent, and the various arguments from the Square of Opposition. We have therefore shown that all the basic elements of $\vdash$ are valid.

It remains then to show the inductive step. In the inductive step we must show that if we feed valid arguments into the various construction rules for $\vdash$ we get out valid arguments. We break the task down into three lemmas. Lemma (1) says in effect that if the inputs of the construction rule h_{RAI} are valid, then so is the output. Lemma (2) ensures that if the inputs of h_{Cut} are valid, then so is its output. Lemma (3) does the same for the rule h_{RO}.

LEMMAS. (1) If $P, \sim R \vDash \sim Q$, then $P, Q \vDash R$.

(2) (a) If $P \vDash Q$ and $Q \vDash R$, then $P \vDash R$.

(b) If $P \vDash Q$ and $Q, R \vDash S$, then $P, R \vDash S$.

(c) If $P, Q \vDash R$ and $R \vDash S$, then $P, Q \vDash S$.

(3) If $P, Q \vDash R$, then $Q, P \vDash R$.

Proof of Lemma (1). We must show that if the first argument is valid so is the second. For CP, assume that the first is valid; i.e., for all R in $[R]$, if $R(P) = R(\sim R) = \mathrm{T}$, then $R(\sim Q) = \mathrm{T}$. Then by propositional logic we know that if $R(P) = \mathrm{T}$ and $R(\sim Q) \neq \mathrm{T}$, then $R(\sim R) \neq \mathrm{T}$. But since $R \in [R]$, $R(\sim Q) \neq \mathrm{T}$ iff $R(Q) = \mathrm{T}$, and $R(\sim R) \neq \mathrm{T}$, iff $R(R) = \mathrm{T}$. Then by substitutivity of equivalents, we know for an arbitrary $R \in [R]$ that if $R(P) = \mathrm{T}$ and $R(Q) = \mathrm{T}$, then $R(R) = \mathrm{T}$, i.e., that $P, Q \vDash R$. QED.

Proof of the other lemmas is similar so that we may conclude that we have in fact established the completeness theorem.

We have in the syllogistic an example of a total metatheory: a fully developed and rigorously defined syntax, semantics, and proof theory. It is, however, very rudimentary. Its syntax is limited and there are many arguments from ordinary language that, though valid, cannot be forced into the form of syllogisms. Nevertheless, the syllogistic has filled the purpose of providing a fairly simple example of the new metatheoretic concepts. As we turn to more complex languages, these ideas will no longer be new, and we can focus instead on novel features of syntax and semantic interpretation.

One serious limitation of the syllogistic as well as of the other theories of the simple sentence we have studied is that none of them allow for simple relational assertions like ‘Socrates loves Plato’.

☐ **EXERCISE**

Prove Lemma (2b).

4.3 RELATIONS

4.3.1 Expressing Relations in Subject-Predicate Sentences

It is commonplace in traditional grammar to distinguish between transitive and intransitive verbs, between those that take an object and those that do not. The sort of object that a transitive verb can take might be any sort of noun phrase including proper and common nouns. We have already seen that, logically speaking, predicates consisting of intransitive verbs, adjectives, or common nouns all behave very much the same. These three are all general and, Ockham's theory apart, are interpreted semantically as standing for universals. Theories differ mostly on what they take universals to be, for example, on whether they are properties or sets. They all agree that these three types of predicate, which one might think on syntactic grounds were rather different, are actually used to say essentially the same sort of thing. Here, in fact, is an example of a syntactic distinction that seems to make little difference semantically. For the purposes of communication we might, so the traditional view goes, dispense entirely with any two of the three types of general predicates and make do with the remaining third. But transitive verbs with proper nouns as objects are quite a different matter.

Aristotelian logic and most logical theories up to the nineteenth century tried to construe such predicates as really fitting the pattern of the other sorts of general predication. One famous example of this conflation is suggested by an argument of Plato's in the *Theætetus* (155b ff.). At issue is knowledge of the sensible world. Socrates is at one point taller than Theætetus when Theætetus is a boy. At another point, however, when Theætetus is a man, Socrates is not taller than Theætetus. If the proper noun following 'taller than' is really part of general predicate we can, without violence to the preceding proposition, conclude that Socrates both is and is not tall. But since this conclusion is a contradiction, and no contradiction can be true, our premises must be false. Indeed, no such changeable Socrates could exist because any similar change would produce contradiction. Generally throughout his philosophy Plato was unable to explain change and was unhappy with the proposition that changeable things exist. He would have it that only immutable things exist, and in his middle years made this thesis part of his famous Theory of Forms.

There is a good deal wrong with treating a relational sentence as the application of a general predicate to a singular subject. It is in general misleading to chop off the proper noun from relational expressions like 'is taller than'. If we grant that Plato was wrong to drop the object 'Theætetus', there are at least two ways to resolve the apparent contradiction. One way is to say that in speaking of two different times one is really speaking of two different possible worlds and that there is nothing at all contradictory about saying that the same sentence is true in one world but false in another. Another analysis is more compatible with Plato's reading and permits both sentences to be true at the same world. We do sometimes speak tenselessly about the actual world, viewing all times as irrelevant to what we are saying. But if we adopt this atemporal stance toward Socrates and Theætetus, we should not use the same term 'Theætetus' to refer to different things in different sentences. In its first use it stands for a boy, and in the second use for a grown man. Using the same term with different referents in the same argument amounts to *equivocation*, the fallacy of changing the meanings of terms in the middle of an argument. In this analysis, then, what is wrong with Plato's argument is that in speaking of the world atemporally, he incorrectly dropped the proper noun 'Theætetus' from the predicate term, leaving the truncated predicates 'is short' and 'is not short' which are indeed contradictory. If he had not dropped 'Theætetus' and further had used a separate term for each meaning, say Theætetus_1 and Theætetus_2, then all he would have established are the quite noncontradictory propositions: 'Socrates is taller than Theætetus_1' and 'Socrates is not taller than Theætetus_2'.

Allowing proper names to occur as part of the predicate requires some sort of account in semantics about how the referent of a proper name within the predicate helps determine the truth-value of the whole sentence. It is difficult to treat these proper names occurring at the end of the sentence, where the traditional predicate occurs, as predicates themselves. Proper names have been traditionally viewed as referring to singular entities like substances, whereas traditional predicates such as intransitive verbs, adjectives, and common nouns are usually understood to be general and to stand for universals. Thus the usual account of general predication could not be used to explain proper nouns as predicates, and a more elaborate theory would have to be invented. In practice theoreticians sidestepped the problem by arguing that relational predications were only superficially different from ordinary predications. Whatever can be truly said, they believed, could be said in terms of general predication alone.

There were various ways in which this thesis was defended. Perhaps the most common was by means of a metaphysical claim that relations are in a sense unreal. Whatever relational truths hold for individuals result from more primary truths about what properties the various individuals have. All that the world consists of are particulars and their properties. Once it is fixed what properties inhere in which individuals then certain relational facts will follow. If I am bright red and you are dull gray, then the relational fact that I am brighter than you will follow, but there is no special brighter-than entity in the world additional to you, me, and our respective properties of redness and grayness. This view is often summarized by saying that all relational predications are accidental. Such relations in later times came to be called *external*, and the belief that all such relational truths may be replaced by more basic talk in terms of more traditional general predication is called the theory of external relations.

Some philosophers could not convince themselves that all relations could be eliminated in this way. One particularly problematic group of relations concerned those that define the various persons of the Blessed Trinity. Surely these, it was thought, were essential. Relations that enter into essences or definitions were called *internal*, and various obscure means of reformulating even these in terms of general predication were proposed. Bertrand Russell attributed many of the more bizarre metaphysical theories found in the history of philosophy to wrong-headed attempts to reduce relational truths to general predications.[12] He claimed that many of the counterintuitive and

[12] For a general discussion of the concept of relation in the history of philosophy see Julius Weinberg, *Abstraction, Relation, Induction* (1965). Russell's first extended argument that relations have confused past philosophers is found in his discussion of Leibniz. See Bertrand Russell, *A Critical Exposition of the Philosophy of Leibniz* (1900). Russell's main arguments that relations cannot be reduced to simple predication, some of which we use here, are developed in *Principles of Mathematics* (1903). See especially Section 48, and Chapter XXVI.

absurd claims of Leibniz and idealists like Hegel and Bradley can be traced to errors much like Plato's. Indeed, Russell was one of the leaders of the rejection by philosophers in Britain and America of nineteenth-century German idealism, and he regarded as among his most important arguments those in which he demonstrated that relational statements cannot in principle be replaced by general predication. His argument is to the effect that if it were true that all relational statements are disguised general predications, then this would have consequences that contradict our intuitions about the logical inferences involving relations.

Let us represent the relational expression that a bears the relation R to b by the shorthand aRb. Let a, b, and c stand for arbitrary subjects and let F, G, and H be typical predicates standing for properties. We shall consider various attempts to translate aRb into subject–predicate sentences.

THEOREM. If aRb means Fa, for some general predicate F, then some sentences which should follow from aRb according to logical intuitions do not.

Proof. Intuitively both the following arguments are valid:

$$\frac{aRb}{\text{For some } x,\ aRx} \qquad \frac{\begin{array}{c} aRb \\ b = c \end{array}}{aRc}$$

Let us assume that we may translate aRb as Fa for some suitable predicate F. The idea is that the information contained in both the R and the b is contained in the F. To translate the first of these arguments, we must render 'For some x, aRx' in the terms of some subject–predicate sentence or sentences. Unless we are to equivocate like Plato, we should translate aRx by something other than Fa, which we have already agreed to use as the translation of aRb. Thus let us use another predicate, call it G, to contain the information from the R and the x, and translate aRx by Ga. But then the argument has the following form, which is invalid.

$$\frac{Fa}{\text{For some } x,\ Ga}$$

The premise does not logically imply the conclusion. Likewise in the second argument, we should translate aRc by something other than Fa, which is already used for aRb. Let aRc be Ha. Then the argument becomes the following, which also is invalid.

$$\frac{\begin{array}{c} Fa \\ a = c \end{array}}{Ha}$$

Again the premises have no bearing on the conclusion. Given these premises we cannot tell from the syntax of the premises alone that the conclusion is true. Hence the translation does not validate two intuitively valid arguments. QED.

A somewhat more subtle attempt to translate relations into simple predication is to understand the same predicate as asserted of both the subject and the object. Let aRb be translated by $Fa \wedge Fb$, for some general predicate F.

DEFINITION: R is *symmetric* iff for any x and y, xRy iff yRx.

THEOREM. If for every relation R, there is some general predicate F such that aRb means $Fa \wedge Fb$, then every relation is symmetric.

Proof. Suppose aRb, then by translation there is some F such that $Fa \wedge Fb$. By commutativity of $\wedge$, $Fb \wedge Fa$. Then by translation of R, bRa. Since a and b are arbitrary (we have assumed nothing special about them), we generalize: for all x and y, if xRy, then yRx. That is, R is symmetric. QED.

But it is fairly easy to find examples of relations that are not symmetric. I may admire you, but you may not return the compliment, and surely if I am taller or richer than you, you cannot be taller or richer than I.

Perhaps what is wrong with our translation into simple predication is that we have used the same general predicate twice. Perhaps a relation between a and b should be traced to different properties in each. Then given the appropriate predicates F and G, whichever these might be, aRb would translate $Fa \wedge Gb$. It is then a fairly straightforward matter to show that every relation is transitive, contrary to intuition.

DEFINITION: R is *transitive* iff for any x, y, and z, if xRy and yRz, then xRz.

THEOREM. If for every relation R, there are some universal predicates F and G such that aRb means $Fa \wedge Gb$, then every relation is transitive, contrary to intuition.

□ **EXERCISES**

1. Find three different two-place relations that intuition says are not transitive.
2. Prove the preceding theorem.

4.3.2 Relations as an Ontological Category in Semantics

It was such considerations that led the founders of modern symbolic logic, like Frege and C. S. Peirce, to introduce into the notation of logic special predicates flanked by proper names as representatives of relations irreducible to other universals. The syntax and semantics of formal languages with atomic sentences made up of relational predicates are now such a standard part of modern logic that they are presupposed by most users of logic and are considered uncontroversial. Although, as we shall soon see, even this standard theory has been reformed in various ways to bring the symbolic language closer to the syntax of natural language, it is important to learn the standard form because it is a kind of *lingua franca* in the logical world.

In the syntax we stipulate two sets of basic lexical items. In the literature of logicians these sets are usually allowed to be infinite in extent, but linguists usually stipulate that these sets are finite because they are concerned about mankind's ability to manufacture the infinite varieties of language from a finite base. Nothing we shall say will depend on how big the sets are, and we shall use the logician's format because it is probably the more common. Accordingly, we stipulate an infinite set of proper names or constants, and then a set of predicates that will include as subsets an infinite number of predicates of each degree. A predicate of degree n, indicated by its superscript, is a predicate that will refer to an n-place relation. The various predicates of degree n are distinguished from one another by their subscripts.

DEFINITION: We stipulate a set of *proper names*: $\text{PN} = \{a, b, c, \ldots\}$. We also stipulate a set Pd of predicates that contains an infinite number of predicates that are one-place, two-place, etc.:

$$\text{Pd} = \{P_1^1, \ldots, P_n^1, \ldots; \ldots; P_1^m, \ldots, P_n^m, \ldots; \ldots\}.$$

We say that an m-place predicate P_i^m is *of degree m*, and use the notation P^m to stand for the set of all predicates of degree m, i.e., $P^m = \{P_1^m, \ldots, P_n^m, \ldots\}$.

Thus Pd as a whole is the union of the various sets P^i; i.e., $\text{Pd} = P^1 \cup \cdots \cup P^i \cup \cdots$. We shall understand predicates of degree 1 to be the traditional one-place general predicates that stand for properties or sets. The set of basic sentences is defined as the result of concatenating a string of n proper names to the right of an n-place predicate. First we define a formation function f_{BS} that attaches a string of n symbols to the right of another symbol. The set of sentences is then defined inductively from the set BS of basic sentences and the formation rule introduced earlier for propositional logic.

DEFINITION: A *syntax for propositional logic with relational atomic sentences* is defined as follows:

$$f_{\text{BS}} = \{\langle x, y_1, \ldots, y_n, z\rangle | z = x^\frown y_1{}^\frown \cdots {}^\frown y_n\}$$

$$\text{BS} = \{z | \text{for some } x \text{ in } P^n \text{ and some } y_1, \ldots, y_n \text{ in PN}, \\ z = f_{\text{BS}}(x, y_1, \ldots, y_n)\}$$

S is such that

(1) $\text{BS} \subseteq S$;

(2) if x and y are in S, then $f_{\sim}(x), f_{\wedge}(x, y), f_{\vee}(x, y), f_{\rightarrow}(x, y)$, and $f_{\leftrightarrow}(x, y)$ are in S;

(3) nothing else is in S.

Semantically all we need to do to interpret this syntax is to decide what sort of thing predicates of degree n stand for and then to define a semantic rule g_{BS} explaining how the referents of the parts of a basic sentence determine the referent of the sentence itself. Some philosophers like Aristotle and Russell happen to think that there is a distinct category of things in the world called relations that inhere in groups of things all at once. Such full-blooded realists might define g_{BS} as follows:

DEFINITION: A *realist's* semantic operation for interpreting atomic sentences is

$$g_{\text{BS}} = \{\langle x, y_1, \ldots, y_n, z\rangle |$$

(1) if $y_1, \ldots, y_n$ are all particulars that bear the relation x to one another in that order, then $z = \text{T}$;

(2) if not, $z = \text{F}\}$.

This definition presupposes some undefined ontological primitives, viz. the notions of particular, relation, and particulars-bearing-a-relation. An alternative account which has become standard is to understand relations set theoretically. Proper names stand for elements of the universal set $\mathbf{V}$ and predicates of degree n for sets of n-tuples, i.e., for elements of $\mathbf{V}^n$. The semantic rule then gives the value T to a pair consisting of an n-tuple and a relation if the n-tuple is a member of the relation, and gives it the value F otherwise.

DEFINITION: A *set theoretic* semantic operation for relational atomic sentences is

$$g'_{\text{BS}} = \{\langle x, y_1, \ldots, y_n, z\rangle |$$

(1) if $\langle y_1, \ldots, y_n\rangle \in x$, then $z = \text{T}$,

(2) if otherwise, $z = \text{F}\}$.

The resulting semantics is quite neat, especially when compared to the previous definition which appeals to ontological unknowns. The definition of possible world is then straightforward.

DEFINITION: The set $[R]$ of possible worlds is defined as

$[R] = \{R | R$ is a function on $\text{PN} \cup \text{Pd} \cup S$ such that

(1) for any x in CN, $R(x) \in \mathbf{V}$,

(2) for any x in P^n, $R(x) \subseteq \mathbf{V}^n$,

(3) for any x in S,
  (a) if some $f_{\mathrm{BS}}(x_1, \ldots, x_n, y) \in \mathrm{BS}$, then
  $R(f_{\mathrm{BS}}(x_1, \ldots, x_n, y)) = g_{\mathrm{BS}}(R(x_1), \ldots, R(x_n), R(y))$,
  (b) if some $f_{\sim}(x) \in S$, then $R(f_{\sim}(x)) = g_{\sim}(R(x))$,
  (c) if some $f_{\vee}(x, y) \in S$, then $R(f_{\vee}(x, y)) = g_{\vee}(R(x), R(y))$,
  (d) if some $f_{\wedge}(x, y) \in S$, then $R(f_{\wedge}(x, y)) = g_{\wedge}(R(x), R(y))$,
  (e) if some $f_{\rightarrow}(x, y) \in S$, then $R(f_{\rightarrow}(x, y)) = g_{\rightarrow}(R(x), R(y))$,
  (f) if some $f_{\leftrightarrow}(x, y) \in S$, then $R(f_{\leftrightarrow}(x, y)) = g_{\leftrightarrow}(R(x), R(y))\}$.

Logical truth and validity are as defined in previous languages.

DEFINITION: An argument $P_1, \ldots, P_n$ to Q is valid (briefly, $P_1, \ldots, P_n \vDash Q$) iff for any R in $[R]$, if $R(P_1) = \cdots = R(P_n) = \mathrm{T}$ then $R(Q) = \mathrm{T}$. The sentence P is a logical truth (sometimes abbreviated $\vDash P$) iff for all R in $[R]$, $R(P) = \mathrm{T}$.

Even this syntax and semantics are not rich enough to show that the intuitively valid arguments of the first theorem above are valid in this language. They are not valid here because there is not enough syntactic richness to express the quantified conclusion of the first argument nor the identity premise of the second. Later when we do add such locutions, the arguments will come out valid. But it is an easy matter to show for this language that not all relations are symmetric and transitive.

THEOREM. Let P_i^2 be in P^2 and a and b in PN. Then the inference from P_i^2ab to P_i^2ba is not valid.

Proof. We find a possible world R such that $R(P_i^2ab) = \mathrm{T}$ but $R(P_i^2ba) = \mathrm{F}$. Let $\mathbf{V} = \{1, 2, 3\}$. Let $R(P_i^2)$ be $\{\langle 1, 2\rangle, \langle 2, 3\rangle\}$, and let $R(a) = 1$ and $R(b) = 2$. Then $\langle R(a), R(b)\rangle \in R(P_i^2)$ and hence by clause (3a) above $R(P_i^2ab) = \mathrm{T}$. But $\langle R(b), R(a)\rangle \notin R(P_i^2)$ and hence again by clause (3a) $R(P_i^2ba) = \mathrm{F}$. QED.

THEOREM. Let P_i^2 be in P^2 and let a, b, and c be in PN. Then the inference from P_i^2ab and P_i^2bc, to P_i^2ac is not valid.

□ EXERCISES

1. Prove the preceding metatheorem.
2. Suppose we stipulate that the first predicate of degree 2 is I (for the identity predicate) and that we add to clause (2) the condition: $R(I) = \{\langle x, x\rangle | x \in \mathbf{V}\}$. Show then that the argument from P_i^2ab and Ibc to P_i^2ac is valid, when $P_i^2 \in P^2$ and a, b, and c are in PN.

What was wrong with the earlier attempts to reduce relational assertions to subject–predicate sentences is that they failed to provide the element of order essential to relations. There would be nothing in principle wrong with some sort of reduction that captured the order of the proper names. Indeed the notation used in set theory $\langle a, b \rangle \in P_i^2$, is a sort of subject–predicate sentence with $\in$ serving as a copula joining a general predicate P_i^2 standing for a set and a name $\langle a, b \rangle$ standing for a pair of elements of **V**. This notation differs from those earlier in that it attributes structure and grammatical complexity to the name itself so that it is in fact made up of two other names a and b given in a certain order. Even the sentence $P_i^2 ab$ of the formal language just defined differs only in unimportant ways from the set theoretic notation $\langle a, b \rangle \in P_i^2$. Let us reserve set theoretic notation for the metalanguage. Thus, in the metalanguage we may refer to sets, ordered pairs, etc. in the usual notation of set theory. Let us also augment the syntax of the relational language we have just defined so that it contains a special type of complex term that stands for pairs. For example, let us add a formation operation f that takes two constants a and b as arguments and yields the complex expression $[a, b]$ as value. Semantically, we add to the definition of a possible world R the condition that $[a, b]$ must stand for the pair $\langle x, y \rangle$ made up of the referent x of a and the referent y of b. That is, we require $R([a, b]) = \langle R(a), R(b) \rangle$. Then the formation rule for basic sentences would need to be adapted so that it consisted of concatenating a complex name made up of two parts with a two-place predicate. Thus, something like $[a, b]P_i^2$ would be a well-formed simple sentence. (One might even insert a copula.) The corresponding semantic rule would give the sentence the value T if the reference of the complex name was contained in the reference of the predicate, and the value F otherwise. Relational assertions of this object language would then be of a special sort of subject–predicate sentence. This particular notation for relations was not discovered until some time after Russell's famous critique of the attempt to reduce relational assertions to general predications. What remains true is that within the limited syntax of Aristotelian logic no adequate reduction is possible. But the construction of relations as sets of n-tuples and the syntactic device of constructing complex subjects standing for the n-tuple of entities are, in fact, greatly simplifying elements of set theory. It is a genuine reduction of relations to the single general category of set. There are equivalent ways of performing the reduction in the opposite direction, of reducing sets to relations, which we shall not investigate here, but the fact that it is possible means that we cannot claim that the reduction of relations to sets imparts to sets any sort of ontological primacy. The whole issue of what are relations, of whether they are reducible to other universals, and of the appropriate logical form of relational assertions is an excellent example of the tendency of metaphysical questions in the history of philosophy to be essentially issues in the syntax and semantics of everyday natural language.[13]

☐ **EXERCISE**

Work out in detail the syntax and semantics outlined here that allow in the syntax complex names which are made up of strings of proper names, in an order, and which refer to the *n*-tuple of entities referred to by those names in that order. Also define a subject–predicate formation rule and corresponding semantic rule explaining the truth assignment to basic sentences. Finally, define the set of possible worlds.

[13] For a discussion of the history of the representation of relations by sets of pairs and the reduction of pairs to sets see Randall R. Dipert, 'Set-Theoretic Representations of Ordered Pairs and Their Adequacy for the Logic of Relations' (1982).

We should also note that the notation of set theory is not the only way to construe relational assertions as subject–predicate sentences. Modern linguistics which views all basic sentences in many languages as constructed from a noun phrase and a verb phrase offers another.

5

Classical Propositional and Quantificational Logic

5.1 CLASSICAL PROPOSITIONAL LOGIC

5.1.1 Review of Syntax and Semantics

In the last chapter we investigated how to combine lexical expressions to form simple sentences. In this chapter we take up how to form complex sentences out of simple ones. One way to make up complex sentences is already familiar. We use the standard logical connectives joining together shorter sentences with the terms 'not', 'and', 'or', 'if...then', and 'if and only if'. These terms, which the traditional grammarian would call conjunctions, are called *connectives* in logic, and the syntax generated by them from simple sentences is what is called *propositional* or *sentential logic*. We have already studied this logic twice, once informally in Chapter 1 and again more carefully in Chapter 3. The informal presentation was necessary in order to equip us to work with these notions in a tentative way as we set about the metatheoretic study of particular object languages. The more formal presentation was provided as a concrete example illustrating general points about what the metatheoretic study of a language should look like. Now it is time to investigate propositional logic for itself, in a serious and rigorous way.

The object language we shall study will obviously need to have expressions designed to represent the propositional connectives of natural language. It is equally obvious that we will need to reason about this object language in the metalanguage and that some of our metatheoretic statements will employ these same connectives. We shall distinguish between object and metalanguage occurrences of the connectives by using a different set of symbols for each. In the metalanguage we shall continue to use the English words 'not', 'and' (or the ampersand &), 'or', 'if...then', and 'if and only if' (shortened 'iff'). The connectives as they appear in the specially constructed object language designed to display their properties in a rigorous way are the symbols $\sim$, $\wedge$, $\vee$, $\rightarrow$, and $\leftrightarrow$. The definitions of sentence, possible world, logical truth, and validity will be the same as those of Chapter 3. Since these are not new, we state them now without further motivation. We allow that there may be an infinite number of atomic sentences, primarily to make clear that none of the results we later prove depend on the fact that there are only a finite number. Syntactic concepts are defined as follows:

DEFINITION: The *syntax for propositional logic*, Syn-PL, consists of the *formation functions* $f_\sim$, $f_\wedge$, $f_\vee$, $f_\rightarrow$, and $f_\leftrightarrow$, the set BS of *atomic sentences*, and the set Sen of *sentences* defined as follows:

$$f_\sim = \{\langle x, y\rangle \mid y = \sim{}^\frown x\}$$
$$f_\wedge = \{\langle x, y, z\rangle \mid z = ({}^\frown x^\frown \wedge {}^\frown y^\frown)\}$$
$$f_\vee = \{\langle x, y, z\rangle \mid z = ({}^\frown x^\frown \vee {}^\frown y^\frown)\}$$
$$f_\rightarrow = \{\langle x, y, z\rangle \mid z = ({}^\frown x^\frown \rightarrow {}^\frown y^\frown)\}$$
$$f_\leftrightarrow = \{\langle x, y, z\rangle \mid z = ({}^\frown x^\frown \leftrightarrow {}^\frown y^\frown)\}$$
$$\mathrm{BS} = \{P_1, P_2, P_3, \ldots, P_n, \ldots\}$$

Sen is such that

(1) $\mathrm{BS} \subseteq \mathrm{Sen}$;
(2) for any x and y, if x and y are in Sen, then $f_\sim(x)$, $f_\wedge(x, y)$, $f_\vee(x, y)$, $f_\rightarrow(x, y)$, and $f_\leftrightarrow(x, y)$ are all in Sen;
(3) nothing else is in Sen.

(As we shall see in the next chapter, it is usual to group the various parts of the syntax into a structure $\langle \mathrm{Sen}, \mathrm{BS}, \{f_\sim, f_\wedge, f_\vee, f_\rightarrow, f_\leftrightarrow\}\rangle$. In this format the first element of the structure is an inductive set, the second is the set of basic elements used to construct it, and the third element is the set of construction rules used.)

The set BS may be understood to be one of the various sets of simple sentences defined in the languages of the last chapter. For our purposes here we are not concerned about the internal grammar or semantics of the basic sentences; we are assuming in effect that the possible alternatives have already been canvassed.

Strictly speaking, the formation functions for the binary connectives ($\wedge$, $\vee$, $\rightarrow$, and $\leftrightarrow$) bracket each sentence they make by putting parentheses on each side. These marks are necessary to show grouping when those sentences are themselves used to make up longer sentences. However, when a sentence stands alone we shall usually drop the outermost pair of parentheses in order to make the sentence easier to read.

In principle we do not need all the connectives listed above because certain connectives may be used to define others, and many presentations of the standard theory of classical logic include just one or two connectives as 'primitive' and introduce the others by definition. For example, given a grammar that uses just $\sim$ and $\wedge$, we could define the other connectives as follows: $P \vee Q$ is defined as $\sim(\sim P \wedge \sim Q)$, $P \to Q$ as $\sim(P \wedge \sim Q)$, and $P \leftrightarrow Q$ as $\sim(\sim(P \wedge Q) \wedge \sim(\sim P \wedge \sim Q))$. In the following we shall use P, Q, and S as variables standing for elements of Sen, and we shall use uppercase letters X, Y, Z, etc. to stand for sets of sentences, i.e., for subsets of Sen.

□ EXERCISES

1. Define the other connectives using just $\sim$ and $\to$ as follows. For a sentence containing P, Q, and one of the other connectives, find a truth-functional equivalent written in terms of P, Q, $\sim$, and $\to$. These symbols may occur more than once in this equivalent. Assure yourself that it is in fact equivalent by doing a truth-table.
2. Let us introduce the connective | (called *alternative denial* or the *Sheffer stroke*, after its inventor Henry Sheffer) by a function in both the syntax and semantics:

$$f_1(x, y) = \{\langle x, y, z\rangle\} | z = (^\frown x^\frown | ^\frown y^\frown)\}, \text{ and}$$

$$g_1 = \{\langle T, T, F\rangle, \langle T, F, T\rangle, \langle F, T, T\rangle, \langle F, F, T\rangle\}.$$

We read $P|Q$ as saying 'not both P and Q'. Define $\sim$ and $\wedge$ in terms of the Sheffer stroke, thereby proving it sufficient for defining all the connectives.[1]

The semantic interpretation for Sen is also unchanged. It is perhaps the most intuitive semantics for the connectives, using as it does only the two values T and F, and conforming to the principle of truth-functionality. This semantics in terms of the standard truth-tables is called *classical* because it has historically dominated discussions of the connectives. It was the first to be studied in modern logic, and was central to the semantics of earlier periods.[2] Since the ideas have been introduced previously, we state the key ideas without further elaboration.

[1] See Henry S. Sheffer, 'A Set of Five Independent Postulates for Boolean Algebras' (1913).

[2] For interesting discussions of the truth-functional tables for the connectives in early logic see Benson Mates, *Stoic Logic* (1961), and Ernest Moody, *Truth and Consequence in Medieval Logic* (1953).

DEFINITION: The *classical semantics for propositional logic* consists of the *semantic operations* $g_{\sim}$, $g_{\wedge}$, $g_{\vee}$, $g_{\rightarrow}$, and $g_{\leftrightarrow}$, and the set $[R]$ of *possible worlds* defined as follows:

$$g_{\sim} = \{\langle T, F\rangle, \langle F, T\rangle\}$$

$$g_{\wedge} = \{\langle T, T, T\rangle, \langle T, F, F\rangle, \langle F, T, F\rangle, \langle F, F, F\rangle\}$$

$$g_{\vee} = \{\langle T, T, T\rangle, \langle T, F, T\rangle, \langle F, T, T\rangle, \langle F, F, F\rangle\}$$

$$g_{\rightarrow} = \{\langle T, T, T\rangle, \langle T, F, F\rangle, \langle F, T, T\rangle, \langle F, F, T\rangle\}$$

$$g_{\leftrightarrow} = \{\langle T, T, T\rangle, \langle T, F, F\rangle, \langle F, T, F\rangle, \langle F, F, T\rangle\}$$

$[R] = \{R \mid R(\text{Sen} \xrightarrow[\text{into}]{} \{T, F\})$ such that

(1) for any $P \in \text{BS}$, $R(P) \in \{T, F\}$, and
(2) R assigns values in $\{T, F\}$ to molecular sentences in Sen as follows:
 (a) if $f_{\sim}(P) \in \text{Sen}$, then $R(f_{\sim}(P)) = g_{\sim}(R(P))$
 (b) if $f_{\wedge}(P, Q) \in \text{Sen}$, then $R(f_{\wedge}(P, Q)) = g_{\wedge}(R(P), R(Q))$
 (c) if $f_{\vee}(P, Q) \in \text{Sen}$, the $R(f_{\vee}(P, Q)) = g_{\vee}(R(P), R(Q))$
 (d) if $f_{\rightarrow}(P, Q) \in \text{Sen}$, then $R(f_{\rightarrow}(P, Q)) = g_{\rightarrow}(R(P), R(Q))$
 (e) if $f_{\leftrightarrow}(P, Q) \in \text{Sen}$, then $R(f_{\leftrightarrow}(P, Q)) = g_{\leftrightarrow}(R(P), R(Q))\}$.

As explained in Chapter 3, a language may be intuitively understood as a syntax interpreted in such a way that it says something about the world. On this understanding we identify the language L of propositional logic with the appropriate pair.

DEFINITION: The *language for propositional logic* is the pair $\langle \text{Sen}, [R]\rangle$.

We let L stand for this language and use the usual Leibnizian definitions for the logical concepts.

DEFINITION: P is a *logical truth* in L (briefly, $\vDash_L P$) iff for any $R \in [R]$, $R(P) = T$. The argument from the set X of sentences to the sentence P is *valid* in L (briefly, $X \vDash_L P$) iff for any R in $[R]$, if (for all Q, if $Q \in X$, then $R(Q) = T$), then $R(P) = T$.

When it is perfectly clear that we are speaking about the language L, we omit the subscript and write simply $X \vDash P$. To avoid the cumbersome formulation in the *definiens* of this last definitions, we introduce the idea of satisfying a set of sentences.

DEFINITION: We say a world R in $[R]$ *satisfies* a set X of sentences iff R assigns T to all elements of X; i.e., for all P, if $P \in X$, then $R(P) = T$.

Hence, another way to say that X logically implies P in L, or in notation $X \vDash_L P$, is to say that for any world R, if R satisfies X, then $R(P) = \mathrm{T}$.

The most general notion of a contradiction is a sentence that is 'logically false' in the sense of being F in every possible world. These include straightforward contradictions like $P \wedge \sim P$ as well as more obscure sentences like $\sim(\sim(P \wedge \sim(P \wedge \sim Q)) \vee Q)$. Since the term 'contradiction' is sometimes used to mean a sentence of narrow form $P \wedge \sim P$, we coin a new word for the semantic idea of being always or necessarily false.[3]

DEFINITION: A set of sentences X is said to be *unsatisfiable* iff for any R in $[R]$, there is some P in X such that $R(P) = \mathrm{F}$ (i.e., for any R, if $R \in [R]$, then there exists a P such that $P \in X$ and $R(P) = \mathrm{F}$).

What we have proved to be logical truths and valid arguments in earlier chapters will clearly remain so.

☐ **EXERCISE**

For practice in understanding these definitions, prove the following metatheorem which will be used at an important point later.

THEOREM. $X \vDash P$ iff $X \cup \{\sim P\}$ is unsatisfiable.

5.1.2 Syntactic and Semantic Accounts of Logical Ideas

In this section we turn to the syntactic notion of proof. What is interesting about the concept is that it provides an alternative characterization of the ideas of logical truth and valid argument that are defined in semantics. In semantics we have managed to define these terms quite satisfactorily from the perspective of traditional conceptual analysis, inasmuch as our formal definitions in set theory are straightforward paraphrases of the possible world definitions found in the logical tradition. In various forms throughout the history of philosophy, we find this semantic idea of a logical or necessary truth as one that is immutable or unchanging throughout a set of alternative possibilities. Hand in hand with the semantic idea of logical truth we find a semantic idea of valid argument as one that preserves truth in reasoning from premises to conclusion in any world. Plato and the Neoplatonic tradition viewed such immutable truths as the only sort of genuine truth and accordingly rejected contingent truths as a genuine category of truth at all. Aristotle understood necessity as invariance of truth with respect to all possible moments in history and denied that there are any possible worlds other than the moments of actual history. Medieval logicians explained

[3] We shall see that the term 'contradiction' is also used in proof theory for a purely syntactic idea of contradictoriness. For example, a set X of sentences is said to be contradictory iff there is a proof tree headed by X that terminates with a contradiction of the form $P \wedge \sim P$.

logical notions semantically and were the first to explicitly introduce the idea of logically possible worlds and to define logical truth and validity in terms of invariance with respect to truth in these worlds. In the modern period Leibniz used these same definitions, and they are expanded and developed in modern semantic theory.

At the same time, however, there has always been in logic the idea that logical truth and validity is a matter of certainty and that this certainty derives from the form of the truths and the arguments. This strand of thought is closely linked to modern proof theoretic definitions, and in order to develop it more fully, we shall pause for a moment to analyze these ideas of truth and validity based on form alone, and the kind of certainty they possess.

The basic notion of a formal truth is that of a sentence that is made true by its grammatical structure. The simplest examples are various sorts of redundancies like 'If P then P' and 'All A is A'. The grammatical structure of these sentences forces them to be true, and so likewise does the grammatical structure of more complicated logical truths that are not simple redundancies, like $\sim P \rightarrow (Q \rightarrow \sim(P \leftrightarrow (Q \vee \sim P)))$ and 'For all x, $P(x)$ only if not for some x, not $P(x)$'.

Certainty is a concept used in traditional philosophy to discuss an important epistemic feature of formal truths. The point has been repeatedly made that it is possible to know in a singularly transparent way, so transparently that many have held there is no possibility of error, that these formal truths are in fact true. Certainty, then, has been held to be a mark of formal truths.

The precise relevance of certainty to distinguishing formal truths may be made clear by referring to the traditional definition of knowledge. Knowledge is standardly defined as justified true belief. More formally the definition may be put this way:

A person S *knows* that P iff
(1) S believes that P;
(2) P is true;
(3) S is well justified in believing that P.

One of the necessary conditions for knowledge, then, is good justification. Justifications, arguments, defenses, proofs—all imprecise names for the same thing—are efforts to ground our beliefs, and they fall fairly naturally into a number of important categories. To put it another way, various varieties of knowledge can be distinguished in terms of the types of justification characteristic of them.

One major category of justification is empirical. Empirical justification consists of demonstrating that the sentences one claims to know are in fact verified by sense experience. Knowledge with this sort of justification is called *empirical* or *a posteriori*, and is usually believed to be the sort of knowledge embodied in the natural sciences. But one of the most striking features of much empirical knowledge is that it is hard to come by, subject to error, and constantly in need of refinement and approximation. Apart from trivial descriptions of what one seems to be presently sensing, it is possible to be skeptical about most empirical claims, and we seem to be certain of very little about the external world.

Formal truths, on the other hand, seem to have quite a different form of justification, one that renders knowledge of them if not completely certain, then quite close to it, and many philosophers class them in a special category of knowledge. Though Plato never clearly distinguished logical or formal truths from other sorts, he does seem to have been very impressed by the success of geometry. What is so striking about geometry is that its truths can be proven by formal techniques. Indeed, the provability of geometry was taken by Plato, Aristotle, and their medieval followers as a paradigm for all knowledge, and the idea of knowledge with a kind of justification different from a formal proof, for example sensory knowledge, was not taken very seriously by many philosophers until the Renaissance. Aristotle was the first to focus on what we call the form of logical argumentation, and invented the use of variables and category letters for abstracting grammatical structure to reveal logical forms. He observed that all the valid syllogisms are reducible to Barbara and Celarent by the rules we have studied. This sort of reduction is formal in the sense that it is a matter of the manipulation of grammatical structures. He also held that knowledge is certain and immutable, though he thought certainty and immutability apply to knowledge of the world as well as to logic. Though medieval logicians very often explained logical truth and validity in semantic terms, they just as often summarized logical facts by talking of the form of sentences, as in the following rule:

> From the opposite of the consequence the opposite of the hypothesis follows.

Such rules can be and often were justified by the medievals in semantic terms but they were very often merely stated without any justification because they are so obvious.[4] Notice that what is said to follow in the rule is stated in terms of its syntactic form. What the example says in more modern terms is that if a sentence of the syntactic form $P \rightarrow Q$ is true then so is that of the form $\sim Q \rightarrow \sim P$.

Modern philosophy discusses logic in terms of the notion of *a priori* knowledge. The *a priori* type of knowledge is usually defined negatively as that variety of knowledge that is justified by means other than an appeal to

[4] For discussion of such medieval *consequentiae* see I. M. Bocheński, *A History of Formal Logic* (1961), and Ernest Moody, *Truth and Consequence in Medieval Logic* (1953).

the senses, and is often understood to include logic as well as other purely rational subjects such as mathematics and definitions. Leibniz thought that all logical truths are varieties of redundancies (what he and his tradition labeled *analytic* truths) and that their certainty or 'aprioricity' derives from their analytical nature.

Kant held that logic is *a priori* and analytical in this sense. The certainty of logic derives, he believed, not from grammatical redundancy but from the fact that the mind forces us to understand things in a certain form. In comprehending the subject and predicate, one sees in the case of an analytic truth that the latter is contained in the former. But in addition to this theory of 'forms of thought' and its accompanying metaphysics, Kant and other philosophers of his day employed a second way of explaining necessity and logical truth, and this second explanation makes use of the idea of form in a more syntactic sense much like the present-day notion of syntactic form. In this approach, a logical truth is defined as one whose negation leads to a contradiction. The idea is that there is a formal technique, something like a proof in the modern sense, for exhibiting in an epistemically transparent way whether a proposition is a logical truth, and this technique involves a reduction to the absurd of the proposition's negation. Thus in explaining logical truth Kant used the notion of form, both in the metaphysical sense of forms of thought and in the sense of syntactic form. He had no need to refer to semantic ideas like truth and possible world.[5]

Another useful way to make the distinction between the semantic and formal approaches to the ideas of logical truth and validity is by means of the ideas of necessity and aprioricity. Necessity is a semantic idea: it is the invariance of truth through possible worlds, however these are understood. Thus the thesis that logical truths are necessary is semantic. The notion of *a priori* knowledge, however, is from epistemology; it is supposed to characterize one variety of knowledge. It is the sort of knowledge supported by certain proof. Proofs in the logical tradition, moreover, are formal. They are linguistic structures of a particular syntactic form. Therefore, the thesis that logic is known *a priori* is grounded in the formal approach to logic. The formal nature of logical truths and valid arguments is what makes them epistemically transparent.

There are, then, two approaches to the same logical ideas, one semantic, the other syntactic or formal. We shall not pursue further here the epistemological issue of whether the formal nature of logic renders it truly certain or *a*

[5] For an account of Plato's idea of knowledge as inspired by geometry see Kenneth M. Sayre, *Plato's Analytic Method* (1969). A discussion of Aristotle's notions of possibility as restricted to possible moments in history is found in Jaakko Hintikka, *Time and Necessity* (1973). For Kant's ideas on the related topics of necessity, analytic truth, logic, and *a priori* knowledge see Arthur Pap, *Semantics and Necessary Truth* (1958).

priori knowledge, but we shall see in detail exactly how to define the logical ideas syntactically.[6]

Syntax in its broadest definition is the study of the properties of expressions which can be fully explained by reference to other properties of expressions, and it may be broken down into two major subdisciplines. The first is grammar, or what may be called syntax 'in the narrow sense'. Grammar in its usual form consists of inductive definitions of classes of well-formed expressions of some language, and these definitions are properly classified as syntactic because all the terms used in the definitions either are borrowed from set theory or refer to the simple syntactic properties of expressions. For each member of an inductive class of expressions it is possible to provide a grammatical tree explaining how it is constructed from atomic or basic elements by the application of formation rules. These rules provide a kind of proof for membership in a grammatical category. Since each stage in the construction consists of the manipulation of expressions in a simple way, the construction itself is epistemically transparent. It is a simple matter of inspection to determine whether a construction is properly executed, and in this sense grammatical knowledge is formal. We shall study grammatical trees in detail in Chapter 6. It should be noted that grammar in this sense is totally independent of semantics, and in this respect is quite different from some usages of the terms 'grammar' and 'syntax' among linguists who sometimes use these terms to include semantics.

The second major branch of syntax, as we shall use the term, is called *proof theory*, which studies in syntactic terms the ideas of logical truth and valid argument. Proof theory presupposes grammar in the sense that its definitions presuppose those of grammar. It then goes on to provide definitions of logical truth and valid argument. These definitions must meet two conditions.

The first condition is that the definitions of the logical terms themselves must be syntactic in the sense just defined; i.e., the terms used in the definitions must describe only relations among symbols. Thus, this is a condition on the theoretical resources appealed to in the definitions. In practice, the restriction amounts to limiting the defining vocabulary to set theory augmented by a few undefined 'primitive' ideas about symbols like that of concatenation.

The second requirement is that the sets defined must have inductive definitions. Thus, this requirement is about the form that the definitions of logical truth and validity will take. An inductive set is defined by first stipulating a grammatical characterization of a set of basic elements and then 'closing' this set under a series of operations all definable syntactically in terms of the grammatical transformations of their arguments. If the inductive

[6] For more on the distinction between semantic and syntactic characterizations of logical ideas see Alfred Tarski's quite readable *Scientific American* article 'Truth and Proof' (1969).

set is properly defined, it will turn out that it coincides exactly with the set of logical truths or valid arguments as defined independently in semantics. If such a perfect match between syntactic and semantic ideas is achieved, then two quite different conceptual routes to the same ideas have been found: one in the traditional vocabulary of expressions describing the world, and one in terms of epistemically transparent and mechanically effective manipulations of symbols. The actual proof of the coincidence is nontrivial, and how to prove the coincidence is just as much an object of our study here as is the format of the proof theoretic definitions.

5.1.3 An Axiom System for Propositional Logic

Historically, the first way to characterize logical truth in modern proof theory was in terms of *axiom systems.* Indeed, the logical truths of propositional logic were axiomatized in inductive sets by modern logicians before the semantic theory for propositional logic was clearly understood. Axiom systems all have a standard form. First a set of basic sentences is defined. These are called the *axioms.* If the set is finite, it is given by a simple enumeration of its elements. If it is infinite, it is usually specified by means of a finite list of what are called *axiom schemata,* sentential forms from which it is possible to construct axioms by the replacement of letters in the schema by sentences, using the same sentence for all occurrences of the letter it replaces. Once the basic axioms are defined, the inductive set of *theorems* is defined as the closure of the axioms under a set, usually finite, of inference rules. The inference rules are functions on sets defined wholly in terms of the manipulation of the grammatical forms of the arguments. The formal transparency of the set of theorems is ensured by our ability to provide a tree structure, what we shall call a *proof tree,* exhibiting how to construct a theorem in a finite number of steps from axioms by the application of inference rules.

DEFINITION:[7] By the *axiom system P for propositional logic,* briefly AS_P-PL, we mean the structure $\langle \text{TH}, \text{AX}, f_{\text{mp}} \rangle$ such that

(1) AX is the set of all sentences meeting the form of one of the following axiom schemata:

(a) $(x \to (y \to x))$,

(b) $((x \to (y \to z)) \to ((x \to y) \to (x \to z)))$, or

(c) $((\sim x \to \sim y) \to (y \to x))$.

[7] This system derives from that in Frege's *Begriffsschrift* (1879). For the present form see Jan Łukasiewicz and Alfred Tarski, 'Untersuchungen über den Aussagenkalkül' (1930). It is also the system P of Alonzo Church, Section 27, *Introduction to Mathematical Logic* (1956). See Section 29 of Church's book for a historical account of the development of the various axiomatizations of propositional logic.

(2) f_{mp} is that function that maps any pair consisting of a conditional and its antecedent to its consequent: for any sentence x and any sentence $x \to y$, $f_{mp}(x, x \to y) = y$.

(3) TH is the inductively defined set which is the closure of AX under f_{mp}; i.e., TH is the smallest set X such that AX is a subset of X, and if x and $x \to y$ are in TH, then so is $f_{mp}(x, x \to y)$.

We now define the notion of a proof tree, assuming an intuitive understanding of what a tree graph looks like. In the definition we adopt the common practice used among mathematicians, and by us in more precise discussions later in this book, of inverting a tree and referring to its single root node as its maximal element and all other nodes of the tree as 'beneath' it. We shall, however, continue to draw proof trees right side up, with root at the bottom and leaves at the top.

DEFINITION: A *proof tree* for AS_P-PL for a sentence P with annotation g is defined as any binary, branching, finite tree T and any function g on the nodes of T such that

(1) P occupies the root (maximal node) of T,

(2) elements of AX occupy the various leaves (minimal nodes) of T and each such node is annotated with the number of the axiom schema to which the sentence occupying the node conforms,

(3) any intermediate node is occupied by a sentence x such that the immediate predecessor (lower) nodes are occupied by sentences of the form x and $x \to y$, respectively. (These nodes would normally be annotated by the rule used to derive them, but since in this system there is only the one rule, *modus ponens*, this information may be omitted.)

EXAMPLE If P is an atomic sentence, the following is a proof tree:

$$\dfrac{\begin{array}{c}(P \to (P \to P))\\ \text{axiom schema 1}\end{array} \qquad \dfrac{\begin{array}{c}(P \to ((P \to P) \to P))\\ \text{axiom schema 1}\end{array} \quad \begin{array}{c}((P \to ((P \to P) \to P)) \to\\ ((P \to (P \to P)) \to (P \to P)))\\ \text{axiom schema 2}\end{array}}{((P \to (P \to P)) \to (P \to P))}}{(P \to P)}$$

□ **EXERCISE**

Construct a proof tree in the sense just defined for the following sentences. From this point on we omit outer parentheses.

$\sim P \to (P \to Q)$

$P \to ((P \to P) \to (P \to P))$

It is possible to provide a completeness proof demonstrating that the set of theorems TH coincides with the set of logical truths, but rather than prove the coincidence of syntactic and semantic ideas in this case, we shall turn to a more general inductive set of acceptable arguments, also defined syntactically, and show that it coincides with the semantic idea of valid argument. The theorems of TH will be contained in the new set as cases of arguments with no premises. The identity of the theorems of AS_P-PL with the logical truths will then follow as a special case of the identity of the syntactically defined set of arguments with the semantically defined set of valid arguments.

5.1.4 Natural Deduction for Propositional Logic

Rather than focusing on logical truths as the proper subject matter of logic, it has proven fruitful to explore the slightly more general idea of valid argument. Both semantically and syntactically logical truths turn out to be the special case of those sentences that follow from (in the appropriate sense) the empty set. We have already seen how this happens semantically, and we explore in this section the syntactic version.

As in axiomatics we shall define an inductive set in syntactic terms. This time the set we shall define is a relation, specifically a set of pairs, the first element of which is a set of sentences and the second element of which is a sentence. The relation will be that of deducibility and will be named by the symbol $\vdash$. We shall let the letters X, Y, and Z stand for arbitrary sets of sentences (subsets of Sen), and let P, Q, and S stand for arbitrary sentences (elements of Sen). We shall read the assertion '$\langle X, P\rangle \in \vdash$' as saying that P is deducible from X, and we shall usually rewrite it in the more customary form '$X \vdash P$'. Our goal is to provide a syntactic definition of deducibility. We shall proceed in two steps. First, we inductively define the related notion of *finite deducibility* which we shall label $\mathrel{\scriptstyle\vdash}$, and again $\langle X, P\rangle \in \mathrel{\scriptstyle\vdash}$ is rewritten in the more customary form $X \mathrel{\scriptstyle\vdash} P$. In terms of it, we then define $\vdash$: we say that $X \vdash P$ iff there is some finite subset Y of X such that $X \mathrel{\scriptstyle\vdash} P$.

For the inductive definition of finite deducibility we need some basic elements and some rules. The basic elements we use, called *basic deductions*, are logical redundancies of an especially trivial and transparently valid type, namely any deduction that repeats as its conclusion a sentence already listed among its premises. The rules under which we close the basic deductions are also chosen for their transparency and usefulness. (Hence the name 'natural deduction'.) We shall postpone their precise statement until after we have stated the general form of the definition of the inductive set $\mathrel{\scriptstyle\vdash}$.

For the sake of simplicity we assume that the syntax contains only the connectives for negation, conjunction, disjunction, and the conditional, and that the possible worlds in $[R]$ are similarly restricted.

DEFINITION:[8] By the *natural deduction system for propositional logic*, briefly NDS-PL, we mean the inductive system $\langle\vdash, \text{BD}, f_1, \ldots, f_{11}\rangle$ such that

(1) BD is $\{\langle X, P\rangle | X \text{ is finite and } P \in X\}$;

(2) $f_1, \ldots, f_{11}$ are respectively the rules for natural deduction defined below; and

(3) $\vdash$ is the set of pairs $\langle X, P\rangle$ inductively defined as the closure of BD under $f_1, \ldots, f_{11}$. That is, $\vdash$ is the smallest set R of pairs such that

(a) $\text{BD} \subseteq R$, and

(b) for any elements $\langle X_1, P_1\rangle, \ldots, \langle X_n, P_n\rangle$ and any of the rules f_i, if $\langle X_1, P_1\rangle, \ldots, \langle X_n, P_n\rangle$ are all in R, then

$$f_i(\langle X_1, P_1\rangle, \ldots, \langle X_n, P_n\rangle) \in R.$$

We need a convenient name for the elements of $\vdash$. Recall that they are all pairs of the form $\langle X, P\rangle$. The idea is that P is supposed to follow logically from X and that this notion of 'following logically' is supposed to be syntactic rather than semantic. The traditional term 'deduction' can be used to express this kind of syntactic dependence because a deduction is supposed to hold as matter of form. Hence we shall call the members of $\vdash$ *deductive assertions* or just *assertions* if the context makes clear we are talking about elements of $\vdash$. We let the letters A, B, C, and D stand for arbitrary elements of $\vdash$.

The rules will be defined as in the syllogistic. The argument forms for which the rule is defined will be written above a horizontal line, and the form of the value assigned to the arguments is specified below the line. For each of the connectives there are two rules. An *introduction* or + rule explains how to add the connective to the conclusion of a deduction, and an *elimination* or − rule explains how to remove the connective from the conclusion of a deduction. To the extent that each connective is explained by using a pair of rules about it alone, the rules are sometimes said to 'explain' the meaning of that connective. The sense in which meaning is explained here, however, must be understood as syntactic and distinguished from the sense in which semantic rules explain meaning. (In Chapter 7 when we discuss intuitionistic logic, we return to the issue of whether syntactic rules like these can properly be said to explain the meaning of the connectives.)

There are also two rules used to explain a new syntactic symbol, $\perp$. This symbol is supposed to represent a typical contradiction or necessarily false sentence. Since it does not matter how $\perp$ is defined as long as it is necessarily false, we choose the atomic sentence P_1 and stipulate that $\perp$ is an abbreviation for the sentence $(P_1 \wedge \sim P_1)$. It must be remembered that $\perp$ is a

[8] The idea of a natural deduction system is due to Gerhard Gentzen, 'Untersuchungen über das logische Schliessen' (1939). The form of natural deduction theory used in this book is explored in detail in D. Prawitz, *Natural Deduction: A Proof Theoretic Study* (1965).

particular sentence with its own grammatical form. In a number of proofs below that detail the properties of $\perp$, this internal grammar is relevant, and we shall have to replace the symbol by the sentence it abbreviates.

To make the statement of the rules more perceptually transparent, we first introduce some notational abbreviations that suppress some of the set theoretic detail. The idea behind these abbreviations is that though we should always understand that it is a set of sentences that appears to the left of $\vdash$, we sometimes name that set by listing the relevant subsets and sentences of which it is composed. It must be stressed that in the notation below everything to the left of $\vdash$ functions grammatically as the name of a set, even if that set is named by listing some of its elements and subsets.

DEFINITION:

$X, Y \vdash P$ means $X \cup Y \vdash P$;

$X, Q \vdash P$ means $X \cup \{Q\} \vdash P$;

$Q, \ldots, S \vdash P$ means $\{Q, \ldots, S\} \vdash P$;

$\vdash P$ means $\varnothing \vdash P$.

DEFINITION: The *rules for natural deduction* are the functions $f_1, \ldots, f_{11}$ defined as follows:

	Introduction rules	Elimination rules
$\perp$	$$\frac{X \vdash P \quad Y \vdash \sim P}{X, Y \vdash \perp}$$	$$\frac{X \vdash \perp}{X \vdash P}$$
$\sim$	$$\frac{X, P \vdash \perp}{X \vdash \sim P}$$	$$\frac{X \vdash \sim\sim P}{X \vdash P}$$
$\wedge$	$$\frac{X \vdash P \quad Y \vdash Q}{X, Y \vdash (P \wedge Q)}$$	$$\frac{X \vdash (P \wedge Q)}{X \vdash P} \qquad \frac{X \vdash (P \wedge Q)}{X \vdash Q}$$
$\vee$	$$\frac{X \vdash P}{X \vdash (P \vee Q)} \qquad \frac{X \vdash Q}{X \vdash (P \vee Q)}$$	$$\frac{X \vdash (P \vee Q) \quad Y, P \vdash R \quad Z, Q \vdash R}{X, Y, Z \vdash R}$$
$\rightarrow$	$$\frac{X, P \vdash Q}{X \vdash (P \rightarrow Q)}$$	$$\frac{X \vdash P \quad Y \vdash (P \rightarrow Q)}{X, Y \vdash Q}$$

Thinning $$\frac{X \vdash P}{X, Y \vdash P}$$

(Since introduction rules are referred to as + rules, $\perp$-introduction is often abbreviated $\perp +$; similarly $\perp$-elimination is abbreviated $\perp -$, etc.) Given these rules, the definition of the system NDS-PL and the set $\vdash$ is complete. We now define the relevant notion of proof tree appropriate to deductive assertions. We use these trees to exhibit the construction of the various assertions in $\vdash$. For each element of $\vdash$ there is in principle at least one proof tree which shows how it is arrived at, either because it is a basic deduction or because it is added to $\vdash$ by one of the rules applied to other deductive assertions already in $\vdash$.

DEFINITION: An *annotated proof tree* for $X \vdash P$ in NDS-PL is a finitely branching finite tree such that

(1) its root (maximal node) is occupied by $\langle X, P \rangle$;

(2) each leaf (minimal node) is occupied by an occurrence of a basic deduction and is annotated with the information 'bd';

(3) each intermediate node is occupied by some A which is such that

(a) its immediate predecessors are each occupied respectively by some $B, \ldots, D$,

(b) there is a natural deduction rule f_i such that $f_i(B, \ldots, D) = A$, and

(c) the node occupied by A is annotated with the information 'f_i'.

In principle every proof tree must by definition have a basic deduction on each leaf. In practice once we have proven a deductive assertion by obtaining it as the root of some proof tree, we may use it as a leaf on a new proof tree. It is clear, after all, that any tree with proven assertions at the tip of every branch can be turned into a proof tree in the strict sense by grafting onto each leaf node the proof tree of the previously proven assertion. Thus in practice we need only construct proof trees with basic assertions or previously proven assertions at the tips of the branches. As in the syllogistic, we must annotate proof trees. To the left of every tip of the tree, we indicate whether it is a basic deduction by writing 'bd', or whether it is previously proven by writing 'pp'. To the right of each horizontal line, we write the name of the rule which justifies the descent from what is above it to what is below. We cite the rule by naming the relevant connective and then indicating $+$ or $-$. Before proceeding with examples it will be useful to define a short cutting rule, called Cut.

THEOREM. *Cut.* For any X, Y, P, and Q, if $X \vdash P$ and $Y, P \vdash Q$ then $X, Y \vdash Q$. The customary form of writing this sort of fact is

$$\frac{X \vdash P \quad Y,P \vdash Q}{X,Y \vdash Q}$$

Proof. Assume $X \vdash P$ and $Y, P \vdash Q$ are previously proven. Then we construct the following which by inspection is a proof tree for $X, Y \vdash Q$:

$$\dfrac{X \vdash P\ (\text{pp}) \qquad \dfrac{Y,P \vdash Q\ (\text{pp})}{Y \vdash (P \to Q)}\ (\to +)}{X,Y \vdash Q}\ (\to -)$$

Now some examples.

THEOREM. $\vdash (P \to P)$.

Proof.

$$\frac{P \vdash P \text{ (bd)}}{\varnothing \vdash (P \to P)}\ (\to +)$$

THEOREM. $P \vdash \sim\sim P$.

Proof.

$$\cfrac{\cfrac{P \vdash P \text{ (bd)} \qquad \sim P \vdash \sim P \text{ (bd)}}{P, \sim P \vdash \bot}\ (\bot +)}{P \vdash \sim\sim P}\ (\sim +)$$

THEOREM. $P, \sim P \vdash Q$.

Proof.

$$\cfrac{\cfrac{P, \sim P \vdash P \text{ (bd)} \qquad P, \sim P \vdash \sim P \text{ (bd)}}{P, \sim P \vdash \bot}\ (\bot +)}{P, \sim P \vdash Q}\ (\bot -)$$

THEOREMS. $(P \to Q), \sim Q \vdash \sim P$.

$P, (P \to Q) \vdash Q$.

$(P \wedge Q) \vdash (P \vee Q)$.

$\sim(P \wedge Q) \vdash (\sim P \vee \sim Q)$.

$\vdash (P \vee \sim P)$.

THEOREMS.

$$\frac{X \vdash \sim Q}{X \vdash (Q \to S)}$$

$$\frac{P \vdash Q}{\vdash (P \to Q)}$$

$$\frac{X \vdash \sim Q \quad X \vdash \sim S \quad X \vdash (Q \vee S)}{X \vdash \bot}$$

$$\frac{X \vdash P}{X, \sim P \vdash \bot}$$

Now we show that the set of valid arguments and the set of provable deductions are the same, and hence that the syntactically defined relation $\vdash$ is adequate in the sense that it is coextensive with the semantic relation $\vDash$.

□ **EXERCISE**

Give proof trees establishing the previous unproven metatheorems.

5.1.5 Soundness and Completeness

Our goal in this section is to establish that the relations $\vdash$ and $\vDash$ are identical. By the principle of extensionality, we must show that each is a subset of the other. We first show in a theorem called the soundness result that $\vdash \subseteq \vDash$. The key idea of the proof is to notice that $\vdash$ is an inductive set. To prove that all members of an inductive set have a certain property, we must employ an inductive proof. We must show first in a basis clause that the basic elements, in this case the basic deductions, all have the property, and then in an inductive step we must show that all the construction rules, in this case the various inference rules f_1–f_{11}, preserve the property. That is, we must show for each rule that if the arguments for the rule have the property, then the rule applied to those arguments yields a value that has that property. The property in question is membership in $\vDash$.

This theorem will actually be the first serious use of a proof by induction in this book, so it will be well for us to review at this point the precise form of an inductive argument. First let us apply the general form of an inductive definition to the special case of a binary relation. The inductive set in this case will have as its elements pairs rather than single individuals, the basic elements will likewise be pairs rather than individuals, and the formation operations will apply to a series of pairs yielding as outputs other pairs. These facts follow directly from the definition of an inductive set and the fact that a relation is a set of pairs, but because they are somewhat complicated it is worth stating these facts in a theorem.

THEOREM. A binary relation R is inductive iff there is a (possibly infinite) set $\{\langle a_1, b_1\rangle, \ldots, \langle a_n, b_n\rangle\}$ of basic elements, and a series (again possibly infinite) of formation functions $f_1, \ldots, f_m$ such that R is the smallest set such that

(1) $\{\langle a_1, b_1\rangle, \ldots, \langle a_n, b_n\rangle\} \subseteq R$; and

(2) for all elements $\langle x_1, y_1\rangle, \ldots, \langle x_n, y_n\rangle$ and any n-placed rule f_i, if $\langle x_1, y_1\rangle, \ldots, \langle x_n, y_n\rangle$ are all in R, then $f_i(\langle x_1, y_1\rangle, \ldots, \langle x_n, y_n\rangle) \in R$.

It is also worthwhile stating the relevant form of an inductive proof in the special case in which the inductive set is a set of pairs. In this case we want to show that every pair $\langle x, y\rangle$ in the inductively defined relation R has a certain property. The property in this case will consist of some relational fact holding between x and y and will be described by some open sentence, say $Q(x, y)$. Thus the goal of the proof is to show that every $\langle x, y\rangle$ in R is such that the condition $Q(x, y)$ holds, or in set theoretic vocabulary that $R \subseteq \{\langle x, y\rangle | Q(x, y)\}$. This proposition is established by showing that each basic pair has the property, and then on the assumption that all the arguments for a formation operation have the property, that its value does too. Again it is worth stating the straightforward application of the proof by induction theorem to the case of binary relations.

THEOREM. Suppose we can establish the following three facts:

(1) R is a set defined inductively relative to the set $\{\langle a_1, b_1\rangle, \ldots, \langle a_n, b_n\rangle\}$ of basic elements and the series $f_1, \ldots, f_n$ of formation operations;

(2) (*basis step*) $\{\langle a_1, b_1\rangle, \ldots, \langle a_n, b_n\rangle\} \subseteq \{\langle z, w\rangle | Q(z, w)\}$;

(3) (*inductive step*) for any m-placed rule f_i, and any $\langle x_1, y_1\rangle, \ldots,$

$\langle x_m, y_m \rangle$, if (*induction hypothesis*) $\langle x_1, y_1 \rangle, \ldots, \langle x_m, y_m \rangle$ are all in $\{\langle z, w \rangle | Q(z, w)\}$, then $f_i(\langle x_1, y_1 \rangle, \ldots, \langle x_m, y_m \rangle) \in \{\langle z, w \rangle | Q(z, w)\}$.

We may then conclude that $R \subseteq \{\langle z, w \rangle | Q(z, w)\}$.

Now we may apply the general form of an inductive proof to the special inductive set $\vdash$. We must establish that all elements $\langle X, P \rangle$ of $\vdash$ have the property of being members of $\models$. That is, we must show $\vdash \subseteq \{\langle X, P \rangle | X \models P\}$.

THEOREM. *Soundness.* The relation $\vdash$ is a subset of the relation $\models$: for any X and P, if $X \vdash P$ then $X \models P$.

Proof. We prove first that $\vdash$ is a subset of $\models$, and since $\vdash$ is an inductive set we prove this by induction. That is, we show by induction that $\vdash \subseteq \{\langle X, P \rangle | X \models P\}$, first showing that every basic deduction $\langle X, P \rangle$ has the property $X \models P$, and then showing for each inference rule in turn that if its arguments are semantically valid then so is its value. The details are left as exercises. Given that $\vdash \subseteq \models$, it follows that $\vdash \subseteq \models$. For suppose $\langle X, P \rangle \in \vdash$. Then $X \vdash P$. Then by definition of $\vdash$ there is a finite subset Y of X such that $Y \vdash P$. Then since $\vdash \subseteq \models$, it follows that $Y \models P$. But if $Y \models P$ and $Y \subseteq X$, then $X \models P$, since any possible world R that assigns T to all elements of X must assign T to all elements of Y. Then since $Y \models P$, R would also assign T to P. End of Proof.

□ EXERCISES

1. Show the basis step of the above inductive proof, namely that any basic $\langle X, P \rangle$ in $\vdash$ is such that $X \models P$. Notice that by definition P must be a member of X.

2. Establish the inductive step of the inductive proof. This step is divided into parts, one for each of the inference rules. We assume in the inductive hypothesis that the inputs of the rule have the property in question, and then show that the output of the rule has the property.

Consider, for example, the rule for $\wedge$-introduction. We assume that two arguments for the rule, say $\langle X, P \rangle$ and $\langle Y, Q \rangle$, are in $\models$, and then show that the output of the rule, in this case $\langle X \cup Y, P \wedge Q \rangle$, is in $\models$. That is, we assume $X \models P$ and $X \models Q$, and then show $X \cup Y \models P \wedge Q$.

Prove a similar result for each of the rules:

a. (i) If $X \models P$ and $X \models \sim P$, then $X \models \perp$.
   (ii) If $X \models \perp$, then $X \models P$.

b. (i) If $X \cup \{P\} \models \perp$, then $X \models \sim P$.
   (ii) If $X \models \sim\sim P$, then $X \models P$.

c. (i) If $X \models P$ and $Y \models Q$, then $X \cup Y \models (P \wedge Q)$.
   (ii) If $X \models (P \wedge Q)$, then $X \models P$ and $X \models Q$.

d. (i) If $X \models P$ or $X \models Q$, then $X \models (P \vee Q)$.
   (ii) If $X \models (P \vee Q)$, $Y \cup \{P\} \models R$, $Z \cup \{Q\} \models R$, then $X \cup Y \cup Z \models R$.

e. (i) If $X \cup \{P\} \models Q$, then $X \models (P \rightarrow Q)$.
   (ii) If $X \models P$ and $Y \models (P \rightarrow Q)$, then $X \cup Y \models Q$.

f. If $X \models P$, then $X \cup Y \models P$.

The converse of the soundness theorem is the completeness result. It says that the semantic entailment relation $\models$ is a subset of the syntactically defined set $\vdash$. A direct proof of this result might take the form of finding some general method for constructing for every valid argument a proof tree from basic deductions. The strategy we shall use, due to Leon Henkin, is a proof by indirection.[9] Let us recast these syntactic and semantic facts in alternative ways. One way to reformulate relations of semantic entailment is in terms of contradictions. If P follows logically from a set X then the simultaneous assertion of X with $\sim P$ would be absurd. More precisely, $X \models P$ if, and only if, the set $X \cup \{\sim P\}$ is unsatisfiable in the sense that there is no world R simultaneously assigning T to all members of X and to $\sim P$. A similar reformulation in terms of a syntactic version of contradiction is open to the syntactic version of 'following from'. It follows from $\sim$-elimination and an earlier exercise that $X \vdash P$ iff $X, \sim P \vdash \perp$. That is, the set $X \cup (\sim P\}$ is syntactically inconsistent iff P is deducible syntactically from X.

Given these equivalences, let us reformulate the problem. We must show, given $X \cup (\sim P\}$ is semantically unsatisfiable, that the set is syntactically inconsistent. One obvious strategy is a reduction to the absurd. We suppose the set is semantically unsatisfiable, but syntactically consistent, and then try to deduce a contradiction. Henkin's key idea was to show that a consistent set can be made true in some world. He showed this by taking a consistent set and from it defining a relation R from sentences to truth-values that both meets the conditions for being a possible world and also assigns T to every element of $X \cup \{\sim P\}$. If any syntactically consistent set can be rendered true in some possible world, we then have a contradiction, because we have on the one hand, the assumption that $X \cup \{\sim P\}$ is unsatisfiable and, on the other, the assumption that since it is syntactically consistent, there is a world in which it is satisfied.

In the case of propositional logic it is not very difficult to describe a general method for defining, for any syntactically consistent set of sentences, a possible world in which all its members are true. The process proceeds in two steps. We first show in the maximalization theorem that we can add to a consistent set enough other atomic sentences or their negations so that the set as a whole remains consistent but also determines a truth-value for each atomic sentence. If an atomic sentence is contained in the set, it determines the value T and if its negation is in the set then it determines the value F. Next we show in the satisfiability theorem that the resulting truth-value assignment to the atomic sentences is both a genuine possible world and assigns T to all the members of the consistent set. Later in this chapter when we consider first-order logic, we shall see that Henkin's method continues to

[9] The completeness proof here and in the later sections on first-order logic is modeled on that of Leon Henkin, 'The Completeness of the First-Order Functional Calculus' (1949).

work in a far less obvious context. It is good preparation for the more complex completeness proof given there, to work through in detail this simpler version for propositional logic.

DEFINITION: X is (syntactically) *inconsistent* iff $X \vdash \bot$. We say X is *consistent* when it is not inconsistent. When X is consistent, we say that it follows *by consistency* that not$(X \vdash \bot)$.

DEFINITION: X is *maximally consistent* iff

(1) X is consistent and

(2) X is maximal in the sense that for any P, either $P \in X$ or $\sim P \in X$.

THEOREM. If X is maximally consistent, then X is 'closed under deducibility', i.e., for any P, if $X \vdash P$, then $P \in X$.

Proof. Assume for arbitrary P that $X \vdash P$ but that $P \notin X$. Then by maximality of X, $\sim P \in X$, and $X \vdash \sim P$ is a basic deduction. Since $X \vdash P$ by assumption, $X \vdash \bot$ by $\bot$-introduction, contradicting the assumption that X is consistent. QED.

☐ **EXERCISES**

1. Show not$(X \vdash \bot)$ iff for some P, not$(X \vdash P)$.
2. Given the inductive definition of Sen, define a function mapping Sen 1-1 and onto the set of positive integers. We use the existence of such a function below.

THEOREM. *Maximalization.* If not$(Y \vdash \bot)$, then for some X, $Y \subseteq X$ and X is maximally consistent.

Proof. Let not$(Y \vdash \bot)$. We construct a set $Y*$ as follows. Since Sen is countably infinite, we can give a list of its members, assigning a numerical subscript to each. Accordingly let Sen be $P_1, \ldots, P_n, \ldots$. We first define inductively the set Y^+ as the set $\{Y_0, Y_1, \ldots, Y_n, \ldots\}$ of subsets of Sen as follows:

Basis clause. We set Y_0 equal to Y and place it in $Y+$.

Inductive clause. We define a rule (construction function) for making up new elements of $Y+$ from elements already in $Y+$: if Y_n is in $Y+$, then we add to $Y+$ the element Y_{n+1} constructed as follows:

$$Y_{n+1} = Y_n \cup \{P_n\} \text{ if not}(Y_n, P_n \vdash \bot),$$

$$Y_{n+1} = Y_n \text{ if } Y_n, P_n \vdash \bot.$$

Clearly, for all i, Y_i is consistent. Consider the cases. We know that for the basic element, not$(Y_0 \vdash \bot)$, since by assumption not$(Y \vdash \bot)$ and $Y_0 = Y$. Further, if Y_n is consistent, so is the element Y_{n+1} constructed from it, for either not$(Y_n, P_n \vdash \bot)$ or $Y_n, P_n \vdash \bot$. In the former case, $Y_{n+1} = Y_n \cup \{P_n\}$ and not$\{Y_{n+1} \vdash \bot)$. In the latter case $Y_{n+1} = Y_n$, and since not$(Y_n \vdash \bot)$, then not$(Y_{n+1} \vdash \bot)$.

We now define $Y*$ as the union of all Y_i; i.e., $Y* = \{P | \text{for some } i, P \in Y_i\}$. We show first that $Y*$ is consistent and then that $Y*$ is maximal. Clearly $Y \subseteq Y*$.

$Y*$ is consistent, for suppose not. Suppose that $Y* \vdash \bot$. Then there is some finite subset X of $Y*$ such that $X \vdash \bot$ is the base of a proof tree. Further since X is finite and $X \subseteq Y*$, there is some Y_i such that $X \subseteq Y_i$. But if $X \subseteq Y_i$ and $X \vdash \bot$, then $Y_i \vdash \bot$ and contrary to what we have already shown, Y_i is inconsistent. Hence $Y*$ must be consistent.

Furthermore, $Y*$ is maximal, for suppose not. Then there is some Q such that neither $Q \in Y*$ nor $\sim Q \in Y*$. Since $Q \in$ Sen, there are some P_i and P_j such that $Q = P_i$ and $\sim Q = P_j$. We show first that both $Y_i, P_i \vdash \bot$ and $Y_j, P_j \vdash \bot$. For the former, observe that since $P_i = Q$ and $Q \notin Y*$, then $P_i \notin Y*$. Thus, for any k, $P_i \notin Y_{k+1}$. In particular, $P_i \notin Y_{i+1}$. But then $Y_i, P_i \vdash \bot$, because suppose not. Then $Y_{i+1} = Y_i \cup \{P_i\}$ and $P_i \in Y_{i+1}$ and $P_i \in Y*$, contrary to what we have shown. Likewise, $Y_j, P_j \vdash \bot$, for since $P_j = Q$ and $Q \notin Y*$, $P_j \notin Y*$ and, for any k, $P_j \notin Y_{k+1}$. In particular, $P_j \notin Y_{k+1}$. But then $Y_j, P_j \vdash \bot$, for suppose not. Then $Y_{j+1} = Y_j \cup \{P_j\}$, and $P_j \in Y_{j+1}$, which we have shown to be false. Hence both $Y_i, P_i \vdash \bot$ and $Y_j, P_j \vdash \bot$. Let k be the greater of i and j. Then since both $Y_i \subseteq Y_k$ and $Y_j \subseteq Y_k$, and since $P_i = Q$ and $P_j = \sim Q$, we have $Y_k, Q \vdash \bot$ and $Y_k, \sim Q \vdash \bot$. From these two we can construct a proof tree for $Y_k \vdash \bot$:

$$\dfrac{\dfrac{Y_k, Q \vdash \bot}{Y_k \vdash \sim Q}\ (\sim +) \qquad \dfrac{\dfrac{Y_k, \sim Q \vdash \bot}{Y_k \vdash \sim\sim Q}\ (\sim +)}{Y_k \vdash Q}\ (\sim -)}{Y_k \vdash \bot}\ (\bot +)$$

But since we have already shown Y_k is consistent, our original assumption that $Y*$ is not maximal must be false. End of Proof.

THEOREM. *Satisfiability.* If X is maximally consistent, there is some R in $[R]$ such that for any P in Sen, $R(P) = \text{T}$ iff $P \in X$ (i.e., R satisfies X).

Proof. Let X be maximally consistent. We define a member R of $[R]$ and then show it has the property claimed. Let $R(\text{Sen} \xrightarrow[\text{into}]{} \{\text{T}, \text{F}\})$ such that

(1) for any sentence $P \in$ BS, $R(P) = \text{T}$ iff $P \in X$, and

(2) if P is a complex sentence, $R(P)$ is calculated as stipulated in the definition of $[R]$ from the R values of P's parts.

Clearly $R \in [R]$. We now show by induction that for any $P \in$ Sen, $R(P) = \text{T}$ iff $P \in X$. The property that we are going to show holds for all sentences is expressed in the following open sentence:

$$R(\ldots) = T \text{ iff} \ldots \in X.$$

Here the ellipsis '...' functions as the free variable showing the positions to be filled in the open sentence. The proof has two parts. We show first (the 'basis' step) that for any $P \in \text{BS}$, $R(P) = \text{T}$ iff $P \in X$. We then show (in the 'inductive' step) the truth of a conditional: if for all immediate parts Q of P, Q has the property, then P does also. That is, if all immediate parts Q of P are such that $R(Q) = \text{T}$ iff $Q \in X$, then $R(P) = \text{T}$ iff $P \in X$. To show this conditional we assume the antecedent, which is the induction hypothesis, and then argue to the consequent. It follows from the basis and inductive steps together that for every P, $R(P) = \text{T}$ iff $P \in X$. The basis step holds trivially by clause (1) of the definition of R. We show the inductive step for a complex sentence P by considering the cases.

Case I: P is a negation, say $\sim Q$. Note that by the induction hypothesis we may assume $R(Q) = \text{T}$ iff $Q \in X$. Now $R(\sim Q) = \text{T}$ iff [by definition of R] $R(Q) = \text{F}$ iff $R(Q) \neq \text{T}$ iff [by induction hypothesis] $Q \notin X$ iff [since X is maximal] $\sim Q \in X$.

Case II: Let $(Q \vee S) \in X$ and thus $X \vdash (Q \vee S)$. Assume for a *reductio* proof that $R(Q \vee S) = \text{F}$. Thus $R(Q) = R(S) = \text{F}$, $Q \notin X$, $\sim Q \in X$, and $X \vdash \sim Q$. Moreover $S \notin X$, $\sim S \in X$, and $X \vdash \sim S$. We now claim that if we know that $X \vdash \sim Q$, $X \vdash \sim S$, and $X \vdash (Q \vee S)$, then it follows that $X \vdash \bot$, which we establish by producing the relevant proof tree:

$$\dfrac{\dfrac{X,S \vdash S\ (\text{bd}) \qquad \dfrac{X \vdash \sim S\ (\text{pp})}{X,S \vdash \sim S}}{X,S \vdash \bot} \qquad \dfrac{X,Q \vdash Q\ (\text{bd}) \qquad \dfrac{X \vdash \sim Q\ (\text{pp})}{X,Q \vdash \sim Q}}{X,Q \vdash \bot} \qquad X \vdash Q \vee S\ (\text{pp})}{X \vdash \bot}$$

Thus $X \vdash \bot$. But we know that not($X \vdash \bot$). Hence by *reductio* proof $R(Q \vee S) = \text{T}$. We also know by the induction hypothesis that $R(Q) = \text{T}$ iff $Q \in X$, and $R(S) = \text{T}$ iff $S \in X$. Now $R(Q \vee S) = \text{T}$, iff [by definition of R] $R(Q) = \text{T}$ or $R(S) = \text{T}$, iff [by induction hypothesis] $Q \in X$ or $S \in X$, iff [by closure of X under $\vdash$] $X \vdash Q$ or $X \vdash S$, iff [by what is shown above] $X \vdash (Q \vee S)$ iff [by closure] $(Q \vee S) \in X$.

Case III: P is some conjunction, say $Q \wedge S$. Now $R(Q \wedge S) = \text{T}$ iff [by definition of R] $R(Q) = \text{T}$ and $R(S) = \text{T}$, iff [by induction hypothesis] $Q \in X$ and $S \in X$, iff [by closure] $X \vdash Q$ and $X \vdash S$, iff [by $\wedge$-introduction and $\wedge$-elimination] $X \vdash (Q \wedge S)$ iff [by closure] $(Q \wedge S) \in X$.

Case IV: P is some conditional, say $Q \rightarrow S$. We know by $\rightarrow$-introduction that if $X \vdash S$ then $X \vdash (Q \rightarrow S)$. We also know by an exercise that if $X \vdash \sim Q$, then $X \vdash (Q \rightarrow S)$. Hence if either $X \vdash \sim Q$ or $X \vdash S$ then $X \vdash (Q \rightarrow S)$. The converse also holds, on the assumption that X is maximally consistent, for assume that X is maximally consistent and that $X \vdash (Q \rightarrow S)$. Assume also that neither $X \vdash \sim Q$ nor $X \vdash S$. Then $\sim Q \notin X$ and $S \notin X$. Hence $X \vdash \sim S$ and $X \vdash S$. But then $X \vdash \perp$, contradicting our assumption that X is consistent. Now, $R(Q \rightarrow S) = \text{T}$ iff, [by definition of R] $R(Q) = \text{F}$ or $R(S) = \text{T}$, iff [by maximality] $\sim Q \in X$ or $S \in X$, iff [by closure] $X \vdash \sim Q$ or $X \vdash S$, iff [by what was just shown] $X \vdash (Q \rightarrow S)$, iff [by closure] $(Q \rightarrow S) \in X$. End of Proof.

THEOREM. *Soundness and Completeness.* For any $X \subseteq \text{Sen}$ and any P in Sen, $X \vdash P$ iff $X \vDash P$.

Proof. The 'if' part has already been proven in the soundness theorem. For the completeness part assume $X \vDash P$. Then by a previous metatheorem $X \cup \{\sim P\}$ is unsatisfiable in the sense that there is no R in $[R]$ that assigns T both to all members of X and to $\sim P$. Moreover, $X \cup \{\sim P\}$ is inconsistent, for suppose it is not. Then by the maximalization theorem we know that there is some maximally consistent set X' such that $X \cup \{\sim P\} \subseteq X'$. Then by the satisfiability theorem X' is satisfiable in the sense that there is some R in $[R]$ that assigns T to all elements of X' including those in $X \cup \{\sim P\}$. But then $X \cup \{\sim P\}$ is satisfiable, which contradicts what has already been shown. Hence $X \cup \{\sim P\}$ is inconsistent, i.e., $X \cup \{\sim P\} \vdash \perp$. But then by an earlier metatheorem, $X \vdash P$, and therefore $X \vdash P$. End of Proof.

5.2 CLASSICAL FIRST-ORDER LOGIC

5.2.1 Quantificational Syntax

In this section we augment the syntax, semantics, and proof theory of propositional logic to include formal versions of the English expressions 'all' and 'some', in what is called *quantificational*, *predicate*, or *first-order logic*. The theory is the core of standard formal logic, and it is this orthodox system that is the basis of newer attempts to match the syntax of natural language more closely. The language builds upon the relational syntax for simple sentences (defined in Chapter 4) by adding to it the formation rules for propositional logic and a new rule introducing a variable binding quantifier. We used an intuitively adequate but rather imprecise version of this language in Chapter 1 and in the metatheory of subsequent chapters. Now we define the syntax more carefully. We use the previously defined formation functions f_{BS}, $f_{\sim}$, $f_{\wedge}$, $f_{\vee}$, $f_{\rightarrow}$, and a new rule generating universally quantified sentences:

$$f_{\forall} = \{\langle x, y, z\rangle \mid z = (^\frown\forall^\frown x^\frown)^\frown y\}.$$

With these rules we may define a syntax. We stipulate a basic lexicon of names, variables, and predicates (of all degrees) and build up sentences from these.

DEFINITION: A *quantificational* or *first-order*[10] syntax, briefly Syn-QL, consists of various elements which we group into the structure ⟨Sen, {PN, Vb, Pd}, Fm⟩ in which Sen is an inductive set constructed from basic elements from the sets of basic elements PN, Vb, and Pd by the construction rules in Fm as follows: We define Fm to be the set $(f_{BS}, f_{\sim}, f_{\wedge}, f_{\vee}, f_{\rightarrow}, f_{\forall}\}$, and

(1) $PN = \{a_1, \ldots, a_n, \ldots\}$ (the set of *proper names* or *constants*).
(2) $Vb = \{x_1, \ldots, x_n, \ldots\}$ (the set of *variables*).
(3) We define the set Tm (of *terms*) to be $PN \cup Vb$.
(4) $Pd = P^1 \cup P^2 \cup \cdots \cup P^n \cup \cdots$, where each P^i is $\{P^i_1, \ldots, P^i_n, \ldots\}$ (the set of *predicates of degree i*).
(5) We define the set BS (of *basic sentences*) as the set containing the results of concatenating n terms behind a predicate of degree n:

$$BS = \{z \mid \text{for some } y_1, \ldots, y_n \text{ and } x, y_1, \ldots, y_n \text{ are all in Tm}, \; x \in P^n, \text{ and } z = f_{BS}(x, y_1, \ldots, y_n)\}.$$

(6) The set Sen (of *sentences*) is defined inductively:
  (a) $BS \subseteq Sen$;
  (b) if P and Q are in Sen, and $v \in Vb$, then $f_{\sim}(P)$, $f_{\wedge}(P, Q)$, $f_{\vee}(P, Q)$, $f_{\rightarrow}(P, Q)$, and $f_{\forall}(v, P)$ are in Sen:
  (c) nothing else is in Sen.

We say v is *free* in P iff there is no part $(\forall v)Q$ of P.

5.2.2 Semantics: The Substitutional Interpretation

The notion of a possible world for this syntax may be understood, as in earlier languages, as a function that assigns a referent to each expression (to proper names, variables, predicates, and sentences). Names and variables will stand for things, predicates of degree n for n-place relations (sets of n-tuples),

[10] The language is called *first-order* to distinguish it from languages, which we will not study in this book, that make use of a hierarchy of quantifiers, each of some order n, that quantify over a hierarchy of domains. Quantifiers of the first-order quantify over individuals, those of the second-order quantify over sets and relations of individuals, and in general those of order $n + 1$ quantity over sets of those objects on level n. Second-order logic, for example, has in addition to the quantifiers we shall study that quantify over individuals a second sort of quantifier that quantifies over sets. The metatheoretic properties of higher order logics prove them to be less tractable than first-order logic. They are, for example, incomplete.

and sentences for truth-values. A variable may be understood as the formal equivalent of the natural language pronouns, like 'it'. If its occurrence is free, its referent is fixed by context like a pronoun, but if it is connected with a quantifier term like 'all', the variable refers to everything in a sense we shall spell out. It is traditional in quantification theory to break up the definition of a reference relation into stages. First, referents of the lexicon (proper names, variables, and predicates) are defined in a concept called a 'model' or 'structure'. Then in a second stage, the referents of sentences are defined by appeal to the model and a series of semantic rules. These rules are functions on referents, and there is one such semantic rule paired with each formation operation in the syntax. Given an expression formed from a formation rule, the corresponding semantic rule takes the referents of the expression's parts as arguments and yields the referent of the expression as a whole as value. In defining the referents of the lexicon, we shall talk about the particular set of things or individuals in the world that are 'picked out' by names and among which relational predicates apply. This set of objects is intended to constitute the set of existing individuals, in that it is to this set that we refer in the semantic rule interpreting the quantifier 'all'. This is the class of objects that counts as 'everything' in a given world. Since the reference relation is defined relative to such a domain we make the domain part of the initial notion of possible world.

DEFINITION: A *model* or *structure* for a quantificational syntax Syn-QL is any $\langle D, R\rangle$ such that

(1) D (the *domain of discourse*) is a nonempty set,

(2) R is a function on $\mathrm{Tm} \cup P$ and

  (a) for any t, if $t \in \mathrm{Tm}$, then $R(t) \in D$,

  (b) for any G, if $G \in P^n$, then $R(G) \subseteq D^n$.

Here D^n is the set of all n-tuples of elements of D, and $R(G) \subseteq D^n$ is the set theoretic way to state that the referent $R(G)$ of the n-place predicate G is an n-place relation on members of D. Thus, given the definition above, terms refer to 'things' in D and predicates to relations among elements in D.

The simplest way to explain the meaning of a universally quantified sentence is the method we used in Chapter 1, which was also exploited by Ockham as discussed in Chapter 4. There we translated 'all' statements into long conjunctions. In order to state this translation more rigorously here, we need to define what it would be to replace a variable by a name. We then translate a universally quantified sentence by the conjunction of all sentences obtained by dropping the quantifier and replacing the variable by a name. Below we define the notation $[P]^x_y$, which is the name for the new expression obtained from P by replacing the free variable y with the free variable x.

DEFINITION: For any sentence P and any terms x and y that are free in P, the result of replacing term y by term x in P, briefly $[P]^x_y$, is defined recursively:[11]

(1) if P is some basic sentence $P^n t_1, \ldots, t_n$, then
  (a) if y is some t_i among $t_1, \ldots, t_n$, then
    $[P]^x_y = P^n t_1, \ldots, t_{i-1}, x, t_{i+1}, \ldots, t_n$,
  (b) if y is not among $t_1, \ldots, t_n$, then $[P]^x_y = P$,

(2) (a) if P is some $\sim Q$ then $[P]^x_y = \sim[Q]^x_y$,
  (b) if P is some $(Q \wedge S)$, then $[P]^x_y = ([Q]^x_y \wedge [S]^x_y)$,
  (c) if P is some $(Q \vee S)$, then $[P]^x_y = ([Q]^x_y \vee [S]^x_y)$,
  (d) if P is some $(Q \rightarrow S)$, then $[P]^x_y = ([Q]^x_y \rightarrow [S]^x_y)$,
  (e) if P is some $(\forall v)Q$, then $[P]^x_y = (\forall v)[Q]^x_y$.

[Note that in (e) neither x nor y is v, for if so they would not be free in P.] In other words $[P]^x_y$ is made by replacing y by x in basic parts and then constructing a whole in the same manner that P is constructed.

The intuitive translation of the universally quantified sentence $(\forall v)P$ may now be written in this notation. Let $\{a, b, c, \ldots, n, \ldots\}$ be the set of all proper names. Then $(\forall v)P$ means that the following long conjunction is true. Here each conjunct is made by dropping the quantifier and replacing the variable by a proper name:

$$[P]^a_v \wedge [P]^b_v \wedge [P]^c_v \wedge \cdots \wedge [P]^n_v \wedge \cdots$$

What is nice about the translation is that we could then explain when $(\forall x)P$ is true in terms of semantic concepts already well understood, namely the rule for subject–predicate sentences and the truth-table for conjunction. But there are at least two important problems with this idea. First, no conjunction is infinitely long: given the rules of grammar, it is possible to show that any conjunction has only finitely many conjuncts. What we need is a way to say the same thing but without requiring that conjunctions be infinite. The following definition of sentence referent does just that. It says $(\forall v)P$ is T in w iff all its substitution instances are T in w.[12]

DEFINITION: The *substitutional extension* of a model $\langle D, R\rangle$ is any function $R+$ such that $D(R) = \text{Tm} \cup P \cup \text{Sen}$, $R \subseteq R+$, and for all P in Sen,

[11] To say that this idea is defined 'recursively' means in our earlier terminology that a relation F, in this case of 4-tuples, is being defined inductively. The definition thus defines what 4-tuples $\langle P, x, y, Q\rangle$ belong to the set F, where P, x, and y are the arguments for F and Q the value; i.e., Q is the result of substituting x for y in P. It should be clear from the definition that for any P, x, and y the result Q is unique, and thus that the relation F is a function. Hence whenever $\langle P, x, y, Q\rangle \in F$ we may write $F(P, x, y) = Q$. But instead of defining F inductively and then using the notation '$F(P, x, y)$', we use the more suggestive and traditional notation $[P]^x_y$, which as defined is just another way to write $F(P, x, y)$.

[12] For early statements of the substitutional interpretation see Rudolf Carnap, *Introduction to Semantics* (1942), and *Meaning and Necessity* (1947).

(1) if P is atomic, say $P^n t_1, \ldots, t_n$, then
$R+(P) = g_{BS}(R(P), R(t_1), \ldots, R(t_n))$; i.e.,
$R+(P) = T$ if $\langle R(t_1), \ldots, R(t_n)\rangle \in R(P)$, and $R+(P) = F$ otherwise;

(2) if P is a negation, say $\sim Q$, then $R+(P) = g_{\sim}(R(Q))$; i.e.,
$R+(P) = T$ if $R(Q) = F$, and
$R+(P) = F$ if $R(Q) = T$;

(3) if P is a conjunction, say $Q \wedge S$, then $R+(P) = g_{\wedge}(R+(Q), R+(S))$; i.e.,
$R+(P) = T$, if $R+(Q) = T$ and $R+(S) = T$, and
$R+(P) = F$, if either $R+(Q) = F$ or $R+(S) = F$;

(4) if P is a disjunction, say $Q \vee S$, then $R+(P) = g_{\vee}(R+(Q), R+(S))$; i.e.,
$R+(P) = T$, if either $R+(Q) = T$ or $R+(S) = T$, and
$R+(P) = F$, if both $R+(Q) = F$ and $R+(S) = F$;

(5) if P is a conditional, say $Q \to S$, then $R+(P) = g_{\to}(R+(Q), R+(S))$; i.e.,
$R+(P) = T$, if either $R+(Q) = F$ or $R+(S) = T$, and
$R+(P) = F$, if both $R+(Q) = T$ and $R+(S) = F$;

(6) if P is a universally quantified sentence, say $(\forall v)Q$, then
$R+(P) = T$ iff (for all c, if $c \in$ PN then $R+([Q]^c_v) = T$).

Clause (6) is the only novel part of the definition, and it clearly captures the intention of making a universal sentence true only when all its substitution instances are true. We could add another rule to the syntax making an *existential* quantified sentence $(\exists v)P$ from a variable v and a sentence P and another semantic rule interpreting it:

(7) If P is an existentially quantified sentence, say $(\exists v)Q$, then $R+(P) = T$ iff (for some c, $c \in$ PN and $R+([Q]^c_v) = T$).

We may, however, accomplish the same thing by introducing $(\exists v)P$ by definition in terms of its equivalent form which we met in Chapter 1:

DEFINITION: Any occurrence of $(\exists v)P$ is an abbreviation for $\sim(\forall v) \sim P$.

☐ **EXERCISE**

1. Explain how to set up an inductive proof to show that any sentence in Syn-QL consists of only a finite number of parts.
2. Given the definition of $(\exists v)P$, show that clause (7) follows as a theorem from the definition of a substitutional extension, clause (6). That is, show that the definition and clause (6) together imply that $R+((\exists v)Q) = T$ iff (for some c, $c \in$ PN and $R+([Q]^c_v) = T$).

We group the set of all substitutional extensions of any model of Syn-QL into the set $[R+]$ of substitutional 'worlds', and identify substitutional language LSub as any $\langle$Syn-QL, $[R+]\rangle$. Validity has the usual definition. Likewise, we retain the usual definition of a function satisfying a set.

DEFINITION: A function R *satisfies* a set X if R assigns T to every member of X.

DEFINITION: $X \vDash_{\text{LSub}} P$ iff, for all $R \in [R+]$, if $R+$ satisfies X, then $R+(P) =$ T.

The substitution interpretation just given is a straightforward application of an intuitive idea, and for most applications it well captures the use of 'all' and 'some'. However, there are important contexts in mathematics and logic in which it is inadequate and because of these contexts, the standard account of the quantifier must be made a bit more complex. The inadequacy lies in the fact that the definition assumes that we have terms for everything we want to talk about. One might think that surely any quantificational syntax has enough terms to talk about any world because, as it is defined, the set Tm has an infinite number of members. This is true, but they may all stand for the same thing in a given world, and the anomalous situation may occur in which everything named happens to have a certain property but the property actually holds for only very few things in the world.

There are also cases in which the reference relation assigns a different object in the domain to each name (i.e., the function $R|\text{PN}$ that results from R by restricting its domain to PN is 1–1), and in which PN and D are countably infinite, yet not everything is named.

□ EXERCISES

1. Let H be a predicate of degree 1 and define a world $\langle D, R\rangle$ such that its domain $D = \{0, 1, 2, 3, \ldots\}$ is the set of natural numbers and there is a one-place predicate, say H, that applies to only the number 1. That is, we require that $R(H) = \{1\}$. Moreover, we also require that all proper names stand for the same thing and that this thing be the number 1. That is, we stipulate that for all $c \in \text{PN}$, $R(c) = 1$. In all other ways let $R+$ meet the conditions for membership in $[R+]$. Show that $R+((\forall x)Hx) = \text{T}$ yet $R(H) \neq D$.
2. We change the previous exercise slightly. We retain the domain $D = \{0, 1, 2, 3, \ldots\}$. But let the predicate H stand for the set of even numbers: $R(H) = \{y|\text{for some } z, y = 2z\}$. Let us set up the assignment of referents to constants in such a way that they all stand for even numbers. For example, let us require that for any constant c_i in PN that $R(c_i) = 2i$. Show that $R+((\forall x)Hx) = \text{T}$, yet not all d in D are even.

One might think that the problem is that we still do not have enough terms, and that we might always in principle add more terms to a world so that everything has a name. In doing so under the substitutional interpretation, one must be careful. Introducing new terms while leaving all the referents of old terms and predicates unchanged can by itself change some sentences from true to false.

☐ **EXERCISE**

Let $L = \langle \text{Sen}, \{\text{PN}, \text{Vb}, \text{Pd}\}, \text{Fm}\rangle$ and $L' = \langle \text{Sen}', \{\text{PN}', \text{Vb}, \text{Pd}\}, \text{Fm}\rangle$ be substitutional languages such that PN is a proper subset of PN′, i.e., $\text{PN} \subseteq \text{PN}'$ but there is some c' in PN′ that is not in PN. Then $\text{Tm} \subseteq \text{Tm}'$, $\text{BS} \subseteq \text{BS}'$, $\text{Sen} \subseteq \text{Sen}'$, and L' is like L except that it contains some new terms. We construct a world $\langle D, R\rangle$ as follows. Let $D = \{0, 1, 2, 3, \ldots\}$ be the set of natural numbers; let us define R so that R assigns each c in PN to some even number. In particular let us require that if $c_n \in \text{PN}$, then $R(c_n) = 2n$. Now let us require that R interpret some one-place predicate, say H, as referring to the set of even numbers; i.e., let $H \in P^1$ and let $R(H)$ be $\{y \mid y \in D \text{ and for some } n, y = 2n\}$. Show first that $R+((\forall x)Hx) = \text{T}$. Now let us define a new model on the same domain. Let R' of $\langle \text{D}, \text{R}'\rangle$ be just like R except that it gives referents to the new constants in $\text{PN}' - \text{PN}$ and assigns at least some of them to odd numbers. That is, if $c \in \text{PN}$, $R'(c) = R(c)$. We also stipulate that R' retain the same interpretations of the predicates and variables. That is, if $G \in P^i$, $R'(G) = R(G)$, and for any $v \in \text{Vb}$, $R'(v) = R(v)$. Further, for some $c \in \text{PN}' - \text{PN}$, let $R'(c)$ be outside $R'(H)$. For example, let $R(c)$ be 3. Show $R'+((\forall x)Hx) = \text{F}$.

There are even domains in which we could not in principle name all the elements. It is possible that the set PN, even if infinite, could not be big enough to name everything in every domain D. The reason is that the set PN, as defined, is what is called *denumerably* or *countably* infinite; i.e., there is a 1–1 function from PN onto the natural numbers $\{0, 1, 2, 3, \ldots\}$, as the subscripts on elements of PN are designed to show. But it is possible to show in set theory that some sets are bigger than countably infinite. We need some definitions. The ideas are due to Cantor.[13]

DEFINITION: A is *equipollent* to B (briefly $A \simeq B$) iff there is a 1–1 function from A onto B (called a *1–1 correspondence* from A to B).
DEFINITION: $A < B$ iff $A \subseteq B$ but not $A \simeq B$.
DEFINITION: The set A is *countable* or *denumerable* iff there is a 1–1 correspondence from A to the set $\{0, 1, 2, 3, \ldots\}$ of natural numbers.

Cantor showed that the set of all subsets of a set A, what we call the power set $P(A)$, is larger than A, even if A is infinite.

THEOREM. $A < P(A)$.

[13] See the references to set theory in Chapter 1.

Proof. Let $f(A \xrightarrow[1-1]{\text{onto}} P(A))$. Consider $B = \{x | x \in A \wedge x \notin f(x)\}$. Clearly B is in $P(A)$, hence for some y in A, $f(y) = B$. But if $y \in f(y)$, then $y \in B$, and $y \notin f(y)$ by definition of B. Conversely, if $y \notin f(y)$ then $y \in B$ and $y \in f(y)$. Hence $y \in f(y) \leftrightarrow y \notin f(y)$, which is absurd. Hence there is no such f, and $A \notin P(A)$. But clearly $A \subseteq P(A)$. Hence $A < P(A)$. End of Proof.

Let ω be the set $\{0, 1, 2, \ldots\}$ of natural numbers. Consider the following series of sets:

$$\omega,\ P(\omega),\ P(P(\omega)),\ P(P(P(\omega))),\ \ldots$$

Each of these sets is infinite, and each is larger than the one before. There are not enough terms in PN to name everything in $P(\omega)$, not to mention the larger sets, so a substitutional language is inadequate for generalizations about such transfinite sets. Among the transfinite sets is the set of real numbers, a class important to standard mathematics and its application in natural sciences such as physics. Thus, the substitutional interpretation appears unequal to the task of explaining the object language used in science. Since much of the motivation for formally defined languages among philosophers, especially early in this century, lay in their use in stating scientific theories, a more powerful interpretation capable of scientific and mathematical uses was developed.

5.2.3 Semantics: The Referential Interpretation

The stronger interpretation explains the variable of a quantified sentence as standing directly for everything in the world without the intermediate step of picking out things in the world by means of taking them as the referents of the language's many terms. Let P be an open sentence containing the variable x. This x functions, in this view, as a pronoun that can refer to different things depending on the context. Imagine evaluating P relative to a world $\langle D, R\rangle$. We can, if we like, alter the referent of x so many times that at one time or another it will have referred to each element of the domain. The idea is that if the sentence P is true in any such context, then its universal quantification $(\forall x)P$ is true in $\langle D, R\rangle$. Intuitively, to say $(\forall x)P$ is simply to say that the sentence P containing x is true, no matter what x stands for.

Given the definition of a model, R assigns a value to the free variable x, as it does to all the variables. Thus, each time we change the referent of x to check the truth-value of P, we must also slightly change R. We keep R the same except for letting x stand for a new object in D. If we make up a relation R' just like R except that it is allowed to assign a new value to x, we call R' an *x-variant* of R. We may then state the new idea briefly: $(\forall x)P$ is true in $\langle D, R\rangle$ iff P is true at all worlds $\langle D, R'\rangle$ such that R' is an x-variant of R. Again in the semantic definition below, all that is new is the interpretation of the quantifier.[14]

DEFINITION: The *referential extension* of a model $\langle D, R\rangle$ is any function $R*$ such that Domain($R*$) = Tm $\cup$ Pd $\cup$ Sen, $R \subseteq R*$, and for any P, if $P \in$ Sen, then (1) through (5) are as in the definition of substitutional extension replacing $R+$ by $R*$.

(6) If P is a universally quantified sentence, say $(\forall v)Q$, then $R*(P) = \text{T}$ iff for any $d \in D$, $R[^d_v] * (Q) = \text{T}$.

DEFINITION: $R[^d_v]*$, called *the variant of* $R*$ *assigning* d *to* v, is defined as follows. First we define $R[^d_v]$ to be the function like R except that it assigns d to v:

$$R[^d_v] = ((R - \{\langle v, R(v)\rangle\}) \cup \{\langle v, d\rangle\}).$$

Then we see that $R[^d_v]*$ is well defined. It is, namely, the referential extension of $R[^d_v]$. Collapsing these steps, $R[^d_v]*$ may be defined in one line as

$$((R - \{\langle v, R(v)\rangle\}) \cup \{\langle v, d\rangle\})*.$$

Then, clause (6) may be stated in a single line:

(6′) if P is $(\forall v)Q$, then
$R*(P) = \text{T}$ iff for any $d \in D$, $((R - \{\langle v, R(v)\rangle\}) \cup \{\langle v, d\rangle\})*(\text{Q}) = \text{T}$.

It follows from this definition that $R[^d_v]$ is like R except that it assigns d to v, and its referential extension $R[^d_v]*$ assigns referents to molecular expressions as determined by its assignment of referents to basic expressions and the rules (1)–(6). Thus, $R[^d_v]*$ is as like $R*$ as possible, compatible with the fact that it assigns d to v and meets the defining conditions for being a referential extension. Note that there are as many v-variants as there are members of D: for each element d of D there is a distinct $R[^d_v]*$ that pairs v with d. For each element d in the domain D there must be one v-variant assigning v to d.

Here the truth conditions for $(\forall v)P$ do not depend on the set Tm, either on what the elements of Tm happen to refer to or on how many terms there are. Rather, for the condition P to hold universally for entities in $\langle D, R\rangle$, all elements of D, no matter how many, must be such that the condition P holds for them. Again we can define a referential language LRef as any $\langle$Syn-QL, $[R*]\rangle$ such that Syn-QL is a quantificational syntax and $[R*]$ is the set of all referential extensions for all models of Syn-QL. As before, $X \vDash_{\text{LRef}} P$ iff for all $R* \in [R*]$, if $R*$ satisfies X then $R*(P) = \text{T}$.

Before turning to the proof theory for the quantifier there are three semantic metatheorems, of some interest in themselves, that must be proven as prerequisites to the utimate completeness proof.

[14] The referential interpretation is due to Tarski. See Alfred Tarski, 'The Concept of Truth in Formalized Languages' (1931).

First, unlike substitutional languages, infinitely many new terms may be introduced to a referential language without altering the truth-value of the original sentences. In the following proof we make use of the notion of the restriction $f|A$ of a function f to a subset A of $D(f)$. By $f|A$ we mean

$$\{\langle x_1, \ldots, x_n\rangle | \langle x_1, \ldots, x_n\rangle \in f \text{ and } \langle x_1, \ldots, x_{n-1}\rangle \in A\}.$$

THEOREM. Let Syn-QL = ⟨Sen, {PN, Vb, Pd}, Fm⟩, Syn-QL′ = ⟨Sen′, {PN′, Vb, Pd}, Fm⟩, such that Tm ⊆ Tm′. Then for any $P \in$ Sen, if $\langle D, R\rangle$ is a model for Syn-QL and $\langle D, R'\rangle$ is a model for Syn-QL′ and $R \subseteq R'$, then $R*(P) = \mathrm{T}$ iff $R'*(P) = \mathrm{T}$.

Proof by induction. We prove by induction that the 'if' clause holds for every element in Sen, both atomic and molecular. For the latter we assume that it holds for their immediate parts. Let Syn-QL and Syn-QL′ be as stipulated.

Atomic case. Let P be some atomic $P^n t_1, \ldots, t_n$. Let $\langle D, R\rangle$ be an arbitrary model of Syn-QL, and $\langle D, R'\rangle$ an arbitrary model of Syn-QL′ such that $R \subseteq R'$. Now, $R*(P) = \mathrm{T}$ iff [by definition of $R*$] $\langle R(t_1), \ldots, R(t_n)\rangle \in R(P^n)$ iff [since for all expressions e of Syn-QL, $R(e) = R'(e)$] $\langle R'(t_1), \ldots, R'(t_n)\rangle \in R'(P^n)$ iff [by definition of $R'*$] $R'*(P) = \mathrm{T}$.

Molecular case. Assume the induction hypothesis, namely that for all sentences Q smaller than P the conditional in the theorem holds for Q.[15] There are various cases depending on the syntax of P. Let $\langle D, R\rangle$ be an arbitrary model for Syn-QL, and $\langle D, R'\rangle$ be an arbitrary model for Syn-QL′ such that $R \subseteq R'$.

(1) P is a negation, say $\sim Q$. Now $R*(P) = \mathrm{T}$ iff [by definition of $R*$] $R*(Q) = \mathrm{F}$ iff [by induction hypothesis] $R'*(Q) = \mathrm{F}$ iff [by definition of $R'*$] $R'*(P) = \mathrm{T}$.

(2) P is some $Q \wedge S$.
(3) P is some $Q \vee S$. } As in case (1).
(4) P is some $Q \rightarrow S$.

[15] Strictly speaking in the metatheory of this chapter we make use of a version of inductive argument that is somewhat stronger than that sketched in Chapter 3 and explained more fully in Chapter 6. Instead of assuming that the induction hypothesis hold for all parts of P, we assume that it holds for all sentences that are shorter than P. If a property holds for all basic expressions, and if it holds for expressions of length L only if it holds for expressions of length $L + 1$, then by induction it holds for all expressions. Given the resources of Chapter 6 and the fact that first-order syntax is monotectonic (as there defined), the relevant concept of length may be defined and induction over expressions of length less than a sentence proven. Though not difficult, we shall not discuss the proof in this book. Rather, in Chapter 9 we explain how to reformulate the syntax and semantics of first-order logic so that the expressions used in the semantic analysis of a universally quantified sentence are indeed its syntactic parts. Given this reformulation, induction over parts of a sentence is sufficient for most purposes.

(5) P is some $(\forall v)Q$. Consider $R[^d_v]*$ and $R'[^d_v]*$ for $R*$ and $R'*$. Now $R[^d_v] \subseteq R'[^d_v]$ and thus by the induction hypothesis $R[^d_v]*(Q) = R'[^d_v]*(Q)$ for any Q smaller than P. Since d is arbitrary this holds for any $d \in D$. Now $R*(P) = \mathrm{T}$ iff (for all $d \in D$, $R[^d_v]*(Q) = \mathrm{T}$) iff (for all $d \in D$, $R'[^d_v]*(Q) = \mathrm{T}$) iff $R'(P) = \mathrm{T}$. End of Proof.

One property which holds for both referential and substitutional interpretations is that terms with the same referent may be substituted *salva veritate*, i.e., without changing the truth-value of the whole.

THEOREM. Let x and y be two distinct terms that are either in PN or free in P, let $\langle D, R\rangle$ be a model, and $R(x) = R(y)$. Then $R+(P) = R+([P]^x_y)$ and $R*(P) = R*([P]^x_y)$.

Proof by induction. *Atomic case.* P is some $P^n t_1, \ldots, t_n$. Case I: y is among $t_1, \ldots, t_n$, say $y = t_i$.

$$R+(P) = R*(P) = \mathrm{T} \text{ iff}$$

$$\langle R(t_1), \ldots, R(t_i), \ldots, R(t_n)\rangle \in R(P^n) \text{ iff}$$

$$\langle R(t_1), \ldots, R(y), \ldots, R(t_n)\rangle \in R(P^n) \text{ iff}$$

$$\langle R(t_1), \ldots, R(x), \ldots, R(t_n)\rangle \in R(P^n) \text{ iff } R+([P]^x_y) = R*([P]^x_y) = \mathrm{T}.$$

Case II: y is not among $t_1, \ldots, t_n$. Then $P = [P]^x_y$ and the result is trivial.

Molecular cases. Let the result hold for sentences of length less than P.

(1) P is some $\sim Q$. $R+(P) = \mathrm{T}$ iff $R+(Q) = \mathrm{F}$ iff [by induction hypothesis] $R+([Q]^x_y) = \mathrm{F}$ iff $R+(\sim[Q]^x_y) = \mathrm{T}$ iff [by the definition of substitution]. $R+([\sim Q]^x_y) = \mathrm{T}$. Likewise for $R*$.

(2) P is some $Q \wedge S$.
(3) P is some $Q \vee S$.
(4) P is some $Q \rightarrow S$.
} As in case (1).

(5) P is some $(\forall v)Q$. Consider $R+$ first. Note that

(a) $R+(P) = \mathrm{T}$ iff for all $c \in \mathrm{PN}$, $R+([Q]^c_v) = \mathrm{T}$, and

(b) $R+([P]^x_y) = \mathrm{T}$ iff $R((\forall v)[Q]^x_y) = \mathrm{T}$ iff for all $c \in \mathrm{PN}$, $R+([[Q]^x_y]^c_v) = \mathrm{T}$). Now consider an arbitrary $c \in \mathrm{PN}$. Then $c \neq v$, since $c \in \mathrm{PN}$ and $v \in \mathbf{V}$. Moreover, $x \neq v$ and $y \neq v$ because x and y would then not be free in P. Hence $[[Q]^x_y]^c_v = [[Q]^c_v]^x_y$, and thus

(c) (for all $c \in \mathrm{PN}$, $R+([[Q]^x_y]^c_v) = \mathrm{T}$) iff (for all $c \in \mathrm{PN}$, $R+([[Q]^c_v]^x_y) = \mathrm{T}$). Moreover by the induction hypothesis $R+([[Q]^c_v]^x_y) = R+([Q]^c_v)$ and hence

(d) (for all $c \in \mathrm{PN}$, $R+([[Q]^c_v]^x_y) = \mathrm{T}$) iff (for all $c \in \mathrm{PN}$, $R([Q]^c_v) = \mathrm{T}$). Putting statements (a)–(d) together we get $R+(P) = R+([P]^x_y)$. Now consider $R*$. $R*(P) = \mathrm{T}$ iff (for all $d \in D$, $R[^d_v]*(Q) = \mathrm{T}$) iff (for all $d \in D$, $R[^d_v]*([Q]^x_y) = \mathrm{T}$) [by induction hypothesis] iff $R([P]^x_y) = \mathrm{T}$. End of Proof.

The following result is rather obvious and not very interesting in itself, but we need it later.

THEOREM. Let $v \in \mathrm{Vb}$, v not occur in P, and $\langle D, R\rangle$ be a model. Then $R*(P) = R[^{d}_{v}]*(P)$.

Proof. *Atomic case.* Let $P = P^n t_1, \ldots, t_n$. $R*(P) = \mathrm{T}$ iff $\langle R(t_1), \ldots, R(t_n)\rangle \in R(P)$. $R[^{d}_{v}](P) = \mathrm{T}$ iff $\langle R[^{d}_{v}](t_1), \ldots, R[^{d}_{v}](t_n)\rangle \in R[^{d}_{v}](P^n)$. But since v does not occur in P, $R(t_i) = R[^{d}_{v}](t_i)$, for each i. Hence, $R*(P) = R[^{d}_{v}]*(P)$.

Molecular cases. Let the result hold for all sentences shorter than P.

(1) P is some $\sim Q$. $R*(P) = \mathrm{T}$ iff $R*(Q) = \mathrm{F}$ iff [by induction hypothesis] $R[^{d}_{v}]*(Q) = \mathrm{F}$ iff $R[^{d}_{v}]*(P) = \mathrm{T}$.

(2) P is some $Q \wedge S$.
(3) P is some $Q \vee S$. } As in case (1).
(4) P is some $Q \rightarrow S$.

(5) P is some $(\forall v')Q$. Note $v \neq v'$. We show first $R*(P) = \mathrm{T}$ only if $R[^{d}_{v}]*(P) = \mathrm{T}$. Let $R*(P) = \mathrm{T}$. Moreover suppose $R[^{d}_{v}]*(P) = \mathrm{F}$. By the latter, for some element of D, let's call it d', $R[^{d}_{v}][^{d'}_{v'}]*(Q) = \mathrm{F}$. By the former, for any element of D, including d', $\mathrm{T} = R[^{d'}_{v'}]*(Q) = R[^{d'}_{v'}][^{d}_{v}]*(Q)$ [by induction hypothesis] $= R[^{d}_{v}][^{d'}_{v'}]*(Q) = \mathrm{F}$. Absurd. Now assume $R[^{d}_{v}]*(P) = \mathrm{T}$ but $R*(P) = \mathrm{F}$. By the latter assumption, there is some element of D, call it d', such that $R[^{d'}_{v'}]*(Q) = \mathrm{F}$. By the former for all $d'' \in D$, $R[^{d}_{v}][^{d''}_{v'}]*(Q) = \mathrm{T}$. Hence, $\mathrm{T} = R[^{d}_{v}][^{d'}_{v'}]*(Q) = R[^{d'}_{v'}]*(Q)$ [by induction hypothesis] $= \mathrm{F}$. Absurd. End of Proof.

We now show that in domains that are finite or denumerably infinite, the substitutional and referential interpretations are essentially equivalent. This result shows that for those philosophers who reject set theory with its 'transfinite' sets, there is really no reason for not accepting the substitutional semantics.

THEOREM. If $\langle D, R\rangle$ is a model and $R(\mathrm{PN} \xrightarrow[\text{onto}]{} D)$, then $R+(P) = R*(P)$.

Proof. *Atomic case.* P is some $P^n t_1, \ldots, t_n$. But $R+(P)$ and $R*(P)$ have exactly the same definitions and hence are the same.

Molecular cases. Assume the result for immediate parts of P.

(1) P is some $\sim Q$. $R+(P) = \mathrm{T}$ iff $R+(Q) = \mathrm{F}$ iff $R*(Q)$ [by induction hypothesis] $= \mathrm{F}$ iff $R*(P) = \mathrm{T}$.

(2) P is some $Q \wedge S$.
(3) P is some $Q \vee S$. } As in case (1).
(4) P is some $Q \rightarrow S$.

(5) P is some $(\forall v)Q$.

Case I: Assume $R+(P) = \mathrm{T}$, but $R*(P) = \mathrm{F}$. By the former for all $c \in \mathrm{PN}$, $R+([Q]^{c}_{v}) = \mathrm{T}$, and by the latter there is some element of D, call it d, such that

$R[^d_v]*(Q) = \mathrm{F}$. Now let c' be that element in PN such that $R(c') = d$. Such a c' exists because $R(\mathrm{PN} \xrightarrow[\text{onto}]{} D)$. Then by universal instantiation, $R+([Q]^{c'}_{v'}) = \mathrm{T}$. Observe that v does not occur in $[Q]^{c'}_{v'}$. Hence, $\mathrm{T} = R+([Q]^{c'}_v) = R*([Q]^{c'}_v)$ [by induction hypothesis] $= R[^d_v]*([Q]^{c'}_v)$ [by an earlier theorem and the fact that v does not occur in $[Q]^{c'}_v$] $= R[^d_v]*(Q)$ [by an earlier theorem] $= \mathrm{F}$, which is absurd.

Case II: For the converse, assume $R*(P) = \mathrm{T}$ but $R+(P) = \mathrm{F}$. By the former for all $d \in D$, $R[^d_v]*(Q) = \mathrm{T}$. By the latter for a given element of PN, call it c', $R+([Q]^{c'}_v) = \mathrm{F}$. Let $R(c')$ be called d'. Hence by instantiation $R[^{d'}_v]*(Q) = \mathrm{T}$. Again v does not occur in $[Q]^{c'}_v$. Hence, $\mathrm{T} = R[^{d'}_v]*(Q) = R[^{d'}_v]*([Q]^{c'}_v)$ [by an earlier theorem] $= R*([Q]^{c'}_v)$ [by the fact that v does not occur and an earlier result] $= R+([Q]^{c'}_v)$ [by induction hypothesis] $= \mathrm{F}$. End of Proof.

☐ **EXERCISE**

In each of the previous four inductive proofs fill out the details of clause (4) for the conditional.

5.2.4 Natural Deduction Proof Theory

The proof theory for quantification that we shall present is an extension of the natural deduction system for propositional logic. Introduction and elimination rules for both the universal quantifiers are added to earlier rules. The definitions of basic deduction, of proof, and of the deducibility relation (i.e., of $X \vdash P$) remain unchanged. We list a separate pair of introduction and elimination rules for the existential quantifier, but given that the existential quantifier is introduced by definition, these rules are really redundant. They are included here for convenience and to show how well the formal statements capture the intuitive ideas of Chapter 1.

DEFINITION: The *natural deduction system for quantificational logic*, briefly NDS-QL, is defined as the inductive system $\langle \vdash, \mathrm{BD}, f_1, \ldots, f_{15} \rangle$ such that

(1) BD, the set of *basic deductions*, is $\{\langle X, P \rangle | P \in X\}$;

(2) $f_1, \ldots, f_{11}$ are as defined in NDS-PL, and $f_{12}, \ldots, f_{15}$ are as defined below;

(3) $\vdash$ is the set inductively defined as the closure of BS under the rules $f_1, \ldots, f_{15}$.

DEFINITION: The *quantificational rules* for natural deduction are the functions $f_{12}, \ldots, f_{15}$ defined as follows. Let v and v' be in Vb and t in Tm, and let both v and t *be free for* v' *in* P in the sense that there is no part $(\forall v')Q$ of P containing v or t.

∀-Introduction (Universal Generalization)

If v is not free in any Q in X, then

$$\frac{X \vdash [P]^{v}_{v'}}{X \vdash (\forall v')P}$$

∀-Elimination (Universal Instantiation)

$$\frac{X \vdash (\forall v')P}{X \vdash [P]^{t}_{v'}}$$

∃-Introduction (Existential Generalization)

$$\frac{X \vdash [P]^{t}_{v'}}{X \vdash (\exists v')P}$$

∃-Elimination (Existential Instantiation)

If v is not free in $(\exists v')P$ and Q, nor in any element of X or Y, then

$$\frac{X \vdash (\exists v')P \quad Y,[P]^{v}_{v'} \vdash Q}{X,Y \vdash Q}$$

The condition on ∀-introduction is the precise rendering of the informal notion that v is 'arbitrary', which we encountered in Chapter 1 and have been using since in a practical way but without a very clear understanding of what we have been doing. The condition on ∃-elimination ensures that v names the individual guaranteed by the existential quantifier in $(\exists v')P$, that nothing else is assumed about v, and that v is not mentioned in the conclusion.

□ EXERCISES

1. Using the syntax of first-order logic and the relation ⊢ of NDS-QL, define the relations on the Square of Opposition from Chapter 4. That is, translate A, E, I, and O sentences into quantificational syntax. Then define in terms of ⊢ what it is for two sentences to be contraries, subcontraries, and contradictories, and for one to 'imply' another. Give natural deduction proof trees in NDS-QL establishing that A, E, I, and O sentences, as translated into first-order syntax, stand in the relations ascribed to them by the Square. For some of the relations you will have to add additional premises making explicit existence assumptions not apparent in the symbolism of the syllogistic.
2. Formulate in first-order logic the valid syllogisms of the first figure and construct natural deduction proof trees in NDS-QL showing that they may be 'reduced' to Barbara and Celarent. That is, for each of the valid syllogisms of the first figure other than Barbara and Celarent, construct a tree with that syllogism as its root and Barbara, Celarent, or basic deductions as its leaves. Show likewise that Bocardo can be deduced from Barbara. Here again you may have to make explicit some existence assumptions left implicit in the symbolism of the syllogistic.

5.2.5 Soundness and Completeness

As in the case of propositional logic, the proof of soundness is a straightforward induction. The basis clause is that every basic deduction is valid, and this follows trivially from the fact that if a set is satisfied, then so is each member of it. The inductive clause establishes that the natural deduction rules preserve validity. If the arguments for any rule are valid, then so are their values.

THEOREM. *Soundness.* If $X \vdash P$ then $X \vDash_{\mathrm{LSub}} P$ and $X \vDash_{\mathrm{LRef}} P$.

Proof. The result follows by induction from the fact that every basic deduction is valid, from the validity-preserving property of the propositional rules, and from the validity-preserving property of the quantifier rules. Since the first two of these facts are proven for the soundness theorem in propositional logic, we need only establish here the last of these, that the quantifier rules preserve validity.

☐ **EXERCISE**

Assume v and t are free for v' in P, and prove

a. if v is not free in X nor $(\forall v')P$ and $X \vDash [P]^{v'}_{v}$, then $X \vDash (\forall v')P$.

b. if $X \vDash [P]^{t}_{v'}$, then $X \vDash (\exists v')P$.

c. if $X \vDash (\forall v')P$, then $X \vDash [P]^{t}_{v'}$.

d. if v is not free in $(\exists v')P$ and Q, nor in any sentences in X or Y, and if both $X \vDash (\exists v')P$ and $Y \cup \{[P]^{v}_{v'}\} \vDash Q$, then $X \cup Y \vDash Q$.

The completeness proof for first-order logic under the referential interpretation is due to Leon Henkin and was previewed in a simplified form in the completeness proof for propositional logic. The main idea of the proof is to transform the problem, by fairly straightforward logical manipulations, into the problem of showing that a consistent set is satisfiable, and then to describe a method for showing that any such set is in fact satisfied in some possible world. As before, this method has two parts. First, every consistent set is shown to be part of a maximally consistent set, and second, every maximally consistent set is shown to be the 'truth set' (set of sentences true) in a referential model.

We retain the previous definition of (syntactic) consistency, namely X is *consistent* iff not($X \vdash \bot$). We must add to the notion of maximally consistent set the idea that a universally quantified sentence should be in such a set if, and only if, all its substitution instances are. That none of the negations of its instances should be in it is required by consistency, and thus it is compatible with consistency that some of its instances are members of the set. That all its instances should be in the set is required by maximality. If some were omitted, there would be some larger consistent set that contained the omissions. The addition of these instances is called *saturation.* It is such a set that we shall use in the completeness proof.

DEFINITION: X is a *saturated maximally consistent* set iff

(1) not $(X \vdash \bot)$,

(2) for all $P \in$ Sen, (either $P \in X$ or $\sim P \in X$), and

(3) for all $(\forall v)P \in$ Sen, $[(\forall v)P \in X$ iff (for all $c \in$ PN, $[P]_v^c \in X)]$.

THEOREM. If X is saturated maximally consistent, then for all $P \in$ Sen, $P \in X$ iff $X \vdash P$.

This theorem is proven as in propositional logic.

THEOREM. *Saturated Maximalization.* If not$(Y \vdash \bot)$ and there are an infinite number of proper names not used in Y, then for some X, $Y \subseteq X$ and X is a maximally saturated set.

Proof. We construct the set $Y*$ as in the case of propositional logic, but with an extra clause in the construction to ensure that the set is saturated. Let $P_1, \ldots, P_n, \ldots$ be the sentences in Sen. We define an inductive set $Y+ = \{Y_0, \ldots, Y_n, A_n, Y_{n+1}, \ldots\}$ such that each element is a subset of its immediate successor in the sequence:

Basis clause. We set Y_0 equal to Y and place it in $Y+$;

Inductive clause. We define a rule for constructing elements of $Y+$ from other elements of $Y+$:

(1) $A_n = Y_n \cup \{(\forall v)P_n\}$, if not$(Y_n,(\forall v)P_n \vdash \bot)$, and
$A_n = Y_n \cup \{[P]_v^c\}$, where $c \in$ PN does not already occur in Y_n, if $Y_n,(\forall v)P_n \vdash \bot$;

(2) $Y_{n+1} = A_n \cup \{P_n\}$, if not$(A_n,P_n \vdash \bot)$, and
$Y_{n+1} = A_n$, if $A_n,P_n \vdash \bot$.

The elements A_n were not present in the series for the proof in the case of propositional logic. We shall see that they are sufficient to ensure saturation. That there are new terms c not present in Y_n is guaranteed by the assumption of the theorem that there are an infinite number of proper names not in Y. Now define $Y*$ as the union of all Y_i, i.e., $Y* = \{P | \text{for some } i, P \in Y_i\}$.

(1) Each Y_i is consistent. Suppose on the contrary that Y_{n+1} is inconsistent. We show that Y_n is inconsistent by an intermediate step of showing first that A_n is inconsistent. Let $Y_{n+1} \vdash \bot$. Now either not$(A_n, P_n \vdash \bot)$ or $A_n, P_n \vdash \bot$. If the former, then $Y_{n+1} = A_n \cup \{P_n\}$ and $Y_{n+1} \vdash \bot$, which is absurd. Hence, $A_n, P_n \vdash \bot$. But then $Y_{n+1} = A_n$ and $A_n \vdash \bot$. Now either not$(Y_n, (\forall v)P_n \vdash \bot)$ or $Y_n, (\forall v)P_n \vdash \bot$. If the former, $A_n = Y_n \cup \{(\forall v)P_n\}$ and thus not$(A_n \vdash \bot)$, which is absurd. Hence the latter is true, $Y_n, (\forall v)P_n \vdash \bot$. Then $A_n = Y_n$ and $Y_n \vdash \bot$. Reasoning in this way we see that if Y_{n+1} is inconsistent, so is $Y_0 = Y$, contrary to our original assumption. Hence every Y_i is consistent.

(2) $Y*$ is consistent. The proof is the same as that of the maximalization theorem for propositional logic.

(3) $Y*$ is maximal. The proof is the same as that of the maximalization theorem for propositional logic.

(4) $Y*$ is saturated. We show $(\forall v)P \in Y*$ iff for all $c \in \text{PN}$, $[P]^c_v \in Y*$. Assume $(\forall v)P \in Y*$. Since $Y*$ is maximal and closed under $\vdash$, $Y* \vdash (\forall v)P$. Hence by $\forall$-elimination, for any $c \in \text{PN}$, $Y* \vdash [P]^c_v$. For the converse let P be P_n, and assume for all $c \in \text{PN}$, $[P]^c_v \in Y*$. We show now that not($Y_n, (\forall v)P_n \vdash \bot$). Suppose $Y_n, (\forall v)P_n \vdash \bot$. Then by definition of A_n, $A_n = Y_n \cup \{\sim[P]^{c'}_v\}$, for some $c' \in \text{PN}$. But then $[\sim P]^{c'}_v \in Y*$ since $A_n \subseteq Y*$. But also $[P]^{c'}_v \in Y*$. Hence $Y*$ is not consistent, which is absurd. Therefore not($Y_n, P_n \vdash \bot$). Thus, by definition of A_n, $A_n = Y_n \cup \{(\forall v)P_n\}$, $(\forall v)P_n \in A_n$, and $A_n \subseteq Y*$. End of Proof.

THEOREM. *Satisfiability.* If X is a saturated maximally consistent set, then there is a model $\langle D, R\rangle$ such that for all $P \in \text{Sen}$, $R*(P) = \text{T}$ iff $P \in X$.

Proof. We construct the model $\langle D, R\rangle$ as follows. The elements of D will be syntactical entities. Let D be the set Tm of terms and let $R(t) = t$. Let $R(P^n_i) = \{\langle t_1, \ldots, t_n\rangle | P^n_i t_1, \ldots, t_n \in X\}$. Thus $\langle D, R\rangle$ is a universe of terms, D^n includes relations that hold among terms, and P^n_i is true conjoined with terms $t_1, \ldots, t_n$ iff the sentence $P^n_i t_1, \ldots, t_n$ is a member of X. Hence $P^n_i t_1, \ldots, t_n$ says in effect that it is in X. We now show in general, for any $P \in \text{Sen}$, $R*(P) = \text{T}$ iff $P \in X$.

Proof by induction. Atomic case. Let P be some $P^n_i t_1, \ldots, t_n$. $R*(P) = \text{T}$ iff $\langle R(t_1), \ldots, R(t_n)\rangle \in R(P^n_i)$ [by definition of $R*$] iff [by definition of R) $P^n_i t_1, \ldots, t_n \in X$.

Molecular case. Let $R*(Q) = \text{T}$ iff $Q \in X$ for all Q shorter than P.

(1) P is some $\sim Q$. $R*(P) = \text{T}$ iff $R*(Q) = \text{F}$ iff [by induction hypothesis] $Q \notin X$ iff [by the fact that X is maximally saturated] $\sim Q \in X$ iff $P \in X$.

(2) P is some $Q \wedge S$. Proof is as in clause (1) above and the satisfiability theorem for propositional logic.

(3) P is some $Q \vee S$. Proof is as in clause (1) above and the satisfiability theorem for propositional logic.

(4) P is some $Q \rightarrow S$. Proof is as in clause (1) above and the satisfiability theorem for propositional logic.

(5) P is some $(\forall v)Q$. Note that Tm is denumerably infinite. Hence referential and substitutional interpretations are equivalent for this model. $R*(P) = \text{T}$ iff $R+(P) = \text{T}$ iff (for all c in PN, $R+([Q]^c_y = \text{T})$ iff (for all c in PN, $R*([Q]^c_v) = \text{T}$) iff [by induction hypothesis] (for all c in PN, $[P]^c_v \in X$) iff [by saturation of X] $(\forall v)P \in X$. End of Proof.

In the next theorem we demonstrate completeness for the referential interpretation and explain why the substitutional interpretation is incomplete for the particular natural deduction rules used in our proof theory.

THEOREM. *Soundness and Completeness.* For any $X \subseteq \text{Sen}$ and any $P \in \text{Sen}$, $X \vdash P$ iff $X \vDash_{\text{LRef}} P$.

Proof. By soundnesss if $X \vdash P$ then $X \vDash_{\text{LRef}} P$. Assume $X \vDash P$. Then there is no $\langle D, R\rangle$ such that $R*({\sim}P) = \text{T}$ and $R*(Q) = \text{T}$, for all $Q \in X$. Moreover $X \cup \{{\sim}P\}$ is inconsistent, for suppose not($X \cup \{{\sim}P) \vdash \bot$). Then since, by an earlier theorem, Syn-QL may always be expanded to some Syn-QL′ with infinitely more constants than Syn-QL and such that there is some R' such that $R \subseteq R'$ and $R'*(P) = R*(P)$ for all P of Syn-QL, we may assume that LRef has an infinite supply of constants not in any sentence in $X \cup \{{\sim}P\}$. (It is this assumption that cannot be met by LSub. The fact that LSub cannot satisfy it is responsible for the result that LSub is sound but not complete for the natural deduction rules given.) Then by the maximalization theorem, there is some saturated maximally consistent set X' such that $X \cup \{{\sim}P\} \subseteq X'$. The proof proceeds just as it does in propositional logic.

One other way the referential interpretation differs from the substitutional is in terms of a special property called finitary semantic entailment or compactness.

DEFINITION: A language L is said to have *finitary semantic entailment* and to be *compact* iff, for any X and P of L,

$$X \vDash P \text{ iff (for some } Y,\ Y \subseteq X,\ Y \text{ is finite, and } Y \vDash P).$$

THEOREM. LRef has finitary semantic entailment.

Proof. Let $X \vDash P$. Then, $X \vdash P$ by completeness, and therefore by the definition of $\vdash$ in terms of $\vdash$, there is some finite subset Y of X such that $Y \vdash P$. Then again by completeness $Y \vDash P$. End of Proof.

THEOREM. LSub does not have finitary semantic entailment.[16]

Thus though simpler and quite intuitive, the substitutional interpretation fails in that it cannot adequately speak about transfinite domains and in that it does not conform to classical proof theory. Matters cannot rest here, however, because of the peculiar fact that in a sense transfinite worlds are reducible to denumerable ones. We state without proof a famous result.

THEOREM. *Löwenheim–Skolem.* A set X of sentences of Syn-QL is satisfiable in some denumerable model of LRef iff it is satisfiable in some nondenumerable model of LRef. More formally, let X be a subset of sentences of Syn-QL. Each of the following holds.

(1) If X is satisfied in a denumerable model, then X is satisfied in a model of any higher cardinality: if there is some model $\langle D, R\rangle$ such that $D \simeq \omega$ and $R*$ satisfies X, then there is a model $\langle D', R'\rangle$ such that $D \leq D'$ and $R'*$ satisfies X.

[16] On the differences between the substitutional and referential interpretations see Saul Kripke, 'Is There a Problem with Substitutional Quantification?' (1976).

(2) If there is a nondenumerable model satisfying X, then there is a denumerable model satisfying X: if there is a model $\langle D', R' \rangle$ such that $\omega \leq D'$ and $R'*$ satisfies X, then there is a model $\langle D, R \rangle$ such that $D \simeq \omega$ and $R*$ satisfies X.

What this theorem says is that there is a cardinality limit on the expressive capacity of first-order logic. In particular, there is nothing that can be said in its syntax with the referential interpretation that if true will distinguish between denumerable and nondenumerable worlds. Given transfinite set theory, however, nondenumerable domains do exist. As we have seen, the substitutional interpretation is inadequate for reasoning logically about them. The referential interpretation captures the right logic, but is expressively limited in the kinds of distinctions it can draw among nondenumerable sets. There are so-called higher order logics, which we will not discuss in this text, which can make these cardinality distinctions.

☐ **EXERCISE**

Prove the metatheorem that LSub does not have finitary semantic entailment. Consider the argument from the set of all substitution instances of a universally quantified sentence to that sentence itself. Clearly in the substitutional interpretation that argument is valid. But deleting any one of the infinite number of premises would render it invalid. This argument is $\{[P]^c_y | c \in \text{PN}\} \vDash (\forall)P$. Show two propositions:

a. The argument is valid in LSub, but
b. if Y is a finite subset of $\{[P]^c_v | c \in \text{PN}\}$, then not($Y \vDash_{\text{LSub}} (\forall v)P$).

6

Inductive Systems and Their Properties

6.1 THE IDEA OF AN INDUCTIVE SYSTEM

Both grammar and proof theory define their key ideas according to a common pattern. Well-formed formulas are defined as the closure of the lexicon under the formation rules. In axiomatic proof theory, theorems are defined as the closure of the axioms under the inference rules, and in natural deduction the set of acceptable deductions is defined as the closure of the set of basic deductions under the introduction and elimination rules. Sets characterized in this way are said to be inductively defined, and discussion of different grammars and proof theories can be greatly simplified by setting forth in a thorough way what an inductive definition is and explaining some of its important consequences. An inductive definition requires, first of all, that some given elements be used as basic building blocks, and we shall allow that there may be a countably infinite number of these. Second, it requires that there be some functions, possibly denumerably many, which are used to build new elements of the set from others already in it. Finally, the inductive set itself is defined as the closure of the basic elements under the operations. The three elements consisting of the inductive set A, the family B of sets of basic elements, and a set F of generating functions constitute a 'structure' or algebra $\langle A, B, F\rangle$ in the sense of Chapter 2.[1]

[1] The theory of inductive sets presented in this chapter is standard and is a fuller statement of ideas presented in Section 2 of John N. Martin, 'Some Formal Properties of Indirect Semantics' (1986). For a fuller account of inductive sets in the context of grammar as done by logicians see Haskell B. Curry, *Foundations of Mathematical Logic* (1963), and for a quite general account of inductive sets adequate to the purposes of mathematics see Yiannis N. Moschovakis, *Elementary Induction on Abstract Structures* (1974).

In the definition of an inductive system below, we make use of some set theoretic notation, which though previously defined, has not been used much. We use $D(f)$ to refer to the *domain* of a function f, defined as the set of all its arguments. We sometimes need to be able to refer not just to the entire domain of a function, but also to the set of objects that may occur at a given rank in the function's argument. If, for example, f is a function from $A \times B \times C$ into D where A, B, and C are different sets, then it is informative to observe that all the objects that occupy the first place in any argument for f are all in A, that those that occupy the second place are all in B, etc. We define a *subdomain* of f to be the set of objects occupying a given rank of one of its arguments.

DEFINITION: By the *ith subdomain* of a function f, briefly $D^i(f)$, we mean the set of all arguments occupying the ith position in any n-tuple in the domain of f:

$$D^i(f) = \{x \mid \text{there exist } y_1, \ldots, y_i, \ldots, y_n \text{ such that } \langle y_1, \ldots, y_i, \ldots, y_n \rangle \text{ is in } D(f) \text{ and } x \text{ is } y_i\}.$$

A set of sets we call a *family*, and we indicate the intersection of all the sets in a family F by $\bigcap F$. That is, $\bigcap F$ is $\{x \mid \text{for any } A \text{ in } F, x \in A\}$. This notation applies even when the family is specified by an abstract, e.g., $\bigcap\{x \mid x \subseteq \mathbf{V}\}$ is the intersection of all sets and is therefore $\varnothing$, and $\bigcap\{x \mid \text{Socrates} = x\}$ is the intersection of all sets containing Socrates and is thus $\{\text{Socrates}\}$. In general, we say that $\bigcap\{x \mid P(x)\}$ is the *least* or *smallest* set such that all its elements have the defining property. The notation permits us then to choose a property of sets, represented by $P(x)$, and then to form the name of the smallest set with that property.

DEFINITION: An *inductive system for* or *on* a set U is any $\langle A, B, F \rangle$ such that

(1) B is a possibly infinite family of subsets of U, each of which is called a *basic set*: B is some $\{B_1, \ldots, B_n, \ldots\}$ such that each B_i is a subset of U;

(2) F is a possibly infinite family of functions on U, each of which is called a *construction operation*: i.e., F is some $\{f_1, \ldots, f_m, \ldots\}$ such that for each f_i, there is an n, such that $f_i(U^n \xrightarrow[\text{into}]{} U)$;

(3) A, called the *inductive set*, is the closure of the basic sets under the construction operations:

$$A = \bigcap\{C \mid \text{(a) for all } B_i \text{ in } B, B_i \subseteq C; \text{ and (b) for all } x_1, \ldots, x_n \text{ in } C, \text{ all } f \text{ in } F, \text{ and all } \langle x_1, \ldots, x_n \rangle \text{ in } D(f), f(x_1, \ldots, x_n) \text{ is in } C\}.$$

In the definition of A, (a) is called the *basis clause* and (b) is the *inductive clause.*

Let us postulate at this point an undefined primitive set of symbols or expressions which we shall call Σ. It is typical of syntax to make this assumption. In all the cases we shall be interested in, the universe of our inductive definitions will be elements or strings of elements in Σ. Moreover, many of the generating functions in F will be definable in terms of the concatenation operation $^\frown$. At various points in proofs about syntax it is legitimate to appeal to the properties of the symbols being concatenated. Very often these properties are self-evident, so self-evident that any attempt to prove them from anything else would be silly. One property of concatenation that is sometimes made explicit is that algebraically it forms what is known as a 'group'. This structure posits the existence of an identity element known as the empty symbol e.[2]

Axiom of Syntax. $\langle \Sigma, {}^\frown, e \rangle$ meets the conditions for being a group with the identity element e: for all elements x, y, and z of Σ:

(1) $(x^\frown y)^\frown z = x^\frown(y^\frown z)$, and
(2) $x^\frown e = e^\frown x = x$.

It is customary in linguistics to refer to the result of concatenating a finite number of symbols as a *string*, and the set of all strings is called $\Sigma*$. Logicians usually refer to strings as *expressions.*

In the special case in which an inductive class has only one set of basic elements, we identify this set with B rather than insisting that B be a family with just one set in it. Likewise if F is small, we shall often merely list its members rather than grouping them into a set.

EXAMPLE 1 The set of natural numbers is inductive. Let $\langle \text{Nn}, \{0\}, \sigma \rangle$ be the inductive system where σ is the successor function: for any x in U, $\sigma(x) = x + 1$. (Here the precise specification of U will depend on the foundational details of the mathematical theory being used to define σ.)

EXAMPLE 2 The set of finite strings of the single stroke symbol '|' is inductive. Let $\langle S, \{|\}, f \rangle$ be the inductive system such that f is a function on the universe $\Sigma*$ of strings defined as follows: for any x in Σ, $f(x) = x^\frown|$. That is, f concatenates a stroke to the right of the string. Unlike the first example,

[2] See Robert Wall, *Introduction to Mathematical Linguistics* (1972). For systematic statements of assumptions about syntax used in logical theory see W. V. O. Quine, 'Syntax', Chapter VII, *Mathematical Logic* (1940); Alonzo Church, Section 7, 'The Logistic Method', *Introduction to Mathematical Logic*, Vol. I (1956); and Haskell B. Curry 'Formal Systems', Chapter II, *Foundations of Mathematical Logic* (1963).

Richard Montague is an exception among logicians to the rule in that he does not require that syntax be constructed from a primitive set of symbols by concatenation. Rather, he abstracts from the specific nature of syntactic entities. His concrete examples of syntaxes, however, are all syntactic in the sense defined here. See Richard Montague, 'Universal Grammar' (1970).

the relevant universe is here explicitly fixed, and for some purposes we may view this structure as capturing all there is to the inductive class of natural numbers.

EXAMPLE 3 The syntax for propositional logic. In this example we take negation and the conditional as 'primitive'. To keep the example simple, we stipulate only a finite number of basic elements. Let Syn-PL be the inductive system $\langle \text{Sen}, B, f_{\sim}, f_{\rightarrow} \rangle$ for the universe $\Sigma*$ such that

(1) B is the finite subset of Σ: $\{P, Q, R, S, T\}$,

(2) $f_{\sim}$ is a one-place function and $f_{\rightarrow}$ a two-place function on $\Sigma*$ defined as follows: for any x, y in $\Sigma*$, $f_{\sim}(x) = \sim{}^\frown x$ and $f_{\rightarrow}(x, y) = ({}^\frown x^\frown \rightarrow {}^\frown y^\frown)$.

Note that in the previous chapter and in those that follow, we follow the more standard practice in logic of assuming that the set of basic elements of Syn-PL is the countably infinite set $\text{BS} = \{P_1, \ldots, P_n, \ldots\}$. We there assume the larger set in order to show that the various properties of the syntax under discussion, like decidability, do not depend on the assumption that it has only a finite number of basic elements.

EXAMPLE 4 The axiom system P of Alonzo Church for propositional logic, discussed in Chapter 5. Let AS_{P}-PL be the inductive system $\langle \text{TH}, \text{AX}, f_{\text{mp}} \rangle$ on the universe Sen of the previous example such that

(1) AX is the set of axioms defined as any member of Sen with one of the following forms:

(a) $(x \rightarrow (y \rightarrow x))$;

(b) $((x \rightarrow (y \rightarrow z)) \rightarrow ((x \rightarrow y) \rightarrow (x \rightarrow z)))$;

(c) $((\sim x \rightarrow \sim y) \rightarrow (y \rightarrow x))$.

[More formally, AX is the family $\{B_1, B_2, B_3\}$ of basic sets such that $B_1 = \{w | \text{for some } x \text{ and } y \text{ in Sen}, w = f_{\rightarrow}(y, f_{\rightarrow}(x, y))\}$, $B_2 = \{w | \text{for some } x \text{ and } y \text{ in Sen}, w = f_{\rightarrow}(f_{\rightarrow}(x, f_{\rightarrow}(y, z)), f_{\rightarrow}(f_{\rightarrow}(x, y), f_{\rightarrow}(x, z)))\}$, and $B_3 = \{w | \text{for some } x \text{ and } y \text{ in Sen}, w = f_{\rightarrow}(f_{\rightarrow}(f_{\sim}(x), f_{\sim}(y)), f_{\rightarrow}(y, x))\}$. Note that each set of axioms is infinite but defined in syntactic terms.]

(2) f_{mp} is a two-place function (called *modus ponens*) that assigns to every pair of sentences of the form x and $(x \rightarrow y)$ the sentence of the form y. [More formally, $f_{\text{mp}} = \{\langle x, z, y \rangle | x \text{ and } z \text{ are in Sen and } f_{\rightarrow}(x, z) = y\}$. Note that here too the definition employs only syntactic terms.]

EXAMPLE 5 The syntax of first-order logic. We redefine the notion of a quantificational syntax Syn-QL given in the last chapter so that it fits the pattern of a general inductive system. Since formation functions must be of a set number of places, we are required to have a distinct formation rule for each n-place basic sentence. Let Syn-QL be $\langle \text{Sen} \cup \text{PN} \cup \text{Vb} \cup \text{Pd}, \{\text{PN}, \text{Vb}, \text{Pd}\}, \text{Fm} \rangle$ where $\text{Fm} = \{f^1_{\text{BS}}, \ldots, f^n_{\text{BS}}, \ldots, f_{\sim}, f_{\rightarrow}, f_{\forall}\}$ such that PN, Vb, and Pd are disjoint sets of expressions and

(1) $\text{PN} = \{a_1, \ldots, a_n, \ldots\}$,

(2) $\text{Vb} = \{x_1, \ldots, x_n, \ldots\}$,

(3) $\text{Tm} = \text{PN} \cup \text{Vb}$,

(4) $\text{Pd} = P^1 \cup \cdots \cup P^n \cup \cdots$, where each $P^i = \{P^i_1, \ldots, P^i_n, \ldots\}$,

(5) for each n, $D(f^n_{\text{BS}}) = (\text{PN} \cup \text{Vb})^n \times P^n$ and $f^n_{\text{BS}}(x_1, \ldots, x_n, y) = y^\frown x_1{}^\frown \cdots {}^\frown x_n$, and $\text{BS} = \{x \mid \text{for some } n, x \text{ is in the range of } f^n_{\text{BS}}\}$,

(6) $\text{BS} \subseteq D(f_\sim)$ and $f_\sim(x) = \sim{}^\frown x$,

(7) $\text{BS}^2 \subseteq D(f_\rightarrow)$ and $f_\rightarrow(x, y) = ({}^\frown x^\frown \rightarrow {}^\frown y^\frown)$,

(8) $D^1(f_\forall) = \text{Vb}$, $\text{BS} \subseteq D^2(f_\forall)$, and $f_\forall(x, y) = ({}^\frown\forall^\frown x^\frown)^\frown y$.

In this example the generation is defined from basic elements of distinct grammatical categories. Moreover, not all of these categories are enlarged by construction. The grammar, for example, does not construct new variables. In the future when referring to inductive systems in which some sets of basic expressions are not subsets of the outputs of the rules, we shall not list the basic expressions as part of the inductive set, though strictly speaking they are included in it. Thus instead of $\langle \text{Sen} \cup \text{PN} \cup \text{Vb} \cup \text{Pd}, \{\text{PN}, \text{Vb}, \text{Pd}\}, \text{Fm}\rangle$, we refer to Syn-QL more perspicuously as $\langle \text{Sen}, \{\text{PN}, \text{Vb}, \text{Pd}\}, \text{Fm}\rangle$.

☐ **EXERCISE**

Add rules to the syntax of the third example for the construction of conjunctions and disjunctions, and state the definition of the expanded inductive system in a formal manner.

6.1.1 Construction Sequences

What is extremely useful about inductive classes is that construction of complex elements from basic ones can be broken down into a series of steps. There are two alternative but essentially equivalent ways in which the breakdown is usually represented in the theory of inductive sets. These are construction sequences and construction trees. Construction sequences are linear representations containing basic elements and elements derived from them by the rules. They terminate with the element being constructed. Linear proofs in axiomatic logic and linear 'derivations' of a terminal string in phrase structure grammar as it is done by linguists are sequences of this sort. Construction trees are branching structures with basic elements as 'leaves', elements on descending nodes which are derived by the rules from the elements on the nodes above them, and the element under construction as the 'root' of the tree. Natural deduction proof trees and grammatical trees in both phrase structure and logical grammars are examples. Both construction sequences and trees are usually 'annotated', i.e., we add information explaining precisely which rule is used at each point in the construction and which arguments the rule is applied to. We begin by defining the abstract notion of construction sequence as a series of elements from the inductive set. We then add a feature capturing the notion of annotation. For this purpose we shall use a function assigning to each line in the series the relevant information.

We wish in general to allow for the same item to be used more than once in a construction, for example, if its use contributes to the construction of collateral branches that culminate in a single item. To achieve this multiple use, we shall consider the steps in a construction to be pairs consisting of a location, viewed as a positive integer, and an item. We first define the more abstract notion of sequence in general and then the particular kind of sequence that is a construction relative to an inductive system.

DEFINITION: We say that a set C is *indexed by a sequence* s iff either

(1) s is a function from a finite subset $\{1, 2, \ldots, n\}$ of the set of positive integers, which we shall call $I+$, onto C (in this case we say that s is a *finite sequence* and refer to s as $\langle s_1, \ldots, s_n \rangle$), or

(2) s is a function from the entire set $I+$ onto C (in this case we say that s is an *infinite sequence* and refer to s as $\langle s_1, \ldots, s_n, \ldots \rangle$).

By this definition a sequence is a set of pairs, each of which consists of a positive integer followed by a member of C. We shall use the usual subscript notation s_i to refer to $s(i)$, the element in C paired in s with the integer i. Occasionally we also wish to refer to the specific pair $\langle i, s(i) \rangle$ in s. When the context of discussion precludes any possibility of confusion, we shall sometimes refer to $\langle i, s(i) \rangle$ also by the notation s_i; however, if the context is ambiguous, we refer to $\langle i, s(i) \rangle$ by $\langle s_i \rangle$.

We now define the particular notion of construction sequence by using the more general idea of sequence just defined.

DEFINITION: Let s be a sequence that indexes some subset of a universe U, let B be a family of subsets of U, let F be a set of functions on U, and let g be a function with domain s. We say that s is a *construction sequence of e relative to* or *on* U, B, and F and that g *analyzes* s iff

(1) the element paired with 1 in s is e, i.e., $s_1 = e$;

(2) for any pair $\langle s_i \rangle$ in s, either

(a) s_i is an element of some B_j in B, and g records the information that s_i comes from this set: for some B_j in B, $s_i \in B_j$ and $g(\langle s_i \rangle) = B_j$, or

(b) s_i is constructed from earlier members of the sequence and g records that information: there are integers $k, \ldots, m$ and a function f in F such that

(i) $i < k, \ldots, i < m$,

(ii) $f(s_k, \ldots, s_m)$ is s_i, and

(iii) $g(\langle s_i \rangle)$ is $\langle f, k, \ldots, m \rangle$.

Usually we shall suppress mention of the universe U unless its properties are relevant to the discussion, and we shall use the shorter form $g(s_i)$ in place of $g(\langle s_i \rangle)$. If the family B contains only one set B_1 of basic elements, we identify B and B_1 and write $g(s_i) = \varnothing$ instead of $g(s_i) = B$.

The generality of this definition allows for construction sequences that would not normally be met in applications of the concept to grammatical constructions or proofs. For example, it is consistent with the definition that one item may be in more than one basic set, that a construction sequence might not terminate in a finite number of steps, that an item occurs at a point in its own generation, and that a single item has more than one construction sequence. We shall discuss these peculiarities in more detail later in order to rule them out. The examples we now give are orderly and do not have these properties.

We adopt the convention of dropping the index numbers from the elements of a short finite sequence if the sequence is short enough for us to see the rank of each element immediately. Thus instead of writing $s = \langle a_1, b_2, c_3, d_4 \rangle$, we suppress the subscripts for legibility and say $s = \langle a, b, c, d \rangle$.

EXAMPLE 1 The series $\langle 5, 4, 3, 2, 1, 0 \rangle$ is a construction sequence for 5 relative to the first example, the inductive system of the natural numbers defined earlier, and its analysis would be as follows:

$$g = \{\langle 5, \sigma, 2 \rangle, \langle 4, \sigma, 3 \rangle, \langle 3, \sigma, 4 \rangle, \langle 2, \sigma, 5 \rangle, \langle 1, \sigma, 6 \rangle, \langle 0, \varnothing \rangle\}.$$

EXAMPLE 2 The series $\langle ||||||, |||||, ||||, |||, ||, | \rangle$ is a construction sequence for the inductive system of iterated strokes, and its analysis is

$$g = \{\langle ||||||, f, 2 \rangle, \langle |||||, f, 3 \rangle, \langle ||||, f, 4 \rangle, \langle |||, f, 5 \rangle, \langle ||, f, 6 \rangle, \langle |, f, \varnothing \rangle\}.$$

EXAMPLE 3 Grammarians typically exhibit the grammatical construction of well-formed expressions by linear derivations which are special cases of construction sequences. A grammatical 'derivation' in the propositional syntax Syn-PL of an earlier example may be illustrated by a generation of the sentence $((\sim P \rightarrow Q) \rightarrow \sim R)$. A common way to display such a derivation is down the page with the analysis to the right:

(7)	P	$\varnothing$
(6)	$\sim P$	$f_{\sim}, 7$
(5)	Q	$\varnothing$
(4)	$(\sim P \rightarrow Q)$	$f_{\rightarrow}, 6, 5$
(3)	R	$\varnothing$
(2)	$\sim R$	$f_{\sim}, 3$
(1)	$((\sim P \rightarrow Q) \rightarrow \sim R)$	$f_{\rightarrow}, 4, 2$

[More formally, the sequence is $\langle((\sim P \rightarrow Q) \rightarrow \sim R), \sim R, R, (\sim P \rightarrow Q), Q, \sim P, P\rangle$, and the analysis function g is

$$\{\langle((\sim P\rightarrow Q)\rightarrow \sim R), f_{\rightarrow}, 4, 2\rangle, \langle \sim R, f_{\sim}, 3\rangle, \langle R, \varnothing\rangle, \langle(\sim P\rightarrow Q), f_{\rightarrow}, 6, 5\rangle, \langle Q, \varnothing\rangle, \langle \sim P, f_{\sim}, 7\rangle, \langle P, \varnothing\rangle\}.]$$

EXAMPLE 4 We now give a traditional proof for $(P \rightarrow P)$ in terms of the inductive system AS_P-PL defined in the earlier example:

(5)	$((P \rightarrow ((P \rightarrow P) \rightarrow P)) \rightarrow ((P \rightarrow (P \rightarrow P)) \rightarrow (P \rightarrow P)))$	axiom schema 2
(4)	$(P \rightarrow ((P \rightarrow P) \rightarrow P))$	axiom schema 1
(3)	$((P \rightarrow (P \rightarrow P)) \rightarrow (P \rightarrow P))$	mp, 4, 5
(2)	$(P \rightarrow (P \rightarrow P))$	axiom schema 1
(1)	$(P \rightarrow P)$	mp, 2, 3

[More formally, the sequence is

$$\langle(P \rightarrow P), (P \rightarrow (P \rightarrow P)), ((P \rightarrow (P \rightarrow P)) \rightarrow (P \rightarrow P)), (P \rightarrow ((P \rightarrow P) \rightarrow P)), ((P \rightarrow ((P \rightarrow P) \rightarrow P) \rightarrow ((P \rightarrow (P \rightarrow P)) \rightarrow (P \rightarrow P)))\rangle.$$

Its analysis is the following function g:

$$\begin{aligned}&\{\langle(P \rightarrow P), f_{\text{mp}}, 2, 3\rangle,\\ &\langle(P \rightarrow (P \rightarrow P)), 1\rangle,\\ &\langle((P \rightarrow (P \rightarrow P)) \rightarrow (P \rightarrow P)), f_{\text{mp}}, 4, 5\rangle,\\ &\langle(P \rightarrow ((P \rightarrow P) \rightarrow P)), 1\rangle,\\ &\langle((P \rightarrow ((P \rightarrow P) \rightarrow P)) \rightarrow ((P \rightarrow (P \rightarrow P)) \rightarrow (P \rightarrow P))), 2\rangle\}.]\end{aligned}$$

□ EXERCISES

1. Give two examples of construction sequences for sentences involving conjunctions and disjunctions from the expanded syntax of the earlier exercise.
2. Provide construction sequences for the following showing that they are members of the set of theorems as defined above:
   a. $(P \rightarrow (Q \rightarrow P))$.
   b. $((P \rightarrow Q) \rightarrow ((R \rightarrow P) \rightarrow (R \rightarrow Q)))$.

6.1.2 Mathematical Induction

Since an inductive system is not defined by a simple abstraction from a defining property, proving that every element in an inductive set has some property requires special argumentation. The form of argument is called *mathematical induction.* (Despite its name, it has nothing to do with varieties of statistical generalization in empirical science.) It consists of showing that all elements have a property if all the basic elements have the property and all the generating functions preserve the possession of the property.[3]

THEOREM. *Induction.* Let $\langle A, B, F\rangle$ be an inductive system on a universe U. Then A $\subseteq$ C if the following two propositions are established:

(1) (*Basis step*) every basic element is in C: for all $B_i \in B$, $B_i \subseteq C$; and

(2) (*Inductive step*) each rule preserves being in C: for all f in F and all arguments $\langle x_1, \ldots, x_n\rangle$ in $D(f)$, if (*induction hypothesis*) $x_1, \ldots, x_n$ are all in C, then $f(x_1, \ldots, x_n)$ is in C.

Proof. The theorem follows directly from the definition of an inductive system. Let $P(y)$ be the property and assume:

(1) for any B_i of B, B_i is a subset of y, and

(2) for any $x_1, \ldots, x_n$ and f in F, $\langle x_1, \ldots, x_n\rangle \in D(f)$ and $x_1, \ldots, x_n \in y$, then $f(x_1, \ldots, x_n) \in y$.

By the definition of inductive system and the assumption that $\langle A, B, F\rangle$ is inductive, it follows that

(3) $x \in A$ iff (for any G, $P(G)$ only if $x \in G$).

Moreover, $P(C)$ holds by assumption. Now let us assume that $x \in A$. Then by clause (3) for any G, $P(G)$ only if $x \in G$. By instantiation, $P(C)$ only if $x \in C$. Since $P(C)$, $x \in C$. Since x is arbitrary, $A \subseteq C$. End of Proof.

6.1.3 Equivalence among Sequences

Just as it does not alter the validity of a proof to list its premises in a different order or to apply one applicable inference rule before another, so too in construction sequences we may construct the same entity by two construc-

[3] The order of analysis here has been from the top down. We first defined the entire inductive system and only then the notion of construction sequence used to manufacture its elements. This order may be reversed and the set defined in terms of its elements. We state the relevant definitions and theorems without proof.

DEFINITION: A *bottom-up inductive system* relative to a universe U is any $\langle A, B, F\rangle$ such that B is a family of subsets of U, f is a set of functions on U of finite degree, and A is

$$\{x \mid \text{for some } s, s \text{ is a finite construction sequence for } x \text{ relative to } B \text{ and } F\}.$$

THEOREM. Every inductive system is a bottom-up inductive system.

It is also possible to show directly that induction holds for a bottom-up inductive set and that these are inductive systems in the original sense.

THEOREM. Let $\langle A, B, F\rangle$ be a bottom-up inductive system. $A \subseteq C$, if both

(1) every B_i of B is a subset of C, and

(2) for any f in F and any $\langle x_1, \ldots, x_n\rangle \in D(f)$,

$$\text{if } x_1, \ldots, x_n \in C, \text{ then } f(x_1, \ldots, x_n) \in C.$$

THEOREM. If $\langle A, B, F\rangle$ is a bottom-up inductive system, then it is an inductive system.

tion sequences that differ only in the order in which the basic elements are listed and the order in which the rules are applied to non-nested parts. We say that two sequences are equivalent when they resemble each other in everything except the order in which earlier members are listed or in the order in which the generation rules are applied to parts that are not nested inside one another.

DEFINITION: A *permutation* is any 1–1 correspondence Π from the set $I+$ of positive integers onto itself.
DEFINITION: Let s and s' be two construction sequences on $\langle A, B, F\rangle$, and let s have analysis g and s' have analysis g'. We say s is *equivalent* to s' iff there is a permutation Π such that for all pairs $\langle s_i\rangle$ in s,

(1) s_i is $s'_{\Pi(i)}$, and
(2) $g(s_i)$ is $g'(s_{\Pi(i)})$.

EXAMPLE The grammatical derivation of the third example above is equivalent to the following:

(7)	R	$\varnothing$
(6)	P	$\varnothing$
(5)	$\sim R$	$f_{\sim}, 7$
(4)	Q	$\varnothing$
(3)	$\sim P$	$f_{\sim}, 6$
(2)	$(\sim P \rightarrow Q)$	$f_{\rightarrow}, 3, 4$
(1)	$((\sim P \rightarrow Q) \rightarrow \sim R)$	$f_{\rightarrow}, 2, 5$

under the permutation Π defined as follows:

$$7 \rightarrow 6$$
$$6 \rightarrow 3$$
$$5 \rightarrow 4$$
$$4 \rightarrow 2$$
$$3 \rightarrow 7$$
$$2 \rightarrow 5$$
$$1 \rightarrow 1$$

☐ **EXERCISE**

Define a sequence equivalent to that of the fourth in Section 6.1.1.

6.2 CONSTRUCTION TREES

6.2.1 Representing Constructions by Trees

A more intuitive way to exhibit constructions is by trees. At the bottom or 'root' node of the tree we write the item to be constructed. The other items from which it is constructed are assigned to progressively higher nodes of the tree in a branching pattern that duplicates the order of construction. The branches of the trees terminate at tips or 'leaves' when a basic expression is reached. Though most of the claims we make about trees need no more than an intuitive understanding of what a tree diagram is, at one or two points we need the more rigorous definition below. Consistent with the customary usage we invert the tree so that its root is the highest element and the leaves are lowest elements.

DEFINITION: By a tree T we shall mean a structure $\langle T, \leq \rangle$ with the following properties:

(1) $\leq$ is a binary relation on elements of T that is reflexive, transitive, and antisymmetric, in which case we call $\leq$ a *partial ordering* on T ($\leq$ is *antisymmetric* iff, $x \leq y$ and $y \leq x$, only if $x = y$);

(2) there is one and only one element of T that is maximal; we name this element $t*$ and call it the *root* (to say of $t*$ that it is *maximal* means that $\forall t(t \in T \rightarrow t \leq t*)$);

(3) for every element t of T, there is a unique branch ending with t, where the notion of branch is defined as follows:

(a) for any x and y in T, we say x is the *immediate predecessor* of y iff
  (i) $x \neq y$,
  (ii) $x \leq y$, and
  (iii) for every z in T, if both $x \leq z$ and $z \leq y$, then either $x = z$ or $y = z$;

(b) by a *branch ending with t* we mean any finite sequence $\langle t_1, \ldots, t_n \rangle$
  (i) $t_1 = t$,
  (ii) $t_n = t*$, and
  (iii) for every t_i in the sequence, t_i is the immediate predecessor of t_{i+1}.

We say that the tree is *finitary* if, and only if, the set T is finite, and that the tree is *finitely branching* if, and only if, the immediate predecessors of any given node are only finite in number. Given these definitions, it is possible for a tree to be finitely branching yet not finitary. Also, it is possible for all branches of a tree to be finite in length, and yet for the tree to be neither finitely branching nor finitary. Relative to a tree, let us call t a *minimal node* or a *leaf* iff it has no immediate predecessors: $\forall t'((t' \in T \wedge t' \leq t) \rightarrow t' = t)$.

A special sort of tree, called a *construction tree*, is used to display a construction of a member of an inductive set. In principle it does not matter what sort of entities we use to make up the tree. The first condition for a construction tree is that an entity to be constructed, let us call it e, is paired with the root $t*$ of the tree. Second, each subsequent node of the tree must be assigned items from the inductive set in a manner that records a construction of e. Consider any node n of the tree with an item i assigned to n, including the case in which n is $t*$, and i is e. If i is a basis element, then n must be a minimal element (a 'leaf') of the tree. If not, then there must be some set $\leq$-immediate predecessors $\{k, \ldots, m\}$ of n, each node of which is occupied by elements which, when taken as arguments for a formation function f, yield i as value. We annotate such a tree by assigning to n the information needed to determine how i was constructed from the items in the immediate predecessors of n. What we need to know is what function is used, and the order of the arguments. Thus, as annotation we need to know the name of a function, say f, and some order of the predecessors of n, let us call this order $\langle k, \ldots, m\rangle$, such that when the items at k through m are fed into f in that order, the value is i.

We have already said that in principle it does not matter what sort of entities we use to make up the trees themselves. These nodes merely serve as points or 'hooks' on which to put the elements from the inductive set. But to make the comparison of construction trees with construction sequences simpler, we shall limit the entities used in construction trees. In particular we shall require that T be itself a subset of the inductive set as indexed by integers. The benefit of doing so is that a construction tree becomes a structure $\langle s, \leq\rangle$ in which s is a sequence of elements from the inductive set. It is then easy to compare s to a construction sequence s'. The two generate the same expression in the same way if s' is s and they have the same annotation. Another way of making this point is that the ordering relation $\leq$ really contributes nothing essential to the analysis of construction. It merely organizes the same information in an intuitively transparent fashion. To any construction sequence we may add an ordering relation that turns it into a tree, and conversely from any tree we may determine a construction sequence.

DEFINITION: Let U be a universe, B a family of subsets of U, F a family of functions on U, and e an element of U. We say that a structure $\langle s, \leq\rangle$ is a *construction tree* for e relative to U, B, and F, and that g *annotates* $\langle s, \leq\rangle$ iff $\langle s, \leq\rangle$ is a tree, g is a function on s, and

(1) there is some subset of U such that s is a sequence (finite or infinite) indexing its members;

(2) for some n, the maximal element of $\langle s, \leq\rangle$ is $\langle s_n\rangle$, and e is s_n;

(3) if $\langle s_i \rangle$ is an arbitrary member of s, then either
 (a) $\langle s_i \rangle$ is a minimal node of $\langle s, \leq \rangle$, and there is some B_j in B such that it contains s_i as an element, and $g(\langle s_i \rangle)$ is B_j; or
 (b) $\langle s_i \rangle$ is not a minimal node of $\langle s, \leq \rangle$, and for some function f of F and some integers $k, \ldots, m$: $f(s_k, \ldots, s_m)$ is s_i, $\langle s_k \rangle, \ldots, \langle s_m \rangle$ each are $\leq$-immediate predecessors of $\langle s_i \rangle$, and $g(\langle s_i \rangle) = \langle f, k, \ldots, m \rangle$.

We usually suppress mention of the universe U unless it is relevant to the issue at hand.

In order to give some examples of construction trees, we lay down some conventions about how to draw graphs of trees on paper. A point representing the maximal element (the root of the tree) appears at the top of the page. Thus mathematicians and linguists usually draw their trees upside down, a convention which is the source of some confusion in that nodes that would be above one another in a right-side-up intuitive drawing are in fact predecessors of that node in the technical representation and accordingly appear beneath it in the graph. A second convention is that the immediate predecessors of a node appear beneath it. Sometimes a node is connected to an immediate predecessor by a line, and then the tree diagram consists of branching lines downward from the root. Linguists usually use this type of diagram to represent grammatical constructions. An alternative convention is to draw a horizontal line beneath a node and then to write in order beneath that line the immediate predecessors of the node above it. Diagrams of this type consist of descending levels of horizontal lines with spaces between sketching out the shape of branches. Such trees are used in proof theory to display the construction or 'proofs' of theorems (we have already used them in their root-downward form), and they are sometimes used by computer scientists to represent grammatical constructions. Either type of diagram may be annotated.

Without the annotation the immediate predecessors of a node fall in no particular order, and in the diagram of an unannotated tree the fact that the diagram places the immediate predecessors in a left to right order on the page does not record a property of the tree itself considered as an abstract object. (In this regard trees as used by logicians and defined in the manner above differ somewhat from trees as defined by linguists; see the exercise below.) The left to right order of the diagram as it appears on paper represents rather some of the information in the annotation of the tree: in a diagram representing an annotated tree, immediate predecessors are written from left to right in the order in which they appear as arguments for the generating function which when applied to them produces the item above the line. (The proof trees used in Chapter 5 conform to this rule but they are there drawn root-downward in deference to ordinary trees.) In a graph diagramming a tree, the function used to produce a node may be represented by writing its name in the vicinity of the instances of its application. (In our earlier proof trees, function names are written to the right of the horizontal lines marking a descent.) The reader is referred to the proof trees of Chapter 5 for examples. Trees capturing essentially the same construction as the contruction sequences exemplified earlier in this chapter are given below.

EXAMPLE A tree representing a grammatical construction.

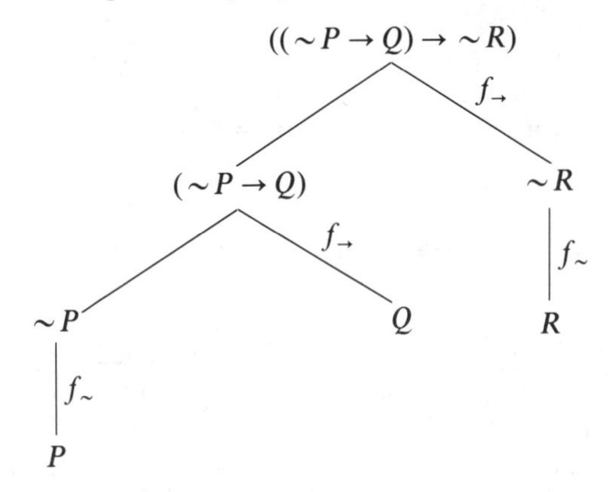

EXAMPLE A root-downward tree representing a proof.

$$\dfrac{(P \to (P \to P))\ [1] \qquad \dfrac{(P \to ((P \to P) \to P))\ [1] \qquad \begin{array}{c}((P \to ((P \to P) \to P))\\ \to ((P \to (P \to P)) \to (P \to P)))\ [2]\end{array}}{((P \to (P \to P)) \to (P \to P))}\ f_{mp}}{(P \to P)}\ f_{mp}$$

As in the case of construction sequences, we can show that every element of an inductive set possesses a finite tree construction. We leave the task as an exercise.

□ **EXERCISE**

Let $\langle A, B, F\rangle$ be an inductive system. Prove the following:

$$A = \{x \mid \text{there exists a finite construction tree of } x, \text{ relative to } B \text{ and } F\}.$$

6.2.2 Equivalence among Trees and Sequences

Two quite different trees may be used to construct the same item, but some variations in construction are so trivial that they are really equivalent in a strong sense. One such trivial difference is the variation in the particular subscripts used to label the nodes. If two trees are exactly alike except that the indices used in one tree are an exact permutation of those in another, then the two trees are distinct rigorously speaking, but in the essential matter of what item is used to construct what, what formation rules are used, what order of the rules are applied in, and what order is taken by the arguments for the rules, the two trees are the same.

DEFINITION: Let $\langle s, \leq \rangle$ with annotation g and $\langle s', \leq' \rangle$ with annotation g' be construction trees relative to U, B, and F. We say $\langle s, \leq \rangle$ is *equivalent* to $\langle s', \leq' \rangle$ if, and only if, for some permutation Π and all values $\langle s_i \rangle$ and $\langle s_j \rangle$ of the sequence s,

(1) s_i is $s_{\Pi(i)}$,
(2) $\langle s_i \rangle \leq \langle s_j \rangle$ if, and only if, $\langle s'_{\Pi(i)} \rangle \leq \langle s'_{\Pi(j)} \rangle$, and
(3) $g(s_i)$ is $g'(s'_{\Pi(i)})$.

Examples of such equivalences are easily constructed simply by erasing the numerical subscripts from the elements of a tree and its annotation function and then replacing them with new numbers in a uniform way.

Construction sequences and trees are two alternative methods for describing the same process of construction, and the information contained in a sequence can be reformulated as a tree, and vice versa. The use of numerical subscripts in the definition of a construction tree makes this equivalence between trees and sequences easy to define. A sequence is equivalent to a tree if its analysis function is literally identical to the annotation function of the tree.

DEFINITION: Let s with analysis g be a construction sequence relative to U, B, and F, and let $\langle s', \leq \rangle$ with annotation g' be a construction tree relative to the same parameters. Then, we say s is *equivalent* to $\langle s', \leq \rangle$ *in a direct sense* if, and only if

(1) s is identical to s', and
(2) g is identical to g'.

DEFINITION: Let s with analysis g be a construction sequence relative to U, B, and F and let $\langle s', \leq \rangle$ with annotation g' be a construction tree relative to the same parameters. Then, we say s is *equivalent* to $\langle s', \leq \rangle$ *in a wide sense* if, and only if, there exists at least one construction sequence s'' and one construction tree $\langle s'', \leq'' \rangle$ both with the same annotation g'' such that relative to U, B, F, and g'',

(1) the sequences s and s'' are equivalent,
(2) the sequence s'' is equivalent in the direct sense to the tree $\langle s'', \leq'' \rangle$, and
(3) the trees $\langle s'', \leq'' \rangle$ and $\langle s', \leq \rangle$ are equivalent.

6.2.3 Restrictions on Syntactic and Proof Theoretic Induction

Like construction sequences, construction trees are defined so as to include bizarre cases that we would not normally meet in the constructions of syntax or proof theory. There may be overlapping basic sets. In grammar this situation would correspond to a single expression counting as falling into more than one part of speech, a feature of natural languages that is usually prohibited in the formal languages of logic. In proof theory axioms are usually either finite in number and listed in a single set of basic elements, or instead of being construed as axioms, the basic elements are stated by means of what are called *axiom schemata*. The axiom system AS_P-PL defined earlier is an example. Each axiom schema specifies that sentences or deductive assertions of a certain form count as basic elements. Usually there are an infinite number of expressions meeting the form of each schema and therefore it is best to think of each axiom schema as determining its own set of basic elements. Usually these forms are unique and no two sets of schema instances would overlap.

There may be elements that are used in the construction of themselves (some item s_i may be such that s_i is a predecessor of itself). But in grammar, expressions are never allowed to be constructed from themselves because if they were, there would be no sure method of testing in a finite number of steps whether an expression was grammatical. In proof theory, circles are possible. Indeed, in axiomatic proof theory $P \vdash P$ is usually a metatheorem.

As the definition stands it is also possible to have branches of a construction tree that are infinitely long. Again, to keep a grammar decidable, such possibilities are usually excluded in syntax, and in proof theory they are ruled out because a proof is supposed to represent the reasoning of finite beings.

The definition permits more than one nonequivalent construction tree for the same item. In natural language syntax, this situation does arise and is known as syntactic ambiguity, but in logical syntax it is usually prohibited. In proof theory, of course, the same item may be proven in numerous ways. Following Curry we shall call systems with unique constructions *monotectonic.*

Last, as defined, constructive systems and the constructive trees generating them may have generating functions with domains and ranges that overlap. In logical syntax, however, it is usually required that a formation rule be defined for an entire part of speech if it is defined for any expressions of that type. Natural language syntax is not so well-behaved. Some verbs, for example, are open to passive formations and others not, and a large number of 'selectional' restrictions are often posited in the grammar of natural languages to indicate for what part of a category a rule is defined. To describe this property more carefully, we need to be able to refer not just to the entire domain of a formation function, but also to the set of objects that are used to make up the ith position in an n-place formation function. Hence we make use of the notion of subdomain. In some nicely behaved cases in grammar, the subdomains of the various formation functions form a partition of the inductive set. We shall call such systems *categorized.*

Proof theory is not categorized in this sense. For example, in the natural deduction proof theory for propositional logic in Chapter 5, the rule $\perp$-introduction is defined for both $X \vdash (P \wedge Q)$ and $X \vdash (P \vee Q)$, but $\wedge$-elimination is defined for just the former.

We now give names to some of these restrictions.

DEFINITION: Let $\langle A, B, F\rangle$ be an inductive system relative to a set U.

(1) We say the system is *syntactic* if, and only if, U is a subset of $\Sigma*$ the set of expressions, and every formation function f in F is definable in terms of the concatenation operation $^\frown$.

(2) We say the system is *finitary* if, and only if, all construction trees (sequences) for the elements of A have only a finite number of members.

(3) We say the system is *noncircular* if, and only if, there does not exist a construction tree $\langle s, \leq\rangle$ and an element e of A such that there are i and j with the following properties:

(a) $e = s_i = s_j$, and

(b) $\langle s_i\rangle \leq \langle s_j\rangle$;

(4) We say the system is *monotectonic* if, and only if,

(a) each formation function f of F is 1–1, and

(b) if the ranges of any two formation functions overlap, then these ranges are identical.

(5) We say the system is *lexically unambiguous* if, and only if, if any two sets of basic categories in B overlap, then these sets are identical.

(6) We say the system is *categorized* if, and only if

(a) if two sets are the subdomains of any function or functions in F and these sets overlap, then they are identical, and

(b) the range of any formation function in F is included as a subset of some subdomain of that or another function in F.

THEOREM. If an inductive system is monotectonic, then any two construction trees for any member of the inductive set must be equivalent.

Proof. Assume (1) that a set $\langle A, B, F\rangle$ is monotectonic, but (2) that not all trees of every element are equivalent, that is, for any permutation Π and some $\langle s_i\rangle$ and $\langle s_j\rangle$, if both $s_i = s_{\Pi(i)}$ and $(\langle s_i\rangle \leq \langle s_j\rangle$ iff $\langle s_{\Pi(i)}\rangle \leq \langle s_{\Pi(j)}\rangle)$, then $g(s_i) \neq g'(s_{\Pi(i)})$. Now consider the identity permutation Π such that $\Pi(i) = i$, for any natural number i. Let us instantiate assumption (2) for this Π and for a given s_i and s_j. Now by the definition of Π, both $s_i = s_{\Pi(i)}$ and $(\langle s_i \rangle \leq \langle s_j \rangle$ iff $\langle s_{\Pi(i)} \rangle \leq \langle s_{\Pi(j)} \rangle)$, because $\Pi(i) = i$ and $\Pi(j) = j$. Hence the 'if' clause of (2) is satisfied; thus by *modus ponens* $g(s_i) = g'(s_{\Pi(i)})$. But since $\langle A, B, F \rangle$ is monotectonic there are unique f and $s_k, \ldots, s_m$ such that $f(s_k, \ldots, s_m) = s_i$ and $g(s_i) \neq \langle f, k, \ldots, m \rangle$. Likewise there are unique $f', s_{k'}, \ldots, s_{m'}$, such that $f'(s_{k'}, \ldots, s_{m'}) = s_{\Pi(i)}$, and $g'(s_{\Pi(i)}) \neq \langle f', k', \ldots, m' \rangle$. But since $s_i = s_{\Pi(i)}$ and $f, s_k, \ldots, s_m, f', s_{k'}, \ldots, s_{m'}$, are unique, $f = f'$, $s_k = s_{k'}, \ldots, s_m = s_{m'}$ and thus $g(s_i) = g'(s_{\Pi(i)})$, contradicting what was proved earlier. End of Proof.

☐ **EXERCISE**

Prove that if an inductive system is monotectonic, then any two construction sequences of any member of the inductive set are equivalent.

6.2.4 The Part–Whole Relation and Substitution

One of the virtues of the theory of construction we have been spelling out is that we may use it to define notions in syntax and proof theory that in earlier chapters have been left intuitive or defined in an *ad hoc* way. One such notion is that of an occurrence of one expression within another. If the syntax is monotectonic and exhibits the history of construction on the face of its expressions, as it does in the logical languages we have been studying, then we can visually scan for the occurrences of one expression within another. Every occurrence is marked by the visual presence of an instance of the expression. However, not all languages are monotectonic. Even in languages that have unique constructions for each expression, it is possible to have outputs of formation operations that do not encode on their faces, as it were, the history of their construction. Linguists and logicians have often suggested that there are cases in which an expression's form masks its true 'deep structure' or 'logical form'. Ockham's translation of subject–predicate sentences into conjunctions and disjunctions of identity statements discussed in Chapter 4 is one example, and we shall meet other important examples later.[4]

One way to define the notion of occurrence that abstracts from the way a construction is carried out is to identify an occurrence of an expression with a node in a construction tree. For each such intuitive occurrence there is one such node, and in cases in which a language is monotectonic a node is an occurrence in one tree if, and only if, it is so in an equivalent tree.

[4] In Chapter 8 we shall study Russell's theory of descriptions in which it is claimed that 'the present king of France is bald' contains no occurrence of a singular term 'the present king of France'. In Chapter 9 we shall discuss Donald Davidson's translations of superficially simple action expressions into complex expressions in first-order syntax.

DEFINITION: Let $\langle s, \leq \rangle$ be a construction tree (equivalently, let s be a construction sequence). Then, we say that a pair $\langle s_i \rangle$ in s is an *occurrence* or *instance* of e in $\langle s, \leq \rangle$ (equivalently, in s) if, and only if, $s_i = e$.

☐ **EXERCISE**

Prove that if a construction tree $\langle s, \leq \rangle$ is equivalent (in either sense) to a construction tree $\langle s', \leq' \rangle$, then there is a permutation Π such that for any i and any e, $\langle s_i \rangle$ is an occurrence of e in $\langle s', \leq \rangle$ iff $\langle s'_{\Pi(i)} \rangle$ is an occurrence of e in $\langle s', \leq' \rangle$.

It is possible to define the notion of syntactic part in a similar way. Relative to a construction tree for e, a part of e is anything that occurs in the tree. If e' occupies a node that leads to the construction of e, then we say that e' is a part of e.

DEFINITION: Let e and e' be members of an inductive set, and let $\langle s', \leq \rangle$ be a construction tree for e (equivalently, let s be a construction sequence for e) relative to that set. Then we say e' is a *part of e relative to* $\langle s', \leq \rangle$ (equivalently, s) if, and only if, for some i and j, $s_i = e$, $s_j = e'$, and $\langle s_i \rangle \leq \langle s_j \rangle$.
DEFINITION: If an inductive system is monotectonic and e and e' are elements of the inductive set, then we say e is a *part of* e' iff relative to all construction trees for e, e' is a part of e.

In earlier chapters we have often used the idea of substituting one expression for another. It figures importantly, for example, in defining the notion of the instance of a universally quantified sentence. Though we defined the relevant sort of substitution at the time, we did not give a general analysis of arbitrary substitution. We may do so by means of constructions.

Intuitively, to substitute one expression for another we erase all or some occurrences of the first in a construction tree and replace them with occurrences of the second. The item constructed by the new tree will then be the 'result' of the substitution process. For this intuitive process to work a condition must be satisfied: the inductive system must be monotectonic. If an item e had more than one nonequivalent construction tree then the process of replacing some part of e would yield more than one result depending on which tree is used. Hence, in the definition below we limit the notion of substitution to monotectonic structures.

Another condition that must be met before we can use trees to define substitution is that the expression doing the replacing must be defined for the same formation functions as the expression it replaces, and moreover the expressions generated from the replacing expression must themselves be defined for the generating functions of the original. If not, then we will not be able to construct a new whole from the new parts. In the languages of formal logic, then, these conditions are met because the syntax is categorized.

Exprcssions fall into parts of speech, and each formation operation is defined for all expressions of a category if they are defined for any. Thus, we impose on the definition of substitution the requirement that the inductive system be categorized.

DEFINITION: Let us assume the following conditions:

(1) let $\langle A, B, F\rangle$ be an inductive system that is monotectonic and categorized,

(2) let x, y, and z be elements of A such that for some f in F and some i, y and z are in $D^i(f)$ (such a subdomain is called a *category*), and

(3) let T be a construction tree $\langle s, \leq\rangle$ of x that has an annotation g.

Then by T_z^y we mean the structure $\langle s', \leq'\rangle$, with the following properties:

(1) s' is the sequence $\langle s'_1, \ldots, s'_n, \ldots\rangle$ defined as follows:

- (a) if $\langle s_i\rangle$ is a minimal element of T and s_i is not z, then $s'_i = s_i$,
- (b) if $\langle s_i\rangle$ is a minimal element of T and s_i is z, then s'_i is y, and
- (c) if $\langle s_i\rangle$ is not a minimal element of T and $g(s_i)$ is $\langle f, k, \ldots, m\rangle$, then s'_i is $f(s'_k, \ldots, s'_m)$; and

(2) we define the relation $\leq'$ over pairs in s' and a mapping g' with domain s' as follows: for any i and j,

$$\langle s'_i\rangle \leq' \langle s'_j\rangle \text{ if, and only if, } \langle s_i\rangle \leq \langle s_j\rangle,$$
$$g'(s'_i) \text{ is } g(s_i).$$

THEOREM. T_z^y is a tree.

Proof. In this proof and subsequent discussion of trees we do not make reference to the expressions occupying their nodes. Thus, we adopt the notation s_i for $\langle s_i\rangle$. It follows directly from the definition of $\leq'$ that $\leq'$ is reflexive, transitive, and antisymmetric. We illustrate the case for anti-symmetry. Let $s'_i \leq' s'_j$ and $s'_j \leq' s'_i$; then $s_i \leq s_j$ and $s_j \leq s_i$ by the definition of $\leq'$. Since $\leq$ is antisymmetric, $s_i = s_j$. Since s'_i and s'_j are unique, we know that $s'_i = s'_j$. Next we show that T_z^y has a maximal element, namely e' where e is the maximal element of T. Let s'_i be in s'. Now $s_i \leq e$ since e is maximal in T. Hence by definition of $\leq'$, $s'_i \leq e'$. Thus e' is maximal. It remains to be shown that for any s'_i, there is a finite sequence starting with s'_i, ending with e', such that each element is an $\leq'$-immediate predecessor of the element to its right. We know that there is such a sequence $s_1, \ldots, s_n$ for s_i of T. We show that $s'_1, \ldots, s'_n$ is such a sequence for s'_i. Consider any s'_j and s'_{j+1} of this sequence. We show $s'_j \leq' s'_{j+1}$. Suppose that for some k, $s'_j \leq' s'_k$ and $s'_k \leq' s'_{j+1}$. Then $s_j \leq s_k$ and $s_k \leq s_{j+1}$. Then either $s_j = s_k$ or $s_k = s_{j+1}$. In the former case $s'_k = s'_{j+1}$, and in the latter $s'_k = s'_{j+1}$. Hence either $s'_j = s'_k$ or $s'_k = s'_{j+1}$. Therefore, not $s'_j \leq' s'_{j+1}$. Thus $s'_1, \ldots, s'_n$ is the sequence claimed. It is, moreover, the only such sequence since for any node there is at most one $\leq'$-immediate predecessor. End of Proof.

☐ **EXERCISE**

Let T_z^y be as defined above. Prove that

a. T_z^y is a construction tree for its $\leq'$-maximal element, which we may call t'; and

b. g' is an annotation for T_z^y.

6.2.5 Construction Trees in Linguistics

At this point it is worthwhile to digress a bit and discuss an alternative definition of tree that is frequently found in linguistics for representing grammatical constructions. This notion is essentially equivalent to the one previously defined except that it adds an additional structural condition that the immediate predecessors of a node are ordered in a relation of precedence and that the predecessors of a preceding node n themselves all precede any predecessors of n. (Recall that we are here using s_i for $\langle s_i \rangle$.)

DEFINITION: A *tree* in linguistics is any $\langle s, \leq, P \rangle$ such that

(1) s is a finite sequence indexing some subset C of the set $\Sigma*$ of expressions;

(2) $\leq$ is a partial ordering on s (i.e., $\leq$ is a binary relation on s that is reflexive, transitive, and antisymmetric);

(3) P is a strict partial ordering on s (i.e., P is a binary relation on s that is transitive and asymmetric in the sense that if $s_i P s_j$ then not$(s_j P s_i)$);

(4) there is some $\leq$-maximal element $e*$ of s;

(5) (*exclusivity*) for any i and j, not$(s_i \leq s_j$ or $s_j \leq s_i)$ iff $(s_i P s_j$ or $s_j P s_i)$;

(6) (*nonentanglement*) for any $i, j, k,$ and m, if $(s_i P s_j$ and $s_i \leq s_k$ and $s_j \leq s_m)$ then $s_k P s_m$.

THEOREM. If $\langle s, \leq, P)$ is a tree in linguistics, then $\langle s, \leq \rangle$ is a tree.

Proof. The facts that $\leq$ is a partial ordering of s and that there is a $\leq$-maximal element $e*$ follow by the definition of linguistic tree. It remains to be shown that for any s_i there is a unique sequence $\langle s_1, \ldots, s_n \rangle$ of immediate predecessors starting with s_i and ending with $e*$. We show first that every item x in s has a unique immediate predecessor under $\leq$, i.e., that there is a unique y such that $x \leq y$. Assume the opposite, that $x \leq y, x \leq z, y \neq z$. Now either $(y \leq z \vee z \leq y)$ or not. If so, by definition of immediate predecessor, $y = z$, which is absurd. If not, then by exclusivity, yPz or zPy. Suppose yPz, then $x \leq y$ and $x \leq z$ and $y \neq z$, and nonentanglement is violated. It is likewise violated if zPy. Hence the assumption is absurd, and immediate predecessors are unique.

Let us define a function f that assigns to each x in s its $\leq$-immediate predecessor. For s_i we now define the sequence $\langle s_1, \ldots, s_n, \ldots \rangle$ such that $s_1 = s_i$, and s_{j+1} in the sequence is defined as $f(s_j)$. Clearly $s_1 = s_i$. Also the sequence is finite because the range of f is a subset of s and s is finite. Finally we argue that its greatest element, call it s_k, is the same as $e*$. Suppose not.

Then s_k is not the last member of the sequence since there exist predecessors of s_k not in the sequence, namely $e*$. The sequence is also unique because the immediate predecessor relation picks out a unique object. Thus, the sequence has all the required properties and $\langle s, \leq \rangle$ is a tree. End of Proof.

As remarked before, annotating a tree does provide a left-to-right order to the nodes, and it can be shown (see the exercise below) that this ordering obeys the properties of the linguists' precedence relation. Moreover, in order to use even their sorts of trees to represent grammatical constructions, linguists annotate by pairing with each node the function generating it. In the exposition here we have chosen to use the more abstract notion of tree for two reasons. First of all, it is the most abstract or general definition possible that captures the properties of a tree capable of representing a construction. This generality is desirable in itself because it provides the simplest analysis of the notions under discussion. Second, there are instances of construction trees found outside the context of grammar that represent genuine constructions but that violate some of the conditions imposed on the linguistic tree. In particular, it is often useful in mathematics to employ infinitary trees and to construct nonsymbolic entities. For almost all the constructions we shall discuss in this book, however, we might equally well have chosen the linguistic idea as fundamental.

☐ **EXERCISE**

Define a precedence relation P for a construction tree $\langle s, \leq \rangle$ with annotation g, relative to inductive system $\langle A, B, F \rangle$, and then prove that $\langle s, \leq, P \rangle$ is a linguistic tree. The proof is not technically difficult but is somewhat tedious. *Hints*: Define iRj relative to a function f iff for some $x_1, \ldots, x_n$, $\langle x_1, \ldots, x_i, \ldots, x_j, \ldots, x_n \rangle \in D(f)$. Then define the precedence relation as follows: $s_i P s_j$ iff

(1) for some s_k, f is the first item in the annotation $g(s_k)$ and iRj relative to f, or

(2) for some s_m, s_n, and s_k, both

  (a) $s_i \leq s_m$ and $s_j \leq s_n$, and

  (b) f is the first item in $g(s_k)$, and mRn relative to f.

We are now in a position to define substitution.

DEFINITION: Let $\langle A, B, F \rangle$ be an inductive system that is monotectonic and categorized, let x, y, and z be elements of A such that some category (subdomain of a formation operation) contains both y and z, and let T be a construction tree of x. Then, by the *result of substituting y for z in x*, which we shall abbreviate $[x]^y_z$, we mean the maximal element $t*$ of T^y_z.

The notion of substitution defined above replaces *all* occurrences of one expression by another, but there are two other notions of substitution that are often used. In the informal statement of the axiom of abstraction in Chapter 2, for example, we used the notion of replacing *some* occurrences of one expression by another, and in Chapter 5 we spoke of replacing *all free* occurrences of a variable. It is a straightforward matter to define these notions by altering the definition of substitutional tree given above and then proving that the result is indeed a tree. Only relatively small parts of the proof need be changed. Note that a simple way to define the idea that x is *free in* A is by the condition that x is not a part of any expression $(\forall x)B$ which is in turn part of A.

□ **EXERCISE**

Define the following notions.

a. The result of replacing some occurrences of y by z in x.
b. The result of replacing all free occurrences of y by z in x.

6.3 THE IDEA OF A CONSTRUCTION

6.3.1 Effective Process

We have now finished the exposition of the more straightforward ideas in the theory of inductive systems. There is a group of more philosophically elusive properties that bear directly on when an inductive set is properly viewed as constructive or, more narrowly, as constructive in the manner typical of actual languages. These are the concepts of effective process, decidability, and learnability.

Our discussion of construction has been quite abstract. In particular, the general notion of construction allows that any sort of finitely valued function may serve as a generating operation. However, in the special constructive sets found in logic and linguistics only certain sorts of generations are permitted. We have already discussed some restrictions typical of syntax and proof theory. There is another restriction which we have postponed discussing until now because it is quite difficult to characterize. This is the condition that the functions be effective processes.

The most basic way to explain an effective process is by examples. The mechanical process we all learned in school for long division, called Euclid's algorithm, is an effective process. So too is the truth-table test for logical truths in propositional logic. Another example is the smart rat's procedure for exiting from any given maze: just keep turning right. In general, any rule-governed method of problem solving that always works will be an example.

But a set of examples is an inferior sort of explanation of any idea. It would be better to have a definition or theory that spells out the properties of an effective process. In modern logic there have been two approaches to a more complete explanation. Perhaps the more successful has been to approach the problem by axiomatics. The idea is to lay down a series of axioms that exhaustively describe the set of effective processes. One measure of success of such a project would be how plausible the axioms are as statements about effective processes. What they say literally must conform to our intuitive understanding of what such a process is. But since the whole point of advancing the theory is that we lack a clear understanding of the notion to begin with, such intuitive appraisals of axioms do not provide enough guidance. A second and, on the whole, just as important measure of success of an axiomatic approach is how well the consequences of the axioms match our judgments about particular examples of effective processes. In particular, we should be able to prove from the axioms that those examples which we intuitively judge to be effective processes are in fact effective processes as that notion is explained within the axiom system. Further, we should not be able to prove within the system that an intuitively noneffective process is effective. In short, the axiom system should entail that the effective processes coincide exactly with our list of intuitive examples.

In the period between the two world wars various attempts were made to characterize the effective functions by what is essentially this method. The problem was limited to the characterization of effective processes like Euclid's algorithm that are functions on positive integers, or on the numerals representing the positive integers. A number of different theories were developed independently. The notion of *recursive function* was axiomatized by Gödel, that of *algorithm* by Markov, that of a *function computable by a Turing machine* by Turing, that of a *function in the calculus of lambda conversion* by Church, and that of a *Post system* by Post. An important branch of mathematical logic was thus born which has at its center the remarkable result that all these independently developed axiomatizations can be proved to define exactly the same set of functions and that all the examples of effective process that people agree about can be shown to fall within this class. The conceptual thesis that this formally definable set coincides with the intuitively characterized set of effective processes is known as *Church's thesis* because of his discussions of the issue. The thesis is widely accepted by students of the subject.[5]

An alternative approach to the problem of characterizing effective process is to try to give a straightforward definition of the form: a function f counts as an *effective process* if, and only if, $\ldots f \ldots$. This principle would be a traditional definition with 'effective process' as its *definiendum* and a sentence '$\ldots f \ldots$' describing the relevant properties of f as its *definiens*. This is the kind of definition or characterization that is typically pursued in the sort of philosophical study called conceptual analysis. The attempt to define

[5] For an exposition of the theory of effective process see Martin Davis, *Computability and Unsolvability* (1958).

'knowledge' as justified true belief, 'truth' as correspondence to the world, and 'the good' as the greatest pleasure for the greatest number are all examples of this sort of definition.

One of the problems facing any attempt to give a direct definition is the choice of vocabulary to be used in the *definiens*. It should be clearer and less problematic than the term it defines, and ideally it should be part of some well-developed branch of science. We shall see that in the case of effective process the defining terms come from epistemology and fall rather short of ideal clarity. In particular, we shall not be able to reduce the idea to mathematically precise ideas like those of set theory. (It is largely for this reason that mathematicians have tended to approach the characterization problem indirectly through axiomatizations which can be stated within a mathematical language.)

One criterion of success for a direct definition is how well they record our intuitive or preanalytical understanding of the term being defined. It should match up well with older, vaguer formulations and definitions. Intuitively clear examples should be captured within the scope of the term as analyzed, and cases that intuitively fall outside the application of the term should likewise fall outside by the definition. If the term has a history of usage in science or philosophy, the proposed definition should correspond to the noncontroversial parts of that usage. In short the analysis should be conceptually adequate as explained in Chapter 3.

Let us try to abstract an intuitively adequate definition of effective process from the examples. One feature to notice first of all is that in each case it is perfectly evident whether we should even start the process on a given occasion. Long division is a process that applies to integers, not to horses. One would not try to divide one horse by another. Likewise, the truth-table test only applies to formulas of sentential logic. One would not write rows of T and F under anything else. We may summarize this property by saying that in an effective process it is always clearly evident whether an object is the sort of thing to which we may start applying the process.

A second feature of our examples is that the process itself breaks down into little steps, and it is perfectly clear how to start the step, when it is finished, and what its result is. Thus, in long division we divide part of the numerator by the denominator, subtract, and then start over again. In truth-tables we calculate the truth-values of progressively larger parts by distinct steps with perfectly evident outcomes.

Another obvious feature of such processes is that they terminate, often quickly and certainly in a finite amount of time. It is also clear when the end is reached and what the final result is.

Common to each of these properties has been the idea that something or other was clear or evident to the person performing the process. The notion of clarity is epistemic. Something is clear to somebody if the person *knows* it easily and reliably. Hence any attempt to directly characterize effective processes must employ ideas from epistemology.

Let us summarize our discussion by offering as a rough definition the following:

DEFINITION: A function f is *analyzed as an effective process* if, and only if, in the analysis, f is broken down into a finite number of steps each of which is such that the following are epistemically evident:

(1) what order the steps fall in,
(2) what arguments the step is defined for,
(3) how to perform the step, and finally
(4) what the result of each step is.

The reason for the qualifier 'as analyzed' in the above definition is that being an effective process is relative to the definition given. Only if the clauses of the definition ensure that the relevant information is obtainable will the function count as effective. Moreover, a function may have one characterization that though providing necessary and sufficient conditions does not show that it is effective, and another that shows that it is.

The tie in logic between the idea of construction and that of knowledge is old and deep. What is it after all that makes proofs interesting? It is that we use them as justifications for our claims to knowledge. Mathematical proofs like those in geometry were viewed by Plato as paradigms of epistemic justification, and indeed much of the history of philosophy was an attempt to understand knowledge by the model of geometry. The idea of proof has built into it constructions from both syntax and proof theory. First we build up the expressions of the language, and we then use them to produce proofs, and both processes are epistemically transparent. It is, of course, interesting to try to explain why. Unfortunately, the mathematical axiomatizations of effective process avoid epistemic issues.

One way to explain the particular transparency of logical constructions is to observe that to a large extent they can be carried out with a pencil and paper. They consist of the manipulation of concrete symbols like pencil markings in simple, clearly defined ways. We can see these marks, we can see the results of manipulating them, and our knowledge has a very high degree of perceptual certainty.

It would, however, be wrong to think that only physical marks are subject to effective processes or that the kind of knowledge in question is in all cases perceptual. The restriction to the realm of the physical is wrong because many, probably most, mathematicians think of effective processes as definable for entities like numbers which they do not regard as physical. For Platonistic mathematicians, for example, who regard numbers as abstract entities, the kind of knowledge attached to the completion of steps in an effective processs is something like that found in executing moves in blindfold chess.

There *is* a link between numbers and physical objects. Let us grant for the moment that numbers are abstract nonphysical objects. Then to each number is paired a name, called a *numeral*. The first positive integer, for example, has paired with it the numeral 1, a linguistic symbol used to refer to that number. Now by the usual Platonistic account, numerals too are abstract objects. A numeral is related in a one–many relationship to its various concrete physical instances, the multitudinous examples of the numeral throughout time and space. These instances are called *inscriptions* of the numeral by philosophers of language. Often the relationship between a numeral and its inscriptions is discussed in the language of type and token. This terminology presupposes that there is a distinction, usually considered to be indefinable and primitive, between a *type* of a symbol and its various physical inscriptions or utterances, called the *tokens* of the type. For most purposes, however, we need not think of these as primitives or resort to concepts outside set theory and syntax. It is usually adequate to define types in terms of tokens: a type is an equivalence class of inscriptions determined by some equivalence relation. The equivalence relation associated with an actual numeral or the psycholinguistic properties that might be needed to restrict the set of possible equivalence relations to those which might actually be used by humans are usually irrelevant to the very abstract points being made in logic and grammar. We may thus think of the type/token relation as a species of set membership.

Abstract numbers, then, are paired with numerals which in turn have various physical instances. Thus it is the case that in all standard examples of effective process, there is a correlation between the effective process on abstract objects and a corresponding mechanical manipulation of inscriptions with its peculiar variety of perceptual certainty. This correlation invites the hypothesis that the reason the abstract function is effective is because of its association with the perceptually certain manipulation of inscriptions and other physical representatives. This speculative thesis is one that Platonic mathematicians have little to say about. That these points depend on the perceptual clarity of inscription, however, goes some way toward explaining why logicians and philosophers have tended to think of language not as spoken but as written, an idealization linguists are not tempted to make.

6.3.2 Decidability

The notion of effective process will help us define another concept needed to restrict inductive systems to the type found in syntax and proof theory. It is not sufficient that the functions used in the construction be effective; the sets that the functions are applied to must also be epistemically evident. In particular we must be able to know whether something counts as a basic element, and whether a construction operation is defined for a given object.

The property of knowing in an evident way whether something is in a set is called *decidability*, and it may be explained by means of effective process. First we define the idea of a set's characteristic function. This is the function that assigns every element in the set T and everything else F. Suppose this function is effective. Then there is a finitely evident procedure for testing whether anything gets T and hence whether anything is in the set.

DEFINITION: If A is a subset of U, then f is the *characteristic function for A in U* iff $f(U \xrightarrow[\text{into}]{} \{\text{T}, \text{F}\})$ and $A = \{x \mid x \in U \wedge f(x) = \text{T}\}$.

DEFINITION: Let A be a subset of a wider set U. We then say that A is *decidable relative to* and *is recursive in* U if, and only if, there is a characteristic function f for A in U such that f may be analyzed as an effective process.

We may now use the notions of effective procedure and decidable set to impose further conditions on the notion of an inductive set to bring it closer to the intuitive idea of a construction as found in logical theory. The first condition we impose is that the generating operations be effective. We also require the following to be evident: what counts as a basic element, what counts as a generating function (when there are an infinite number of basic expressions or generating functions, these questions are not trivial), and what counts as an acceptable argument for these functions. We ensure these last conditions by requiring that the sets in question be decidable.

DEFINITION: Let $\langle A, B, F\rangle$ be an inductive system on U. We say that the system is *constructive* if, and only if, it meets the following conditions:

(1) each set in the family B, each subdomain of the operations in F, and both B and F themselves are decidable sets, and

(2) all the formation operations contained in F are analyzable as effective processes.

We conclude the discussion of decidability by mentioning the important fact, which we cannot prove here, that a constructible set need not be decidable. The set of acceptable deductive assertions of first-order logic, for example, is constructive but in principle lacks a decision function. Conversely, a set may be decidable yet not be constructive. For example, there is a decision procedure for testing whether an integer is a prime, but there is no known way of constructing all the primes.

6.3.3 Logistic Grammar and Proof Theory Defined

We are now in a position to summarize the discussion in this chapter by stating definitions restricting the general form of syntax and proof theory as done in the tradition of symbolic logic.

DEFINITION: By a *logistic syntax* we mean any inductive system $\langle A, B, F\rangle$ that is

(1) syntactic,
(2) finitary,
(3) noncircular,
(4) monotectonic,
(5) lexically unambiguous, and
(6) constructive.

Compared to syntax, proof theory is much less restricted. A proof, however, must obviously be constructed from elements of some syntax.

DEFINITION: A *logistic proof theory* relative to a logistic syntax and inductive set S is any inductive system $\langle A, B, F\rangle$ such that A is a set or relation on elements of S and $\langle A, B, F\rangle$ is

(1) syntactic,
(2) finitary, and
(3) lexically unambiguous.

Notice that as defined neither a syntax nor a proof theory automatically contains an inductive set that is decidable, and it is often a major result to show for a particular structure that it is decidable or, alternatively, that it is undecidable. The syntax of both propositional and first-order logic and the classical proof theory for propositional logic are decidable, but the notion of provable deductive assertion in first-order logic is not. The nontriviality of the so-called *decidability question* is a major motivation for not adding decidability as an extra condition in the definitions of the two sorts of systems. However, in linguistic discussions of natural languages, it is usual to add a restriction that at once ensures the grammar is comprehensible to finite humans and that decidability is trivially satisfied. We complete our discussion of inductive structures by defining this additional constraint.

6.3.4 Learnability

The third and last concept relevant to the characterization of linguistic construction is one needed to distinguish mathematical constructions in general from the subspecies of constructions important to natural languages. The concept is sometimes called *learnability*, and is probably best viewed as psychological. The core phenomenon that it is used to explain is the fact that with finite experience and psychological resources we are able to utter and decipher a potentially infinite collection of grammatical expressions. Chomsky discussed the situation in terms of his famous competence/performance distinction, which was mentioned in Chapter 3. We never actually utter or entertain in our thoughts an infinite number of sentences. Thus the linguistic data that are open to empirical observation are always finite in number. Nevertheless, there is a wider sense of data in which the data to be explained are infinite. This potentially infinite set of expressions is that which we could express or understand. It is by drawing attention to the need to explain this larger set that Chomsky motivated the use of constructive methods in grammar and departed in an important way from earlier structuralist grammarians who attempted to explain only the linguistic acts that are actually observable.[6]

For our purposes it will be useful to distinguish two aspects of language use. First is the construction or utterance of a grammatical expression by a speaker, which we might call *encoding*, and second is the understanding or deciphering of an utterance by a listener, which we might call *decoding*. Exactly what physical mechanisms might be required for these processes is the subject of a now large literature in phonology and psycholinguistics, and the nature of the physical instruments actually used in the production and perception of language imposes very restricted conditions on any theory that is going to describe correctly how human language works. It is customary in linguistic research to abstract some very general conditions necessary for encoding and decoding and to require that these be met in any inductive system used to represent a possible language. The condition which is imposed to ensure the possibility of encoding a potentially infinite number of expressions is that the set of grammatical utterances be viewed as a constructive set with a finite number of basic expressions and a finite number of generating rules.

DEFINITION: An inductive system $\langle A, B, F\rangle$ is said to be *learnable* if, and only if, each basic set in B and the family F of formation operations are all finite in number.

The process of decoding imposes additional structure. In particular it is assumed that a message is broken down into the basic bits from which it was manufactured together with a determination of the form used in manufacturing it. The basic elements and the grammatical structure organizing the basic elements are thus recoverable from the message itself. Semantically, the basic elements together with the structure are supposed to determine the meaning of the whole, and we are presumed to decipher the meaning of an expression

[6] Noam Chomsky, *Aspects of the Theory of Syntax* (1965). The need for a finitary basis for learnable languages is argued for in the philosophical literature in a well-known paper by Donald Davidson, 'Theories of Meaning and Learnable Languages' (1964). For an account of how important infinite competence was in Chomsky's rejection of the earlier and more positivistic grammars of the American structuralists see Frederick J. Newmeyer, *Linguistics in America* (1980).

by reducing it to these more basic semantic features. A given element of the inductive set then must have one or at most a limited number of different ways of being constructed. Thus, ideally, the grammar would be unambiguous, but a certain amount of ambiguity could presumably be processed by a listener if he or she reviews the possible constructions and then selects from these the one the speaker most likely intends to mean. At this level of abstraction we need not specify the amount of ambiguity communication will tolerate, nor the method of disambiguation. We already have in hand the concept of monotectonic structure by which we may limit inductive systems to those in which decomposition is unique. As we have seen in the study of classical propositional and first-order logic, the grammars defined by logicians are indeed monotectonic in this way.[7] Nevertheless, the grammars studied by linguists (and computer scientists) allow for some degree of ambiguity so as to match natural languages more accurately.

[7] In linguistics and computer science it is customary to define particular grammars within a wider covering theory known as formal or phrase structure grammar. Within this theory important varieties of grammar are defined by imposing increasingly greater restrictions on the basic notion of a *context-sensitive grammar*. That species of formal grammar closest to the kind of grammar found in logic is called a *context-free* grammar. The main differences between context-free and the logistic grammars we have been studying are

(1) context-free grammars are generated from basic elements by construction relations that are not functions, and

(2) they are learnable in our sense: their basic sets and set of formation relations are finite.

But the different ways that logicians and linguists have come to talk about grammar are largely equivalent: every context-free grammar may be shown to be translatable into a logistic grammar, and conversely every learnable logistic grammar may be formulated as a context-free grammar.

See M. Gross and A. Lentin, *Introduction to Formal Grammar* (1970) for an exposition of the theory of formal grammar. The basic ideas were first formulated in Noam Chomsky, 'On Certain Properties of Grammar' (1959) and 'Formal Properties of Grammars' (1965). The first explicit statement of a fully defined logistic grammar is found in Rudolf Carnap, *The Logical Syntax of Language* (1934). On the equivalence of the two traditions see John N. Martin, 'Some Formal Properties of Indirect Semantics' (1986).

7

Alternative Semantics for Propositional Logic

7.1 THREE-VALUED LOGIC

7.1.1. The Third Value

One way that logicians often depart from classical semantics in the history of logic is to question the assumption that all sentences are either true or false. Such theories reject the fundamental principle of classical semantics, called variously *Tertium Non Datur*, the *Law of Excluded Middle*, or the *Principle of Bivalence.*

The Principle of Bivalence. Every sentence in every world is either true or false: for any $P \in \text{Sen}$, and any $R \in [R]$, $R(P) \in \{T, F\}$.

Such revisions face some major difficulties which we may group into three sorts. First, the theory must plausibly explain what the third kind of sentence is and how it differs from genuinely true and false sentences. Doing so adequately requires a close conceptual analysis of the key ideas—truth, falsity, and the concept represented by the third value. Providing this analysis is sometimes called the *problem of defining the third truth-value.* Second, given the new truth-value, the theory must reconstruct the truth-tables for the sentential connectives or otherwise explain how to assign truth-values to molecular sentences. Again, doing so is a matter of conceptual analysis, but this time the analysis concerns the meaning of the sentential connectives themselves. Defining the assignment of truth-values to the connectives in many-valued semantics is often called the *projection problem.* Last, given the revision of the idea of truth-value, the theory must redefine the notions of logical truth and valid argument. Again the definitions must conform to the conceptual content of these traditional ideas. Moreover, the classes delineated by the proposed definitions must have the right extensions as judged on the basis of logical intuition. We should not be able to find any intuitively valid arguments or logical truths excluded by the definitions, and all those embraced by the definition should be intuitively valid and logically true. Discussion of three-valued logic within the tradition of formal semantics centers on these three problems, and we shall discuss each in turn.

Claiming that there are three kinds of sentence—the true, the false, and something else—presupposes a fact about the meanings of words or, to put it another way, about the geography of concepts. Just as it is a linguistic fact about the meanings of the English words 'red', 'green', and 'blue' that they are mutually exclusive and that in a given world different things may be properly called by each, so it is a conceptual claim about the meanings of 'true', 'false', and the third category that they are exclusive and satisfiable. Obviously in order for these conceptual claims to be established, a meaning for the third category must be fixed. In the long tradition of the subject various different interpretations for the third value have been proposed. The important point theoretically is that once an interpretation is decided upon, an exercise in discussing the meanings of words is in order. Such a discussion usually makes two points. First it shows that given their ordinary meanings, the three categories divide up sentences much as color words divide up physical objects. Second, it shows that there are in fact important examples of the new category in ordinary speech—that there really is a difference in the linguistic data sufficient to justify the new distinction.

Before giving a list of the various meanings attached to the third value and examples of each, we must mention several challenges facing any such revision of classical semantics. Any such theory, first of all, must argue that given the meanings of basic semantic ideas, it is appropriate to divide up the category of the nontrue into two mutually exclusive subtypes. In addition, it must show that given the meaning of the term 'false', it is right to apply it to only one of these types. Last, it must establish that given the definition of the third value, however it is defined in that theory, it is correct to apply it to the remaining type.

Thus, the false sentences and those receiving the third value are viewed as proper subsets of the wider category of nontrue sentences. All such theories face a common objection to the effect that falsity really means nontruth, and that it does violence to the meaning of the word 'false' to distinguish a variety of nontrue sentences which are not false. In short, the objection claims that any threefold classification of sentences into true, false, and other is incoherent. In this view 'falsity' is claimed to mean nontrue, and therefore a third category is inconsistent with the meanings of the theoretical terms used.

Defenders of the third value usually respond that the ordinary meaning of the term 'false' is somewhat vague and that it is only specialized theories in formal logic that rigorously divide all sentences into true and false. Ordinary speech, it is argued, allows for many unclear and borderline cases. Given this latitude in the ordinary language idea of falsity, the theorist of language may justifiably clarify the ordinary language idea if he or she has good theoretical reasons for doing so. These theoretical reasons usually consist of the claim that some phenomenon previously unremarked or unexplained in semantic theory can be adequately treated by clarifying the nontrue in such a way that it consists of two subspecies, one of which is the false.

Moreover, the point is also made that not only is ordinary language usage not clear enough in itself to resolve the issue of whether the nontrue is identical to the false, the more sophisticated usage of 'true', 'false', and 'nontrue' in works from the history of philosophy and grammar is no more definitive. We might call this usage *technical* or *theoretical* to distinguish it from that in ordinary language, and it might be thought that if ordinary language cannot fix the relative meaning of 'falsity' and 'nontruth' then technical usage might. The facts of intellectual history say otherwise. Though it is true that there have been many theorists who have held that the two are the same, there have also been numerous thinkers who have defended the opposing view that falsity is a proper subcategory of the nontrue. Among the latter are Aristotle, Ockham, Buridan, Hegel, Frege, and literally hundreds of twentieth-century logicians. Thus, the issue of the propriety of positing a third value turns not on general considerations about the meaning of the single term 'false', but on a detailed consideration of the meaning of the third value and on the cases that might be successfully explained by its means. We shall now review some of these cases and the category terms used to draw them together.

7.1.2 Category Mistakes

Some terms, it is held, are limited in the spheres of their meaningful usage. A given term can be correctly asserted or denied only for a restricted class of things. To attempt to apply it outside this class is nonsensical. In this view truth corresponds to correct assertion, falsity to correct denial, and the third value to meaningless uses.[1] For example, 'deductible' correctly applies to some expenses and not to others, but it is a conceptual mistake to think the question even arises whether anything other than an expense is deductible. Sentences that are grammatically correct but that link words together in a way that violates their restricted ranges of meaningfulness are called *category mistakes*. Here are some cases:

EXAMPLES Triangularity drinks procrastination. (Russell)
Colorless green ideas sleep furiously. (Chomsky)
Einstein's most important discovery supports combustion. (Thomason)

7.1.3 Vagueness

Words, especially those used to describe ordinary things, are *vague* in the sense that there is a large class for which it is unclear whether they fall under the term or not. When, it is argued, does it become true that I am in the corner as I advance toward it? There is a fuzzy border to the phrase 'in the corner'. Here are two cases that are often alleged to be so vague that they are not really either true or false.[2]

EXAMPLES France is hexagonal.
Italy is boot-shaped.

7.1.4 Presupposition Failure

Issues often presuppose facts, and often a question cannot arise without certain presuppositions being true. Both the meaningful assertion and denial of a sentence may presuppose the truth of another sentence, and if that presupposition is false, then any attempt to assert or deny the original

[1] In modern logic perhaps the first important statement of this idea was by Sorën Halldén, *The Logic of Nonsense* (1949). A much more developed treatment is found in L. Goddard and Richard Routley, *The Logic of Significance and Context* (1973). In both these works standard three-valued matrix theories (explained below) are used. For less standard many-valued semantics of category mistakes see Richmond Thomason, 'A Semantics of Sortal Incorrectness' (1972), John N. Martin, 'A Many-Valued Semantics for Category Mistakes' (1975), and Merrie Bergmann, 'Logic and Sortal Incorrectness' (1977).

[2] Perhaps the most interesting paper on a three-valued semantics of vagueness as distinct from nonsense is that by Hans Kamp, 'Two Theories about Adjectives' (1975), in which supervaluations are used. Vagueness is also the main inspiration for the movement known as 'fuzzy logic', which proposes a semantics similar to Łukasiewicz's infinitary-valued logic studied below. On fuzzy logic see L. Zadeh, 'Fuzzy Sets' (1965), and for a critical review of the movement see Charles Grady Morgan and Francis J. Pelletier, 'Some Notes Concerning Fuzzy Logics' (1977), and Alasdair Urquhart, 'Many-Valued Logic' (1986).

sentence, in this view, is meaningless.[3] The idea is important enough to merit a formal definition.

DEFINITION: *P presupposes Q* iff in any world *w*, if *P* is either T or F in *w*, then *Q* is T in *w*.

The definition assumes that assignments of T and F do not exhaust all the possible cases and that the law of bivalence is false. Here are two common examples. Each is presented as a set of three sentences. The first consists of an assertion and its denial, and both are said to presuppose the third sentence of the triple. Neither of the first two is true—indeed the question whether they are true does not arise—if the third is not true.

Existential Presupposition of Singular Terms

John is a bachelor.
John is not a bachelor.
John exists.

The king of France is bald.
The king of France is not bald.
The king of France exists.

Examples of this sort are the subject of a famous debate between Bertrand Russell and P. F. Strawson.[4] Russell argued that the affirmation 'The king of France is bald' may be false because it fails of presupposition but that its negation 'The king of France is not bald' would then be true or false depending on what one means by 'not'. If one means 'not' in the sense of 'it is not true that' then the negation is true. But if the negation means 'The king of France exists but is not bald' then this too is false because it fails of presupposition. In either case, claimed Russell, the negation does not violate the law of excluded middle. Strawson reserved the term 'false' for the subspecies of nontruth that satisfies its presuppositions. He held that in fact neither the affirmation nor the denial is true or false when the presupposition

[3] Some readers find this idea in Frege, 'On Sense and Reference' (1892), but it is first clearly distinguished in P. F. Strawson, *Introduction to Logical Theory* (1952), pp. 20–21, 175. The literature on presupposition is vast. The first clear use of presupposition as a motivation for a many-valued projection to molecular sentences was an application of the semantics of Bochvar to presupposition by T. J. Smiley, 'Sense Without Denotation' (1960). For some recent general discussions of semantic theories of presupposition using many-valued logic see John N. Martin, 'Some Misconceptions in the Critique of Semantic Presupposition' (1979), and William Lycan, *Logical Form in Natural Language* (1984).

[4] See Bertrand Russell, 'On Denoting' (1905), and 'Descriptions' (1919), and P. F. Strawson, 'On Referring' (1950) and 'Identifying Reference and Truth-Values' (1964). The logical literature on existential presupposition, both of singular and general terms, is described in the later sections on supervaluations and free logic.

fails. In such cases, to use his terminology, neither sentence can be used to make a meaningful statement. The debate is a good example of disagreement about the viability of three-valued logic in terms of a dispute about the scope of the term 'false'.

Another important kind of existential presupposition is that which is sometimes carried by common nouns. These cases will be discussed more fully in Chapter 8 under the topic of free logic. Here is a typical case:

Existential Presupposition of Class Terms

All the senators are crooks.
Not all the senators are crooks.
There are some senators.

One of the interesting discrepancies between Aristotelian and modern logic is that Aristotle captured this presuppositional inference in his logic in a way modern logic does not. In the syllogistic, in order for either an A or an O statement to be true, its subject term must stand for a nonempty set, and hence it would be true to say that there was something for which the subject term was true whenever either statement was true. But in modern logic predicates and class terms may have empty extensions, and the inference from $(\forall x)(Fx \rightarrow Gx)$ to $(\exists x)Fx$ is invalid.

A third kind of presupposition requires that the sentence complement of some verbs, like 'discover', 'regret', and 'is surprised', must be true whether the sentence as a whole is an affirmation or a denial. Such verbs are called *factives*, and here is an instance:[5]

Factive Presupposition

He discovered she was there.
He did not discover she was there.
She was there.

Last some individual words (*lexical* items in linguistic jargon) carry their peculiar presuppositions. Here is a well-known case.

Presupposition of the word 'stop'

He stopped beating his wife.
He did not stop beating his wife.
He beat his wife.

[5] See C. A. S. and R. P. V. Kiparsky, 'Fact' (1970), and Lauri Karttunen, 'Some Observations on Factivity' (1971).

7.1.5 Future Contingents

Aristotle reasoned that if the law of excluded middle were true, then the future tense sentence 'There will be a sea battle tomorrow' is either true or false, and the fact it describes is therefore determined. But matters that depend on human decision are not determined. Hence, the law must be false. Medieval philosophers were greatly exercised over whether God's foreknowledge is compatible with human freedom. Like Aristotle's examples of future contingent sentences, these facts about the future were classified as undetermined rather than true or false. These cases are interesting because the need to find an alternative to truth and falsity arises from a philosophical conundrum rather than a straightforward attempt to classify examples of sentences on the fuzzy border between truth and falsity.[6] In classifying their values as indeterminate rather than meaningless, they also offer quite a different conceptual account of the meaning of the new category.

7.1.6 Paradoxes

If the sentence below is true, it is false, and if it is false, it is true:

This sentence is false.

This sort of absurdity led Jean Buridan in the fourteenth century and D. A. Bochvar in the twentieth century to classify this and similar paradoxes as neither true nor false.[7] In this way they attempted to explain away apparent exceptions to another traditional principle of logic, the law of noncontradiction (i.e., $\models \sim (P \wedge \sim P)$). Whether such attempts succeed is controversial, but they are interesting because in the concept of paradoxicalness they have quite a new meaning for the third value. Like the case of future contingents this departure from the law of excluded middle is motivated by logical puzzles.

[6] See the discussion of Aristotle in William and Martha Kneale, *The Development of Logic* (1962), and the application of Aristotle's ideas on nonbivalence to many-valued logic in Bas van Fraassen, 'Singular Terms, Truth-Value Gaps, and Free Logic' (1966).

[7] For discussion of Buridan's solutions to the 'sophismata' see James Cargile, *Paradoxes: A Study in Form and Predication* (1979), and Hans G. Herzberger, 'Dimensions of Truth' (1973). See also D. A. Bochvar, 'On a Three-Valued Logical Calculus and Its Application to the Analysis of the Paradoxes' (1937). There is quite a large literature on the application of many-valued logic to the paradoxes. Many of the most important papers may be found in Robert L. Martin, ed., *The Paradox of the Liar* (1970), and *Recent Essays on Truth and the Liar Paradox* (1984), as well as in the special issue on the paradoxes, Vol. 13 (1984), of the *Journal of Philosophical Logic*.

□ **EXERCISES**

1. Show that if the law of bivalence were true, then presuppositions would all be trivial in the sense that only logical truths could be presuppositions. That is, given bivalence and the formal definition of 'presupposition', show that if P presupposes Q, then in all R, $R(Q) = \mathrm{T}$.
2. Find some examples of the use of common nouns in which the sentences clearly presuppose that the extensions of the nouns are nonempty, and then other examples of the use of the same or other common nouns in which it clearly remains an open question whether the extensions of the terms are nonempty.
3. Find some examples using the verb 'to report' in which the complement is clearly presupposed to be true, and other examples in which it remains an open question whether the complement is true.

7.1.7 The Projection Problem

Once a meaning for the third value, which we shall call N, is decided upon and defended, both in its compatibility with truth and falsity and in its ability to cover important examples, one must then explain how the truth-values of molecular sentences are determined. One way to do so is to assume that essentially the same mechanisms will work in many-valued semantics that apply in classical semantics. In particular, Jan Łukasiewicz at the beginning of this century supposed that many-valued semantics would remain truth-functional. On this view there are rules for determining the truth-value of a whole sentence given the truth-values of its immediate parts, and these rules may be formulated in many-valued truth-tables. These tables must pass what is really a conceptual test. It must be convincingly argued that the connectives as interpreted by the tables are being used in a way consistent with their ordinary meanings. We have a rough idea of the meaning of the ordinary words 'not', 'and', 'or', 'if...then', etc. We also know roughly what we mean by 'true', 'false', and whatever we are choosing as our rendering of N. This linguistic knowledge must be consistent with the relations stated in a given truth-table. We must intuitively agree that the whole has the values assigned in the various cases. Such judgments depend on our intuitive understanding not only of the connective but of the concepts represented by the truth-values. Below are three of the best known three-valued tables for the connectives.

	$\sim$
T	F
F	T
N	N

$\wedge$	T	F	N
	T	F	N
	F	F	N
	N	N	N

$\vee$	T	F	N
	T	T	N
	T	F	N
	N	N	N

$\rightarrow$	T	F	N
	T	F	N
	T	T	N
	N	N	N

Kleene's weak connectives
(Bochvar's internal connectives)

	~
T	F
F	T
N	N

∧	T	F	N
	T	F	N
	F	F	F
	N	F	N

∨	T	F	N
	T	T	T
	T	F	N
	T	N	N

→	T	F	N
	T	F	N
	T	T	T
	T	N	N

Kleene's strong connectives

	~
T	F
F	T
N	N

∧	T	F	N
	T	F	N
	F	F	F
	N	F	N

∨	T	F	N
	T	T	T
	T	F	N
	T	N	N

→	T	F	N
	T	F	N
	T	T	T
	T	N	T

Łukasiewicz's three-valued connectives

The weak connectives treat N as an infection that corrupts the whole if any part is affected, and they seem to conform best with the reading of N as meaningless. They are, therefore, often defended as the tables most suitable for theories for category mistakes and vagueness. Bochvar viewed paradoxicalness as a kind of infection and thus used the first tables in his explanation of the semantic paradoxes, and Buridan seems at times to have had something similar in mind.

Presupposition failure has sometimes been explained as a kind of corruption of this sort, but just as frequently it is explained by the second set of tables. These strong connectives are usually explained by reading N as 'unknown'. If one part of a conjunction is false, then regardless of what we know about the other part the whole must be false. Likewise a disjunction with a true disjunct must be T. Of the readings given to N earlier, this treatment conforms best to that taking N as marking indeterminateness because indeterminateness may be understood in the quasi-epistemic sense of undecided.

Łukasiewicz's tables are explained, with one exception, just like those of the strong connectives. In the case of the conditional, when both parts are N the whole is T. The motivation for this analysis seems to reside in intuitions about logical truth. Unless the truth-table for the conditional yields T for the arguments N and N, it looks like the obvious logical truth $P \rightarrow P$ would sometimes not be T, viz. when P is N. This bow in the direction of capturing an adequate logic raises the whole question of how logical truth and validity are to be defined in a three-valued logic. The adequacy of these definitions of logical ideas constitutes a major problem for a many-valued theory to which we shall return in a moment. First, however, we must discuss in some detail the use of epistemic ideas in truth-tables.[8]

7.1.8 Epistemic Readings of Truth-Values

Let us grant for the sake of argument that the strong tables correctly describe how to determine the epistemic status of a whole expression from the status of its sentential parts. Even if this supposition were true, there would remain the prior question of what these epistemic facts have to do with truth. Is it proper to use epistemic ideas in truth theory?

Explanations that define truth-values in terms of epistemic ideas have been open to a traditional challenge. Given the traditional definition of knowledge as justified true belief, a vast difference exists between a state of knowledge and a fact about the world. The truth or falsity of a sentence is a function of how it corresponds to the world. Knowledge, on the other hand, is a function of what reasons a person can advance for his or her beliefs. It is perfectly possible and indeed highly likely, in the traditional view, that something could be true but unknown. To translate the truth-value T as 'known', then, seems to collapse two quite different ideas. Epistemology, in this view, has nothing to do with the theory of truth, and it is a confusion to use a truth-value to represent an epistemic category. This traditional analysis of truth and knowledge is sometimes called *realism.*[9]

The reply to this objection consists of rejecting the traditional definition of truth as correspondence to the world, and with it the definition of knowledge as justified belief that corresponds to the world. The alternative conception of

[8] The projection problem is so named by Lauri Karttunen, 'Presuppositions of Compound Sentences' (1973). The original source of the weak connectives is S. C. Kleene, 'On a Notation for Ordinal Numbers' (1938). That of the strong connectives is S. C. Kleene, *Introduction to Metamathematics* (1959). For early statements of Łukasiewicz's three-valued matrix see Jan Łukasiewicz, 'On 3-Valued Logic' (1920), 'On Determinism' (1923), and 'Philosophical Remarks on Many-Valued Systems of Propositional Logic' (1930). Though we shall not study the proof theory corresponding to these matrices in this book, their characteristic logical truths and valid arguments can be completely specified both by axioms and in natural deduction systems. For a natural deduction account using much the same terminology as that of the classical proof theory given in Chapter 5 but applied to Łukasiewicz's matrix (which has Kleene's strong connectives as a part) and generalizations from it, see Richard B. White, 'Natural Deduction in the Łukasiewicz Logics' (1980).

[9] For references to the philosophical literature on coherence theories and antirealism see Chapter 3. References to the literature on intuitionistic logic and its semantics are given below. For varieties of many-valued logics with epistemic interpretations see the probabilistic semantics of Hartry Field, 'Logic, Meaning, and Conceptual Role' (1977), and an epistemic interpretation of supervaluations is developed in John N. Martin, 'Epistemic Semantics of Classical and Intuitionistic Logic' (1984).

truth is that of coherence, and holds that the truth of a sentence is a function of its place in a larger systematic body of sentences that, as a whole, has the property of coherence. Thus, there would be no need to posit a world beyond language to serve as the measure by which we evaluate sentences. Knowledge, then, collapses into truth. To know something is to believe it as a part of a larger coherent set. This view has come to be called *antirealism.*

It is hard at first glance to see the attraction of antirealism. It is open to two major objections that it has never satisfactorily answered. The theory should be able to define its central idea of coherence, but beyond the notion of consistency there is little agreement about what coherence amounts to, and clearly consistency itself is an insufficient explanation of a notion of coherence that aspires to be equivalent to truth. Second, given a coherence theory of truth, it appears that more than one set of sentences could be coherent and hence true. Moreover, nothing in the idea of coherence seems to preclude the possibility that these sets could be mutually contradictory. If so, their simultaneous truth would violate the law of noncontradiction, and a theory that violates this law clashes with very deep logical intuitions.

The turn to antirealism came as the outcome of long discussions in two related areas of philosophy, the philosophy of mathematics and epistemology. Plato held the rather implausible view that mathematical objects such as triangles exist on some special level of reality specific to them, and that it is the task of mathematics to describe this special world. This view that mathematical truth is a special case of correspondence to abstract mathematical objects is known in the philosophy of mathematics as *Platonism.* But these mathematical objects are not part of common sense, and it strains plausibility, to say the least, to say that mathematicians investigating objects such as imaginary numbers are *describing* the entities of a world. Thus Platonism in mathematics has never been a particularly convincing application of the correspondence theory of truth. What, then, is truth in mathematics? Coherence is an obvious candidate, and here the idea seems to make a good deal of sense. There is a tradition called *constructivism* in mathematics and *intuitionism* in logic that says that a sentence is true in mathematics if, and only if, it has been proven, and is false if, and only if, it has been refuted. Because being proven or refuted is a matter of justification and is epistemic, in this tradition the theory of truth and epistemology merge.

Difficulties in mainstream epistemology have also led philosophers to take the coherence theory seriously, not only as a model for knowledge in mathematics, but for all knowledge. The traditional view of knowledge as justified true belief has always had the problem of explaining what justification means. Classical philosophers thought justification makes use of some kind of special access to the truth that is so foolproof that it imparts certainty. Modern philosophers have generally backed away from the claim that all knowledge is certain, but most have held that what knowledge we do have is based in some remote way on a foundation of certainties. The rationalists of the Renaissance believed these foundations were truths of reason that we grasp by the intellect alone; more recently the general view has been that most knowledge is built upon sensation. In this view, our senses make reports that we are constrained to accept as 'givens', and we then make inferences or inductions on the basis of these reports. We construct a world view, a body of scientific knowledge and common sense, that is compatible with and ultimately verified by a foundation of sensation. Such is the empiricist view of knowledge accepted by most scientists and by the movement known as *logical positivism* earlier in this century. It is now generally admitted that this sort of *foundationalism* in epistemology has not been worked out. In the theory there is an important relation between the foundation of knowledge and the larger body of scientific theory and common sense based upon it. But the theory has not been able to explain what that relation is and how it works. In particular, many attempts to explain the relation seem to lead to skepticism, the denial that there is any knowledge at all. There is, then, the temptation to think that the whole idea of foundationalism is misconceived, that perhaps knowledge is not based on indubitable links to an external world. The alternative seems to be some kind of coherence theory.

In this book we cannot pursue epistemology nor the philosophy of mathematics, and these remarks will have to suffice as a sketch of what is at issue in using epistemic ideas to explain truth-values. Some such rejection of traditional realism underlies many of the developments of nonclassical semantics and many-valued logics. Intuitionism, which is one such view, is discussed in some detail shortly.

□ **EXERCISES**

1. Using the syntactic definition of 'consistent' from Chapter 5, make up two sets of sentences from propositional logic that are each consistent, but which contradict each other in the sense that they could not be put together in a consistent set.
2. Describe a simple situation in which somebody has a very good justification for believing something, good enough to satisfy the ordinary requirements for expert knowledge of the subject, yet he is mistaken because what he is justified in believing happens to be false.

7.1.9 The Importance of Explaining Logical Intuitions

In three-valued logic we continue to use essentially Leibniz's definitions of logical truth and validity. There are two ways to read Leibniz's definitions once two kinds of nontruth have been distinguished. A logical truth may be either one that is always true or one that is never false, one that is always T, or always either T or N. Likewise a valid argument may be either one that whenever its premises are true so is its conclusion, or one in which whenever its premises are not false, its conclusion is not false. That is, it is one in which whenever the premises are T the conclusion is T, or one in which whenever the premises are either T or N, the conclusion is T or N. In what follows we allow for these various possibilities by singling out a subset of truth-values, called the *designated values*, as those relevant to defining logical truth and validity. A logical truth will be one that always has a designated value, and a valid argument will be one in which whenever the premises are designated so is the conclusion. Then we specify whether we mean $\{T\}$ or $\{T, N\}$ as the set of designated values.

Once the logical notions are defined, they are tested to see if they conform to our logical intuitions. In practice this testing amounts to seeing how the new notions correspond to their classical counterparts: does the new theory agree with classical logic? This comparison with classical logic may be done with mathematical rigor, and we now turn to the techniques used to make the comparison. As we have seen, the evaluation of many-valued semantics involves conceptual issues and the collection of different kinds of examples from usage that might reasonably be candidates for sentences having a value other than T or F. Many-valued truth-tables also are supposed to serve as explanations of the ordinary meaning of the connectives. Much more than we have space to discuss can be said about the strengths and weaknesses of many-valued semantics from the perspective of these criteria. Here, however, we shall focus most of our discussion on the appraisal of three-valued semantics from a logical point of view. We do so because the proper place for discussing the methodology for appraising the conceptual adequacy and accuracy of a semantic theory is theoretical linguistics and the philosophy of language. But one of the most important kinds of critique of many-valued semantics has focused on its logic. The concepts and techniques used in this logical appraisal are a special case of the general methods we shall see applied again and again in this book. They consist of studies in the way the structure of syntax relates to that of semantics, and the ideas used are drawn from abstract algebra. We pause in the next section to state in general terms the concepts needed to evaluate the logics of specific many-valued theories.

□ EXERCISE

Assume that the relation of valid argument is defined by reference to a set D of designated values as follows: $P \vDash Q$ iff for all $R \in [R]$, if $R(P) \in D$ then $R(Q) \in D$. Show that the relation $\vDash$ is transitive.

7.2 COMPARING LOGICAL ENTAILMENT RELATIONS IN DIFFERENT MANY-VALUED LOGICS

7.2.1 The Idea of a Matrix Language

Many-valued logic studies the semantics and proof theory of the highly simplified and abstract syntax of the sentential logic, the formal language built up from atomic sentences by the sentential connectives.[10] For the purposes of this chapter we may use a rather abstract notion of sentential syntax:

DEFINITION: A *sentential syntax* Syn is any structure $\langle \text{Sen}, B, F \rangle$ such that

(1) B is an ordered set of basic sentences (called *atomic* and usually countably infinite in number);

(2) F is an ordered family of 1-1 syntactic functions of various finite degrees (called *formation rules*, usually finite in number);

(3) Sen is the inductive set formed by closing B under the operations in F.

In the examples we shall discuss we shall assume a single set of atomic sentences $B = \{P_1, \ldots, P_n, \ldots\}$, and frequently make use of the formation rules $f_{\sim}, f_{\wedge}, f_{\vee}, f_{\rightarrow}$ for negation, conjunction, disjunction, and the conditional as well as a few new rules. To simplify our presentation, we shall let the index of the function stand for the function as a whole and write $\wedge(x, y)$ for $f_{\wedge}(x, y)$, $\vee(x, y)$ for $f_{\vee}(x, y)$, $\rightarrow(x, y)$ for $f_{\rightarrow}(x, y)$, and $\sim(x)$ for $f_{\sim}(x)$.

Semantically a syntax will be interpreted by a structure of truth-values organized by truth-functions which are intended to interpret the various connectives. The structure specifies, in order, the truth-values used in the semantics, the set of truth-values used in the definition of logical entailment, and the truth-functions corresponding to the formation operations. Possible worlds are then defined as functions which map atomic sentences into truth-values and then project truth-values to complex sentences by applying to the truth-values of its immediate parts the truth-function corresponding to the connective. A language could be defined as we have in the past as a pair consisting of a syntax and its set of possible worlds, but the custom in many-valued semantics is to identify a language with the syntax paired with its semantic structure.

[10] The major extended studies of the semantic theory of many-valued logics are those by J. B. Rosser and A. R. Turquette, *Many-Valued Logics* (1952), Nicholas Rescher, *Many-Valued Logic* (1969), and George Epstein, ed., *Multiple-Valued Logic* (1976). A good review of the technical issues in many-valued logic, which is, however, somewhat too dismissive of its conceptual and linguistic motivation, is by Alasdair Urquhart, 'Many-Valued Logic' (1986). Another critical discussion from a logical perspective is that of Dana Scott, 'Does Many-Valued Logic Have Any Use?' (1976). The metatheory presented in this section is a development of that in John N. Martin, 'The Semantics of Frege's *Grundgesetze*' (1984).

As explained earlier, there are two possible ways to define valid argument once three values are allowed. Such an argument may be defined as one that always takes you from premises that are T to a conclusion that is T. That is, it may be defined as truth-preserving. Alternatively, it may be defined as non-falsity-preserving, as one in which whenever the premises are not F then the conclusion is not F. In classical semantics in which the only value other than F is T, the two definitions are equivalent, but they are not so when three or more values are allowed. To state the definition in general terms, we set aside a subset of truth-values as those preserved in logical inference, and define validity by reference to this set of 'designated' values.

DEFINITION: A *logical matrix* M is defined as any structure $\langle U, D, G\rangle$ such that

(1) U is a nonempty set (called the set of *truth-values*);
(2) D is a subset of U (the set of *designated values*);
(3) G is an ordered set of finitely valued functions on U.

DEFINITION: A *sentential matrix language* L is any structure $\langle \text{Syn}, M\rangle$ such that

(1) Syn is some sentential syntax $\langle \text{Sen}, B, F\rangle$;
(2) M is some logical matrix $\langle U, D, G\rangle$, such that
  (a) F and G contain the same number of functions and
  (b) for any f_i in F, if f_i is of degree n, so is g_i, and if f_i is nonempty, so is g_i.

DEFINITION: For a sentential matrix language $L = \langle \text{Syn}, M\rangle$ where Syn $= \langle \text{Sen}, B, F\rangle$ and $M = \langle U, D, G\rangle$, we define the set $[R]$ (called the *set of possible worlds for L*) as follows:

$$[R] = \{R|(\text{Sen} \xrightarrow[\text{into}]{} U) \text{ such that}$$

$$\begin{aligned} &(1)\ \text{if } P \in B, \text{ then } R(P) \in U;\\ &(2)\ \text{if } f_i \in F \text{ and } P_1, \ldots, P_n \in \text{Sen, then}\\ &\quad R(f_i(P_1, \ldots, P_n)) = g_i(R(P_1), \ldots, R(P_n))\}. \end{aligned}$$

In the following definition we introduce the abbreviation $R(X) \in D$ for the condition in which all the sentences in a set X are assigned designated elements in D by R.

DEFINITION: For any set X of sentences and any reference relation R, we define $R(X) \in D$ to mean that for any element P of X, $R(P)$ is in D.

DEFINITION: For a matrix language L and a subset X of Sen of L and a sentence P in Sen, we say

X logically entails P in L (briefly, $X \vDash_L P$) iff
for all R in $[R]$ of L, $R(X) \in D$ only if $R(P) \in D$.

From this point on we shall assume that L ranges over sentential matrix languages, and that Syn = $\langle$Sen, B, $F\rangle$ is its syntax, $M = \langle U, D, G\rangle$ is its matrix, and $[R]$ is its world set. Distinct languages, their syntaxes, matrices, world sets, and entailment relations will be distinguished by subscripts and prime marks. As we have in the past we let X, Y, and Z range over the subsets of the set Sen under discussion, and P, Q, and S over its members. We let f range over the set F of operations, and g over the operations of the set G of a matrix.

Our goal in this section is to define the relevant concepts and prove the necessary theorems for the systematic comparison of the entailment relations of various many-valued languages. The need to make such comparisons is dictated by the theoretical goal of maintaining an entailment relation that approximates that recognized by our logical intuitions. One way to make such comparisons is to evaluate directly a proposed entailment relation by comparison with our raw intuitions. If some arguments which we intuitively accept fall outside the entailment relation as defined, the definition is too narrow, and if the definition sanctions some arguments rejected by intuition, it is too broad. In practice we often compare a new entailment relation with another that is already formally defined, especially that of classical two-valued semantics. We know the classical entailment relation very well. We know its strengths and weaknesses. Even though there are some intuitively strange arguments sanctioned by classical logic (e.g., the argument from P to $Q \vee {\sim}Q$, or that from P to $P \vee Q$), classical logic is an impressive theory. Any competitor would do well to equal classical logic at capturing logical intuitions, and it is usual practice to contrast new semantics with the standard classical account. We shall see that it is a far from trivial matter to introduce new truth-values and preserve a truth-functional logic that even approximates classical logic.

To carry out the comparison we need some theory. Our procedure will be to introduce a series of new concepts, some syntactic and some semantic, and along with each concept we shall prove the relevant metatheorem which explains how the concept is to be used in comparing entailment relations.

7.2.2 The Part-Of Relation among Syntaxes

A natural way to think of one syntax as being part of another is that the larger syntax contains all the atomic sentences of the smaller, and all the sentences built up from them. The larger syntax might also contain atomic sentences not present in the smaller, as well as the molecular sentences built up from these. The formation rules of the larger would accordingly be defined for the additional sentences not present in the smaller.

DEFINITION: A Syn is *part of* Syn′ iff $B \subseteq B'$, and for each i, $f_i \subseteq f'_i$.

The notion of part as defined here allows for the possibility that a given f_i might be empty, and indeed we shall consider one matrix to be a part of another if it can be made a part in the sense just defined by the addition of various empty formation rules and re-indexing the set F. Note also that a matrix for a syntax will also count as a matrix for all syntaxes of which it is a part.

THEOREM. Let Syn be a part of Syn′ and let M be a matrix for both. For any R in $[R]$, there is some R' in $[R']$ such that $R \subseteq R'$. Likewise, for any R' in $[R']$, there is an R in $[R]$ such that $R \subseteq R'$.

Proof. For the first part, we assume R, define R' in terms of R, and then show by induction that for any P in Sen, $R(P) = R'(P)$. We define R' as follows: for any atomic P in B of Syn, we require that $R'(P) = R(P)$ and that for any P in $B' - B$, $R'(P)$ is in U'. For any molecular $P = f_i(Q_1, \ldots, Q_n)$, we define $R'(P) = g_i(R'(Q_1), \ldots, R'(Q_n))$. We have defined R' so that it trivially meets the conditions for membership in $[R']$. For induction consider the following property of sentences in Sen:

(1) $R(P) = R'(P)$.

We show that it holds for all P in Sen by induction.

Atomic case. Let P be atomic. Then by definition of R', $R(P) = R'(P)$.

Molecular case. Let P be $f_i(Q_1, \ldots, Q_n)$, and we assume as our induction hypothesis that (1) holds for all sentences shorter than P. In particular, we assume that (1) holds for its immediate parts: for any j, $R(Q_j) = R'(Q_j)$. Now,

$R(P) = g_i(R(Q_1), \ldots, R(Q_n))$ [by the assumption that R is in $[R]$]

$= g_i(R'(Q_1), \ldots, R'(Q_n))$ [by the induction hypothesis and substitution of identities]

$= R'(P)$ [by the definition of R'].

Proof of the second part of the theorem is left for the reader.

□ **EXERCISE**

Prove the second part of the previous theorem by assuming R', defining R so as to be in $[R]$. Show by induction that for any P in Sen, $R(P) = R'(P)$.

We now state the results which show how to employ the notion of syntactic part in comparing entailment relations.

THEOREM. If Syn is a part of Syn′ and $M = M'$, then $X \vDash_L P$ only if $X \vDash_{L'} P$.

Proof. For some R' of $[R']$ of L' assume for a *reductio* proof that $R'(P) = \mathrm{F}$ but $R'(X) = \mathrm{T}$. Since $X \vDash_L P$, X is a subset and P an element of Sen of L. Then, by the previous metatheorem, there is some R of $[R]$ that agrees with

R' such that $R(X) = \text{T}$ and $R(P) = \text{F}$, contradicting our assumption that $X \vDash_L P$. End of Proof.

THEOREM. If Syn is a part of Syn′, $M = M'$, and P is in B of Syn, then $X \vDash_{L'} P$ only if $X \vDash_L P$.

☐ **EXERCISE**

Prove the previous theorem.

7.2.3 Sameness of Syntax

The next concept we shall use to compare logics is a variety of sameness of syntax. Clearly if all that differentiates two syntaxes is the shape of the connectives, they differ only in style, not substance. The formal idea of sameness in this sense is that of isomorphism. It is also possible to show rather easily that if one syntax differs from another only in having more atomic sentences but is otherwise the same, then the logic of the two will at least agree on the expressions they share. This variety of sameness is discussed under the concept of homomorphism.

DEFINITION: A function h is a *homomorphism* from a structure $\langle X, O_1, \ldots, O_n \rangle$ to a structure $\langle X', O'_1, \ldots, O'_n \rangle$, where each of O_i is an operation on X, each O'_i is an operation on X', and O_i is of the same degree as O'_i, iff

(1) h maps X into X', and

(2) for any i, $h(O_i(x_1, \ldots, x_n)) = O'_i(h(x_1), \ldots, h(x_n))$.

DEFINITION: A function h is an *isomorphism* iff h is a 1–1 ‘onto’ homomorphism.

THEOREM. If h is a homomorphism from Syn to Syn′ and $M = M'$, then for any R' in $[R']$, there is an R in $[R]$ such that for any P in Sen, $R(P) = R'(h(P))$.

Proof. Assume h is such a homomorphism. We assume R' and define R: for any P in B, $R(P) = R'(h(P))$. We now show by induction that for any P in Sen, $R(P) = R'(h(P))$.

Atomic case. Trivially true by definition of R.

Molecular case.

$$\begin{aligned} R(f_i(P_1, \ldots, P_n)) &= g_i(R(P_1), \ldots, R(P_n)) \text{ [by definition of } R \text{ and } R'] \\ &= g_i(R'(h(P_1)), \ldots, R'(h(P_n))) \text{ [by induction hypothesis]} \\ &= R'(f'_i(h(P_1), \ldots, h(P_n))) \text{ [by definition of } R'] \\ &= R'(h(f_i(P_1, \ldots, P_n))) \text{ [since } h \text{ is a homomorphism].} \end{aligned}$$

End of Proof.

THEOREM. If h is a homomorphism from Syn to Syn′ and $M = M'$, then $X \models_L P$ only if $h(X) \models_{L'} h(P)$. (Here $h(X) = \{h(P) | P \in X\}$.)
THEOREM. If h is a homomorphism from Syn to Syn′ and $h(P)$ is in B' of Syn′, then P is in B of Syn.

□ **EXERCISE**

Prove the previous two theorems. The proof strategy for the first is similar to that of previous results. The second can be shown by a straightforward *reductio* proof.

THEOREM. h is a homomorphism from Syn to Syn′ and for any atomic P in B, $h(B)$ is a unique element of B' (i.e., h restricted to B is 1–1 and onto B') iff h is an isomorphism from Syn to Syn′.

Proof. *'If' part.* We need only show that h is 1–1 and onto molecular sentences since it is so by definition for atomic sentences. We shall show by induction that h assigns a unique value to every element in Sen. Clearly the basis step is satisfied because by definition h assigns unique values to all atomic elements in B. For the inductive step we assume h assigns unique values to the parts of the whole sentence $f_i(P_1, \ldots, P_n)$ and then show it assigns a unique value to the sentence itself. Now, $h(f_i(P_1, \ldots, P_n))$ is the composition value $f'_i(h(P_1), \ldots, h(P_n))$. By the induction hypothesis these h values are unique (i.e., h restricted to the parts of the whole is 1–1) and f'_i is a 1–1 function by definition. Thus their composition function is unique.

'Only if' part. It follows trivially from the definition of isomorphism that h is a homomorphism from Syn to Syn′. We now show that h restricted to B is 1–1 and onto B'. It is 1–1 by definition. Since h is by assumption an 'onto' function, it assigns values to all elements in its domain Sen′, including the subset B' of Sen′. By a previous metatheorem, we also know that if $h(P)$ is in B', then P is in B. Thus for every value in B' there is a unique argument in B assigned to it by h. It remains to be shown that h restricted to B assigns values only in B'. Suppose otherwise, that for some f'_i, $P'_1, \ldots, P'_n$, and some P in B, $h(P) = f'_i(P'_1, \ldots, P'_n)$. Then for some $P_1, \ldots, P_n$ of Sen, $h(P_1) = P'_1, \ldots, h(P_n) = P'_n$ and then $h(P) = f'_i(h(P_1), \ldots, h(P_n))$ [by substitution of identities] $= h(f_i(P_1, \ldots, P_n))$ [by definition of homomorphism], contradicting our assumption that h is 1–1. End of Proof.

THEOREM. If h is an isomorphism from Syn to Syn′ and $M = M'$, then for any R in $[R]$, there is an R' in $[R']$ such that for any P in Sen, $R(P) = R'(h(P))$.

Proof. Assume h is such an isomorphism and that R is in $[R]$. We define R'. If P' is in B', there is a unique P in B such that $h(P) = P'$. We define $R'(P') = R'(h(P))$ to be $R(P)$. Likewise for the molecular case. For any molecular $f'_i(P'_1, \ldots, P'_n)$, there are unique $P_1, \ldots, P_n$, such that $h(P_j) = P_j$. We defne $R'(f'_i(P'_1, \ldots, P'_n)) = g'_i(P'_1, \ldots, P'_n))$. We show by induction that for all P in Sen, $R(P) = R'(h(P))$. The reader may fill out the details as an exercise.

THEOREM. If h is an isomorphism from Syn to Syn′ and $M = M'$, then $X \vDash_L P$ iff $h(X) \vDash_{L'} h(P)$.

☐ **EXERCISE**

Prove the previous two theorems. Note that half of the latter result has in effect been proven earlier.

7.2.4 Part–Whole among Matrices

Thus far we have compared two languages by varying their syntaxes but keeping the matrix determining their semantics fixed. We can also compare languages by varying their matrices. We begin by defining a part–whole relation for matrices. It will turn out that possible worlds according to the smaller matrix also count as worlds according to the larger and that entailments valid under the larger hold also for the smaller.

DEFINITION: M is a *part of* M' iff $U \subseteq U'$, $D \subseteq D'$, and for each i, g_i is nonempty and a subset of g'_i.

THEOREM. If Syn = Syn′ and M is a part of M', then $[R] \subseteq [R']$.

Proof. Assume the antecedent, and that R is in $[R]$. It is evident that R meets the defining conditions for membership in $[R']$. For any atomic P, $R(P)$ is in U' because the fact that R is in $[R]$ entails that $R(P)$ is in U and $U \subseteq U'$. Similarly in the molecular case $R(f_i(P_1, \ldots, P_n)) = g_i(R(P_1), \ldots, R(P_n))$ [since R is in $[R]$] $= g'_i(R(P), \ldots, R(P_n))$ [since g_i is contained in g'_i]. Therefore R is in $[R']$. End of Proof.

THEOREM. If Syn = Syn′ and M is a part of M', then $X \vDash_{L'} P$ only if $X \vDash_L P$.

☐ **EXERCISE**

Prove the last theorem.

7.2.5 Sameness of Matrix

Just as similarity of structure among syntaxes forces similarity of entailment, so too does structural sameness among matrices. The general concepts of morphism defined for arbitrary structures will serve as the relevant notions of sameness of structure but we must adjust them slightly since matrices have the extra set of designated elements not allowed for in the general case. We do so with the following definitions.

DEFINITION: h is a *morphism* from M to M' iff h is a morphism from

$$\langle U, g_1, \ldots, g_n \rangle \quad \text{to} \quad \langle U', g'_1, \ldots, g'_n \rangle.$$

DEFINITION: A morphism h from M to M' is said to *preserve designation* iff for any x, $x \in D$ only if $h(x) \in D'$, and is said to *preserve nondesignation* iff for any x, $x \notin D$ only if $h(x) \notin D'$.

THEOREM. If Syn = Syn′ and h is a homomorphism from M to M', then $\{h \cdot R \mid R \text{ is in } [R]\} \subseteq [R']$.

Proof. Here $h \cdot R$ is the composition function of R and h defined in the usual way: $h \cdot R(x) = h(R(X))$. Assume the antecedent of the theorem, and consider an arbitrary $h \cdot R$ such that R is in $[R]$. We show that it meets the conditions of membership in $[R']$. For an atomic P, we need note only that h is defined for $R(P)$ and that the range of h is included in U'. Hence $h(R(P))$ is in U'. For the molecular case we note that $h(R(f_i(P_1, \ldots, P_n))) = h(g_i(R(P_1), \ldots, R(P_n)))$ [since R is in $[R]$] $= g'_i(h(R(P_1), \ldots, h(R(P_n)))$ [since h is a homomorphism]. Thus $h \cdot R$ meets the conditions for membership in $[R']$. End of Proof.

THEOREM. If Syn = Syn′ and h is a homomorphism from M to M' that preserves both designation and nondesignation, then $X \models_{L'} P$ only if $X \models_L P$.

Proof. Assume the condition that $X \models_{L'} P$, and assume for a *reductio* proof that for R in $[R]$, $R(X) \in D$ but that $R(P) \notin D$. We know from the last theorem that $h \cdot R$ is in $[R']$. Since h preserves designation, $h \cdot R(X) \in D'$, and since h preserves nondesignation, $h(P) \notin D'$. But this contradicts the assumption that $X \models_{L'} P$. Thus if $R(X)$ is in D, so is $R(P)$. End of Proof.

THEOREM. If Syn = Syn′ and h is a homomorphism from M onto M', then $\{h \cdot R \mid R \text{ is in } [R]\} = [R']$.

THEOREM. If Syn = Syn′ and h is a homomorphism from M onto M', then $X \models_L P$ iff $X \models_{L'} P$.

☐ **EXERCISE**

Prove the previous two theorems.

7.2.6 Sublanguages and Conservative Extensions of Entailment

Thus far we have allowed structures to be extensions of one another if their various features are subsets of one another. There is another sense of part–whole that is useful when considering matrices. It is frequently the case that we want to compare one language with another like it except that the second contains some additional connectives and corresponding truth-functions.

Normally we should not expect the addition of some new connectives to alter the meaning of the old. In particular, we would expect that the logical relations validated in the restricted language would remain valid in the new, and any argument in the new language formulated solely in terms of the old would be valid in the extended language only if it had been so in the original. To express these ideas, we first define the relevant notion of part–whole and then the idea of being faithful in the whole to the logic of the part.

DEFINITION: L is a *sublanguage* of L' iff Syn is a part of Syn′, $U = U'$, $D = D'$, and for each i, either g_i is empty or identical to g'_i.

DEFINITION: L' is a *conservative extension* of L iff Syn is a part of Syn′ and the logical entailment relation of L' restricted to Sen is identical to that of L (i.e., for any subset X of Sen and any P in Sen, $X \vDash_{L'} P$ iff $X \vDash_L P$).

Notice that for any language it is required that if f_i is nonempty, so is g_i. Thus, if g_i is empty, so is f_i. Intuitively, an empty formation operation is equivalent to no operation at all, and we shall in fact identify any structure with empty operations with the structure obtained by deleting the empty operations and renumbering. The idea is intuitive enough but its formal statement is a bit baroque.

DEFINITION: A *deflation* of a structure $\langle X, O_1, \ldots, O_m\rangle$ is the structure $\langle X, O'_1, \ldots, O'_n\rangle$ such that there is a function p on $\{1, \ldots, m\}$ such that $\{0, 1, \ldots, n\}$ is the range of p, $O'_{p(i)} = O_i$, and p is defined (recursively) as follows:

(i) $p(1) = 1$ if Q_1 is nonempty and $p(1) = 0$ otherwise, and
(ii) $p(i + 1) = p(i) + 1$ if Q_{i+1} is nonempty and $p(i + 1) = 0$ otherwise.

When convenient we shall assume without comment that a structure is identical with its deflation.

THEOREM. If L is a sublanguage of L', then
(1) for any R in $[R]$, there is an R' in $[R']$ such that for any P in Sen, $R(P) = R'(P)$, and
(2) for any R' in $[R']$, there is an R in $[R]$ such that for any P in Sen, $R(P) = R'(P)$.

Proof. We prove part (2). Assume the antecedent of the theorem and that R' is in $[R']$. We define R as the restriction of R' to Sen. Since Sen is a subset of Sen′, R' is defined for Sen, and since R is the restriction of R' to Sen, R and R' agree on all values assigned to elements in Sen. What remains to be shown is that R meets the conditions for membership in $[R]$. Clearly, R assigns atomic elements values in U because R' does. Moreover, for the molecular case consider a function f_i of F that is nonempty, $R(f_i(P_1, \ldots, P_n)) = R'(f_i(P_1 \ldots, P_n))$ [since R is the restriction of R' to Sen] $= g_i(R'(P_1), \ldots, R'(P_n))$ [since R' is in $[R']$] $= g_i(R(P_1), \ldots, R(P_n))$ [since R is the restriction of R' to Sen]. Hence R is in $[R]$. End of Proof.

THEOREM. If L is a sublanguage of L', then L' is a conservative extension of L.

☐ **EXERCISE**

Prove the last theorem and part (1) of the one that precedes it.

Yet another technique for constructing logically similar languages is to introduce into a new language explicit connectives for truth-functions expressible in the original but only by means of molecular sentences. For example, we know that it is sufficient for classical propositional logic to have only negation and the conditional as primitive connectives in the syntax. We could then 'introduce' connectives for conjunction and disjunction by using $P \wedge Q$ as an abbreviation of the longer expression $\sim(P \rightarrow \sim Q)$ and $P \vee Q$ as short for $\sim P \rightarrow Q$. In such a theory a distinction is made between, on the one hand, the primitive notation defined as any sentence of the syntax and, on the other, the abbreviated forms. An abbreviated expression is not really a sentence of the syntax, though a genuine sentence of the syntax that it abbreviates is in principle obtainable from it. Thus an expression employing the defined forms is translated into primitive notation in order to transform it into a genuinely well-formed expression. It follows that the nonprimitive forms receive no direct semantic interpretation because in the matrix for the syntax there is no semantic operation corresponding to or interpreting the defined connectives. The expressions introduced by definition must be interpreted indirectly by first transforming them into primitive notation. A language using primitive and defined notation may be contrasted with one in which the syntax has a separate formation operation for all the connectives. Each of these connectives has its own syntactic operation in the syntax that generates genuine sentences, and each of these syntactic operations is interpreted by a corresponding semantic operation in the matrix. Of course, both sorts of language are in a deep sense capable of saying the same thing. We now take up discussion of this equivalence and how to formulate it. The first idea we need is that of a truth-function definable in terms of the other truth-functions of a matrix. It is a property of the abbreviated forms that their truth-functions are definable in this way.

DEFINITION: We define the notion of a function $[k]$ *constructible in a structure* $S = \langle X, O_1, \ldots, O_n \rangle$ inductively.

(1) (*Basis clause*) Any of the functions O_i of S is constructible in S; and

(2) (*Inductive clause*) if g, $h_i, \ldots, h_j$ are functions constructible in S and $\langle x_1, \ldots, x_m \rangle = \langle x_q, \ldots, x_r, \ldots, x_s, \ldots, x_t, x_u, \ldots, x_v \rangle$, then the function $[k]$ defined on X as follows is constructible in S:

$$[k](x_1, \ldots, x_m) = g(h_1(x_q, \ldots, x_r), \ldots, h_j(x_s, \ldots, x_t), x_u, \ldots, x_v).$$

(In this case we refer to $[k]$ as $[g \cdot h_i \cdot \ldots \cdot h_j]$).

We shall apply this definition to matrices in the obvious way by calling a function constructible in M iff it is constructible in the structure obtained by deleting D.

DEFINITION: L' is a *definitional extension* of L iff L is a sublanguage of L', B of Syn is identical to B' of Syn$'$, and for each i, if g_i is empty but g'_i is nonempty, then g'_i is constructible in M.

THEOREM. If L' is a definitional extension of L, then there is a translation function t from Sen$'$ onto Sen such that $X \vDash_{L'} P$ iff $t(X) \vDash_L t(P)$.

Proof. First, for a function $[k]$ constructible in M we define by recursion the function $*$ that assigns to $[k]$ a function constructible in Syn such that $[k]$ intuitively interprets the grammatical operation $[k]*$. If $[k]$ is constructible in M, we define $[k]*$ recursively.

(1) if for some i, $[k] = g_i$, then $[k]* = f_i$; and

(2) if $[k] = [g \cdot h_i \cdot \ldots \cdot h_j]$ for some functions g, h_i, h_j constructible in M, then $[k]* = [g* \cdot h_i * \cdot \ldots \cdot h_j *]$.

We make the claim that embodies the intuitive interpretation of $*$:

(I) for any R in $[R]$, $R([k]*(P_1, \ldots, P_n)) = [k](R(P_1), \ldots, R(P_n))$.

Proof of claim (I) is by induction on the inductive set of sentences in Syn and is left as an exercise. We define by recursion the relevant translation function t from Syn$'$ onto Syn:

(1) if P is in B', $t(P) = P$;

(2) if P is some $f'_i(P_1, \ldots, P_n)$, then $t(P)$ is $[g'_i]*(t(P_1), \ldots, t(P_n))$.

It is clear that t is an 'into' function, but we also claim that

(II) t is an 'onto' function from Sen$'$ to Sen.

Proof is again by induction on the set of sentences in Sen and is also left as an exercise. Now, let us use the usual notation $f \mid A$ for the restriction of the function f to A, i.e., $f \mid A = \{\langle x, y\rangle \mid \langle x, y\rangle \in f \wedge x \in A\}$. Note that below in the notation $f \mid A(x)$, $f \mid A$ is grouped together as a function name, and the whole $f \mid A(x)$ refers to the value of that function for the argument x. We are now ready to make our final claim:

(III) for any R' in $[R']$, $R'(P) = R' \mid \text{Sen}(t(P))$.

Proof is by induction on the set of sentences in Sen$'$. For brevity let $R' \mid S$ be $R' \mid$ Sen.

Atomic case. Since $B' = B$, if P is in B', $R'(P) = R' \mid S(P) = R' \mid S(t(P))$ [since $t(P) = P$].

Molecular case.

$$\begin{aligned} R'(f'_i(P_1, \ldots, P_n)) &= [g'_i](R'(P_1), \ldots, R'(P_n)) \text{ [since } R' \text{ is in } [R']] \\ &= g'_i(R'|S(t(P_1)), \ldots, R'|S(t(P_n))) \text{ [by induction hypothesis]} \\ &= R'|S([g_i]*(t(P_1), \ldots, t(P_n)) \text{ [by claim (I)]} \\ &= R'|\text{Sen}(t(f'_i(P_1, \ldots, P_n)) \text{ [by definition of } t]. \end{aligned}$$

End of Proof.

We are now suitably armed to attempt a broad review of how the logical entailment relations of various many-valued logics compare to that of classical logic.

☐ **EXERCISE**

Prove claims (I) and (II) in the preceding proof.

7.3 EXAMPLES OF MANY-VALUED LOGICS

7.3.1 Kleene's Weak and Strong Connectives

S. C. Kleene is responsible for two quite interesting three-valued matrix semantics. In the first the classical truth-values are augmented by a third that may be read as representing meaninglessness. A sentence assigned T is true in the usual sense, and one assigned F is false in the usual sense, but a sentence assigned the third value (we shall use N), though grammatical and hence genuinely a member of Sen, is supposed to be semantically ineffectual. Questions of its truth or falsity do not arise. This idea alone does not tell us how to project truth-values to molecular sentences. We need a second idea. Kleene proposed that any sentential whole containing a meaningless part is itself meaningless. Thus the semantic imperfection of the part affects the whole, and this idea is sufficient for completely determining a set of three-valued truth-functions for the usual connectives:

	$\sim$
T	F
F	T
N	N

$\wedge$	T	F	N
T	T	F	N
F	F	F	N
N	N	N	N

$\vee$	T	F	N
T	T	T	N
F	T	F	N
N	N	N	N

$\rightarrow$	T	F	N
T	T	F	N
F	T	T	N
N	N	N	N

Kleene's weak connectives

In another context Kleene proposes another reading of the third value and a correspondingly different projection of it to molecular sentences. The theory is meant to apply to those sorts of sentences in mathematics that can in principle be decided by an algorithm. Kleene's idea is to divide the mathematically relevant sentences into three classes: those for which there is a mathematical algorithm showing that it is true, those for which there is one showing that it is false (i.e., that its negation is true), and those which are undecided in the sense that there is no algorithm establishing either it or its negation. Here an algorithm is meant to be what we have called an effective process in Chapter 6. In the vocabulary of that discussion, we may express

Kleene's idea as follows. There is, he suggests, a decidable subset A of the set U of all mathematical propositions. Thus, the characteristic function f of A is definable as an effective process. For any P in U, if f is defined for P and $f(P) = \mathrm{T}$, then we say that the sentence is 'true'; if f is defined for P and $f(P) = \mathrm{F}$, then we say P is 'false' and $\sim P$ is 'true'; and if P is in $U - A$ and f is undefined for P, we suspend judgment on P. A computer program that answers mathematical inquiries for defined inputs with either a 'yes' or 'no' in a finite period of time would be an example. Such a testing procedure for mathematical truths would be, if accurate, a justification for believing those sentences that pass the test and for disbelieving those that fail. Thus, classification of sentences according to their status as decidable by an algorithm may be viewed as an epistemic semantics.

A more general reading of the truth-values as recording epistemic status is a natural abstraction from Kleene's particular application to sentences in mathematics. By this three-valued generalization any sentence receives one of the three values according to whether it is justified, refuted, or neither. There are those sentences that are fully justified and receive T, those which are fully refuted (their negations are fully justified) and receive F, and the remainder about which we are still in epistemic doubt. We shall find similar ideas underlying the semantics for intuitionistic logic when we discuss it later in this chapter.

The projection to molecular sentences that Kleene proposed for such truth-values is one that preserves a feature of the classical truth-tables. If the truth-value of one part of a sentence is enough to determine that of the whole, then it should remain so even when an additional value is introduced. Thus a conjunction with a false conjunct should be false regardless of whether the other conjunct is true, false, or neither. Likewise, a disjunction with a true disjunct is true, and a conditional with a false antecedent or a true consequent is true. Using this principle, which seems to be quite reasonable under an epistemic reading of the truth-values, we arrive at the following operations:

	$\sim$
T	F
F	T
N	N

$\wedge$	T	F	N
T	T	F	N
F	F	F	F
N	N	F	N

$\vee$	T	F	N
T	T	T	T
F	T	F	N
N	T	N	N

$\rightarrow$	T	F	N
T	T	F	N
F	T	T	T
N	T	N	N

Kleene's strong connectives

In order to define the matrices in the customary way, we shall use numbers as truth-values. It is customary to regard 1 as T, 0 as F, and 1/2 as N. We will also follow the usual practice in mathematics of identifying a (natural) number with the set of all its predecessors. For example, 0 is the empty set, $1 = \{0\}$, $2 = \{0, 1\}$, $3 = \{0, 1, 2\}$, etc. We define KW, the matrix for the weak connectives, to be the matrix $\langle\{0, 1/2, 1\}, \{1\}, \sim, \wedge, \vee, \rightarrow\rangle$ such that the operations $\sim$, $\wedge$, $\vee$, and $\rightarrow$ are as defined in the tables for the weak connectives. Similarly, KS, the matrix for the strong connectives, is defined as $\langle\{0, 1/2, 1\}, \{1\}, \sim, \wedge, \vee, \rightarrow\rangle$ such that the operations are defined by the truth-tables for the strong connectives. We shall now compare the logics of these matrices with those of classical logic. Let C be the matrix $\langle\{0, 1\}, \{1\}, \sim, \wedge, \vee, \rightarrow\rangle$ such that the operations conform to the classical truth-tables. Let us further assume Syn $= \langle$Sen, $\sim, \wedge, \vee, \rightarrow\rangle$ is a syntax for propositional logic, and the following languages are defined: LC $= \langle$Syn, $C\rangle$, LKW $= \langle$Syn, KW$\rangle$, and LKS $= \langle$Syn, KS$\rangle$.

THEOREM. (1) If $X \vDash_{\text{LKW}} P$ or $X \vDash_{\text{LKS}} P$, then $X \vDash_{\text{LC}} P$;
(2) there is an X and P such that $X \vDash_{\text{LC}} P$ and not($X \vDash_{\text{LKW}} P$); and
(3) there is an X and P such that $X \vDash_{\text{LC}} P$ and not($X \vDash_{\text{LKS}} P$).

Proof. Proof of clause (1) follows directly from the fact that there are homomorphisms from KW and KS into C that preserve designation and nondesignation. Clauses (2) and (3) are proven by finding the right examples. Consider the argument from P to $(P \wedge Q) \vee (P \wedge \sim Q)$. End of Proof.

Though there are interesting generalizations of these matrices to more than three values, we shall not consider them here but turn instead to some other three-valued theories that readily lend themselves to comparison with classical logic by the techniques we have developed.

☐ **EXERCISE**

By KW* let us mean the matrix like KW except that both 1 and 1/2 are designated (i.e., $D = \{1/2, 1\}$). Likewise, let KS* be like KS except that both 1 and 1/2 are designated. Let LKW* be $\langle$Syn, KW*$\rangle$, and LKS* be $\langle$Syn, KS*$\rangle$. Prove that a metatheorem just like that above continues to hold with the * matrices replacing the original versions.

7.3.2 Lukasiewicz's Three-Valued Logic

One of the earlier versions of three-valued logic was developed by the Polish logician Jan Łukasiewicz to deal with problems like future contingents. Those sentences that are not determined receive the third value. The matrix he proposed is quite like that of the strong connectives except for the conditional which has the special feature that if both the antecedent and consequent are undetermined, the whole is true:

	∼
T	F
F	T
N	N

∧	T	F	N
T	T	F	N
F	F	F	F
N	N	F	N

∨	T	F	N
T	T	T	T
F	T	F	N
N	T	N	N

→	T	F	N
T	T	F	N
F	T	T	T
N	T	N	T

Łukasiewicz's three-valued connectives

Again let us use numbers for truth-values and define the matrix L3, Łukasiewicz's three-valued matrix, to be $\langle\{0, 1/2, 1\}, \{1\}, \wedge, \vee, \rightarrow\rangle$, and set LL3 = ⟨Syn, L3⟩. Likewise, let L3∗ and LL3∗ be like their unstarred originals except that both 1 and 1/2 are designated.

THEOREM. The logical entailment relations $\vDash_{\text{LL3}}$ and $\vDash_{\text{LL3*}}$ are proper subsets of $\vDash_{\text{LC}}$.

Proof. The examples for LKS and LKS∗ will work for Łukasiewicz's matrix because they do not make use of the conditional.

It is possible to generalize the ideas in this matrix to arbitrarily many values. Let min be a function that pairs with any two arguments their minimum, and let max be the function that pairs with them their maximum.[11]

DEFINITION: By Ln we mean the matrix $\langle U_n, \{1\}, \sim, \wedge, \vee, \rightarrow\rangle$ such that
(1) $U_n = \{n/n, \ldots, 0/n\}$;
(2) $\sim(x) = 1 - x$;
(3) $\wedge(x, y) = \min(x, y)$;
(4) $\vee(x, y) = \max(x, y)$; and
(5) $\rightarrow(x, y) = \min(1, (1 - x) + y)$.

DEFINITION: By Lω we mean the matrix $\langle R, \{1\}, \sim, \wedge, \vee, \rightarrow\rangle$ such that R is the set of rational numbers (ratios of positive integers), and the operations are as defined in clauses (2)–(5) above. (Here ω is the limit ordinal representing the set of all natural numbers $\{0, 1, 2, \ldots\}$.) These matrices may be used to form a sequence of languages with increasingly strong entailment relations culminating in classical logic. Let LLω be ⟨Syn, Lω⟩, LLn be ⟨Syn, Ln⟩, etc.

THEOREM. The logical entailment relation $\vDash_{\text{LL}\omega}$ is a proper subset of any $\vDash_{\text{LLn}}$; $\vDash_{\text{LLn}}$ is a proper subset of any $\vDash_{\text{LLm}}$ such that $m < n$; and L2 = C.

[11] The following results are due to techniques of Gödel and Dugundi. See Nicholas Rescher, *Many-Valued Logic* (1969), pp. 188–195.

Proof. Proof that the relations are subsets follows from the fact that there are relevant homomorphisms from the larger matrices into the smaller that preserve designation and nondesignation. However, proof that the subsets are proper is more difficult and will not be attempted here.

7.3.3 Product Logics

Product logics, first developed by the Polish logician Stanisław Jaskowski, are another kind of logic that illustrates the technique of comparing entailment relations through structural similarities among matrices.[12] First we define the general idea and then illustrate it by an example.

DEFINITION: M^n, relative to a matrix $M = \langle U, D, g_1, \ldots, g_m \rangle$, is that matrix $\langle U^n, D^n, h_1, \ldots, h_m \rangle$ such that

(1) U^n and D^n are the sets of n-tuples of U and D respectively; and

(2) for each i, $h_i(\langle x_{1,1}, \ldots, x_{1,n} \rangle, \ldots, \langle x_{m,1}, \ldots, x_{m,n} \rangle) = \langle g_i(x_{1,1}, \ldots, x_{m,1}), \ldots, g_i(x_{1,n}, \ldots, x_{m,n}) \rangle$.

A special case is the matrix C^2, which interested Łukasiewicz a good deal because its logic is classical. Indeed it is possible to show by structural similarities among matrices that M and M^n have the same logic. Let $LM^n = \langle Syn, M^n \rangle$.

	~
11	00
10	01
01	10
00	11

∧	11	10	01	00
11	11	10	01	00
10	10	10	00	00
01	01	00	01	00
00	00	00	00	00

∨	11	10	01	00
11	11	11	11	11
10	11	10	11	10
01	11	11	01	01
00	11	10	01	00

The four-valued tables for C^2

THEOREM. $X \vDash_{LM^n} P$ iff $X \vDash_{LM} P$.

Proof. The theorem holds because there are relevant 'onto' homomorphisms from M^n to M.

So far our comparison of languages has employed homomorphism among matrices only. For examples of the use of the other structural properties, we

[12] See S. Jaskowski, 'Investigations into the System of Intuitionist Logic' (1936). For more recent applications of product logics to problems in the philosophy of language, see Hans Herzberger, 'Dimensions of Truth' (1973), John N. Martin, 'A Many-Valued Semantics for Category Mistakes' (1975), and Merrie Bergmann, 'Presupposition in Two Dimensions' (1981).

now turn to an interesting attempt by the Russian logician D. A. Bochvar to introduce a third value and retain precisely classical logic.

7.3.4 Bochvar's Internal and External Connectives

Bochvar's idea is that sentences with meaningless parts are indeed meaningless, as Kleene suggested in his interpretation of the weak connectives. We can however render the parts of a sentence bivalent (i.e., either true or false) by first affixing a truth operator to them. The operator assigns any true sentence the value true, and any sentence that is not true, whether it be false or something else, the value false. Frege had used a similar operator in his formalizations of mathematics, and Bochvar showed that the portion of the language rectified by having its atomic sentences prefixed by the truth operator consitutes a perfectly classical fragment of the language. All that is necessary, then, for logic to be perfectly classical is that we ensure that our atomic sentences be bivalent by prefixing them with a truth operator meaning the same as the English phrase 'It is true that...'.

Historically, the sort of meaninglessness that Bochvar was concerned with is that characteristic of paradoxes. He marked with the third value the semantic deviance of sentences (like the liar paradox or the paradoxes of naive set theory) that are provably both true and false. Later, in an important paper, Timothy Smiley interpreted Bochvar's third value as marking the failure of presupposition, thus beginning a long discussion among logicians of the proper way, if any, of representing presuppositions within many-valued semantics.

Bochvar's result is developed in stages. We first introduce a language using essentially Kleene's weak connectives, though our version will generalize the idea to arbitrarily many values.[13] First, let SynC be the syntax for classical logic using only negation and conjunction formation operations, let MC be the classical matrix for these connectives, and let LC = ⟨SynC, MC⟩. We shall use the same names $\sim C$ and $\wedge C$ for the operations of the two structures. Though we shall suppress mention of the other connectives, all the results continue to hold if, relative to each syntax, they are introduced by the usual definitions in terms of negation and conjunction. We now give names to two important ways in which a many-valued matrix may resemble the classical two-valued matrix. First of all, it may treat the classical values in the same way that the classical matrix does, and second, it may assign classical values only to wholes which have classical values as parts.

DEFINITION: The operations $\sim$ and $\wedge$ of a matrix are called *normal* iff whenever x and y are in $\{0, 1\}$, then $\sim(x) = \sim C(x)$, and $\wedge(x, y) = \wedge C(x, y)$; and they are called *sensitive* iff whenever x and y are not in $\{0, 1\}$, then $\sim(x)$, and $\wedge(x, y)$ are not in $\{0, 1\}$.

[13] These generalizations are from John N. Martin, 'The Semantics of Frege's *Grundgesetze*' (1984).

DEFINITION: An internal language is any LI = ⟨SynI, MI⟩ such that

(1) SynI, which we shall assume is ⟨Sen, B, $\sim I$, $\wedge I$⟩, is any propositional logic syntax such that $\sim I$ is unary and $\wedge I$ is binary; and

(2) MI is ⟨U, {1}, $\sim I$, $\wedge I$⟩ (called an *internal matrix*) such that U is a set of values including 0 and 1, and the operations $\sim I$ and $\wedge I$ are normal and sensitive.

The reader can easily verify that if U is the three-valued set {T, F, N} then MI determines the same tables as Kleene's weak connectives:

	~
T	F
F	T
N	N

∧	T	F	N
	T	F	N
	F	F	N
	N	N	N

∨	T	F	N
	T	T	N
	T	F	N
	N	N	N

→	T	F	N
	T	F	N
	T	T	N
	N	N	N

Bochvar's internal connectives

DEFINITION: An *extension* LI+ of an internal language LI is any ⟨SynI+, MI+⟩ such that

(1) SynI+ = ⟨SenI+, B, $\sim I$, $\wedge I$, τ, $\sim E$, $\wedge E$⟩, τ is a one-place operator (the truth operator), and $\sim E$ and $\wedge E$ are new one-place and two-place operators, respectively.

(2) MI+ = ⟨U, {1}, $\sim I$, $\wedge I$, τ, $\sim E$, $\wedge E$⟩ such that

(a) for any x, if $x = 1$, $\tau(x) = 1$, and $\tau(x) = 0$ otherwise;

(b) for any x and y, $\sim \mathrm{E}(x) = \sim \mathrm{I}(\tau(x))$ and $\wedge E(x, y) = \wedge I(\tau(x), \tau(y))$.

DEFINITION: By the *external language* LE relative to an internal language LI and its extension LI+ we mean ⟨SynE, ME⟩ such that

(1) SynE is ⟨SenE, B, $\sim E$, $\wedge E$⟩; and

(2) ME is ⟨U, {1}, $\sim E$, $\wedge E$⟩.

In the three-valued case in which U is {T, F, N} it is straightforward to verify that the truth operator and the external connectives conform to the following tables:

	T
T	T
F	F
N	F

	~
T	F
F	T
N	T

∧	T	F	N
	T	F	F
	F	F	F
	F	F	F

∨	T	F	N
	T	T	T
	T	F	F
	T	F	F

→	T	F	N
	T	F	F
	T	T	T
	T	T	T

Bochvar's truth operator and external connectives

THEOREM. There is some isomorphism from SynE to SynC such that $X \vDash_{\mathrm{LC}} P$ iff $t(X) \vDash_{\mathrm{LI}} t(P)$.

THEOREM. ME is homomorphic onto MC in a way that preserves designation and nondesignation, and hence $X \vDash_{\mathrm{LE}} P$ iff $X \vDash_{\mathrm{LI+}} P$.

THEOREM. LE is a sublanguage of LI+ and hence $X \vDash_{\mathrm{LE}} P$ iff $X \vDash_{\mathrm{LI+}} P$.

☐ **EXERCISE**

Prove the previous three metatheorems by using the results of the previous section.

THEOREM. There is a translation function t from SenC to SenI such that $X \vDash_{LC} P$ iff $t(X) \vDash_{LI} t(P)$.

Proof. The previous results establish that there are homomorphisms h and h' such that for any X and P of SynE:

$$h(X) \vDash_{LC} h(P) \text{ iff } h'(X) \vDash_{LI} h'(P).$$

Assume for arbitrary Y and Q of SenC that $Y \vDash_{LC} Q$. Then since h is an isomorphism, its inverse h^{-1} is also, and $h(h^{-1}(Y)) \vDash_{LC} h(h^{-1}(Q))$. Then by the previous results $h'(h^{-1}(Y)) \vDash_{LI} h'(h^{-1}(Q))$ and the function t defined as $t(P) = h'(h^{-1}(P))$ is the translation desired. End of Proof.

7.4 NON-TRUTH-FUNCTIONAL SENTENTIAL LOGICS

7.4.1 The Issue of Truth-Functionality

The motivation for many-valued semantics lies in the desire to classify sentences into more categories than just the true and the false, but as the survey of the last section shows, introducing new truth-values as representatives of the additional classes has unwanted consequences for logical entailment. In most cases the entailment relations of the new languages reject some classically valid arguments. The rejection of classical validities can be responded to in various ways. One reply is to maintain that the rejected validities are nonintuitive anyway, and it is fair to say that there is at least some plausibility to this view inasmuch as arguments rejected by the strong connectives and Łukasiewicz' matrices often depend on unintuitive features of classical logic. Among these are the paradoxes of material implication (Chapter 1) and arguments that introduce in the conclusion new sentences that do not even appear as parts of those sentences in the premises. It is, moreover, possible to characterize exactly what the rejected arguments are, though we shall not do so here.[14] It is also possible to experiment with novel ways to define logical entailment while retaining a matrix semantics.[15] In this

[14] For example, Bas van Fraassen has shown that

$$P \vDash_{LKW} Q \leftrightarrow (\vDash_{LC} P, \text{ or all atomic sentences in } Q \text{ are in } P \text{ and } P \vDash_{LC} Q).$$

It is also fairly easy to show that $P \vDash_{LKW*} Q$ iff ($P \vDash_{LC} Q$ and (if not $P \vDash_{LC} Q$, then all the atomic sentences of P are in Q)). Less obvious results of a similar nature may be found in John N. Martin, 'A Syntactic Characterization of Kleene's Strong Connectives' (1975), and Merrie Bergmann, 'Logic and Sortal Incorrectness' (1977).

[15] For example, it can be shown that $\vDash_{LKW*} P$ iff $\vDash_{LKS*} P$ iff $\vDash_{LC} P$.

chapter the response we shall discuss in detail involves the rejection of the matrix format for semantical theory. If we abandon the assumption that semantics is truth-functional, we may be able to obtain a more adequate logic.

Before discussing some examples of such theories, we should pause first to explain the nature of the assumption that they sacrifice. What is truth-functionality and why is it important? Briefly put, truth-functionality is the property which reference relations possess when they assign truth-values to a whole in a manner uniquely determined by the truth-values assigned to its immediate parts. The formal idea of a truth-functional semantics is captured in the concept of a matrix language. Intimately tied to truth-functionality is a logical property characteristic of classical logic and lost in non-truth-functional semantics. This is the property of the valid substitutability of one sentence for another of like truth-value in a larger sentence, or what is called *substitutability salva veritate*. This property fails if the reference relations are non-truth-functional.

THEOREM. *Substitutability of Material Equivalents.* Make the following assumptions: L is a matrix $\langle \text{Syn}, M \rangle$, S is some sentence of Syn that contains the sentence P, $[S]^P_Q$ is like S except for containing the sentence Q at one or more places where S contains P, and R is a member of the set $[R]$ of possible worlds for L. It follows then that if $R(P) = R(Q)$, then $R(S) = R[S]^P_Q)$.

This theorem is really a special case of a more general property of abstract algebras proven in Chapter 2. If the matrix relations g_i are functions, then each reference relation R is a homomorphism from Syn to M, and the relation $P \equiv Q$ defined as $R(P) = R(Q)$ is a congruence relation admitting substitutability of coreferential parts without altering the reference of the whole.

When pressed, however, it is difficult to know how much importance to attach to this sort of substitutability, and individual cases of nonmatrix languages are appraised in terms of their various compensating virtues. This kind of substitutability is part of what is meant when classical logic is said to be *extensional*, and we shall find other examples, especially in modal and intensional logic where the property is abandoned in order to enrich semantic theory.

7.4.2 Intuitionistic Logic

Historically, intuitionistic logic was developed first as a particuar theory of proof motivated by perceived weaknesses in classical proof theory. It was provided with a semantics only much later. Let us begin then by discussing intuitionistic ideas of proof.

Mathematically minded logicians concerned with codifying not reasoning in general but the particular sort of reasoning done in mathematics observed that mathematicians often encountered nonintuitive results when they used some questionable reasoning techniques of classical logic, and especially when they assumed the law of excluded middle, which in its syntactic form is $\vdash(P \vee \sim P)$. This group of logicians, whose views came to be known as *intuitionism*, observed that in mathematics it is inappropriate to assume that every sentence is either true or false. It may well be possible, they reasoned, that there may be some mathematical questions that are not resolvable in principle. Certainly, it is the case that there are still open questions, and it is only a matter of classical dogma, they suggested, to assume that these open questions can all ultimately be decided one way or the other.

These ideas were developed and explained by making them a part of a wider theory of mathematical truth. Truth, at least in mathematics, they claimed, may be analyzed through the concept of proof. A sentence is true if it is proven, false if it is refuted, and neither true nor false otherwise. Moreover, negation is interpreted as saying 'this sentence is refuted'. Hence, to prove $\sim P$ is the same as refuting P. The other connectives are explained in a similar way. A conjunction is proven iff both its conjuncts are, a disjunction is proven iff either of its disjuncts are, and a conditional is proven iff there is a proof that attaches to a proof of the antecendent so as to yield a proof of the consequent.

These semantic ideas defining truth and provability were only used informally to explain the more formal statement of the theory which was proof theoretic. The earliest formulations were in terms of axiom systems, but the same ideas are usually expressed today in the more general form of natural deduction systems.

Proof theoretically, the way to eliminate exluded middle must proceed indirectly by eliminating one or more of the classical assumptions used in proving it. As established in an earlier exercise, one classical rule used in its derivation, negation elimination (or more familiarly, double negation), is doubtful for the same reason excluded middle is. To have proven $\sim\sim P$ is to have refuted the proposition that P is false. But that does not entail that P is true because the possibility remains that P is neither. Thus the intuitionistic adjustment to classical proof theory is to replace $\sim$-elimination with

$$\frac{X \vdash P \qquad Y \vdash \sim P}{X, Y \vdash Q}$$

Intuitionistic $\sim$-elimination

We keep the other rules the same. This one change results in quite major changes in the resulting notion of $\vdash$. We now list some of the classical results that fail in the new theory and some that remain true. Let $\vdash$ remain as defined in classical proof theory as the closure of the basic deductions under the classical rules amended to include the intuitionistic version of $\sim$-elimination.[16]

THEOREM. The following are not true in intuitionistic natural deduction:

(1) $\vdash P \vee \sim P$

(2) $\dfrac{\sim\sim P}{P}$

(3) $\vdash \sim\sim P \rightarrow P$

(4) $\dfrac{\sim P \vdash \bot}{\vdash P}$

(5) $P \rightarrow Q, \sim P \rightarrow Q \vdash Q$

(6) $\dfrac{\sim(\sim P \wedge \sim Q)}{P \vee Q}$ $\quad$ $\dfrac{\sim(\sim P \vee \sim Q)}{P \wedge Q}$

(7) $\dfrac{\sim P \rightarrow \sim Q}{Q \rightarrow P}$ $\quad$ $\dfrac{\sim P \rightarrow Q}{\sim Q \rightarrow P}$

(8) $\dfrac{\sim\sim P \rightarrow P}{P \vee \sim P}$ $\quad$ $\dfrac{P \rightarrow Q}{\sim P \vee Q}$

(9) $\dfrac{P \rightarrow (Q \vee S)}{(P \rightarrow Q) \vee (P \rightarrow S)}$

THEOREM. The following classical results continue to hold in intuitionistic natural deduction:

(1) $\vdash \sim(P \wedge \sim P)$ and $\vdash \sim\sim(P \vee \sim P)$

(2) $\dfrac{P}{\sim\sim P}$

(3) $\vdash (P \rightarrow \sim\sim P)$

[16] For an introduction to the ideas motivating intuitionistic logic see Chapter 1 of Michael Dummett, *Elements of Intuitionism* (1977), and Section 13 of S. C. Kleene, *Introduction to Metamathematics* (1971). For a fuller exposition of the natural deduction system see Dummett, Chapter 4, and for a detailed comparison to classical natural deduction see Section 4.5 of Neil Tennant, *Natural Logic* (1978), as well as Chapter VI of Kleene.

(4) $\dfrac{P \vdash \bot}{\vdash \sim P}$

(5) $\dfrac{\sim(P \vee Q)}{\sim P \wedge \sim Q}$ $\quad$ $\dfrac{\sim P \wedge \sim Q}{\sim(P \vee Q)}$

(6) $\dfrac{P \rightarrow Q}{\sim Q \rightarrow \sim P}$ $\quad$ $\dfrac{P \rightarrow \sim Q}{Q \rightarrow \sim P}$

(7) $\dfrac{P \vee \sim P}{\sim\sim P \rightarrow P}$

(8) $\dfrac{\sim P \vee Q}{P \rightarrow Q}$

THEOREM. If $\vdash \sim P$ in classical natural deduction, then $\vdash \sim P$ in intuitionistic natural deduction.

□ **EXERCISE**

Prove the last metatheorem as well as results (1)–(3) of the one preceding it.

7.4.3 Beth's Semantics for Intuitionistic Logic

We can conclude from the foregoing discussion that there is a clear sense in which intuitionistic logic rejects some doubtful classical inferences, but what remains unclear is the semantics of the natural deduction proof theory. In particular, how is the semantic theory to be developed so that its valid inferences coincide exactly with the provable deductions of the system? It must be done, moreover, by means of a conceptually plausible analysis of truth in terms of a proof that rejects the law of excluded middle.

Conceptually, the whole idea of a semantics for intuitionistic logic is somewhat strange if not incoherent. The argument for this view runs as follows. What is characteristic of intuitionism is the rejection of a classical tenet of philosophy that there is a difference between truth, understood as sentences corresponding to an objective real world, and knowledge, consisting of true, well-justified beliefs about the world. In intuitionism truth and knowledge are collapsed inasmuch as a sentence being true is conceptually identical to the epistemic state of it being proven. Indeed, it is perfectly consistent with the intuitionistic explanation of mathematical truth that there is no external world for sentences to correspond to, but only a mental life with its various epistemic states of possession of proof, possession of refutation, and ignorance. Some philosophers like Michael Dummett have even taken the intuitionistic conception of mathematical truth as a key to the understanding of all truth, and have accordingly raised doubts about the need to posit a real world at all for the purposes of semantics and logical theory. A second reason for being skeptical of the project of developing a semantics for intuitionistic logic is a technical result by Gödel that shows that there is no finitely valued matrix language whose logical entailment relation is that of intuitionistic logic.[17] A straightforward two- or three-valued matrix semantics is therefore impossible.

Nevertheless, there are semantical accounts of the intuitionistic connectives, but they differ from traditional many-valued logic in being nontruth-functional. Here we shall present an interpretation due to E. W. Beth. The fundamental idea of this semantics is to evaluate sentences relative not to possible worlds in a robust realistic sense but rather to worlds understood epistemically as states of information. The supposition is that relative to these states it is possible to classify sentences according to whether they are provable or not. Those that are so are true (in the intuitionistic sense) and are assigned 1, those that are not are assigned 0. The semantics is epistemic in the sense that the intended readings of the truth-values are provided by concepts from traditional epistemology, but it is at the same time two-valued. The law of excluded middle nevertheless fails because, given the special non-truth-functional way truth-values are projected onto molecular sentences, both the sentences P and $\sim P$ may be 0.

This twofold classification of atomic sentences is then projected to molecular sentences, but in ways significantly different from matrix semantics. In particular, the truth-value of the whole relative to a 'world' is no longer completely determined by those of its parts. The details of this projection deserve some special comment because it is both new and not very intuitive.

Worlds in the relevant sense are understood to be states of information. It is assumed that these states are ordered in the sense that information can only increase. What information we have we do not lose, and the information we have may be augmented in various possible ways. Hence, these states form a tree structure such that if a sentence is provable relative to any state of information it remains provable at any states subsequent to or 'beneath' it on the tree. We also add an assumption that from a mathematical perspective any finitely distant improvement in information is in principle accessible. (We could, for example, just wait around until it comes.) The theory therefore assumes that any sentence P that is true at a finite distance in every possible refinement of an information state is also true at that state. We shall call such a sentence *finitely inevitable*. Moreover, if a sentence is finitely inevitable from

[17] See Michael Dummett, *Elements of Intuitionism* (1977), p. 172.

a state w, then we can collect a set of all worlds with a special property. Each of these worlds is a world in which P is true, and each is only a finite distance beneath w. This set in a sense forms a barrier across the tree structure beneath w. No matter which branch you descend from w, you will in a finite time run into at least one world in the barrier set. This set is said to 'bar' w. We begin by defining the general ideas necessary for talking about ordering states of information on trees. We assume a propositional logic syntax with the connectives $\sim$, $\wedge$, $\vee$, and $\rightarrow$.[18]

DEFINITION: A structure $\langle A, \leq \rangle$ is said to be a *partial ordering* iff $\leq$ is
(1) reflexive, i.e., for any x in A, $x \leq x$;
(2) transitive, i.e., for any x, y, z in A, if $x \leq y \wedge y \leq z$, then $x \leq z$; and
(3) antisymmetric, i.e., for any x and y in A, if $x \leq y \wedge y \leq x$, then $x = y$.

DEFINITION: For x and y in A, if $x \leq y$, x is said to *precede* y and y to *succeed* x, and if in addition there is no z between them (for any z in A if $x \leq z$ or $z \leq y$, then $x = z$ or $z = y$) then we say x is the $\leq$*-immediate predecessor* of y and y is the $\leq$*-immediate successor* of x.

As is customary in the subject, we refer to the set of possible worlds as K and to the possible worlds in K by lower case k, with and without prime marks and subscripts.

DEFINITION: A *world structure* is any $\langle K, \leq \rangle$ such that
(1) $\leq$ is a partial ordering on K;
(2) there is a unique maximal element E in K (i.e., E is in K, and all elements in K are $\leq$-predecessors of E);
(3) for each element k of K, there is a unique finite chain $k_n, \ldots, k_1$ such that $k = k_n$, $E = k_1$, and each element of the chain is an $\leq$-immediate successor of the previous element. (This chain is said to be the *branch ending with* k and to *contain* the branch $k_m, \ldots, k_1$ such that $m < n$.)

Let us adopt the convention that $\langle K, \leq \rangle$ ranges over world structures and k, k', k'' over elements of K. We are now in a position to define the assignment of truth-values to worlds. In the definition below the requirements on the assignment of values to atomic sentences state in a slightly more formal idiom the ideas that information does not degenerate and that finitely inevitable information is accessible.

The clauses assigning values to molecular sentences are less transparent. Their justification is in part that they work in the sense of yielding the later completeness result. But one of the requirements of semantic theory is

[18] See E. W. Beth, *The Foundations of Mathematics* (1968). The presentation here follows that of Dummett, *Elements of Intuitionism* (1977). Kripke has also proposed an alternative semantics which differs from Beth's in a number of important technical ways but which retains the intuitive interpretation of 'worlds' as states of information. See Saul Kripke, 'Semantical Analysis of Intuitionistic Logic, I' (1965).

supposed to be conceptual adequacy. The various clauses are supposed to state plausible analyses of the connectives, given the intended readings of the truth-values. In this theory, then, the clause for negation should say that we have a proof that the unnegated sentence is absurd. The clause for conjunction should embody the idea that given a proof for each part of a conjunction we may turn them into a proof for the whole conjunction. That for disjunction should say that a proof for either part of a disjunction may be transformed into a proof for the whole. That for the conditional should say that given a proof for the antecedent we may transform it into a proof of the consequent. Whether they do in fact express these ideas in a more formal idiom is somewhat doubtful.

DEFINITION: A subset K' of K is said to *bar* k relative to $\langle K, \leq\rangle$ iff there is some branch b of $\langle K, R\rangle$ ending with k such that for any branch b' of $\langle K, R\rangle$ containing b there is an element k' of K' that is a strict $\leq$-predecessor of k.

DEFINITION: The set $[R]$ of *possible worlds* relative to $\langle \mathrm{K}, \mathrm{R}\rangle$ is defined as $\{R | R(K \times \mathrm{Sen} \xrightarrow[\text{into}]{} \{0, 1\})$ such that for any P and k,

(1) if P is atomic, then
  (a) $R(k, P) = 1$ only if $R(k', P) = 1$ for all $\leq$-precedessors k' of k;
  (b) if some subset K' of K bars k and all k' of K' are such that $R(k', P) = 1$, then $R(k, P) = 1$;
(2) if P is molecular, then
  (a) if P is some $\sim Q$, $R(k, P) = 1$ iff, for all $\leq$-predecessors k' of k, $R(k', Q) \neq 1$;
  (b) if P is some $Q \wedge S$, $R(k, P) = 1$ iff $R(k, Q) = R(k, S) = 1$;
  (c) if P is some $Q \vee S$, $R(k, P) = 1$ iff there is some subset K' of K that bars k and is such that for any k' of K', either $R(k', Q) = 1$ or $R(k', S) = 1$;
  (d) if P is some $Q \rightarrow S$, $R(k, P) = 1$ iff, for all $\leq$-predecessors k' of k, $R(k', Q) = 1$ only if $R(k', S) = 1\}$.

Let R range over possible worlds, and instead of writing $R(k, P)$ we shall write $R_k(P)$. We may identify the (Beth) *intuitionistic language* (briefly, LI) with $\langle \mathrm{Sen}, [R]\rangle$.

We now state two useful and interesting properties of world structures.

DEFINITION: We define P to be *finitely inevitable* relative to $\langle K, \leq\rangle$, R, and k iff

(1) some subset K' of K bars k and
(2) for all k' of K', $R_{k'}(P) = 1$.

THEOREM. (1) If k is a least element of K, then R_k is classical (i.e., it is bivalent and assigns values to molecular sentences in accordance with the matrix C); and (2) $R_k(P) = 1$ iff P is finitely inevitable relative to $\langle K, \leq\rangle$, R, and k.

□ **EXERCISES**

1. Prove the last metatheorem.
2. Explain which clause for molecular sentences in the defintion of [R] best captures the intuitive ideas about proof underlying intuitionistic semantics. Which clause seems to do least well?

We now state but do not prove Beth's completeness theorem.[19]

THEOREM. $X \vdash P$ (in intuitionistic natural deduction) iff $X \vDash_{\text{LI}} P$.

7.4.4 Supervaluations

In all the examples of nonstandard semantics which we have so far considered, some classically valid inferences are rejected. The theory we shall now discuss has as its main virtue that it simultaneously allows for three truth-values and retains a perfectly classical account of entailment. The theory is due to Bas van Fraassen, and makes use of a special notion of a non-truth-functional reference relation. Before beginning our discussion, we shall adopt a change of vocabulary so as to use here the terms commonly found in the literature. In particular, it is common in logic generally, and always true in discussions of supervaluations, to call what we have been referring to as a reference relation, a function from sentences to truth-values, by the term *valuation*. A valuation is some assignment of truth-values to sentences of a propositional syntax, which we have hitherto been calling a 'possible world' or reference relation.

The theory of supervaluations was originally developed to represent failures of presupposition, but has been applied in interesting ways to all the problems that have motivated three-valued semantics. Suppose, for whatever reason, that some of the atomic sentences lack a classical truth-value. The remaining sentences that are bivalent (are either T or F) determine in a straightforward sense a partial world. Some but not all the facts of that world are decided. Those which are decided are the ones described by the bivalent sentences; those as yet undecided are those corresponding to the sentences that lack either T or F. We might attempt to complete a semantic theory with this information alone by proposing some way to calculate the truth-values for molecular sentences from this partial atomic valuation. The various three-valued matrix theories offer alternative ways to do this. Van Fraassen's idea is to retain as much of classical semantics as possible. He observed that any partial assignment, call it $R*$, of T or F to atomic sentences determines a

[19] For an explanation of how Beth's semantics may be reformulated in an equivalent, non-truth-functional three-valued epistemic logic, that is a special case of supervaluations, see John N. Martin, 'Epistemic Semantics for Classical and Intuitionistic Logic' (1984).

unique set of classical reference relations (valuations), namely the set of all classical valuations R that agree with $R*$ as far as $R*$ is defined. A novel, for example, is determinate only about some elementary facts, those which it explicitly says are true or false. There will also be other facts about which we may speculate but which the novel leaves open. The set of classical worlds consistent with the novel may be quite large. What is interesting is that, in a sense, this set of worlds contains all the information of the novel itself. Given the novel we can define the set of worlds and given a set of classical worlds we can determine a novel.[20]

DEFINITION: By a *partial atomic valuation* relative to a propositional syntax Syn $= \langle Sen, B, F \rangle$ is meant any function $R*$ such that for some B', B' is a subset of B and $R*(B' \underset{\text{into}}{\longrightarrow} \{\text{T}, \text{F}\})$.

DEFINITION: If $R*$ is a partial atomic valuation, then the set $[[R*]]$ of completions of $R*$ is defined as

$$\{R \mid R \in [\text{RC}] \text{ and for any } P \text{ in } B, \text{ if } R*(P) \in \{\text{T}, \text{F}\}, \text{ then } R(P) = R*(P)\}.$$

Here [RC] is the familiar set of two-valued classical valuations determined by the classical matrix C for Syn. Clearly a partial atomic valuation $R*$ determines a unique set of classical completions. A set of classical completions also determines a unique partial atomic valuation.

THEOREM. For every subset X of [RC], there is a partial atomic valuation $R*$ such that X is $[[R*]]$, the set of classical completions of $R*$.

☐ **EXERCISE**

Prove the metatheorem.

Mathematically, then, a set of classical worlds can be understood as representing a single partially undefined world, namely that world that all the classical worlds agree about. Van Fraassen's idea is then to let this agreement determine an assignment to molecular sentences as well. A molecular sentence is assigned T or F if the classical worlds consistent with a partial atomic valuation are unanimous in assigning it T or F, and it is not assigned anything (or, equivalently, is assigned N) if there is no unanimity among its classical completions. A three-valued assignment (called a *supervaluation*) is thus defined in two steps. First a partial atomic valuation $R*$ is given, then its set of classical completions $[[R*]]$ is determined, and finally a supervaluation S is defined as the function recording the unanimous assignments

[20] For the theory in its original form see Bas C. van Fraassen, 'Singular Terms, Truth-Value Gaps, and Free Logic' (1966), and *Formal Semantics and Logic* (1968). The presentation here follows that of Hans G. Herzberger, 'Canonical Superlanguages' (1975).

of [[$R*$]]. To sentences for which there is no unanimity, the supervaluation does not assign either T or F.

In the usual development of the theory the fact that the function assigns neither T nor F to a sentence P is formalized by making S a partial function on Sen and making S undefined for P. That is, P is placed outside the domain of S. In this case the domain of S is some proper subset of Sen, P is not a member of the domain, and S is literally undefined for P. If S is undefined in this way for some sentence P, S is said to have a *truth-value gap.* The same idea might equally well be formalized by making S a three-valued function and having it assign a third value N in those cases in which it would be undefined by the usual theory. Thus, in all important respects the semantics is three-valued.

DEFINITION: A *base for a superlanguage* is any family B such that each element of B is some set [[$R*$]] of classical completions of some partial valuation $R*$.

DEFINITION: If X is a subset of [RC], then the supervaluation $X+$ established by X is defined as that function from a subset A of Sen into {T, F} such that

(1) for any P of Sen, if for all R of X, $R(P) = \text{T}$, then $X+(P) = \text{T}$;
(2) for any P of Sen, if for all R of X, $R(P) = \text{F}$, then $X+(P) = \text{F}$;
(3) $X+$ is undefined for all other sentences.

A simplifying advantage obtained from representing non-unanimity by undefinedness rather than the assignment of a third value is the result that a supervaluation turns out to be merely the intersection of the family of classical completions establishing it.

THEOREM. For any subset X of [RC], $X+ = \bigcap X$. (Here, $\bigcap X$ is defined in the usual set theoretic way as $\{x \mid \text{for any } R \text{ in } X, x \in R\}$.)

DEFINITION: The set [S] of supervaluations established by elements of a base B for a superlanguage is defined as

$$\{[[R*]]+ \mid [[R*]] \in B\}.$$

DEFINITION: The superlanguage LS relative to the superlanguage base B is defined as ⟨Syn, [S]⟩ such that [S] is the set of supervaluations established by elements of B.

Two of the most important features of superlanguages are that they preserve classical logic and are non-truth-functional. We define entailment for a superlanguage as a truth-preserving relation.

DEFINITION: $X \vDash_{\text{LS}} P$ iff for any S in [S] of LS, if $S(X) = \text{T}$, then $S(P) = \text{T}$.

THEOREM. If $X \vDash_{LC} P$ then $X \vDash_{LS} P$.

Proof. Assume the antecedent and that for an arbitrary supervaluation S, $S(X) = T$. Then relative to some $[[R*]]$ of B, all R in $[[R*]]$ are such that $R(X) = T$. But since $[[R*]]$ is a subset of [RC]. and $X \vDash_{LC} P$, each such R must be such that $R(P) = T$. Then elements of $[[R*]]$ are unanimous and $S = [[R*]]$ is such that $S(P) = T$. End of Proof.

THEOREM. Some superlanguage is not truth-functional.

Proof. Let B be any superlanguage base in which there are atomic sentences P and Q, and an atomic partial valuation $R*$ such that $R*$ is not defined for either. Then consider the supervaluation $S = [[R*]]+$ and the evaluation of conjunctions. $S(P \wedge Q)$ is undefined because there are classical completions R and R' of $R*$ in $[[R*]]$ such that $R(P) = R(Q) = T$, and $R(P \wedge Q) = T$, and $R'(P) = R'(Q) = F$ and $R'(P \wedge Q) = F$. Thus there is a case in which $S(x)$ is undefined, $S(y)$ is undefined, and $S(x \wedge y)$ is undefined. Now consider the conjunction $P \wedge {\sim}P$. Clearly $S({\sim}P)$ is undefined, because those completions in $[[R*]]$ that disagree about P will also disagree about ${\sim}P$. Moreover, $S(P \wedge {\sim}P) = F$, because all completions R in $[[R*]]$ are such that $R(P \wedge {\sim}P) = F$ since they are all in [RC]. Hence there is a case of x and y such that $S(x)$ is undefined, $S(y)$ is undefined, yet $S(x \wedge y) = F$. Thus the S-assignments to the immediate parts of a conjunction do not determine in a unique way the S-assignment to the whole. End of Proof.

□ EXERCISES

1. Prove the metatheorem that for $X \subseteq [RC]$, $X+ = \bigcap X$.
2. Prove that some superlanguages are truth-functional by proving the following more general theorem.

   There is a superlanguage $LS = \langle \text{Syn}, [S] \rangle$ relative to a base B such that $[S] = [RC]$. (That is, some superlanguage has as its valuations exactly the classical valuations.)

8

Nonclassical Quantificational Logic

8.1 FREE LOGIC

8.1.1 The Nonempty Domain

The semantics of classical quantification theory begins by defining a model $\langle D, R \rangle$, which specifies a nonempty domain D and a function R, and interprets both constants and predicates by assigning each constant a member of D and each predicate a set or relation on D. Free logic departs from classical logic in questioning two assumptions of classical quantificational semantics:

(1) There always exists something or other.
(2) Singular terms always refer to existing things.

Let us begin by discussing the first of these.

Assumption (1), that what we quantify over exists, is articulated in classical semantics by the defining condition on a model:

(1*) $D \neq \varnothing$.

Consider the consequences of (1*). Its requirement that the domain is nonempty joins with the fact that we quantify over D to ensure the truth of (1). Let us stop for a moment to see why it is that we 'quantify over' D. It is of the objects in D that we speak when we say 'all' and 'some' in the quantifiers.

The precise content of this idea is contained in the clause for the quantifier in the recursive definition of truth:

Substitutional interpretation. Every member of D is the value under R for some argument c, and

$$R+((\forall x)P) = \text{T iff, for all } c \in \text{PN}, R+([P]^c_x) = \text{T}.$$

Referential interpretation. $R*((\forall x)P) = \text{T}$ iff, for all $d \in D$, $R[^d_x]*(P) = \text{T}$.

(Here $R[^d_x]$ is like R except perhaps in what it assigns to x.) Thus it is D that we quantify over under either of the two kinds of interpretation, and this D is required by definition to be nonempty. We can recast this fact in terms of the notion of 'existence' by means of the existential quantifier. Recall that, as introduced, $(\exists x)P$ is short for $\sim(\forall x)\sim P$. We have already proven the following theorem.

THEOREM. For any substitution interpretation $R+$, $R+((\exists x)P) = \text{T}$ iff, for some $c \in \text{PN}$, $R+([P]^c_x) = \text{T}$; and for any referential interpretation $R*$, $R*((\exists x)P) = \text{T}$ iff, for some $d \in D$, $R[^d_x]*(P) = \text{T}$.

One intended reading of $(\exists x)P$ is 'there exists an x such that P'. Hence one way of reading $(\exists y)y = x$ is 'x exists'. To use this idea to introduce an existence predicate in quantificational syntax, we first augment the syntax to include a two-place predicate '$=$', perhaps by stipulating that P^2_1 is '$=$'. Recall the definition of model as in Chapter 5 (Section 5.2.2). We now expand the definition of model to require that '$=$' always means identity, by adding this clause to the original two clauses of the definition:

(3) $R(=)$ is the identity relation on D.

(When '$=$' is added to Syn-QL we should speak of Syn-QL$_=$ and of 'quantification with identity' but we shall not need such precision here.) Accordingly we can now introduce the existence predicate '$E!$' (called *E-shriek*).[1]

DEFINITION: Let $t \in \text{Tm}$. Then, $E!t$ is an abbreviation for $(\exists y)y = t$.

Now we can say that classical semantics obeys assumption (1) because of the following metatheorem. We use the notation $\vDash P$ of previous chapters to say P is a logical truth: $\vDash_L P$ iff for all reference relations R of L, $R(P) = \text{T}$.

THEOREM. (1**) $\vDash_{\text{LSub}}(\forall x)E!x$, and $\vDash_{\text{LRef}}(\forall x)E!x$.

Free logic typically rejects all of (1)–(1**) merely by omitting (1*), that $D \neq \varnothing$, from the definition of model.

[1] '$E!$' was first introduced into logic by Whitehead and Russell, *Principia Mathematica* Vol. I (1910), definition *14.02, but there it was not applied to constants but to definite descriptions, as explained below.

We should note that even when (1*) is dropped, it is possible to give a proof theoretic account of the notion of valid argument.[2]

We shall let P and Q be arbitrary sentences, t an arbitrary term (proper noun or variable), c an arbitrary proper noun (a 'constant'), and P_i^n a predicate of degree n. As we go along we shall be altering the definition of a quantificational syntax in various ways, as we have already done in specifying that the first monadic predicate is '='. Likewise, we shall also be redefining the concept of model in various ways, though the concepts defined in terms of model shall keep their original definitions. In particular the definitions of referential and substitutional extension, language, and semantic entailment remain as before. Since nothing we shall say about free logic depends on the difference between referential and substitutional interpretations, we shall refer to the set of possible extensions (of the variety of model currently in question) as $[R]$ and we may understand it as either $[R+]$ or $[R*]$. Likewise we shall let R range over $[R]$, and R may be considered either as an arbitrary element of $[R+]$ or as an arbitrary element of $[R*]$. We let L stand for the language $\langle$Syn-QL, $[R]\rangle$ and use $\models$ for $\models_L$.

☐ **EXERCISE**

Prove statement (1**) on the basis of (1*).

8.1.2 Nonreferring Singular Terms: Frege's Formal Trick

A second assumption of classical quantificational semantics that is typically rejected in free logic is

(2) Singular terms always refer to existing things.

This informal principle finds its precise expression in that part of the definition of a model which requires constants to refer to objects in D:

(2*) $R(c) \in D$.

Two consequences of (2*) for semantic entailment are frequently used to illustrate how assumption (2) is captured in classical semantics. If constants are thought to stand for proper names of a natural language like English,

[2] For axiomatic formulations see Robert K. Meyer and Karel Lambert, 'Universally Free Logic and Standard Quantification Theory' (1968), Hugues Leblanc and Richmond Thomason, 'Completeness Theorems for Some Presupposition-Free Logics' (1968). For a Gentzen-style natural deduction system of the sort we have studied see Richard Routley, 'Some Things Do Not Exist' (1966). For more references on both sorts of systems see Ermanno Bencivenga, 'Free Logics' (1986).

then the following are entailed by (2∗) but are highly questionable as a recording of preanalytic logical intuition:

(2∗∗) $\vDash E!c$
(2∗∗∗) $P \vDash (\exists x)P$

☐ **EXERCISE**

For each of (2∗∗) and (2∗∗∗) find four examples of proper names from ordinary speech, two that confirm and two that appear to be counterexamples. Use as much detail as necessary to make the examples convincing.

Before explaining the various ways free logic rejects (2), we should comment on the connection between (1) and (2). In general if (1∗) is dropped, we cannot tell what will happen to (2∗) unless we know what happens to $R(c)$ and $R(=)$ when $D = \varnothing$. Suffice it to say that there are various alternatives. Conceptually it is best to keep the arguments for and against (1) and (2) separate, though on some accounts rejecting one entails rejecting the other.

The intuitive unacceptability of (2) has been recognized since the start of classical logic, and we shall begin our study by reviewing the various attempts to both reject (2) and keep classical semantics.

Frege proposed representing in a formal language the intuition that a constant c need not refer by stipulating that $R(c)$ need not be defined. To develop this idea we must ask what are the truth-values of atomic sentences containing nonreferring singular terms. There are various answers, but the typical classical answer is that they are all false. The way this is usually argued is via the concept of presupposition, which was introduced in the last chapter as one motivation for many-valued logic. We repeat the definition here but in an informal language intended to capture the idea as it is understood intuitively, prior to any serious logical analysis.

DEFINITION: P presupposes Q iff whenever P is true or false, Q is true.

Using this idea, it is argued that if P presupposes Q and Q is false, then P is not true. In classical two-valued logic, if P is not true it is false. This line of reasoning may then be applied to nonreferring singular terms. Consider the sentences 'Pegasus is white' and 'Pegasus is not white'. Clearly, 'Pegasus' does not refer. It is also claimed that both these sentences presuppose 'Pegasus exists', which is false. Hence, atomic sentences with nonreferring singular terms should be assigned F for not-true. Their negations would then by the classical truth-table for negation be T. Such is the classical analysis.

A three-valued semantics, on the other hand, does not require that a nontrue sentence be F. Hence if these atomic sentences are nontrue because their presuppositions are false, it does not follow that they are F. Rather, it is argued, it makes more sense to assign them the third value, say N. There is thus a distinction drawn among the nontrue sentences, one category which is identified as the genuinely false because, though meaningful, its members fail to correspond to the world, and the other category which contains meaningless sentences. On this theory then all atomic sentences which fail of existential presupposition are N, and by the usual three-valued truth-table for negation, it follows that the negations of these sentences are N as well.

A third point of view is that some such sentences are true, e.g., 'Pegasus has wings', and that some like 'Pegasus has horns' are false. A theory that is unable to distinguish between such true and false sentences with nonreferring singular terms is imperfect.

Frege ensured that a constant c need not refer, i.e., that $R(c)$ need not be defined, by making $R(c)$ for those cases identical to a distinguished element which we shall call $*$. He ensured that all atomic sentences with nonreferring constants are false by requiring this artificially constructed entity $*$ to be outside the extension of every predicate (except perhaps $=$). If c refers to $*$ and $*$ is outside the extension of the predicate of an atomic sentence, then that sentence will be false by the classical analysis of truth for atomic predications.[3] Thus, we add to the definition of a model a new clause:

(4) $*$ is a member of D and for any predicate P_i^n,

$$\langle d_1, \ldots, *, \ldots, d_n \rangle \notin R(P_i^n).$$

From this amendment alone we get the following results:

(I) There is a semantic correlate to the idea that c does not refer, viz. $R(c) = *$.

(II) $P \vDash (\exists x)P$.

(III) Atomic sentences with nonreferring singular terms, like 'Pegasus is white', are false: if $R(P_i^1) = \varnothing$, then $R(P_i^1 c) = \text{F}$.

(I) is desirable, (III) can be argued for even if somewhat unconvincingly, but (II) is a holdover from classical logic and seems to be against the spirit of rejecting (2). This particular theory is only partly complete because there are various alternatives for the treatment of $=$ and $E!$. We shall call the three alternatives (i), (ii), and (iii):

(i) Require that $\langle *, * \rangle \in R(=)$ and that $E!t$ be an abbreviation for $(\exists y)y = t$. These requirements are consistent with classical theory but they imply one of the propositions free logic is designed to reject: $\vDash E!c$.

[3] See Gottlob Frege, 'On Sense and Reference' (1892). Frege calls the distinguished element ε. In using $*$, we follow Rudolf Carnap, whose account of Frege is now a classic. See *Meaning and Necessity* (1947).

(ii) Require that $\langle *, * \rangle \notin R(=)$ and that $E!t$ be an abbreviation for $(\exists y)y = t$. Then, we obtain the desirable result from the point of view of the ideas motivating free logic, namely not($\vDash E!c$). However, we also obtain the rejection of one of the most fundamental laws of logic: not($\vDash t = t$).

(iii) Require that $\langle *, * \rangle \in R(=)$ but make $E!$ a special predicate with its own interpretation fixed by the definition of model. We specify that P_1^1, i.e., the first predicate of degree 1, be $E!$, and add to the definition of model the following clause that makes $E!$ always refer to everything in the domain except $*$:

(4′) $R(E!) = D - \{*\}$.

We have, then, improved upon both the earlier versions: not($\vDash E!c$) and $\vDash t = t$. However, $\vDash (\exists y) \sim E!y$. That is, we have lost the intuitive reading of the existential quantifier. $(\exists x)P$ cannot be read 'there exists an x such that P'. If the existential quantifier does not represent existence, what does it represent? Clearly some explanation is in order.

In summary, we have the following results:

	Intuition	(i)	(ii)	(iii)
(I) Some nonreferring singular terms c	Desirable		$R(c) = *$	
(II) Existential generalization: $P \vDash (\exists x)P$	Dubious		Valid	
(III) Truth-value of				
'Pegasus has wings'	Odd, true		Always false	
'Pegasus has horns'	Odd, false		Always false	
(IV) Necessary existence: $\vDash$Pegasus exists	Very dubious	Valid	Valid	Invalid
(V) Law of identity: $\vDash t = t$	Desirable	Valid	Invalid	Valid
(VI) Existential reading of $(\exists x)P$, i.e., $E!t$ means $(\exists y)y = t$	Desirable	Valid	Valid	Invalid

Thus, all these alternatives have significant problems. But Frege's theory is a classical theory, and we shall use it to introduce into the semantics and syntax a locution called the definite description.

8.1.3 Russell's Theory of Descriptions

In English we are familiar with singular noun phrases modified by relative clauses, e.g., 'the man who corrupted Hadleyburg'. Grammatically these may be analyzed as forming a singular term from an open sentence. We take the open sentence 'x is a man and x corrupted Hadleyburg' and put the variable binding expression (called an *operator* in logical syntax) 'the x such that' in front of it to obtain the complex singular term 'the x such that x is a man and x corrupted Hadleyburg'. We now add to our quantificational syntax the mechanisms for forming such expressions. First we add a formation rule that takes a variable v and a sentence P as arguments and yields the expression $[\imath v|P]$ as value. Here the expression '$[\imath\,|\,]$' is called the *definite description operator* that combines with a variable v and a sentence P to form a complex singular term $[\imath v|P]$. The whole expression $[\imath v|P]$ is read 'the one and only v such that P'. In all useful cases the sentence P will contain the free variable v.

DEFINITION: The formation rule $f_\imath$ is defined as $\{\langle x, y, z\rangle | z = [{}^\frown\imath^\frown x^\frown|^\frown y^\frown]\}$. A *quantificational syntax with definite descriptions*, briefly Syn-$\mathrm{QL_{Des}}$, is defined as $\langle$Sen, {PN, Vb, Pd}, Fm$\rangle$ such that PN, Vb, and Pd, are as defined in a quantificational syntax, $\mathrm{Fm} = (f_{\mathrm{BS}}, f_\sim, f_\wedge, f_\vee, f_\rightarrow, f_\forall, f_\imath\}$, BS is the set of all expressions formed by applying f_{BS} to n terms from Tm and an n-place predicate, Sen is the closure of BS under the rules $f_\sim, \ldots, f_\forall$, and Tm is defined as follows:

(1) (*Basis clause*) PN $\subseteq$ Tm and Vb $\subseteq$ Tm;
(2) (*Inductive clause*) if $v \in$ Vb and $P \in$ Sen, then $f_\imath(v, P) \in$ Tm;
(3) Nothing else is in Tm.

We must now explain the semantic interpretation of the new term phrases. It is obvious that if there is a unique object d in the domain D of a model $\langle D, R\rangle$ such that $R[^d_v]*(P) = \mathrm{T}$, then its referential extension $R*$ should assign d to $[\imath v|P]$. But what happens if there is no such unique d? What happens if there is more than one member of D meeting the description P, or if there are no elements of D meeting P? In Frege's theory the description should then stand for the element $*$. The precise statement of the semantics differs under the substitutional and referential interpretations, so we give both.

DEFINITION: *Substitution interpretation.* We add a clause to the definition of $[R+]$:

$$R+([\imath v|P]) = d, \text{ if } \{d\} = \{d' | \text{for some } c \text{ in PN}, R(c) = d' \text{ and } R+([P]^c_y) = T\};$$
$$R+([\imath v|P]) = *, \text{ otherwise.}$$

Referential interpretation. We add a clause to the definition of $[R*]$:

$$R*([\imath v|P]) = d, \text{ if } \{d\} = \{d' | R[^{d'}_v]*(P) = \mathrm{T}\};$$
$$R*([\imath v|P]) = *, \text{ otherwise.}$$

We may identify a *Fregean quantificational language with definite descriptions* with $\langle \text{Syn-QL}_{\text{Des}}, [R+] \rangle$ or $\langle \text{Syn-QL}_{\text{Des}}, [R*] \rangle$. It follows directly from the above definition that if a description fails of its presupposition for either uniqueness or existence, then it refers to $*$:

THEOREM. *Referential interpretation.*

(1) *Uniqueness.* If for some d and d', $d \neq d'$ and $\{d, d'\} \subseteq \{d'' \mid R[^{d''}_{v}]*(P) = \text{T}\}$, then $R*([\imath x \mid P]) = *$.

(2) *Existence.* If $\text{R}*(\text{E}![\imath x \mid P]) = \text{F}$, then $R*([\imath x \mid P]) = *$. (Here, $E![\imath x \mid P]$ is short for $(\exists y)(y = [\imath x \mid P])$.)

☐ **EXERCISES**

1. Prove (I) on page 266.
2. Prove (II) on page 266.
3. Prove that given the conditions of (ii) that neither $\vDash E!c$ nor $\vDash t = t$.
4. Prove the uniqueness and existence results of the last theorem using the referential interpretation.

Bertrand Russell advanced a famous account of definite descriptions in which he simultaneously retained a classical two-valued logic and yet captured two features that motivate free logic. In his account, definite descriptions need not refer and when they fail to refer they do so because their presuppositions are not met. An extension of the theory is to reformulate ordinary proper names as definite descriptions. If a proper name can be so interpreted, then it too may fail of reference and presupposition in the bivalent manner of Russell's descriptions. Indeed the philosopher W. V. O. Quine has gone so far as to claim all proper names are disguised descriptions.[4]

Russell's idea is to treat any sentence containing a definite description as equivalent by definition to a longer sentence of the language. If an expression of a language is 'defined' in this way, it is viewed not as part of the genuinely well-formed expressions of the syntax, but rather as an abbreviation for a longer well-defined expression.

We have already met such definitions in other contexts. In propositional logic, for example, we may begin with a syntax and semantics that employs only negations and conjunctions. The other connectives may then be introduced as abbreviations for longer sentences expressed in terms of negation and conjunction. We have also used this device to introduce the existential quantifier. In our official presentation of quantificational syntax and semantics, existentially quantified sentences are not part of the syntax of

[4] See Bertrand Russell 'On Denoting' (1905) and 'Introduction', in Whitehead and Russell, *Principia Mathematica*, second edition (1927), and W. V. O. Quine, 'On What There Is' (1948).

the formal language. Rather they are abbreviations for longer sentences expressed in terms of the universal quantifier and negation (although, as we noted, there is an alternative way to present the theory in which existentially quantified sentences are given formation and semantic rules of their own and are then officially well-formed sentences). Such definitions are conveniences of syntax and are called *abbreviative definitions.*

It sometimes happens that in an abbreviative definition a new symbol is used as an internal part of the abbreviation. Such symbols are useful to make clear to the reader which abbreviative definition should be used in translating an expression into the official ('primitive') notation of the syntax. For example, let us stipulate in what we may call *definition 1* that $(P \vee Q)$ is short for $\sim(\sim P \wedge \sim Q)$, and in what we may call *definition 2* that $(P \rightarrow Q)$ abbreviates $\sim(P \wedge \sim Q)$. Then because the symbols $\vee$ and $\rightarrow$ are introduced only by their respective definitions, they signal which definition should be used if we wish to translate an expression containing them into the forms which they abbreviate. We might have used $(P, Q)_1$ instead of $(P \vee Q)$ and $(P, Q)_2$ for $(P \rightarrow Q)$, but such abbreviations, though they meet the requirement of exhibiting what definition should translate them, fail to suggest the natural language expressions they approximate in the way the symbols $\vee$ and $\rightarrow$ do. The symbols $\vee$ and $\rightarrow$ stand in a 1–1 relation with the definitions that introduce them, and also suggest the natural language expression that the definitions ensure they approximate.

Some lessons follow from these observations. First, notice that the symbols $\vee$ and $\rightarrow$ do not themselves have any semantic content. They are not referring expressions of the official syntax, but function rather as orthographic conveniences to help us identify which abbreviative definition we should use in translating into official vocabulary. Clearly the symbol '1' from '$(P, Q)_1$' is a feature of the orthography with no semantic content. Certainly, it is not a referring expression. The symbols $\vee$ and $\rightarrow$, if introduced by abbreviation, are similarly without direct semantic content. If $\vee$ and $\rightarrow$ are introduced by definition, then $R(\vee)$ and $R(\rightarrow)$ are undefined.

Of course there is more to the definition of expressions like $(P \vee Q)$ than that. We also happen to think that $\sim(\sim P \wedge \sim Q)$ is a fair translation of the English expression 'P or Q'. Thus it is common to use abbreviative definitions as an indirect way to provide semantic analysis. If the abbreviation is intended to represent expressions from ordinary language, then it is required that the definition given provide an analysis that conforms with ordinary usage. It nevertheless remains the case that the new symbols that occur in the abbreviation do not themselves have meaning alone. They make sense only as part of the whole abbreviation, and then only as a shorthand for a more complex formula in primitive notation. Russell's idea is to view definite descriptions as orthographic pieces of longer abbreviative definitions.

It follows that the descriptions themselves, considered as pieces of a longer abbreviating string of symbols, have no individual semantic content. Specifically, $[\imath v|P]$ will occur, but only as part of a longer abbreviation, and $R([\imath v|P])$ will not be defined in the semantics.

Grammatically, the ordinary language form of assertions using definite descriptions appear to be subject–predicate sentences. If, for example, we assert the sentence '$[\imath x|P]$ is Q', it looks as if $[\imath x|P]$ is the subject and Q is the predicate. Indeed, we shall write this in the form '$Q[\imath x|P]$'. Consider one of Russell's own examples. Let us apply as a predicate the open sentence 'y is bald' to the description 'the present king of France' to obtain what appears to be a predication of a property to a subject 'The present king of France is bald'. In Russell's theory, however, the application of Q to $[\imath x|P]$ really abbreviates a longer sentence of first-order logic that says 'There is one and only one thing that is P and it is such that Q', which we may write in first-order logic as $(\exists x)(P \wedge (\forall z)([P]^z_x \rightarrow z = x) \wedge [Q]^x_y)$. Moreover, the definite description $[\imath x|P]$ does not occur in the longer formulation, and hence cannot count as a referring expression of the language. In our example, the apparent predication is really short for the longer 'There is one and only one present king of France and he is bald', within which the definite description 'the present king of France' does not occur.

DEFINITION: We return to quantification with identity but without definite descriptions in the syntax or semantics. Specifically, we drop the formation function $f_\imath$ and the additional clause in the definition of R that assigns a value to definite descriptions. We retain $=$ as the first two-place predicate, and clause (3) in the definition of model, the clause interpreting identity sentences. Last we lay down the following abbreviative definition: $[Q]^{[\imath x|P]}_y$ is an abbreviation for $(\exists x)(P \wedge (\forall z)([P]^z_x \rightarrow z = x) \wedge [Q]^x_y)$. The resulting languages $\langle$Syn-QL, $[R+]\rangle$ and $\langle$Syn-QL, $[R*]\rangle$ we may call *Russellian quantificational languages with definite descriptions.* For simplicity we shall usually assume that the variable y is clear from context. When we suppress its mention, we rewrite $[Q]^{[\imath x|P]}_y$ as $Q[\imath x|P]$.

EXAMPLE In the following series of sentences we begin with an ordinary English sentence, transform it into the logical syntax of an abbreviating definite description, and finally replace this abbreviation by the longer sentence in first-order syntax that it abbreviates:

The present king of France is bald.

The one and only x such that x is a present king of France is bald.

There exists an x such that x is a present king of France, and for any y, if y is a present king of France then y is x, and x is bald.

That the longer expression really means the same as the shorter in ordinary usage was argued by Russell as follows. The expression $Q[\imath x|P]$ means, he claimed, three things. First, at least one subject that is P exists. This Russell called the existence claim, and it is captured in the longer expression by its initial clause $(\exists x)(P \wedge \cdots)$. Second, the expression asserts that only one thing has the property described in P. This claim he called the uniqueness condition and it is rendered by the phrase $(\forall z)([P]^z_x \rightarrow z = x)$. Last, the sentence asserts that the object in question has the property described in Q, and this part is contained in the clause $[Q]^x_y$.

It should also be observed that as originally intended $[\imath x|P]$ has no meaning apart from the sentence $Q[\imath x|P]$. Since $[\imath x|P]$ has no meaning, the question of whether it can refer never arises. Hence, we ensure that not all descriptions need refer, by ensuring that none of them ever refers. The least plausible part of Russell's theory is this thesis that definite descriptions are never referring expressions.

THEOREM. (I$*$) For any P and R, $R([\imath x|P])$ is undefined.

We also obtain the classical result that atomic sentences with descriptions that fail of either the existence or uniqueness presuppositions are false.

THEOREM. (1) $\sim(E![\imath x|P]) \vDash \sim(Q[\imath x|P])$;
(2) $(\exists x)(\exists y)(x \neq y \wedge P \wedge [P]^y_x) \vDash \sim(Q[\imath x|P])$.

This falsity of $Q[\imath x|P]$ when $E![\imath x|P]$ is false can be defended by appeal to the notion of presupposition. There is a nice way in which the truth and falsehood of $Q[\imath x|P]$ presupposes $E![\imath x|P]$. Suppose we use $\vDash$ and $\sim$ to define presupposition as follows.

PROPOSAL. P presupposes Q iff $P \vDash Q$ and $\sim P \vDash Q$.

THEOREM. Given the proposal: (1) If P presupposes Q, then Q is a logical truth, and (2) if P presupposes Q, then every sentence presupposes Q.

These consequences follow from the proposal using rather simple logical steps. But these results contradict our intuitions about presuppositions and render the idea rather trivial. Taking note of these consequences Russell proposed introducing a second idea of negation and then defining presupposition in terms of it.

DEFINITION: By the negation of $Q[\imath x|P]$ with $[\imath x|P]$ in *primary occurrence*, written $(\sim Q)[\imath P])$, is meant

$$(\exists x)(P \wedge (\forall z)([P]^z_x \rightarrow z = x) \wedge \sim[Q]^x_y).$$

By negation of $Q[\imath x|P]$ with $[\imath x|P]$ in *secondary occurrence*, written $\sim(Q[\imath x|P])$, is meant

$$\sim(\exists x)(P \wedge (\forall z)([P]^z_x \rightarrow z = x) \wedge [Q]^x_y).$$

(Here the full form mentioning y of $(\sim Q)[\imath x|P]$ would be $[\sim Q]_y^{[\imath x|P]}$.) It turns out that only negations of secondary occurrences render presupposition trivial in the sense of limiting presuppositions to tautologies. Negations with descriptions in primary occurrence yield nontrivial presuppositions.

THEOREM. (1) $Q[\imath x|P] \vDash E![\imath x|P]$;
(2) $(\sim Q)[\imath x|P] \vDash E![\imath x|P]$; and
(3) not($\vDash E![\imath x|P]$).

Russell's notion of presupposition is derived from the above:

DEFINITION: *P presupposes Q* (à la Russell) iff the arguments from P to Q and from the negation of P with descriptions in primary occurrence to Q are both valid.

Notice, however, that existential generalization remains valid:

THEOREM. (II*) $P \vDash (\exists x)P$.

This result is perhaps no longer so counterintuitive, for suppose $Q[\imath x|P]$ is true. Then $E![\imath x|P]$ is true. So existential generalization appears acceptable. Let us note for the record the fact that in Russell's theory atomic sentences with descriptions that fail of presupposition are false, so that we can easily compare it to (III) in the Fregean theory:

THEOREM. (III*) $\sim(E![\imath x|P]) \vDash \sim(Q[\imath x|P])$.

In terms of other principal points of comparison the Russellian theory fares rather well. We can, for example, prove the following theorem.

THEOREM. (IV*) Not($\vDash E![\imath x|P]$) (see above).

But on identity, Russell's theory has the unfortunate consequence:

THEOREM. (V*) not($\vDash [\imath x|P] = [\imath x|P]$).

Proof. For example, let P be the sentence $[\imath x|P_i^1 x]$ such that $R(P_i^1) = \varnothing$. We do retain the following.

THEOREM. (VI*) $\vDash E![\imath x|P] \leftrightarrow (\exists y)(y = [\imath x|P])$.

A major success of the theory that we shall use as a point of comparison later is that it provides a nontrivial analysis of presupposition:

THEOREM. (VII*) $Q[\imath x|P]$ presupposes $E![\imath x|P]$.

☐ **EXERCISE**

Prove the unproven theorems.

8.1.4 Classical Theories with Inner and Outer Domains

A third type of classical theory of singular terms rejects the idea that names always refer, as captured in (2*) and (2**) of Section 8.1.2, by distinguishing between two sorts of domains. The first is that set over which the quantifiers range, which we shall call the *domain of quantification*, and we represent it by U. The second is the set of entities to which names may refer, and this we shall call the *domain of reference* and represent it by D. In classical semantics these two sets are identical. But one way to express the idea that names may be meaningful yet not refer to existing entities is to distinguish the two domains and allow that a name might refer to something in D but outside the domain of quantification U.[5] The details of the account require that $U \subseteq D$ and that we interpret both constants and predicates over D. Interpreting predicates over D has the nice consequence that some atomic sentences with non-referring singular terms (i.e., with $R(c) \in D - U$) are T and others F. The appropriate concept to alter is that of model:

DEFINITION: A *model* (in the relevant sense) is any $\langle U, D, R \rangle$ such that
(1) $U \neq \varnothing$
(2) $U \subseteq D$;
(3) for any $c \in$ PN, $R(c) \in D$ and, for any n-place predicate P_i^n, $R(P_i^n) \subseteq D^n$; and
(4) $R(=)$ is the identity relation on D.
(Usually clause (1) is dropped in frcc logic.)

We must also amend the clauses interpreting the quantifiers in the definition of the extension of R so that U and not D is the domain of quantification. Let u range over entities in U.

DEFINITION: In each of the definitions of extension from Chapter 5 (Sections 5.2.2 and 5.2.3), we replace clause (6) interpreting the quantifier as follows:
Substitution interpretation

$$R+((\forall x)P) = \text{T iff for all } c \text{ such that } R(c) \in U,\ R+[P]_x^c = \text{T}.$$

Referential interpretation

$$R*((\forall x)P) = \text{T iff for all } u \in U,\ R[^u_x]*(P) = \text{T}.$$

Let $E!t$ remain $(\exists y)y = t$. The resulting languages $\langle$Syn-QL, $[R+]\rangle$ and $\langle$Syn-QL, $[R*]\rangle$ we may call *quantificational languages interpreted by outer domains*. Then, as desired, we have this result:

THEOREM. (I**) There is a model $\langle U, D, R \rangle$ such that for some but not all c in PN, $R(c) \in U$.

[5] For an exposition of this sort of theory and of the modal semantics discussed below, see Richmond H. Thomason, 'Modal Logic and Metaphysics' (1969).

Further since $R(P_i^1)$ may be a proper subset of D and overlap U, some sentences with nonreferring singular terms will be T and some F.

THEOREM. (III**) There exists some model $\langle U, D, R\rangle$, some c in PN, and some one-place predicates P_i^1 and P_j^1 such that $R(E!c) = \text{F}$, $R(P_i^1) = \text{T}$, and $R(P_j^1) = \text{F}$.

Proof. Consider this model: $\langle U, D, R\rangle$ such that $R(c) = d$ and d is in D and $R(P_i^1)$, but not in either U or $R(P_j^1)$.

Also, existential generalization fails.

THEOREM. (II*) For some model $\langle U, D, R\rangle$, some c in PN, and some P_i^1, $R(P_i^1 c) = \text{T}$ and $R((\exists x)P_i^1 x) = \text{F}$.

On other points of comparison the theory does rather well:

THEOREM. (IV**) Not($\vDash E!c$);
(V**) $\vDash t = t$; and
(VI**) $\vDash E!t$. (In other words, $\vDash (\exists y)y = t$.)

But all presupposition is trivial:

THEOREM. (VII**) Neither $P_i^1 c \vDash E!c$ nor $\sim P_i^1 c \vDash E!c$.

☐ **EXERCISE**
Prove (II**), (VI**), and (VII**) as stated above.

8.1.5 Supervaluations

In the last chapter we met the device of supervaluation. In that theory partial worlds are defined in the sense of assignments of interpretations to atomic sentences so that some are true, some false, and some neither true nor false. Each partial world w determines the set of its classical completions. These are possible worlds that are just like w in all the sentences that are true and false, but which go beyond its partial specification in two ways: (1) they fill in the truth-value gaps by assigning a definite truth-value to the sentences previously neither true nor false, and (2) they assign truth-values to the molecular sentences in accordance with the classical truth-tables for the connectives. For each partial world w, a supervaluation representing w is defined as that function which assigns to each sentence (atomic or molecular) one of the three truth-values T, F, or N according to this rule: those sentences are T which are true in every classical completion of w, those are assigned F which are false in every classical completion, and those are assigned N which are true in some classical completions and false in others. Given this chapter's semantic concepts for interpreting subject–predicate and quantificational expressions, we can now develop a fully detailed application of the idea of supervaluations to the representation of existential presuppositions. Indeed, though supervaluations have since been applied in the explanation of diverse varieties of nontruth, the idea was originally fashioned by van Fraassen to represent the failure of existential presupposition. The theory, as we shall present it here, will not presuppose any of the technical content of Chapter 7.[6]

Let us call a sentence P *bivalent* relative to a possible world w iff it is either T or F in that world. Then the motivating idea is to limit bivalence to those sentences that have all their existential presuppositions satisfied: P is bivalent in a model iff for any sentence Q, if P presupposes Q, then Q is true. Semantically, we define a new notion of partial model in which sentences are partitioned into those that are true, those that are false, and those that are neither (for which a truth value is not defined). To be consistent with the notation used in this chapter, we continue to represent by U the domain of quantification. In a partial model nonreferring terms do not refer to something outside U; rather, R is merely undefined for them.

DEFINITION: A *partial model* is any $\langle U, R\rangle$ such that

(1) $U \neq \varnothing$;
(2) R is a partial function on PN such that if $R(c)$ is defined, $R(c) \in U$;
(3) $R(P_i^n) \subseteq U^n$.

Again, clause (1) is usually omitted in free logic.

The notion of the extension of R must also be adapted to the new notion of partial model. Each such extension will assign a referent to each predicate, but it will be undefined for some constants and for any sentence containing a constant that does not refer. There are actually two notions of extension depending on whether the substitutional or referential interpretation of the quantifier is used. For simplicity we state both definitions in full. Let $\text{Tm} = \text{PN} \cup \text{Vb}$.

DEFINITION: The set $[[R+]]$ of *classical substitutional extensions* of R relative to the partial model $\langle U, R\rangle$ is
$\{R+ \mid R+$ is a function on $\text{PN} \cup \text{Pd} \cup \text{Sen}$ such that

(1) if $R(c)$ is defined, then $R+(c) = R(c)$, but if $R(c)$ is undefined, then $R+(c)$ is defined but not necessarily in U, and we define the *outer domain* D for the model as $U \cup \{x \mid \text{for some } c \text{ in PN}, R(c) = x\}$;
(2) $R+(P_i^n) = R(P_i^n)$;
(3) $R+$ maps Sen onto $\{T, F\}$ as follows:
  (a) $R+(P_i^n c_1, \ldots, c_n) = T$ iff $\langle R(c_1), \ldots, R(c_n)\rangle \in R(P_i^n)$, and $R+(c = c') = \text{T}$ iff $R(c) = R(c')$;

[6] See the references in Chapter 7, and Bas C. van Fraassen 'Non-classical Logics', Chapter 5, *Formal Semantics and Logic* (1971).

(b) $R+(\sim P) = \mathrm{T}$ iff $R+(P) = \mathrm{F}$;
(c) $R+(P \wedge Q) = \mathrm{T}$ iff $R+(P) = R+(Q) = \mathrm{T}$;
(d) $R+((\forall x)P) = \mathrm{T}$ iff for any c in PN, if $R(c) \in U$, then $R+([P]^c_x) = \mathrm{T}\}$.

DEFINITION: The set $[[R*]]$ of *classical referential extensions* of R relative to a partial model $\langle U, R\rangle$ is
$\{R* | R*$ is a function R on Tm $\cup$ Pd $\cup$ Sen such that

(1) for any v in Vb, $R*(v) = R(v)$, and if $R(c)$ is defined, then $R*(c) = R(c)$, but if $R(c)$ is undefined, then $R*(c)$ is defined but not necessarily in U, and again we define the *outer domain* D for the model as $U \cup \{x | \text{for some } c \text{ in PN}, R(c) = x\}$;
(2) $R*(P^n_i) = R(P^n_i)$;
(3) $R*$ maps Sen onto $\{\mathrm{T}, \mathrm{F}\}$ as follows:
 (a) $R*(P^n_i t_1, \ldots, t_n) = \mathrm{T}$ iff $\langle R(t_1), \ldots, R(t_n)\rangle \in R(P^n_i)$, and $R*(t = t') = \mathrm{T}$ iff $R(t) = R(t')$;
 (b) as in the previous definition, replacing $R+$ by $R*$;
 (c) as in the previous definition, replacing $R+$ by $R*$;
 (d) $R((\forall x)P) = \mathrm{T}$ iff for any $u \in U$, $R[^u_x]*(P) = \mathrm{T}\}$.

Thus each classical extension supplies referents to those constants left uninterpreted by R, and thus ensures a classical bivalent treatment. Since there is more than one way to fill in the missing values of R for constants, there is more than one classical valuation, regardless of whether we are employing the substitutional or referential sense of classical valuation. Since nothing here depends on the difference between substitutional and referential interpretations, we shall refer to both $[[R+]]$ and $[[R*]]$ as $[[R]]$, and let R range over $[[R]]$. Notice first that the classical valuations generated by classical logic are special cases of those generated by partial models.

THEOREM. If $\langle D, R\rangle$ is a model of classical quantificational logic as defined in Chapter 5 and $R+$ is its unique bivalent substitutional extension, also as defined there, then by setting $U = D$, we see that $\langle D, R\rangle$ (which is the same as $\langle U, R\rangle$) meets the defining conditions for being a partial model, as defined in this section, and $R+$ meets the conditions for being its classical substitutional extension, as here defined. Furthermore, in this case $\langle U, R\rangle$ has only one such extension, i.e., $[[R]]$ in this case is $\{R+\}$. This result also holds for the referential interpretation if $R+$ is replaced everywhere by $R*$.

We proceed now to define for each partial $\langle U, R\rangle$, a unique nonclassical valuation with truth-value gaps, called a supervaluation. While $\langle U, R\rangle$ captures the notion of a possible world to the extent that it interprets constants and predicates, the supervaluation associated with $\langle U, R\rangle$ completes the picture by assigning truth-values to sentences. The rationale behind the way supervaluations assign truth-values requires a little discussion.

First, we observe that some sentences receive T from some members of $[[R]]$ and F from other members of the same $[[R]]$. We may justly say of these sentences that classical intuitions do not determine for them a unique truth-value; such classically indeterminate sentences may be grouped into a special category. This category then represents a genuine semantic concept. Second, observe those classically indeterminate atomic sentences, e.g., 'Pegasus is white', which are T for some $R \in [[R]]$, but are F for another $R' \in [[R]]$. These atomic sentences are exactly those with nonreferring singular terms. This coincidence on the level of atomic sentences of classical indeterminacy with presupposition failure suggests that presupposition failure may coincide with indeterminacy for arbitrarily complex sentences also. The theory of supervaluations asserts just this coincidence and semantically distinguishes the category of classically indeterminate sentences relative to $\langle U, R\rangle$ by assigning just these sentences a truth-value gap. On the assumption that classical indeterminacy is the mark of presupposition failure, these truth-value gaps fall to all and only the sentences with presupposition failure.

Let us pause to ask, why opt for the criterion of classical indeterminacy in assigning truth-value gaps to complex sentences? After all, you might point out, we have three-valued matrix logic. Why not use the matrix for the weak or strong connectives of Kleene, for example? The reply is that the several three-valued matrix theories have an unacceptable logic or, in other words, a counterintuitive analysis of semantic entailment. As we saw in detail in the last chapter, they all reject some arguments of classical logic. But supervaluations have the desirable property that every classically valid argument remains valid in a language interpreted by supervaluations. If F is a family of sets (i.e., a set whose elements are themselves sets), recall that $\bigcap F$ is $\{x | \text{for some } X \text{ in } F, x \in X\}$.

DEFINITION: The set $[S]$ of supervaluations is defined as

$\{S | S$ is a function from some subset of sentences into $\{T, F\}$
such that there is a partial model $\langle U, R\rangle$ and $S = \bigcap[[R]]$, i.e.,
(1) if for all $R \in [[R]]$, $R(P) = T$, then $S(P) = T$;
(2) if for all $R \in [[R]]$, $R(P) = F$, then $S(P) = F$;
(3) $R(P)$ is undefined otherwise$\}$.

In the language of the last chapter, each R restricted to sentences forms a partial valuation for sentences, and each $[[R]]$ is its set of classical completions. The family B consisting of all such sets $[[R]]$ generated from partial models (i.e., B defined as $\{[[R]] | \langle U, R\rangle$ is a partial model$\}$) is a base for a superlanguage, and $[S]$ is the set of all supervaluations established by each element of the base.

DEFINITION: By the *quantificational superlanguage with nonreferring constants*, briefly LS, let us mean $\langle$Syn-QL, $[S]\rangle$.
DEFINITION: Let $X \vDash_{LS} P$ iff for all $S \in [S]$, if S satisfies X, then $S(P) = T$. In this section let us use LC to refer to the classical bivalent language $\langle$Syn-QL, $[R]\rangle$ defined in Chapter 5, for either the substitutional or referential interpretation.

THEOREM. If $X \vDash_{LC} P$, then $X \vDash_{LS} P$.

Let us now see how supervaluation theory accounts for the intuitions behind singular terms. First of all, constants need not refer.

THEOREM. (I***) In LS, there is some c and partial model $\langle U, R\rangle$, such that $R(c)$ is undefined.

The theory validates existential generalization.

THEOREM. (II***) $P \vDash_{LS} (\exists x)P$.

But the rationale is similar to that in Russell's theory: $[P]^c_x$ presupposes $(\exists x)P$ and hence entails it. To explain this relation we must first define presupposition.

DEFINITION: *P presupposes Q* iff $P \vDash_{LS} Q$ and $\sim P \vDash_{LS} Q$.

THEOREM. $[P]^c_x$ presupposes $E!c$.

Thus we justify existential generalization as follows. Suppose $[P]^c_x$. Hence by presupposition $E!c$; hence $[P]^c_x \wedge E!c$; and thus $(\exists x)P$.

THEOREM. (III***) If P presupposes B and $S(B) \neq T$, then $S(P)$ is undefined.

Also, c need not refer in some possible world S.

THEOREM. (IV***) Not($\vDash_{LS} E!c$).

Identity is classical, and the quantifiers continue as in classical logic to range over the existing things because we retain the usual definition of $E!t$ as $(\exists x)x = t$.

THEOREM. (V***) $\vDash_{LS} t = t$.
(VI***) $E!t$ iff $(\exists x)x = t$.

We may summarize the discussion in the following table.

	Intuition	Russell	Inner and outer domains	Supervaluations
(I) Some nonreferring singular terms c	Desirable	Constants refer, not descriptions	Constants may or may not refer	Constants may or may not refer
(II) Existential generalization: $P \vDash (\exists x)P$	Dubious	Valid, due to presupposition	Invalid	Valid, due to presupposition
(III) Truth-value of		Both false		Both undefined
'Pegasus has wings'	Odd, true		True	
'Pegasus has horns'	Odd, false		False	
(IV) Necessary existence: $\vDash$Pegasus exists	Very dubious	Invalid for descriptions	Invalid	Invalid
(V) Law of identity: $\vDash t = t$	Desirable	Invalid for descriptions	Valid	Valid
(VI) Existential reading of $(\exists x)P$, i.e., $E!t$ means $(\exists y)y = t$	Desirable	Valid	Valid	Valid

□ **EXERCISE**

Prove the unproven metatheorems stated above.

8.2 QUANTIFIED MODAL LOGIC

8.2.1 Semantics of 'Necessarily' and 'Possibly'

As semantic theory has developed in this book, the notion of possible world has become more refined and detailed. At first, for propositional logic, a possible world was presented in the set theoretic terms of semantic theory by a function from sentences to truth-values. In quantificational logic possible worlds received a more complex representation. A world there was specified by first defining a model that fixed the domain of quantification and the references of atomic expressions, and then by associating with each such model an extension assigning truth-values to all the sentences. In the semantics of modal logic it is usual to make explicit the fact that these models and reference relations record the facts of various possible worlds. We do so by stipulating in the semantic theory that there is a set W of possible worlds and we then assign to each world w in W a model, and from the model we determine a full reference relation interpreting all sentences.[7]

There are two immediate benefits that derive from distinguishing between possible worlds, on the one hand, and models with their associated reference relations, on the other. First of all, if we assign to each world a model, we may then represent the intuitively attractive idea that two worlds might be different yet accurately represented by the same model. Certain philosophical theories are even centered on this possibility, as does the Stoic theory of eternal return in which the world exactly as it is now is supposed to recur again and again in the future.

A second advantage is that by distinguishing worlds from models we may impose structure on the set of worlds and investigate the consequences of this structure on the references of expressions in the language. Thus far we have discussed expressions for which the principle of the compositionality of reference (Chapter 3) holds. For such an expression it is possible to determine its reference in a world w by looking only at the referents of its parts in w and applying the right semantic rule. Some expressions violate this pattern and seem to depend for their truth-value in a world w on facts about the referents of its parts not in the world w, but in some other possible world related in a structural way to w.

The best example is probably tenses. A standard analysis of the future tense inflection is to treat it as a sentential operator. Let us have a formation rule that attaches to any sentence P the future tense sign 'F' to yield the whole FP. We read FP as saying 'It will be the case that P' or 'In the future, P'. Now let us think of possible worlds as times in history. Then the natural account of the truth conditions of FP are these: FP is true at time t iff P is true at some time later than t.

Notice first of all that the truth of FP at t depends on the truth of its part P, and second that the relevant time at which this part is evaluated is some time different from the original t. Notice also that the account presupposes that times fall in a structural order such that some are 'later than' others. The past tense is similar. A sentence in the past tense is true at t if its immediate

[7] Our concern here is with aspects of modal logic that exhibit general features of semantic theory. For the special properties of classical modal logic, both its proof theory and possible world semantics, see G. E. Hughes and M. J. Cresswell, *An Introduction to Modal Logic* (1968). For a more reflective appraisal of its importance to logic see Dana Scott, 'Advice on Modal Logic' (1970).

sentential part is true at some earlier time. Languages with such operators are called *tense logics.*[8]

Another class of expressions that behave in this way are the sentence adverbs 'necessarily' and 'possibly' and their corresponding modal auxiliary verbs 'must' and 'might'. These are called by logicians the *alethic modalities.* It is customary to represent the former by the operator '$\Box$' and the latter by '$\Diamond$'. Thus $\Box P$ is read 'Necessarily, P' or 'It must be the case that P', and $\Diamond P$ is translated 'Possibly, P' or '*It* might be the case that P'. To say P is necessary, it has long been held, means that P must always be true. Thus $\Box P$ is true in a world w iff its immediate part P is true in all worlds w'. On the other hand, $\Diamond P$ is true in w iff there is at least one w' such that P is true at w'.

By imposing structural conditions on the worlds relevant to appraising claims of necessity, interesting facts emerge. If, for example, we limit possible worlds to times, in particular future times, then the future tense operator and $\Diamond$ collapse. Another way to say this is that F is a possibility operator over future times. Likewise, expressions like 'It has to be the case that...' work like necessity operators over future times.

Another interesting kind of expression that works in a similar way is the moral auxiliary verb 'ought', which we may represent by the operator O. One account of OP, read 'You ought to bring it about that P', is what is called *consequentialism* in ethics, the view that moral action is to be appraised by its consequences in the future. This idea may be put semantically as follows. OP is true at t if those future times t' at which the immediate part P is true are better than those times t' at which the part P is false. Such an account seems to presuppose quite an elaborate structure of times, perhaps a treelike organization in which each time has just one immediate past but a series of alternative immediate futures. Such analyses are studied in *deontic logic*.[9]

All such logics are broadly called *modal logic* and here we cannot investigate the interesting properties of various kinds. Rather, we shall concentrate on features common to them all. For this purpose it is best to discuss the alethic modalities, since their properties are basic to the others.

The first basic idea we define is the notion of a 'modal' structure. This is a set of worlds organized by a structural relation, and a function I assigning to each world a model in the classical sense. Given that model, a fully defined reference relation for the sentences is determined in the usual way. In order to avoid any dubious metaphysical claims about the actual existence of possible

[8] A good example of such a semantic theory is Richmond Thomason, 'Indeterminist Time and Truth-Value Gaps' (1970), in which Thomason discusses William of Ockham's nonbivalent theory of future contingents as an example of modal tense logic with times structured as trees branching toward the future.

[9] For a consequentialist semantics for deontic logic see R. E. Jennings 'A Utilitarian Semantics for Deontic Logic' (1974).

worlds, we may assume that the set of possible worlds is drawn from any previously constructed set postulated in set theory or mathematics. The only requirement of such a set is that it be large enough for our purposes. We use the real numbers.[10]

The usual way to discuss the structure on possible worlds is in terms of an ordering relation $\leq$ holding among worlds. The later-than relation is such an ordering in tense logic, and by imposing special conditions on such orderings they can also be turned into tree structures of the sort suggested for deontic logic.

DEFINITION: By a *modal quantificational syntax* (*with identity*), briefly Syn-QL$_\Box$, we mean a quantificational syntax QL-Syn with identity that we have been using up to now but augmented so that Fm includes two additional formation rules $f_\Box$ and $f_\Diamond$ under which the set Sen of sentences is closed. These rules are defined as follows:

$$f_\Box = \{\langle x, y\rangle | y = \Box^\frown x\} \quad \text{and} \quad f_\Diamond = \{\langle x, y\rangle | y = \Diamond^\frown x\}.$$

The concept of model is the same as that of classical logic, but we shall reserve U as the name of the set of all possible objects and refer to the domain of quantification of a particular world w as U_w. We shall not assume that U_w is identical to the domain of reference for singular terms. We define the notion U_w in two stages. First we define a first-order model as before, and then within a wider system of possible worlds we assign to each world one such model.

DEFINITION: A *model* for Syn-QL$_\Box$ is defined (as before) as any $\langle D, R\rangle$ such that D is nonempty (this condition is usually omitted in free logic) and R maps Tm into D and n-place predicates into subsets of D^n.

DEFINITION: A *model structure* is an $\langle W, I, U, \leq\rangle$ such that

(1) W is a nonempty set of real numbers (the set of *possible worlds*);
(2) I is a function with domain W such that $I(w)$ is a model for Syn-QL$_\Box$;
(3) $U = \{I(w) | w \in W\}$; and
(4) $\leq$ is a binary relation on W (sometimes called the *accessibility* or *alternativeness* relation).

We let w range over W, and if $I(w) = \langle D, R\rangle$, we refer to the D as U_w and to R as R_w.

DEFINITION: Sets $[R+]_{MS}$ and $[R*]_{MS}$ of substitutional and referential extensions respectively, relative to a model structure $\langle W, I, U, \leq\rangle$, are

[10] A number of philosophers are quite willing to argue that possible worlds exist and on this view it would be legitimate to merely posit the set of possible worlds as an undefined primitive term of semantic theory. See, for example, Robert C. Stalnaker, 'Possible Worlds' (1976).

defined as the set of all extensions $R+$ and $R*$ that are extensions of some model $\langle U_w, R_w \rangle$ in the range of I; to define $R+$ and $R*$ here, we add clauses for the interpretation of the new sentences to the definitions of extensions in Sections 5.2.2 and 5.2.3. It will suffice to state the rules for R_w+. Those for $R*$ are the same using R_w* to replace R_w+:

(7) if P is a necessity statement, say $\Box Q$, then $R_w+(P) = \text{T}$ iff for all w' such that $w \leq w'$, $R_{w'}+(Q) = \text{T}$; and

(8) if P is a possibility statement, say $\Diamond Q$, then $R_w+(P) = \text{T}$ iff for some w', such that $w \leq w'$, $R_{w'}+(Q) = \text{T}$.

Instead of $R_w+(P)$ and $R_w*(P)$ we shall just write $R_w(P)$, and in general we shall use R instead of $R+$ or $R*$ with the understanding that R should be interpreted in one of these two senses. [In place of a distinct formation rule for $\Diamond$ and the corresponding clause (8), $\Diamond P$ may be introduced by abbreviative definition as short for $\sim\Box\sim P$.]

It is the properties of the alternativeness relation $\leq$ that determine the structure of W, and there are customary names for standard combinations of properties.

DEFINITION: Let $\text{MS} = \langle W, I, U, \leq \rangle$ be a model structure. Then, MS is called

(1) *an* M *system* iff $\leq$ is reflexive;
(2) *a* B *system* iff $\leq$ is reflexive and symmetric;
(3) *an* S4 *system* iff $\leq$ is reflexive and transitive;
(4) *an* S5 *system* iff $\leq$ is reflexive, symmetric, and transitive;
(5) a *weak tense system* iff $\leq$ is a linear ordering (i.e., is reflexive, transitive, and asymmetric);
(6) *a strong tense system* iff $\leq$ is a dense linear ordering (i.e., is a linear ordering such that if $x \leq y$, then for some z, $x \leq z$ and $z \leq y$).

We may then joint together in one large set all the reference relations generated by any of these systems. For example, by $[R]_{\text{M}}$ let us mean the set of all reference relations generated by any M model system. Then the *modal language M* would be $\langle \text{Syn-QL}_\Box, [\text{R}]_M \rangle$.

DEFINITION: By $[R]_X$ is meant $\bigcup\{[R]_{\text{MS}} | \text{MS is an } X \text{ system}\}$, and by L_X is meant $\langle \text{Syn-QL}_\Box, [\text{R}]_X \rangle$.

Since we wish to go on to discuss in some depth the interaction of the quantifiers with the modal operator we shall only list some of the most basic validities of the various modal systems. We first list a series (P1)–(P4) of logical truths:

(P1) $\models \Box P \rightarrow P$

(P2) $\models \Box(P \rightarrow Q) \rightarrow (\Box P \rightarrow \Box Q)$

(P3) $\models \Box P \rightarrow \Box\Diamond P$

(P4) $\models \Box P \rightarrow \Box\Box P$.

THEOREM. (1) In the language L_M both (P1) and (P2) hold;
(2) in the language L_B all of (P1), (P2), and (P3) hold;
(3) in the language L_{S4} all of (P1), (P2), and (P4) hold;
(4) in the language L_{S5} all of (P1)–(P4) hold.

□ EXERCISES

1. By appeal to clause (8) in the definition of the extension of a model, prove that for any extension R of a model $\langle U_w, R_w \rangle$ and any world structure $\langle W, I, U, \leq \rangle$, $R(\Diamond P) = R({\sim}\Box{\sim}P)$.
2. Prove clause (4) in the last theorem.
3. Another way of stating the defining conditions on $\leq$ in the system S5 is that $\leq$ is an equivalence relation. Moreover, every equivalence relation determines a partition of W, and conversely every partition of W determines an equivalence relation on W. Last, the trivial partitioning of W into the single set W is nevertheless a partitioning. On the basis of these facts show that there is an S5 system in which $R_w(\Box P) = \text{T}$ iff for all w in W, $R_w(P) = \text{T}$.

The last exercise shows that $[R]_{S5}$ generates the same validities as the set of all reference relations of any model structure. This set of all reference relations is formally defined as $\bigcup\{[R]_{MS} \mid \text{MS is a model structure}\}$, and we may call it briefly $[R]$. When the differences between the various systems are irrelevant, it is common to refer to a modal language as that interpreted by this wide set.

Since the differences among these systems are irrelevant to what we shall say in this introduction, we shall refer to the *modal quantificational languages* as $\langle \text{Syn-QL}_\Box, [R+] \rangle$ and $\langle \text{Syn-QL}_\Box, [R*] \rangle$.

We shall return in Chapter 9 to general structural features of modal semantics when we discuss intensional logics and how they fail to observe the principle of compositionality of reference. In the rest of this chapter we shall investigate how quantifiers, variables, and constants interact with modal operators, and in particular how the singular reference of expressions in one world can be relevant to the truth-value in a second world of a modal sentence containing these expressions.

8.2.2 Sameness, Difference, and Change

Within classical quantification theory it is perfectly possible to state an adequate theory of identity so long as we talk about only those objects that currently exist. The usual theory is to view $R(=)$ as the identity relation on U_w. Specialized theories might differ by holding to one or another form of a quite different analysis of identity known as the *identity of indiscernibles.* This theory holds that two things are identical if they share all the same properties. The properties in question may be monadic or relational, and thus there are really two varieties of the identity principle.

DEFINITION: A language is said to hold to the doctrine of the *identity of indiscernibles* iff in the definition of model the interpretation of '$=$' takes either of the following forms:

(1) (*Weak form*) $R(t = t') = \text{T}$ iff for all P_i^1, $R(P_i^1 t) = R(P_i^1 t')$; or

(2) (*Strong form*) $R(t = t') = \text{T}$ iff for all sentences P and variable x, $R([P]_x^t) = R([P]_x^{t'})$.

(In classical first-order logic, interpreting '$=$' by the identity of indiscernibles rather than assigning it the identity relation on the domain yields inexpressibility results such as the Löwenheim–Skolem theorem even for domains of finite cardinality. For example, one cannot say in such a language that there are exactly three things and be sure that it will be true only in models with just three things in the domain.) Thus, in classical first-order logic various accounts of sameness for objects in the domain are possible. The case is different when we try to compare the sameness of objects across worlds or through times. The fundamental property of such transworld comparisons is that two objects may be the same yet their properties differ. Such cannot hold for identities within a world. Unfortunately classical quantificational semantics alone cannot account for sameness through time together with alteration of properties. It cannot, in short, distinguish between change and mere difference of properties through time.

EXAMPLE *Inexpressibility in first-order logic of the difference between change and renaming.* Consider two models $\langle U_w, R_w \rangle$ and $\langle U_{w'}, R_{w'} \rangle$ as represented in Fig. 8.1 with the same domain $U_w = U_{w'} = \{u, u', u''\}$ but with different interpretations of descriptive terms, two constants a and b, and one monadic predicate G. In $\langle U_w, R_w \rangle$, $R_w(a) = u$, $R_w(b) = u'$, and $R_w(G) = \{u, u''\}$. Thus $R_w(Ga) = R_w(Gb) = \text{T}$. In $\langle U_{w'}, R_{w'} \rangle$, a continues to refer to the same individual, but b is shifted so that it names an entirely different thing. Moreover, the object referred to by a in the first model changes and ceases to fall under G, whereas the object that b refers to in the first model does not change: $R_{w'}(a) = u$, $R_{w'}(b) = u''$, and $R_{w'}(G) = \varnothing$. Hence $R_{w'}(Ga) = R_{w'}(Gb) = \text{F}$. Let us assume that G continues to have the same meaning in

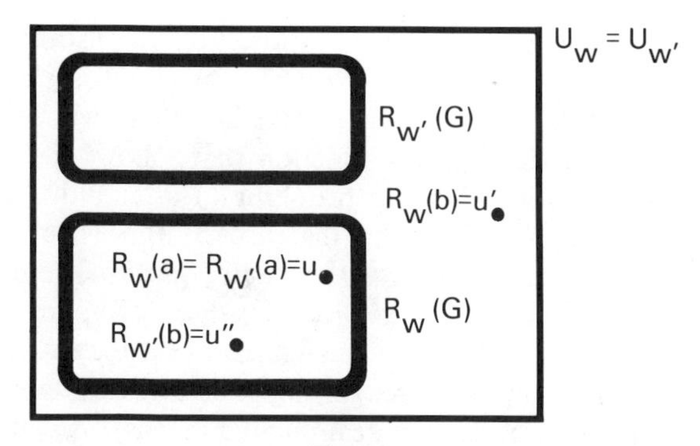

Fig. 8.1

both models.[11] In this situation the individual u undergoes a genuine change, but neither u' nor u'' changes. These facts are not reflected in the truth-values of the sentences of the language. Both Ga and Gb go from T to F. In the first case the switch is due to a genuine change in the referent of a, but in the second it is due to assigning a new object to the constant b. This latter is a change in language rather than a change in the world, and we may call such shifts in the reference of constants *renaming*. The lesson, then, is that first-order languages as they stand cannot discriminate in the object language between genuine change and renaming.

A preferable theory would be one in which a change in the truth-value of a subject–predicate sentence reflects a change in the objects named, rather than a shift in the properties of distinct objects or the shuffling of names. What we want is some concept of 'same individual' through which we could require constants to refer to the same individual throughout worlds. Sameness here will clearly not be sameness of attached predicate.

One way a formal theory could require constants to refer to some individual is just by requiring all constants to always refer to the same entity throughout every world.

Principle of Overlapping Domains. For any models $\langle U_w, R_w \rangle$ and $\langle U_{w'}, R_{w'} \rangle$, and any c in PN, $R_w(c) = R_{w'}(c)$.

If such a condition were imposed, it would make the reference of a constant itself persist as a kind of 'bare particular' or as something like Aristotle's prime matter.

Let us express the idea of 'sameness' in a slightly different way. The semantic behavior of a constant determines a function from possible worlds

[11] The exact content of this assumption about sameness of meaning of predicates, even though their extensions differ across worlds, is discussed in Chapter 9.

into objects in the domains of those worlds. For a constant c, there is a function f on W such that $f(w)$ is $R_w(c)$. Conversely, it is clear that every persisting individual, as we intuitively understand that idea, determines one such function, namely the tracking function that follows it from world to world regardless of how it changes its properties. For an individual i, there is a function f on W such that $f(w)$ is the 'instance' or 'time slice' of i in w. Such functions are variously called *individual concepts* (Carnap, Montague), *individuating functions* (Hintikka), *transworld heir lines* (Kaplan), or *tracking functions.*[12] What is interesting about such functions is that we may use them to represent an individual that passes through possible worlds and times, and to represent the difference between real change in this individual and mere shifting of names.

Let f be such a function representing such an individual i, and let us pair a constant c with f. Then $f(w)$ is an instance or time slice of i in w. Now consider the reference of constant c in two worlds w and w'. If there is a single individual function f such that instances of that individual are picked out in both worlds (i.e., if for some f, $R_w(c) = f(w)$ and $R_{w'}(c) = f(w')$, then regardless of what new predicates apply to c, c continues to represent the 'same' object, and any change in truth-values of atomic sentences using c represents real changes. If, however, there is no such function, if the best that can be said is that there are two individual functions, say f and g, such that c picks out an instance of f in w and an instance of g in w', then changes in truth-values of atomic sentences with c represent linguistic change: c then picks out different individuals in the two worlds.

Likewise we may represent 'sameness of property' by a function from possible worlds to relations in those worlds. In the semantic theory we have developed thus far, we know that the reference of a predicate in each world is a relation, and that this set in general differs from world to world because the extensions of predicates from world to world contain different individuals. Does such a change reflect a change in the world or a change in language? Does it mean, on the one hand, that the predicate corresponds to a genuine property and that the extension of that property has altered from one world to another or, on the other hand, that the predicate has to be paired first with one property and then another, each of which may have extensions which remain unchanged in the two worlds?

Following Carnap and Montague we may identify *properties* with functions from possible worlds to relations on objects in those worlds, and use these functions to distinguish between real and linguistic change. To each

[12] Individual functions were first discussed by Rudolf Carnap in *Meaning and Necessity* (1947), and a good exposition of the idea in more recent logic is found in Jaakko Hintikka, 'Semantics for Propositional Attitudes' (1969).

genuine property in the intuitive sense there corresponds one such set theoretic proxy, and we say a change in the extension of a predicate reflects a genuine change between two worlds w and w' if its referent is an instance in each world of the same property-tracking function, but that it reflects only a linguistic change if there is no such function such that both referents are instances of it.

DEFINITION: A *world system with individual concepts and properties* for a quantified modal syntax is any $\langle W, U, \text{Int}, I, \leq \rangle$ such that

(1) W is a nonempty set of real numbers (*possible worlds*);

(2) U is a nonempty set (the set of *possible objects*);

(3) Int (called the *intension assignment to constants and predicates*) is a function from Tm $\cup$ Pd such that for any t in Tm, Int(t) is a function f from W into U (such functions are called *individual concepts*), and for any P_i^n in Pd, Int(P_i^n) is a function g from W into subsets of U^n (such functions are called *properties*);

(4) I is a function on W such that $I(w)$ is some pair $\langle D, R \rangle$ (called a *model*) with the following properties:

(a) D is nonempty (omitted in free logic);

(b) for any t in Tm, $R(t)$ is $\text{Int}(t)(w)$ and $R(t) \in D$; for any n-placed predicate P_i^n, $R(P_i^n)$ is $\text{Int}(P_i^n)(w)$ and $R(P_i^n) \subseteq D^n$

(as before, if $I(w) = \langle D, R \rangle$, we refer to D as U_w and R as R_w);

(5) $\leq$ is a binary relation (the *alternativeness relation*) on W.

It follows directly that the objects referred to by a constant in a world are members of the domain of that world, and that predicates refer to relations on objects in that domain.

THEOREM. For any c in PN, any individual concept Int(c) and any world w, $\text{Int}(c)(w) \in U_w$, and for any predicate P_i^n, any property $\text{Int}(P_i^n)$, and any world w, $\text{Int}(P_i^n)(w) \subseteq U_w^n$.

DEFINITION: An *extension* $R*$ for a model $\langle D, R \rangle = \langle U_w, R_w \rangle$ and a world system $\langle W, U, \text{Int}, I, \leq \rangle$ is defined just like an extension for the model as before, except that clause (3a) now reads

$$R(P_i^n t_1, \ldots, t_n) = \text{T iff } \langle R_w(t_1), \ldots, R_w(t_n) \rangle \in R_w(P_i^n).$$

An immediate consequence is that references of constants and predicates in a world w are determined by intensions, and that an atomic sentence is true if the objects determined by the intensions of the constants stand in that relation which is determined by the intension of the predicate.

THEOREM. For any constant c and any world w, $R_w(c) = \text{Int}(c)(w)$; for any predicate P_i^n and world w, $R_w(P_i^n) = \text{Int}(P_i^n)(w)$; and for any atomic sentence $P_i^n t_1, \ldots, t_n$, $R(P_i^n t_1, \ldots, t_n) = \text{T iff } \langle \text{Int}(t_1)(w), \ldots, \text{Int}(t_n)(w) \rangle \in \text{Int}(P_i^n)(w)$.

The earlier idea that constants refer to the same individual in all worlds may now be seen to be captured in the fact that constants are assigned individual concepts. More generally, we may investigate various alternative ways to explain sameness as restrictions on the ideas of individual concept and property.

8.2.3 Necessary Identity

One important modification of the basic idea of individuating function applies to it a plausible additional intuition that identity within a world and identity through worlds are both part of the same great identity relation. If X at time t is the same persisting individual as Y at t, and Y at t is the same persisting individual as Z at t', then X at t is the same persisting individual as Z at t'. To put it another way, if X is ever identical to Y, it always is. Transworld lines as representatives of individuals should coincide everywhere if they intersect at all.

Notice that the unrestricted concept of individual concept seems to outrun the preanalytic idea of individual as substance. While for every individual there is an individual concept, it seems that some of these concepts do not really correspond to an individual. This situation is well illustrated by those tracking functions corresponding to definite descriptions: 'the President of the United States' determines a function from possible worlds to objects in their domains, but this function does not correspond to any one individual because different individuals in the intuitive sense move into and out of the office. If, on the other hand, we do not allow distinct individual concepts to intersect, then each such concept does determine an individual in a more intuitive sense. Thus, a theory may require that constants or variables (usually both if either) refer to individual concepts that are identical if they coincide at all.

DEFINITION: A quantified modal language with a world structure with intensions for constants and predicates is said to have *rigid* terms iff for any individual concepts $\mathrm{Int}(t)$ and $\mathrm{Int}(t')$ in its world system, if for some w, $\mathrm{Int}(t)(w) = \mathrm{Int}(t')(w)$, then $\mathrm{Int}(t) = \mathrm{Int}(t')$.

THEOREM. In a quantified modal language with rigid terms, for any constants c and c', and any variables x and y,

$$c = c' \vDash \Box(c = c')$$
$$x = y \vDash \Box(x = y).$$

If variables are required to be rigid, then $(\forall x)P$ reads 'for all substances' or 'for all persisting individuals'.

Frequently, the idea of rigid constants is built into a theory by identifying the individual concepts corresponding to constants with constant functions and then identifying the constant function itself with its unique value. That is, frequently theories obtain the result of rigid constants by forcing constants to have the same instance in all worlds; they therefore require overlapping domains, which is the idea we started with before reformulating the semantics using tracking functions. Certainly, having a name always pick out the same object in the intersection of the various domains is simple, and if variables are treated likewise, there need be only one domain shared with all possible worlds. But we have already seen that tracking functions allow us to state the difference between real and linguistic change and to represent persisting individuals. Moreover, we shall see that limiting our constants and variables to a domain of incorruptible, necessarily existing entities yields quite implausible logical truths. A richer semantics is one in which there is real change, in which some expressions stand for persisting individuals and others do not, and in which we quantify over objects that come into and pass out of existence.

8.2.4 Counterparts

David Lewis has argued for a particularly interesting enrichment. He believed that the notion of 'same individual' through worlds does not in general pick out a unique instance in every world. Though there is only one of me in this world, there may be more than one thing such that it is as similar to me as anything else in some subsequent world.[13] A persisting individual i, in this view, determines not a function from possible worlds to objects in their domains, but rather a relation R. Thus if i determines R and there are two entities u and u' in U_w such that both $\langle w, u\rangle \in R$ and $\langle w, u'\rangle \in R$, we think of u and u' as similar in all relevant respects, each having an equal right to be called an instance of i. Here, 'same as' means roughly 'as similar to as anything else', and the relation is reflexive, symmetric, but not transitive. Normally we would wish constants and variables to be rigid in the sense that individuals even in this relational sense are identical if they coincide at all.

DEFINITION: A modal quantificational language with intensions for constants and predicates is said to be a *counterpart theory* iff individual concepts are allowed to be relations rather than functions, and is in addition said to have *rigid* terms if for any two individual concepts $\text{Int}(t)$ and $\text{Int}(t')$, whenever there is a world w and object u such that $\langle w, u\rangle \in \text{Int}(t)$ and $\langle w, u\rangle \in \text{Int}(t')$, then $\text{Int}(t) = \text{Int}(t')$.

[13] See David Lewis, 'Counterpart Theory and Quantified Modal Logic' (1968).

☐ **EXERCISE**

Suppose L is a modal quantificational language with intensions for constants and predicates, and is also a counterpart theory with rigid terms. Let us define a relation $\equiv_w$ *on* U_w for any model as follows:

$$x \equiv_w y \text{ iff for some } t, \langle w, x\rangle \in \text{Int}(t) \text{ and } \langle w, y\rangle \in \text{Int}(t).$$

Show that $\equiv_w$ is an equivalence relation on U_w. (It is the 'sameness' relation as restricted to the domain of a single world.)

Counterpart theory, however, presents a problem for the theory of truth. Should 'Socrates is black' be T or F in a world in which Socrates has two counterparts, one black and one not? There are at least three answers possible. First, the theory may be bivalent and an atomic sentence true if the predicate applies to even just one of the instances of the individual concept associated with the subject. Second, the theory may be bivalent and the sentence true only when the predicate applies to all the instances of the subject. Thirdly, the theory may be nonbivalent, reserving truth for cases in which all instances of the subject fall under the predicate, falsity for cases in which all instances fail to fall under the predicate, and the third value or undefinedness for the non-unanimous cases. The clause (3a) in the definition of the extension R of a model (on page 276) would have these possible versions:

(1) $R_w(P^n_i t_1, \ldots, t_n)$ is T iff for some $x_1, \ldots, x_n$, $\langle w, x_1\rangle \in \text{Int}(t_1), \ldots, \langle w, x_n\rangle \in \text{Int}(t_n)$ and $\langle x_1, \ldots, x_n\rangle \in R_w(P^n_i)$; or

(2) $R_w(P^n_i t_1, \ldots, t_n)$ is F iff for all $x_1, \ldots, x_n$, if $\langle w, x_1\rangle \in \text{Int}(t_1), \ldots, \langle w, x_n\rangle \in \text{Int}(t_n)$, then $\langle x_1, \ldots, x_n\rangle \in R_w(P^n_i)$; or

(3) $R_w(P^n_i t_1, \ldots, t_n)$ is T if for all $x_1, \ldots, x_n$, if $\langle w, x_1\rangle \in \text{Int}(t_1), \ldots, \langle w, x_n\rangle \in \text{Int}(t_n)$, then $\langle x_1, \ldots, x_n\rangle \in R_w(P^n_i)$, and is F if for all $x_1, \ldots, x_n$, if $\langle w, x_1\rangle \in \text{Int}(t_1), \ldots, \langle w, x_n\rangle \in \text{Int}(t_n)$, then $\langle x_1, \ldots, x_n\rangle \in R_w(P^n_i)$.

Perhaps (2) is the most natural classical counterpart theory, and (3) is a good basis for supervaluations since it permits truth-value gaps in cases of classical (noncounterpart) indeterminateness.

A last point about counterpart theory is that it clearly cannot be simplified by taking terms to stand for unique persisting individuals in the overlap of the domains of diverse possible worlds. Here individual concepts play an essential role.

8.2.5 Generation and Corruption

A third important issue is basically an issue in free logic: does an individual exist in all worlds if in any? Are individual concepts ever partially defined on W? Intuitions strongly suggest yes, though modal logics that are strictly classical say no. For simplicity let us assume that individual concepts are functions. Reformulations in terms of relations for counterpart theory are straightforward. If we take the reference of a term to be determined by its individual concept and we combine this fact with the various different treatments we have seen in free logic for the possibility of nonreferring terms, we see that there are four alternative restrictions on individual concepts.

DEFINITION: A modal quantificational language with intensions for terms and predicates is said to be

(1) *classical* iff for all constants or variables t and worlds w, $\text{Int}(t)(w)$ is defined and in U_w (this is the restriction used previously);

(2) *Fregean* iff the language is a modal quantificational language except that it is stipulated that the entity $*$ is in each U_w, that for any predicate P_i^n and any $x_1, \ldots, x_n$ in U_w, $\langle x_1, \ldots, *, \ldots, x_n \rangle \notin R_w(P_i^n)$, and $\text{Int}(t)(w)$ is in U_w;

(3) *an outer domain theory* iff for any constant or variable t and world w, $\text{Int}(t)$ is defined though it is not necessarily in U_w;

(4) *providing a base for a superlanguage* iff for any constant or variable t and world w, $\text{Int}(w)$ need not be defined, but if it is defined it is in U_w.

Which of these policies is best is usually discussed in terms of two formulas:

(A) $(\forall x)\Box P \to \Box(\forall x)P$ (Barcan formula);
(B) $\Box(\forall x)P \to (\forall x)\Box P$ (converse Barcan formula).

Let us consider a special case in which entities may come into being. Suppose that everything that now exists is 1, 2, or 3. Thus everything that now exists is less than 4, and is so necessarily. But if things may come into existence, then everything may not be less than 4 in some world. Hence given generation, (A) is not valid. Likewise consider a typical case in which things pass out of existence. Everything in a given world is necessarily self-identical, but if one of these things passes out of existence, it cannot always be self-identical. Hence corruption shows (B) is not valid.

THEOREM. Let L be a quantified modal language with intensions for terms and predicates.

(1) If L is classical in the sense just defined, then both the Barcan formula and its converse are valid:

$$\vDash (\forall x)\Box P \to \Box(\forall x)P, \text{ and}$$
$$\vDash \Box(\forall x)P \to (\forall x)\Box P.$$

(2) If the terms in L are rigid, then identities may be substituted even into modal sentences *salva veritate*:

$$t = t' \vDash \Box(t = t');$$
$$t = t' \vDash P \leftrightarrow [P]^t_{t'}.$$

□ **EXERCISE**
Prove the previous theorem.

We conclude by stating the syntax and semantics of a modal language containing definite descriptions that are interpreted in the manner of Frege. Even this classical interpretation is rather complex. We leave to the reader as an exercise the task of formulating a supervaluational semantics for a quantified modal syntax that allows for both nonreferring constants and definite descriptions.

DEFINITION: By a *modal quantificational syntax with definite descriptions*, briefly Syn-$QL_{Des,\Box}$, we mean a quantificational syntax with descriptions Syn-QL_{Des} augmented to contain sentences expressing possibility and necessity. Specifically, it is any syntax like Syn-QL_{Des} except that Fm contains in addition $f_\Box$ and $f_\Diamond$, and Sen is the closure of BS under the new rules as well.

DEFINITION: A *Fregean world system with individual concepts and properties* for a quantified modal syntax with definite descriptions is any $\langle W, U, \text{Int}, I, \leq, [R*]\rangle$ such that

(1) W is a nonempty set of real numbers (*possible worlds*);

(2) U is a nonempty set (the set of *possible objects*);

(3) Int (called the *intension assignment to constants and predicates*) is a function from Tm $\cup$ Pd such that for any t in Tm, Int(t) is defined as follows:

- (a) if $t \in \text{PN} \cup \text{Vb}$, then Int($t$) is a function f from W into U (such functions that are values for constants or variables are called *individual concepts*), and
- (b) if t is some $[\iota x|P]$ then Int(t) is that function f from W to U such that $f(w) = R_w([\iota x|P])$ (such functions are not in general individual concepts because they are not in general identical to Int(t) for some *constant* or *variable* t), and

for any P_i^n in Pd, Int(P_i^n) is a function g from W into subsets of U^n (such functions are called *properties*);

(4) I is a function on W such that $I(w)$ is some pair $\langle D, R\rangle$ (called a *model*) with the following properties:

- (a) D is nonempty (omitted in free logic);
- (b) for any t in PN $\cup$ Vb, $R(t)$ is Int(t)(w) and $R(t) \in D$; for any n-placed predicate P_i^n, $R(P_i^n)$ is Int(P_i^n)(w) and $R(P_i^n) \subseteq D^n$

(as before, if $I(w) = \langle D, R\rangle$, we refer to D as U_w and R as R_w);

(5) $\leq$ is a binary relation (the *alternativeness relation*) on W.

(6) $[R*]$ is $\{R*|R*$ meets all the conditions for being a referential extension of a model $\langle U_w, R_w\rangle$ as defined for a modal quantification language except that a clause is added defining $R*(t)$ for any term t in Tm:

- (a) if $t \in \text{PN} \cup \text{Vb}$, then $R*(t) = R(t)$, and

(b) if t is some $[\iota x|P]$ then $R*(t) = u$ if $\{u\} = \{u'|R[^{u'}_{x}]*(P) = \text{T}$ and $R[^{u'}_{x}]* = u'\}$, if otherwise then $R*(t) = *$, where $*$ is an entity such that it is in each U_w and for any P^n_i and any $x_1, \ldots, x_n$ in U_w,

$$\langle x_1, \ldots, *, \ldots, x_n\rangle \notin R_w(P^n_i)\}.$$

By the *language* relative to such a system we would mean $\langle \text{Syn-QL}_{\text{Des},\Box}, [R*]\rangle$ with $[R*]$ as defined above.

□ EXERCISE

Define a supervaluational semantics for $\text{Syn-QL}_{\text{Des},\Box}$ in the following way. Define a world system $\langle W, U, \text{Int}, I, B, \leq, [S]\rangle$ as follows.

(1) For a constant c, $\text{Int}(c)$ may be a partial function from W into U, and $\text{Int}([\iota x|P])$ is the partial function f such that if $R_w([\iota x|P])$ is defined, $f(w) = R_w([\iota x|P])$, and $f(w)$ is undefined otherwise.

(2) I assigns to each w a partial model in the supervaluational sense, i.e., a pair $\langle D, R\rangle$ such that $D \subseteq U$ and for a constant or variable t, $R(t) = \text{Int}(t)(w)$ if defined and $R(t)$ is undefined otherwise, and for a predicate P^n_i, $R(P^n_i) = \text{Int}(P^n_i)(w)$.

(3) For each model there is a partial extension $R*$ of R such that for any expression e there are two cases.

Case I. e is not a definite description. Then, $R*(e)$ is calculated from the values R assigns to the immediate parts of e if these are all defined. The calculation is exactly that used in the interpretation of e in a modal quantificational language. If the $R*$ value of some immediate part of e is undefined, so is that of e.

Case II. e is some $[\iota x|P]$. Then, if there is one and only one object u such that $R[^{u}_{x}]*(P) = \text{T}$, then $R*(t) = u$. Otherwise, $R*(t)$ is undefined.

(4) For each such $R*$ there is a set $[[R]]$ of functions that are fully defined for every part of speech, bivalent, and classical in the sense of obeying the classical truth-tables for the connectives. (That there is such a set must be proven.) B is the superlanguage base formed as the family of all such sets $[[R*]]$, and $[S]$ is the set of supervaluations established by each set in the base.

9

Intensional Logic and Situational Semantics

9.1 EXTENSIONALITY IN CLASSICAL LOGIC

9.1.1 Extensionality and Semantic Structures

One of the most important properties of classical propositional and first-order logic is that coreferential expressions may be substituted one for another in longer expressions without altering the referent of the whole. Within propositional logic, sentences with the same truth-value in a world (both 'refer' to T or F in *w*) are said to be materially equivalent, and the substitution property is sometimes referred to as the valid substitutability of material equivalents. The property is closely tied to truth-functionality. Indeed, we shall see that the reason such substitution preserves truth-value in classical propositional logic, as well as in any many-valued matrix theory, is that the semantics of such theories project truth-values by means of truth-functions. Moreover, if truth-values of wholes are not uniquely determined by those of their immediate parts, as in intuitionistic logic and supervaluations, coreferential parts cannot be validly substituted. As explained in Chapter 3, truth-functionality is a special case of the more general property of compositionality of reference. What we shall see is that valid substitution of coreferential parts holds in a semantic theory if, and only if, its reference assignments are compositional in this sense.

First-order logic is a good example. It has a richer syntax than propositional logic and more parts of speech. There are not only open and closed sentences, but also proper names (constants), variables, predicates, and sometimes definite descriptions. Expressions from each of these parts have 'referents' in the standard semantics, and moreover two of them from the same part of speech sometimes stand for the same referent. Within classical semantics it is in fact valid to substitute coreferential parts from the same part of speech. We shall see that this property depends on the fact that the referent of a whole expression is functionally determined by those of its parts.

It is traditional to apply the term *extensional* to those complex expressions that have parts that may be validly substituted one for another when they are coreferential. If every expression in the language admits valid substitution of coreferential parts, i.e., if every expression of the language is extensional in the sense just defined, then we call the language as a whole *extensional.* What we shall explore, then, is the fact that a language as a whole is extensional if, and only if, its semantics conforms to the principle of compositionality of reference.

We have discussed in Chapter 3 why compositionality of reference is a theoretically attractive feature of language. The fact that it entails extensionality ensures that compositional languages validate a large class of intuitively acceptable inferences. More importantly, however, is the shape imposed on semantic theory by compositionality. If the language is extensional, then the semantic theory will be like that of classical logic in that parallel to the various formation rules of the syntax, there will be semantic rules, one corresponding to each formation rule. Each of these rules will be functional. In addition, the definition of possible reference relation will proceed in the recursive manner of first assigning referents to the basic expressions of the language and then projecting assignments of referents to molecular expressions. The referents of these molecular expressions are calculated by appeal to the referents of their immediate parts and to the semantic rule corresponding to the formation function producing them. Since each semantic rule is a function, the referents of an expression's parts taken as arguments for the rule will yield a unique value.

This functional determination of semantic value is elegant, but it is also important as a principle of how language users understand language. It is a reasonable speculation that language speakers have somehow internalized some such set of rules for the languages they know. We use rules to encode messages in speech formulation and to decode the messages we hear from others. These rules might be learned or innate, or both. But what is quite interesting is the proposal that some kind of functional parallelism between syntax and semantics underlies the way language works.

9.1.2 Extensionality and Abstract Structures

The idea that validity of substitution is linked to functional determination of referents can be developed precisely with the tools of abstract algebra.

Frege originally conceived the idea through metaphors, but by using the concepts of inductive set, homomorphism, and congruence relations, it is possible to explain the validity of substitution as a special case of a congruence relation determined by a homomorphism holding between the two abstract structures of syntax and referents. We repeat here the relevant definitions from Chapter 2, adapting them to the special sorts of structures we shall be discussing:

DEFINITION: A logical structure is any $\langle A, R_1, \ldots, R_n \rangle$ such that $R_1, \ldots, R_n$ are relations on A. If each R_i is a function, we call the structure *functional.*
DEFINITION: $\equiv$ is an *equivalence relation* on a set A iff $\equiv$ is a relation on A and for any x, y, and z in A,

(1) $x \equiv x$ (reflexivity),
(2) if $x \equiv y$, then $y \equiv x$ (symmetry),
(3) if $x \equiv y$ and $y \equiv z$, then $x \equiv z$ (transitivity).

DEFINITION: If $S = \langle C, f_1, \ldots, f_n \rangle$ and $S' = \langle D, g_1, \ldots, g_n \rangle$ are functional structures such that f_i and g_i of the same subscript are both functions of the same number of places on their respective sets, then the function h is called a *homomorphism* from S into S' iff

(1) h is a function from C into D, and
(2) $h(f_i(x_1, \ldots, x_m)) = g_i(h(x_1), \ldots, h(x_m))$, where f_i and g_i are m-place functions.

Notice that if a homomorphism h exists, then each object x from the first structure is mapped onto an object $h(x)$ in the second structure. Moreover, if x is defined for any function f_i in the first structure, then $h(x)$ is defined for the corresponding function g_i in the second structure.

Often homomorphisms are 'onto' functions, and sometimes they are 1–1 and 'onto' in which case they are called *isomorphisms.*

DEFINITION: $\equiv$ is a congruence relation on $S = \langle C, f_1, \ldots, f_n \rangle$ iff

(1) $\equiv$ is an equivalence relation on C, and
(2) $\equiv$ has the substitution property for each operation f_i of S: if $x_1 \equiv y_1, \ldots, x_m \equiv y_m$, then $f_i(x_1, \ldots, x_m) \equiv f_i(y_1, \ldots, y_m)$, where f_i is m-placed.

Recall that every homomorphism h determines a congruence relation $\equiv_h$ defined as follows: for any x and y, $x \equiv_h y$ iff $h(x) = h(y)$.

These ideas are applied to languages by organizing syntax and semantics into structures and construing reference relations as homomorphisms from one to the other. Our procedure thus far in the book has been to identify a syntax with an inductive set $\langle A, B, F \rangle$, where A is the set formed by closing the basic elements from the sets in B under the formation functions in F. Let

F be $\{f_1, \ldots, f_n\}$. Then, each such syntax determines a functional structure $\langle A, f_1, \ldots, f_n \rangle$ in the current sense. It is this structure that in extensional languages can be mapped homomorphically into a semantic structure. But which semantic structure?

Our practice has been to represent semantic theory by a set $[R]$ of possible reference relations or 'worlds' using that term in a rather abstract sense. We then defined a language as a pair $\langle \text{Syn}, [R] \rangle$ and a logical entailment relation $\models$ in terms of it as a relation preserving truth (or 'designated value') in all worlds in $[R]$. We have used this format because it is the customary one in the field. However, there is a feature of the theory that the presentation does not exhibit clearly, namely the fact that $[R]$ is defined by reference to a set of semantic rules parallel to those in syntax. In the case of extensional languages these rules are functions on semantic values, and they may be organized into a functional structure of semantic values. It turns out that when this is done the set $[R]$ is nothing more than the set of possible homomorphisms from syntactic structure to semantic structure, and the substitutability of coreferential terms reduces to the fact that coreferentiality is a congruence relation determined by a homomorphism.

EXAMPLE *Classical Propositional Logic.* Let $\langle \text{Sen}, \text{BS}, \{f_\sim, f_\rightarrow\} \rangle$ be a Syn-PL as defined in Chapter 7. This determines the unique syntactic functional structure $\langle \text{Sen}, f_\sim, f_\rightarrow \rangle$. Then, the relevant semantic structure is $\langle \{\text{T}, \text{F}\}, g_\sim, g_\rightarrow \rangle$ where $g_\sim$ and $g_\rightarrow$ are the truth-functions for negation and the conditional, respectively. (These have been defined in Chapters 4 and 5, and more generally in connection with the classical matrix C in Chapter 7.) We now define the set of possible worlds.

DEFINITION: $[R]$ is the set of all homomorphisms R from $\langle \text{Sen}, f_\sim, f_\rightarrow \rangle$ into $\langle \{\text{T}, \text{F}\}, g_\sim, g_\rightarrow \rangle$.

It follows from the definition of homomorphism that sentences are mapped only onto truth-values and that the referent of every sentence is defined. It also follows directly that the set of possible worlds under this new definition coincide exactly with those under the one we have been using to this point.

THEOREM. $[R] = \{R \mid R(\text{Sen} \xrightarrow[\text{into}]{} \{\text{T}, \text{F}\})$ such that

(1) for any $P \in \text{BS}$, $R(P) \in \{\text{T}, \text{F}\}$,
(2) for any P and Q in Sen,
  (a) $R(f_\sim(P)) = g_\sim(R(P))$, and
  (b) $R(f_\rightarrow(P, Q)) = g_\rightarrow(R(P), R(Q))\}$.

Substitution of coreferential parts then follows as a special case of homomorphisms determining congruence relations.

THEOREM. For any R in $[R]$, there is a congruence relation $\equiv_R$ defined as follows: for any P and Q in Sen, $P \equiv_R Q$ iff $R(P) = R(Q)$. That is, $\equiv_R$ as defined has the following properties:

(1) $\equiv_R$ is an equivalence relation on Sen, and

(2) $\equiv_R$ has the substitution property, i.e.,

(a) if $P \equiv_R Q$, then $f_{\sim}(P) \equiv_R f_{\sim}(Q)$, and

(b) if $P \equiv_R P'$ and $Q \equiv_R Q'$, then $f_{\rightarrow}(P, Q) \equiv_R f_{\rightarrow}(P', Q')$.

Thus, the extensionality of classical propositional logic is seen as a direct consequence of the fact that its semantic structure functionally parallels its syntactic structure.

□ EXERCISES

1. Rigorously define for an arbitrary language the two ideas of extensionality. First define what it is for an expression of a language to be extensional, and then using this idea define what it is for a language as a whole to be extensional. Use the general notions of logistic syntax, substitution, and part–whole from Chapter 6, the notion of a language as a pair$\langle$Syn, $[R]\rangle$ consisting of a syntax Syn and a set $[R]$ for functions from the sentential expression of Syn into a set of truth-values, and a Leibnizian definition of the semantic entailment relation $\vDash$ as a relation preserving designated truth-values as defined in Chapter 7.
2. Define the relevant semantic structure for the language LKW of Kleene's weak connectives, redefine its set of possible worlds as the homomorphisms on this structure, and prove that the language is extensional.

9.1.3 Tarski's Sequence Algebra for First-Order Logic

As in propositional logic, it is possible to define the syntax and semantics of classical first-order logic so that semantic structure perfectly parallels syntax. Validity of substitution then follows from the substitutivity of a congruence relation. The definition of the parallel semantic structure is due to Alfred Tarski. Its form is not as straightforward as that for propositional logic, because in the case of a quantified sentence it is not quite clear how we should break it down into parts and how we should go about explaining how the referents of these parts determine the referent of the whole.

Since nothing we shall say depends on the fact that, strictly speaking, there is a unique formation rule for each set of n-placed predicates, we shall assume for simplicity that there is a single rule f_{BS} that concatenates any n terms behind an n-place predicate to yield a basic sentence. Thus, we may understand the syntax Syn-QL for first-order logic to be, as defined in Chapter 5, the structure $\langle$Sen, $\{\mathrm{PN} \cup \mathrm{Vb} \cup \mathrm{Pd}\}$, Fm$\rangle$ where Fm $=$ $(f_{\mathrm{BS}}, f_{\sim}, f_{\wedge}, f_{\vee}, f_{\rightarrow}, f_{\forall})$. The rule that requires scrutiny is $f_{\forall}$ which forms quantified sentences. As defined, this rule takes a variable v and a sentence P

and forms the quantified sentence $(\forall v)P$. Thus by the analysis of the part–whole relation given in Chapter 6, we should say that v and P are the immediate parts of $(\forall v)P$. But do their referents determine those of the whole?

Let us consider the substitutional interpretation first. By this interpretation it is not the referents of v and P that determine that of $(\forall v)P$ but rather those of the various substitution instances $[P]^c_v$, but none of these instances are used to generate $(\forall v)P$ in the syntax and thus cannot count as its part. Nor could we easily reformulate the syntax so that the relevant expressions that determine the referent of $(\forall v)P$ would all count as genuine parts. If we were to try to make each substitution instance an immediate part of the quantified sentence, the whole would in general have an infinite number of immediate parts, violating a condition on inductive sets that the generating functions have only a finite number of argument places.

The referential interpretation at first glance appears to lead to similar problems. By this interpretation what we need to know in order to determine the truth-value under $R*$ of $(\forall v)P$ is not just the referents under $R*$ of v and P, but rather the referents of P throughout the set of all v-variants $R[^d_v]*$ of $R*$. It is perfectly possible to have a model $\langle D, R\rangle$ and two sentences, say the sentences $(\forall x)Fx$ and $(\forall x)Gx$, such that their parts have the same referents under R but the wholes do not. Hence the referential interpretation of a whole is not in general functionally determined by that of its immediate parts.

☐ **EXERCISE**

Define a model $\langle D, R\rangle$ such that $R*(Fx) = R*(Gx)$ but $R*((\forall x)Fx) \neq R*((\forall x)Gx)$. *Hint*: Let $R(x)$ be something in $R(F) \cap R(G)$.

Tarski, who was the first to offer a set theoretic semantics for first-order logic using the ideas of the referential interpretation, ensured the correct functional parallelism between syntax and semantics by choosing a slightly different entity to serve as the referent of sentences. We begin the discussion of his semantics by slightly altering the notion of a model. First of all we remove the task of assigning values to the variables from the interpretation function R. The reason for doing this is that we shall later want to associate with each model the set of all ways the variables can be interpreted. We will then be able to assign to each sentence relative to a model those interpretations of the variables that make the sentence true and those that make it false. These sets play the key part in the semantics of complex expressions because Tarski gave to them the role of referent for sentences in a manner we shall shortly explain.

Let D be the domain of a model, and let D^{Vb} be the set of functions from Vb into D, each of which is called a *variable assignment*. The idea is to use subsets of D^{Vb} as the referents of sentences. Though these sets will be called the 'referents' of the sentences, they are such only in an abstract formal sense. Sets of variable assignments are rather like truth-values in that nobody seriously thinks that they count as objects in the world according to either common sense or traditional metaphysics. Like truth-values, however, if they are assumed to be the referents of sentences, a simple and elegant structure of referents genuinely homomorphic to syntax is definable. We shall now explain the details of how to pair with each sentence of the language a unique set of such assignments.

For some sentences the interpretation of the variables is irrelevant to determining their truth-value. This is true, for example, of open sentences that are tautologies. According to Tarski, one way to say that these sentences are true independently of how the variables are interpreted is to say that they are true under all variable assignments. Accordingly these sentences receive the entire set D^{Vb} as their referent.

Other sentences that either lack free variables or are contradictions are false independently of how the variables are interpreted. This fact is represented by assigning such sentences the empty subset of D^{Vb}, namely $\varnothing$.

A third category of sentence, including most of those with free variables, are T or F relative to the interpretation of their variables. Under some interpretations they are true and under others false. To these are assigned the subset of D^{Vb} which contains all and only the interpretations that make it true.

Thus, in this interpretation, some sentences are assigned the whole set D^{Vb}, which represents a property of truth *simpliciter*, some are assigned $\varnothing$, which represents a property of falsity *simpliciter*, and others are assigned subsets of D^{Vb}, which represents a relativized notion of truth: the sentence is true relative to each of the variable assignments in the set.

A second way the concept of model is revised is by abandoning the convention of listing the domain of the model separately from the relation R. The role of the domain is to fix for the world the domain of quantification which differs from world to world and must be specified in calculating the truth-value of quantified sentences. In order that the domain be specified in this calculation, we shall make the quantifier itself a referring expression and assign the domain to it as its referent. To maintain the parallelism between syntax and semantics we must also redefine the formation rule $f_\forall$ so that it is a four-place relation:

$$f_\forall = \{\langle w, x, y, z\rangle \mid w = \forall \;\&\; z = ({}^\frown w^\frown x^\frown)^\frown y\}.$$

We amend the definition of Syn-QL so that it is $\langle$Sen, $\{$PN $\cup$ Vb $\cup$ Pd $\cup$ $\{\forall\}\}$, Fm$\rangle$ where Fm contains $f_\forall$ as defined above and $\{\forall\}$ is a category of basic expressions containing the single quantifier symbol $\forall$.

The semantic function $g_\forall$ parallel to $f_\forall$ will accordingly be a four-place relation. It will take as inputs the domain of quantification, the referent of the variable, and the referent of the sentence quantified, and yield as its output the referent of the whole universally quantified sentence. (As we shall see, the referent of the variable makes no significant contribution to this calculation.)

What is interesting about this semantics is that there are simple semantic functions that explain how the referent of a whole is determined by those of its immediate parts. Before we state the relevant semantic operations parallel to syntax, the intuitions guiding them must be put into a suitable set theoretic idiom.[1]

So far we have spoken about variable assignments as functions from Vb into *D*. But if these functions are to be the actual stuff of the 'world', if they are to serve as semantic values of expressions, they have the defect that they mention the parts of the expression they interpret. Ideally, semantic entities should be describable in the metalanguage completely independently of the language they interpret so that we might define semantic operations on these entities and organize them into a structure which we then use to interpret the syntax. Tarski solved this problem by using a slightly different notion of variable assignment which has the virtue of assigning to each variable in Vb an entity in *D* but without mentioning variables. For this purpose he used as variable assignments infinite sequences of elements of *D*.

Recall from Chapter 6 that a sequence is literally an indexing function on integers. Here we shall consider a sequence to be a mapping from the set ω of natural numbers into *D*, and hence is an element of the set of all functions from ω into *D*. In set theory this set of all functions from ω into *D* is named D^{ω}. Let us now suppose that the set Vb is indexed by some function *I* so that it is meaningful to speak of the *i*th variable in Vb. With this assumption it is possible to view each sequence *s* in D^{ω} as determining an interpretation of variables: the *i*th variable v_i is understood to refer to the *i*th element s_i of *s*. In the definition below we allow the indexing sequences to be 'into' and many-one functions so that they replicate features of variable assignments. They are allowed to be 'into' because we want to leave open the possibility that a given variable interpretation may not assign a variable to everything in the domain *D*. We do not require that it be 1–1 because we do not want to rule out the possibility that two variables may be assigned to the same entity.

DEFINITION: The set of all *variable sequences* D^{ω} on a domain *D* is the set of all functions from ω, the set of natural numbers $\{0, 1, 2, \ldots\}$, into *D*.

The task of the semantics is to define semantic operations on subsets of arbitrary D^{ω} that parallel the structure of syntax. The only one of these

[1] For the original statement of this semantics see Alfred Tarski, 'Contributions to the Theory of Models' (1954).

semantic operations that needs explanation is that for basic sentences. Intuitively a basic sentence without variables is true or false in a model with reference relation R and domain D no matter what items are assigned to the variables, and hence it is assigned either D^{ω} or $\varnothing$. But if the sentence contains variables, then its truth or falsity will depend on the referents of these variables. If it contains proper names it will also depend on their referents as determined by R. We must then employ some means of simultaneously talking about the referents of proper names relative to R and the referents of variables relative to some variable sequence s. We do so by exploiting a feature that both constants and variables have in common. Both are species of expressions that pick out individuals in the domain. The difference between the two is that while constants pick out the same individual regardless of the variable assignment in use, variables pick out different individuals in different assignments. The semantic behavior of a constant c may then be thought of as represented by a constant function δ from D^{ω} to D: for all s in D^{ω}, $\delta(s) = R(c)$. Variables, on the other hand, may be represented semantically by a variable function from D^{ω} to D. Let v_i be a variable. Then the semantic behavior of v_i is represented by that function δ from D^{ω} to D such that for any s in D^{ω}, $\delta(s) = s_i$. By using such functions δ it is possible to state the semantic rule for basic sentences in a simple and elegant way.

Suppose Fcx is an atomic sentence made up of a constant c, a variable x and a two-place predicate F. Suppose further that the semantic behavior of c is recorded by the constant function δ and that of x by the variable function δ'. F is understood, as in the original semantics, as standing for a binary relation D' on the domain. Then, Fcx is satisfied by any sequence s meeting the following conditions, which we formulate in two equivalent ways:

(1) the object $\delta(s)$ referred to by c under s bears the relation D' referred to by F to the object $\delta'(s)$ referred to by x under s, or

(2) $\langle \delta(s), \delta'(s) \rangle \in D'$.

In a free logic we would allow the referents of constants and free variables to stand for things outside the domain of quantification D so long as the interpretation of the quantifier itself is restricted to that domain. In the semantics below we permit such freedom.

The operations for the connectives correspond neatly to the set theoretic operations on D^{ω}, and a universally quantified sentence is satisfied by every sequence of the domain of quantification if and only if its open sentence is also. Recall that the domain of quantification is specified explicitly as an argument of the operation. Let δ range over the set $\mathbf{V}^{\omega}$ of all possible infinite sequences.

DEFINITION: By a *Tarski structure* for Syn-QL we mean the structure

$$\langle \mathbf{V}, g_{BS}, g_{\sim}, g_{\wedge}, g_{\vee}, g_{\rightarrow}, g_{\forall}\rangle \text{ such that}$$

(1) $g_{BS} = \{\langle R, \delta_1, \ldots, \delta_n, X\rangle | R \subseteq \mathbf{V}^n \ \& \ X = \{s | \langle \delta_1(s), \ldots, \delta_n(s)\rangle \in R\}\}$;
(2) $g_{\sim} = \{\langle X, Y\rangle | Y = \mathbf{V}^{\omega} - X\}$ (i.e., $g_{\sim}(X) = \mathbf{V}^{\omega} - X$);
(3) $g_{\wedge} = \{\langle X, Y, Z\rangle | Z = X \cap Y\}$ (i.e., $g_{\wedge}(X, Y) = X \cap Y$);
(4) $g_{\vee} = \{\langle X, Y, Z\rangle | Z = X \cup Y\}$ (i.e., $g_{\vee}(X, Y) = X \cup Y$);
(5) $g_{\rightarrow} = \{\langle X, Y, Z\rangle | Z = (\mathbf{V}^{\omega} - X) \cup Y\}$ (i.e., $g_{\rightarrow}(X, Y\rangle = (\mathbf{V}^{\omega} - X) \cup Y$);
(6) $g_{\forall} = \{\langle W, X, Y, Z\rangle |$ if $W^{\omega} \subseteq Y$ then $Z = W^{\omega}$, and if $Y \neq W^{\omega}$ then $Y = \varnothing\}$.

(Note that in clause (6) the referent X of the variable makes no contribution to calculating the referent Z of the whole.)

DEFINITION: The set $[R]$ of *free Tarski interpretations* for Syn-QL is defined as the set of all homomorphisms from $\langle \text{Sen}, f_{BS}, f_{\sim}, f_{\wedge}, f_{\vee}, f_{\rightarrow}, f_{\forall}\rangle$ into the Tarski structure for Syn-QL $\langle \mathbf{V}, g_{BS}, g_{\sim}, g_{\wedge}, g_{\vee}, g_{\rightarrow}, g_{\forall}\rangle$.

It follows directly from the definition of homomorphism that each expression is assigned a value, which is defined for the semantic operation corresponding to any formation rule the expression is defined for. Showing that the resulting semantics is equivalent to the referential interpretation is left as an exercise.

The repackaging of the referential interpretation in this form is mainly of theoretical interest. It shows that in fact first-order logic conforms to the principle of compositionality of reference and is therefore extensional. As in the case of propositional logic, each homomorphism R determines a congruence relation $\equiv_R$ of material equivalence. These classical extensional languages form the norm in logic. It is in comparison to them that nonextensional expressions appear semantically deviant. Just how deviant they are, i.e., to what extent they may be brought within a general framework of parallel syntactic and semantic structures, is our next topic.

□ EXERCISES

1. Let R be a free Tarski interpretation of Syn-QL. Let D be its outer domain defined as the set of all objects that is either referred to by some term or quantified over, i.e., $D = \{x | x$ is in $R(\forall)$ or for some t in PN $\cup$ Vb and some i, $R(t) = s$ and $s_i = x\}$, and define $U = R(\forall)$ as its inner domain. Prove there is a model $\langle U, D, R'\rangle$ with inner and outer domains (as defined in Chapter 8) such that for any closed sentence P, $R(P) = U^{\omega}$ iff $R'*(P) = \text{T}$.
2. Let $\langle U, D, R'\rangle$ be a model with inner and outer domain for Syn-QL as in Chapter 8. Show that there is a free Tarski interpretation R such that $R(\forall) = D$, and for any closed sentence P, $R'*(P) = \text{T}$ iff $R(P) = U^{\omega}$.

3. In order to build into Tarski interpretations the existential presuppositions of singular terms from classical logic and still define a possible model as any homomorphism from Syn-QL to a Tarski structure, one must build into the function g_{BS} the restriction that the arguments of the function all fall into the domain of quantification. Thus, the framework dictates that there should be some syntactic marker in the basic sentence that refers to the domain of quantification and that the same marker occurs in a quantified sentence performing the same role there. Clearly Syn-QL as it stands lacks such a syntactic feature. One candidate is suggested by the natural language copula. The verb 'to be' occurs in English in both sorts of sentence. Redefine f_{BS} and $f_{\forall}$ so as to contain such a marker; then redefine g_{BS} and $g_{\forall}$ so as to get a Tarski semantics that is equivalent to the nonfree classical referential interpretation.

9.2 INTENSIONAL LOGIC

9.2.1 Data: Nonextensional Contexts

The elegant picture of communication and metatheory suggested by extensional languages is challenged by a set of famous counterexamples. A large number of expressions from natural languages such as English are not extensional in the relevant sense. Intuitively, it is not always possible to substitute within them coreferential parts *salva veritate*. Extensionality fails particularly for the modal sentence adverbs 'necessarily' and 'possibly', and the so-called propositional attitude verbs like 'to believe' and 'to desire'. To see that necessity sentences do not admit valid substitution of coreferential parts consider the following invalid inference:

$9 =$ the number of planets
$\Box(9 = 9)$
Therefore, $\Box(9 =$ the number of planets$)$

Nor is this argument stated in modal propositional logic any better:

$P \leftrightarrow Q$
$\Box(P \leftrightarrow P)$
Therefore, $\Box(P \leftrightarrow Q)$

One way to explain this failure of substitution is that the semantic rule defining the reference of $\Box P$ in terms of that of P is not functional. Intuitively, the former is T in w just in case P is true in every world. But knowing just the value of P in a world w will not in itself let us know the value of $\Box P$ in w. Suppose P is an atomic sentence, and consider the two sentences P and $P \vee {\sim}P$. Suppose that P is T in w. Then according to the intuitive semantics $P \vee {\sim}P$ is T in w, $\Box P$ is F in w, and $\Box(P \vee {\sim}P)$ is T in w. In the former case the value of the part P of the whole $\Box P$ is T and the value of the whole is F. In the latter case the value of the part $P \vee {\sim}P$ is T and the value of the whole

$\Box(P \vee \sim P)$ is T. Thus, in one case T goes to F and in the other case T goes to T, and the value of the part alone clearly does not determine that of the whole.

The case is similar with the epistemic attitudes of belief and knowledge. Consider these two arguments adapted from Frege and Russell, respectively:

I believe the morning star = the morning star.
The morning star = the evening star.
Therefore, I believe the morning star = the evening star.

I know Scott = Scott.
Scott = the author of Waverley.
Therefore, I know Scott = the author of Waverley.

Neither of these arguments follows. The first may fail because of ignorance of astronomy and the second because of ignorance of literature. Thus, the evidence of intuitive data about cases seems to suggest that modal and epistemic contexts are nonextensional.

Logicians in the main have followed an idea of Frege that these contexts must be explained by hypothesizing a structure of 'senses' or intensions mediating between language and the world.

☐ EXERCISES

1. Using the definition in Chapter 7 of the languages LI and LS, show that propositional logic under the interpretations for intuitionistic logic and supervaluations is nonextensional. Do so by finding examples of parts that are coreferential within wholes that are not.
2. Show that the verbs 'to desire' and 'to explain' are nonextensional by finding examples of arguments using these verbs in which substitutivity is intuitively invalid.

9.2.2 Frege's Theory of Sense and Reference

Complex sentences that employ verbs like 'believe', 'know', 'understand', and 'explain' are sometimes called *epistemic contexts*. Frege observed that expressions falling within the complements or 'that' clauses of such contexts have referents that do not appear to uniquely determine the referent of the whole sentence, as in the above examples. The compositional nature of meaning may nevertheless still be true, depending on what is meant by 'meaning'. This key semantic idea is itself ambiguous, and there are two possible interpretations of the idea as it is used in the principle that the meaning of a part determines the meaning of the whole. In one sense, meaning may be understood as reference, and if so there are apparent counterexamples to extensionality and compositionality of meaning. Drawing on his own version of an old idea, Frege pointed out that in another sense the meaning of a term is quite different from its referent. This is the sense of meaning as intension. But intensions are not common or ordinary objects that are well understood, and explaining just what intensions are supposed to be and how they are thought to work raises many interesting issues.

Probably the best way to explain intensions is as hypothetical entities. It is common practice in science to explain an observed phenomenon by hypothesizing the existence of some underlying entity conforming to certain laws and structures which if true would account for the observations. There are lots of examples, some more successful than others: genes, enzymes, atoms, ether, the Big Bang, phlogiston, the homunculus, universals, prime matter, God, the soul, the superego, the social contract, Proto-Indo-European, Homer, deep structure. In all such explanations there is a clear set of phenomena to be explained and there are some detailed properties attributed to the hypothesized entity which if true are supposed to entail the phenomena to be explained. Often a good deal of controversy surrounds the ontological status of the hypothesized entities, and the verification of their existence is a major goal of the theory. In some of the more successful cases, as in genetic theory, the explanatory entity was actually found and observed independently. In historical and metaphysical theories such direct confrontation is often impossible, and philosophers are often skeptical about whether the entities postulated really exist. In philosophical debates about existence several distinct issues usually arise which we should outline and apply to the case of intensions.

One issue concerns simplicity of explanation. If there are two competing theories one of which is simpler, then scientific practice prefers the simpler. A measure of complexity is how many kinds of entities the theory postulates. Hence, all things being equal, a theory that postulates fewer kinds of things is preferable. One of the most interesting features of intensions is how difficult it is to do semantic theory without them. It proves quite hard to do as well at explaining what intensions are designed to explain without postulating something like intensions.

Another important philosophical issue is at root a concern about clarity, but it is often formulated in terms of identity. If one is postulating an unknown entity to explain something, then one has an obligation to be clear about what sort of thing it is. One of the most unsatisfactory parts of early metaphysics and psychology is a lack of such precision. Aristotle's idea of the active intellect and Plotinus' concept of the One are famous sources of vexation. One way to be precise is to define the entities postulated in a neat biconditional, using clear vocabulary in the *definiens.* The call for such a definition in terms of identifying conditions is what is meant by the philosophical maxim, 'no entity without identity'. What one often finds, however, is that the theory is unable to give an ordinary definition or even if it can, the terms used in the definition are also obscure. Newton's mechanics, for example, does not explicitly define its primitive ideas, among which are time. Set theory does not define membership. In psychology there is a large literature on whether and how psychological entities should be defined.

Intensions as postulated by Frege and others are somewhat obscure. Frege himself did not attempt an explicit definition. The best he did was to describe some of the properties of what he called 'senses'. These properties may be viewed as axioms or basic principles of his theory which even if they fail to define explicitly the terms used in their formulation, they nevertheless provide a kind of 'implicit definition' in much the way the axioms of set theory explain the ideas of set and membership.

There are two important properties that Frege attributed to senses.[2] The first is a compositionality principle that says that we figure out the meaning of a whole expression by applying semantic rules to the meanings of its parts.

Principle of the Compositionality of Intensions. The intension of a whole expression is determined in a rulelike manner from the intensions of its parts.

This principle offers a picture of language as being essentially independent of the particular sounds used. Intensions, in this view, are in some sense public entities that are accessible to all language users. These intensions form structures and point to things in the world. The various spoken languages merely consist of assignments of various spoken words to these intensions, and what word is used is merely a matter of local convention. Words carry meaning only to the extent that they are paired with an intension, and we determine the meaning of a whole spoken message by reconstructing its intension from the intensions of the meaningful atomic parts of the message in a manner parallel to the grammatical structure of the message as a whole.

Given what we know about the relation of part to whole and the functional determination of homomorphic structures, this principle invites an elaboration in terms of abstract semantic structures. In the precise development of the theory below, we shall in fact define semantic structures of intensions that are homomorphic to syntax. These will in turn determine a congruence relation of 'being paired with the same intension'. The existence of this congruence relation then allows us to explain the valid substitutivity of co-intensional parts.

[2] See Gottlob Frege, 'On Sense and Reference' (1892). For an extended discussion of Frege's theory as it is interpreted by modern logicians see Rudolf Carnap, *Meaning and Necessity* (1947). On the historical question of how accurate such modern interpretations are to Frege's own views see John N. Martin, 'The Semantics of Frege's *Grundgesetze*' (1984).

The second important property Frege attributed to senses is contained in his claim that the sense of an expression determines its reference.

Principle of Intensional Reference. There is a relation in nature between intensions and referents such that every intension determines a unique referent.

The vision of language captured in this principle is that intensions are responsible for the fact that we can use language to talk about the world. Much of the detail about how they do so is left open, but there is no mistaking the fact, according to Frege, that they do stand for things in the world, no matter how mysterious this relation is.

One detail about the relation of intensions to referents in the world that Frege did take a stand on is a claim that the referents themselves sometimes form a structure parallel to that of intensions. In those cases in which language is genuinely extensional Frege held that there is a structure on referents that is itself compositional and mirrors the structure of intensions. In such cases extensionality understood as substitutability of coreferential parts may be explained algebraically. Valid coreferential substitution may then be viewed as a special congruence relation determined by a homomorphic mapping.

What we have been doing so far is sketching some of the basic properties that intensions are supposed to have. In describing these properties we have not been defining the concept of intension so much as limiting it, much as axioms limit the primitive ideas of an axiom system. Admittedly the properties as described are vague, but they are not hopelessly so, and a great deal of effort has been put into making them more precise.

The process of clarifying Frege's intensions even further rests on a key aspect of the properties Frege attributed to them. All the restrictions Frege placed on intensions are relational. They concern how intensions relate to one another and to entities in other relational structures. These restrictions therefore are suitable to more precise formulation in the language of abstract algebra. When we say that syntax and intensions fall into homomorphic structures and that there is a functional relation between intensions and referents, what we are doing is recasting a vague idea in more precise mathematical terms.

Second, since Frege only restricted intensions in terms of their relational properties, he bequeathed us the powerful idea of trying to find for intensions a direct definition that would entail these relational properties. In a sense, the entire content of the idea of intension, as Frege conceived it, is exhausted in its relational features. If we could find a precisely defined structure of entities that behave in all relational ways in just the way Frege said intensions do, then for many serious intellectual purposes, perhaps all, this structure could be identified with the structure of intensions.

Similar techniques are frequently used in mathematics. It does not matter particularly what the positive integers are so long as they conform to all the laws of integer arithmetic. In the example below nobody seriously believes that in any intuitive sense the number 1 means the same as $\{\varnothing\}$, but if it and the other numbers are identified in the way described, they have all the important properties of inequalities possessed by the numbers.

EXAMPLE Let the *inequality structure of the natural numbers* be defined as $\langle \text{Nn}, \leq \rangle$ where Nn is the inductive system $\langle A, \{\varnothing\}, f \rangle$ such that $f(x) = x \cup \{x\}$ and $\leq$ is $\subseteq$ on A. Thus, $\varnothing$ is the unique basic element used to generate members of A. Let us identify $\varnothing$ with 0. The first element so generated is $\varnothing \cup \{\varnothing\}$, which is identical to $\{0\}$, and this we call the number 1. Likewise $\{\varnothing\} \cup \{\{\varnothing\}\} = 2$ is in A, etc. Clearly, $1 \leq 2$ because $1 \subseteq 2$.

Given that all the relevant properties of intensions are structural in this way, it is open to us to increase the precision of the theory by giving explicit set theoretic definitions to intensions. These definitions must entail that intensions do in fact possess the relational properties Frege attributed to them.

Before clarifying the Fregean theory, we should review the phenomena it is supposed to explain.

Communication. The same motivation underlies the compositionality of intension as that which led us earlier to postulate the compositionality of reference for extensional contexts. If such a compositionality of intensions is true and at work in all instances of linguistic usage, then there is a simple and elegant explanation of how communication works. A speaker encodes a message by functional rules, and the hearer decodes the same message by the same rules. In the theory of compositional intension, moreover, there is a possibility not present in the theory of reference alone. Using intensions we may provide an analysis of the ideas of information and understanding. The information content of an expression is its sense, and understanding an expression consists of standing in some special cognitive relation with its sense. Moreover, since intensions are public nonmental entities, more than one person can understand the same thing.

Synonymy, Translatability, Ambiguity. Frege's theory of senses, like the Stoic theory of *lecta* and Ockham's theory of mental language before it,[3] is supposed to give a simple and intuitive explanation of the three intuitive phenomena of synonymy, translatability, and ambiguity. Such phenomena, if they genuinely exist, would be classified as semantic, and would be exhibited

[3] See Benson Mates *Stoic Logic* (1953), and Philotheus Boehner, *Ockham's Philosophical Writings* (1957), as well as references on Ockham in Chapter 4.

in our semantic intuitions about proper definitions. The explanations of these phenomena would run as follows. Two expressions are synonymous if, and only if, they are paired with the same sense. An expression from one language may translate an expression from another if both are paired with the same language-independent sense. Two expressions are ambiguous if they are paired with more than one sense, a possibility usually prohibited in formal languages.

Sameness of Reference with Difference of Sense. One specific problem that Frege explicitly used to motivate his theory is the phenomenon that two sentences may have the same referent but different information content. Take, for example, the two sentences 'the morning star = the morning star' and 'the morning star = the evening star'. Both being true, they are coreferential, but they clearly are not synonymous because the first is trivially true while the second had to be established by empirical science.

Frege's explanation is as follows. The terms 'the morning star' and 'the evening star' are coreferential, but we understand by them different things. This state of divergent understanding is explained by appeal to the distinct senses of the two expressions. The mind of the language user relates the different terms to the different senses. The senses of the sentences 'the morning star = the morning star' and 'the morning star = the evening star' are then distinct because their senses are made up of different parts. Hence we have a way of explaining why the two sentences can both be true (have the same referent) yet have different information content.

The same point may be made by using a case from propositional logic. Notice that 'the morning star is hot' has the same referent (namely, T) as 'the evening star is hot' but distinct senses, and thus the trivial sentence 'the morning star is hot iff the morning star is hot' has the same referent but quite a different sense from the nontrivial 'the morning star is hot iff the evening star is hot'. On Frege's theory the mind understands senses and, as it were, thinks in terms of them, much as the Stoics envisaged *lecta* and Ockham mental language.

Substitution, Extensionality, and Nonextensionality. The theory attempts to explain the logical intuitions we have about substitution in nonextensional contexts. The explanation in modern dress goes as follows. The relation of language to the world is such that there are three abstract structures. The first of these is syntax, the next is intensional structure, and the last is a structure of referents or 'extensions'. In any given (nonambiguous) language, syntax is always homomorphic to intensional structure, and the homomorphic mapping is the relation that assigns to each expression of the language its meaning or sense. Moreover, in any language and any possible world there is a function pairing intensions with unique referents in that world.

In the case of extensional languages or extensional fragments of larger nonextensional languages, the structure of intensions is also homomorphic to that of referents. It follows that in extensional languages there is a homomorphism from syntax to the structures of extensions, namely the composition function of the homomorphism from syntax to intensions and that from intensions to extensions. This homomorphism in turn determines a congruence relation of sameness of referent and thus ensures the valid substitutability of coreferring parts definitive of extensional languages.

In the case of nonextensional languages, the mapping from intensions to extensions exists but does not determine a true homomorphism, and hence valid substitutivity of coreferential parts fails. The best that can be said for nonextensional languages is that the homomorphism from syntax to intensions determines a congruence relation of synonymy, and thus ensures that expressions that are synonymous are validly substitutable.[4]

9.2.3 The Algebra of Sense and Reference

We may now sketch a Fregean intensional semantics for a propositional syntax containing the modal operator $\Box$ and some propositional attitude verbs $V_1, \ldots, V_n$. The syntax is like that of propositional logic except that it contains the formation function $f_\Box$ for necessity statements and a new rule f_{Att} that concatenates an attitude verb V to a sentence:

DEFINITION: An *intensional propositional syntax* Syn–IPL is an inductive system $\langle \mathrm{Sen}, \{\mathrm{BS}, \mathrm{Att}\}, \mathrm{Fm} \rangle$ such that

(1) BS is some set of expressions $\{P_1, P_2, P_3, \ldots, P_n, \ldots\}$,

[4] To be strictly accurate, Frege's own view about nonextensional contexts was a bit more complex. He held that even in the case of what appear to be nonextensional languages, the structure of intensions is homomorphic to that of extensions. Thus he would hold that the composition function from syntax to intensions and intensions to extensions would be a homomorphism from syntax to extensions and that this homomorphism determines a congruence relation of coreferentiality. Thus, he would say that there are no genuinely nonextensional languages. In his view, the reason belief and propositional attitude sentences appear to be nonextensional is that what looks like nonextensionality is really a kind of systematic ambiguity. Expressions in the complements of such verbs, he held, do not have their usual senses or referents. Rather the sentential complement P of the belief sentence 'I believe that P' is supposed to have as its referent what would normally be its sense in other contexts. He called the sense of a sentence a *proposition*. Thus a first-person belief sentence as a whole asserts that a relation holds between the speaker and a proposition. Thus any sentence is systematically ambiguous. When it stands alone or in ordinary first-order contexts, it has its usual sense and referent, but when it stands in epistemic contexts, it takes on a new sense and has as its referent what is its normal sense. On the divergence of Frege's views from the standard restricted homomorphic account we shall be using, see David Kaplan, 'Quantifying In' (1969).

(2) Att is some set of expressions $\{V_1, \ldots, V_n, \ldots\}$ (called *attitude verbs*) disjoint from BS, and

(3) $\text{Fm} = \{f_{\sim}, f_{\rightarrow}, f_{\Box}, f_{\text{Att}}\}$ such that

(a) $f_{\sim}$, $f_{\rightarrow}$, and $f_{\Box}$ are functions on expressions that are defined for BS such that $f_{\sim}(x) = \sim^{\frown}x$, $f_{\rightarrow}(x, y) = ({}^{\frown}x^{\frown}\rightarrow{}^{\frown}y^{\frown})$, and $f_{\Box}(x) = \Box^{\frown}x$, and

(b) f_{Att} is a binary function on expressions such that its subdomains D^1 and D^2 are disjoint, $\text{Att} = D^1$, $\text{BS} \subseteq D^2$, and $f_{\text{Att}}(x, y) = x^{\frown}y$.

The semantics for the theory posits a structure on intensions homomorphic to syntax. Following Frege we shall call the intensions of sentences *propositions* and group them into a set Prop. The intensions of attitude verbs we shall call *attitudes* and group them into a set Attitudes. For the moment we shall not try to define either Prop, Attitudes, or the relevant structural operations $h_{\sim}$, $h_{\rightarrow}$, $h_{\Box}$, and h_{Att} on them.

DEFINITION: An *intensional structure* of an intensional propositional syntax relative to sets Prop and Attitudes and functions $h_{\sim}$, $h_{\rightarrow}$, $h_{\Box}$, and h_{Att} is the structure $\langle \text{Prop} \cup \text{Attitudes}, h_{\sim}, h_{\rightarrow}, h_{\Box}, h_{\text{Att}} \rangle$ such that $h_{\sim}$ and $h_{\Box}$ are 1-place functions on Prop, $h_{\rightarrow}$ is a binary function on Prop, and h_{Att} is a binary function from Attitudes and Prop into Prop.

Thus, an intensional interpretation is any homomorphism from syntax into intensional structure.

DEFINITION: The set [Int] of *all possible intensional interpretations* of a propositional intensional syntax $\langle \text{Sen}, \{\text{BS}, \text{Att}\}, \{f_{\sim}, f_{\rightarrow}, f_{\Box}, f_{\text{Att}}\} \rangle$ and the intensional structure $\langle \text{Prop} \cup \text{Attitudes}, h_{\sim}, h_{\rightarrow}, h_{\Box}, h_{\text{Att}} \rangle$ for that syntax is defined as the set of all homomorphisms Int from $\langle \text{Sen} \cup \text{Att}, f_{\sim}, f_{\rightarrow}, f_{\Box}, f_{\text{Att}} \rangle$ to $\langle \text{Prop} \cup \text{Attitudes}, h_{\sim}, h_{\rightarrow}, h_{\Box}, h_{\text{Att}} \rangle$.

In addition to compositionality of intension, the theory also postulates that intensions determine referents. In extensional semantics, we make use of only two levels of structure, namely syntax and referents, but in intensional semantics we add a third mediating level of senses. A major point of doing so is to explain the mechanism of linguistic reference. In Frege's theory the reason why a syntactic entity can refer to something in the world is that it is first paired with an intension, and intensions are such that they pick out objects in different worlds in a manner independent of syntax. That intensions can so determine referents in various possible worlds is what is required by the principle of intensional reference. Set theoretically, then, there is for each possible world a function independent of syntax that maps intensions into referents in that world. We can be a little more precise. Let Γ be the set of intensions and let K be the set of all possible worlds. The principle of intensional reference requires that for each k in K there is a function which we shall call H from Γ into entities in the world.[5]

DEFINITION: Let k be in the set K of possible worlds and Γ a set of intensions. Then, by the *reality function* for Γ relative to k is meant a function H with domain Γ.

It is possible now to define the set of all reference relations as the composition functions determined by intensional assignments and reality functions.

DEFINITION: Let Syn-IPL be an intensional propositional syntax, [Int] its set of intensional interpretations relative to an intensional structure, and $[H]$ a family of reality functions for that structure.

(1) We call $\langle$Syn-IPL, [Int], $[H]\rangle$ an *intensional propositional language.*

(2) Let Int $\in$ [Int]. Then, by the set $[R]_{\text{Int}}$ of all *reference relations relative to* Int is meant

$$\{H \cdot \text{Int} \mid \text{the range of Int is } \Gamma \text{ and } H \text{ is a reality function for } \Gamma\}.$$

(3) Let $L = \langle$Int-IPL, [Int]$\rangle$ be an intensional propositional language. Then, by the set $[R]$ of all *reference relations* of L is meant $\bigcup\{[R]_{\text{Int}} \mid \text{Int} \in [\text{Int}]\}$.

(4) We say a set X of sentences logically implies a sentence P in L (briefly $X \vDash P$) if, and only if, for any R in $[R]$, if R assigns T to each element in X, then R assigns T to P.

The referents picked out by the various reality functions are elements out of which worlds are formed. In the well-behaved semantics of extensional languages, referents of this sort form a compositional structure homomorphic to syntax, but in intensional semantics it is not possible in general to determine uniquely the referent of a whole from the referents of its parts. For example, the truth-value T is sometimes paired with T and other times with F in the semantic analysis of necessity sentences. Therefore, it is not possible in general to think of referents as organized by functions mirroring those in intensional or syntactic structure. Nevertheless, referents can be organized into structures. What binds them together, however, are not functions but relations. Even though the referents of parts may not be uniquely paired with a referent for a whole, they are paired in a many–many relation with various referents for the whole. For example, corresponding to the function $f_{\Box}$ in syntax and its parallel intensional function $h_{\Box}$, there is the relation $g_{\Box}$ on referents as described below:

$$g_{\Box} = \{\langle \text{T, T}\rangle, \langle \text{T, F}\rangle, \langle \text{F, F}\rangle\}$$

[5] Such functions are sometimes called *reality functions.* See John Roy Wallace, *Philosophical Grammar* (1964).

Indeed, that there exists for each formation rule and corresponding intensional operation one such structural many-many relation follows trivially by the principle of abstraction. We merely define it. A relation on referents g pairs x with y if the corresponding intensional operation h maps one intension γ to another ξ, and some reality function H assigns γ to x and y to ξ.

DEFINITION: Let $\langle \text{Sen}, \{\text{BS}, \text{Att}\}, \{f_{\sim}, f_{\rightarrow}, f_{\Box}, f_{\text{Att}}\}\rangle$ be an intensional propositional syntax, and let $\langle \text{Prop} \cup \text{Attitudes}, h_{\sim}, h_{\rightarrow}, h_{\Box}, h_{\text{Att}}\rangle$ be its intensional structure. Then *the referential structure* relative to them is defined as $\langle U, g_{\sim}, g_{\rightarrow}, g_{\Box}, g_{\text{Att}}\rangle$ such that

(1) for each i, $g_i = \{\langle x_1, \ldots, x_n, y\rangle \mid$ there is a reality function H for $\text{Prop} \cup \text{Attitude}$ such that for some $\gamma_1, \ldots, \gamma_n, \xi$ in $\text{Prop} \cup \text{Attitudes}$, $H(\gamma_1) = x_1, \ldots, H(\gamma_n) = x_n$, $H(\xi) = y$ and $h_i(\gamma_1, \ldots, \gamma_n) = \xi$, and

(2) U is the union of all the subdomains and ranges of the various g_i.

Such, then, is a rendering of Frege's intensional semantics in a metatheory using algebraic ideas to explain parallel structure. It follows from the general definitions already given that such a language need not be extensional. Valid substitutability fails because the relations on referential structures need not be functions, the various reference relations do not qualify as homomorphisms from syntax to referential structure, and hence the reference relations do not in general determine a congruence relation of coreferentiality.

9.2.4 Intensional Logic

The intensional semantics just defined is an improvement on the vaguely formulated version originally proposed by Frege. In particular, the inchoate notion of parallel semantic structure has been reformulated more precisely in terms of abstract structures and mappings among them. But the theory is still very abstract, and several key semantic ideas are left undefined. No explicit definition has been given for propositions or attitudes, and no attempt has been made to explain how the set of intensions determines the various reality functions.

As the theory stands, it appears quite metaphysical. What exactly are these entities called senses and what in detail is the theory of mental understanding that it posits in holding that language users understand senses? Does not this theory take much too seriously the informal way of talking in which we speak about 'the meaning' of a term as if it were a real thing? Surely to be justified in taking such talk as more than just a *façon de parler* should we not know more about senses? Is it not bad science to explain a phenomenon by hypothesizing an entity and then have nothing more to say about that entity than that it is the thing that explains the phenomenon?[6] These questions are largely metaphysical in the sense that they are about the entities presupposed by semantic theory. Whether they can be adequately answered is a legitimate concern in the overall evaluation of the theory.

Exactly what sort of entity intensions should be thought to be is difficult to say. The fact that they are public and accessible to many speakers at once seems to disprove the proposition that they are parts of an individual's mind. Perhaps they are best construed as a social phenomenon, like a complex pattern of linguistic practice, a convention, or a language game in Wittgenstein's sense. Perhaps this is the sort of question that we should set aside until we understand language better. Fortunately, however, semantic theory may in a legitimate way sidestep some of these issues. All we need do is accept as a working hypothesis that intensions, whatever they are, exist and have the relational properties Frege attributed to them. We solve the problem that they lack explicit definitions by replacing them with well-defined set theoretic entities that have the same relational properties. The set theoretic semantics for nonextensional languages modeled on Frege's ideas is called *intensional logic*.

The key idea is that intensions in general are quite like functions from possible worlds to referents in those worlds. The idea is due to Carnap, and is largely a generalization of Tarski's theory of systems which we shall study later in this chapter. The version of the theory we will now sketch is due to Richard Montague.[7]

Let us begin by sketching the intuitive basis for identifying intensions with functions from possible worlds to objects in those worlds. We have already used essentially this idea in the semantics of modal logic. There we represented the 'concept' of an individual by a function from possible worlds to individuals in those worlds. In a similar manner we represented a property by a function from possible worlds to sets in those worlds. Here we shall represent the sense of a sentence likewise. By a proposition we shall mean a function from possible worlds to truth-values. From the point of view of using these functions as proxies for Frege's senses, the important feature that they have in common is that, like Frege's undefined senses, they each determine a referent in a world. Let γ be a function from the set K of possible worlds to referents in those worlds. Then given k and γ, a referent $\gamma(k)$ is fixed. Senses in this sense do determine for each world a referent in that world. Another way of expressing this point is that intensions in this sense determine

[6] For an extended development of this sort of criticism of Frege's notion of sense see Hilary Putnam, "The Meaning of 'Meaning'" (1975).

[7] See Rudolf Carnap, *Meaning and Necessity* (1947), and Richard Montague, 'Pragmatics' (1968) and 'Pragmatics and Intensional Logic' (1970).

reality functions in a straightforward way: H_k is a reality function for a set Γ of intensions iff H_k is that function on Γ such that $H_k(\gamma) = \gamma(k)$. Montague's idea is to define intensional structure as a set of intensions of this sort, organized by operations on these intensions. The notion of a reality function and with it the notion of a reference relation are, then, readily definable.

Consider now the special case of a proposition. Intuitively the sense of a sentence is supposed to determine the reference or truth-value of each sentence in each possible world. Wittgenstein expressed essentially the same idea when he said that a proposition contains 'the expression of "truth-conditions" of a sentence'.[8] The construct consisting of a function from possible worlds to truth-values behaves just this way. Let K be the set of possible worlds. Now, suppose we associate with a sentence P a function γ from K to $\{T, F\}$. Clearly, γ functions as a proposition is supposed to. For any possible world k in K, γ determines a truth value for P, namely $\gamma(k)$. It is standard, therefore, in set theoretic semantics to use such functions as the intensions of sentences.

DEFINITION: By the set $\{T, F\}^K$ of *propositions* for the set K of all possible worlds is meant the set of all functions from K into $\{T, F\}$.

We let α, β, and γ range over $\{T, F\}^K$.

DEFINITION: If γ is a proposition, we define the set $\gamma*$ to be the set of worlds in K characterized by γ, i.e., $\gamma* = \{k \mid \gamma(k) = T\}$.

Below we shall find that it is sometimes easier to describe the properties of a proposition γ indirectly by explaining those of $\gamma*$. Indeed, anything we say about propositions as characteristic functions on K may be straightforwardly reformulated in terms of propositions as subsets of K. The reason we opt for the characteristic function analysis as the 'official' definition is that it better exhibits the similarity of propositions to other sorts of intensions, such as individual concepts and properties. We shall find that the simplest way to explain these is as functions from K to referents.

In the normal case a sentence P is contingent in the sense that it is true in some worlds but false in others. Its proposition is a nonempty proper subset of the set of all possible worlds. In the case in which P is necessary, it corresponds to the whole set of possible worlds, and in the case in which P is contradictory it corresponds to the empty set.

In this way we substitute talk about sets of possible worlds for talk about propositions. Conceptually speaking, this switch may not seem to amount to much progress. Proposition was an undefined idea and thus far so is the idea of possible world. Indeed, philosophers of language have made the point that

[8] Ludwig Wittgenstein, *Tractatus Logico-Philosophicus* (1918), paragraph 4.431.

possible world semantics is not very much more illuminating than semantics in terms of undefined intensional primitives like senses and propositions. But one advantage of using possible worlds is that they allow for rather simple definitions of structural relations, whereas we have no clue about how to start defining structural relations joining Frege's undefined senses. What rule do we use, for example, to find the sense of a conjunction given the senses of its parts? It is, however, quite simple to define the relevant structural operations on set theoretic intensions. A conjunction is true in any world in which both its conjuncts are, and thus the intension corresponding to a conjunction is just the intersection of the two sets of worlds corresponding to its immediate parts.

We now define some structural relations on $\{T, F\}^K$ corresponding to those of syntax. The functions for the connectives are straightforward. A negation is true in a world in which the contained sentence is false, conjunctions are true in worlds in which both conjuncts are true, etc. Let us adopt the simplest intuititive interpretation of necessity, namely that a necessity statement is true if its contained sentence is always true, and is false otherwise. Also for simplicity let us assume that attitude verbs stand in a world for a set of propositions, namely those propositions toward which the speaker bears that attitude in that world. Thus, the sense or intension of an attitude verb will be a function F taking arguments from K and pairing them with families of propositions.

DEFINITION: By the set $P(K)^K$ of *attitudes* we mean the set of all functions F from the set K of possible worlds into the family of subsets of K (i.e., $F(K \xrightarrow[\text{into}]{} P(K))$, where $P(K)$ is the power set of K).

DEFINITION: The *Montague intensional structure* for Syn-IPL is the intensional structure $\langle \{T, F\}^K \cup P(K)^K, h_{\sim}, h_{\rightarrow}, h_{\Box}, h_{\text{Att}} \rangle$ such that[9]

(1) $h_{\sim}(\alpha*) = K - h(\alpha*)$;

(2) $h_{\rightarrow}(\alpha*, \beta*) = (K - \alpha*) \cup \beta*$;

(3) $h_{\Box}(\alpha*) = K$ if $\alpha* = K$, $h_{\Box}(\alpha*) = \varnothing$ otherwise;

(4) $h_{\text{Att}}(F, \alpha*) = \{k \mid \alpha* \in F(k)\}$.

DEFINITION: The set $[H]$ of *Montague reality functions* for the Montague intensional structure is the set of all H such that for some k in K, F is a function with domain $\Gamma = \{T, F\}^K \cup P(K)^K$ and for any $\gamma \in \Gamma$, $H(\gamma) = \gamma(k)$. Equivalently,

$$[H] = \{H \mid \exists k \in K, H = \{\langle \gamma, x \rangle \mid \gamma \in \{T, F\}^K \cup P(K)^K \,\&\, \gamma(k) = x\}\}.$$

[9] If we were to add the other propositional connectives, their corresponding intensional operations would be defined as follows:

(5) $h_{\wedge}(\alpha*, \beta*) = \alpha* \cap \beta*$;

(6) $h_{\vee}(\alpha*, \beta*) = \alpha* \cup \beta*$.

DEFINITION: By a *Montague intensional language for a propositional syntax* we mean any ⟨Syn-IPL, [Int], [H]⟩ such that [Int] is the set of intensional interpretations for a Montague intensional structure for Syn-IPL and [H] is the set of Montague reality functions for that structure.

With these definitions the notions of reference relations $[R]_{\text{Int}}$ and [R] and logical entailment for such a language are all well defined. Moreover, Frege's intuitive vision of language is satisfied: senses of parts determine the senses of wholes, and sense determines reference.

THEOREM. Let ⟨Syn-IPL, [Int], [H]⟩ be a Montague intensional language in the sense just defined. Then, Int in [Int] is a homomorphism from the syntactic structure to its intensional structure, and for each R in [R], there is some Int in [Int] and some H in [H] such that $R = H \cdot \text{Int}$.

It is not hard to check that the extensional relations determined for the connectives are in fact the classical truth-functions and that the extensional relations corresponding to necessity and attitude sentences are non-functional.

THEOREM. The relations $g_{\sim}$ and $g_{\rightarrow}$ as defined in the extensional structure of a Montague intensional propositional logic are the classical truth-functions, and the relations $g_{\Box}$ and g_{Att} are nonfunctional.

Thus, though modal syntax is not, strictly speaking, homomorphic to extensional structure, a compositional semantics is possible because it is homomorphic to intensional structure.

Although we shall not attempt it here, it is possible to give a similar semantics for first-order logic with the syntactic rules for necessity and attitude verbs added. In order to keep extensional structure as parallel as possible with intensional structure, Montague employed the Tarski interpretation of first-order logic, with the result that the semantics though elegant is rather technical. We shall complete our discussion by adding two refinements to the theory.

9.2.5 The Intensions of Subjects and Predicates

Though extending the Frege–Montague semantics for intensional logic to all of first-order syntax is rather technical, it is straightforward and informative to add subject–predicate sentences. To the propositional syntax we add the set PN of basic expressions for proper names, the various sets P^n of predicates of degree n, and a formation rule f_{BS} generating the set BS of basic sentences. In the intensional semantics, we must then stipulate in set theoretic terms what the intensions of these new categories are, and define an intensional operation h_{BS} for calculating the intension of a subject–predicate sentence from those of its parts. We shall use Carnap's representations that we first met in the semantics of modal logic. Carnap represented Frege's idea of the sense of a proper name by what he called an *individual concept*, a function from possible worlds to objects in the domains of those worlds. The concept, as it were, follows the individual from world to world pointing out exactly what entity in the domain counts as that object in that world. Similarly, the intension of a predicate is identified by Carnap with a function from possible worlds to relations of objects in those worlds, and he called these functions *properties*. The idea is that the function goes from world to world pointing out which relation is to count as the extension of the predicate in that world. It should be noted that propositions do much the same thing.

The intensional function corresponding to the formation rule for basic sentences merely assigns that proposition to the whole that gives the value T to all those worlds in which the intensions of the referents of the parts, as determined by their extensions, stand to one another as the sentence describes, i.e.,

$$h_{BS} = \{\langle X_1, \ldots, X_n, Y, \alpha\rangle | \alpha(k) = \text{T iff } \langle X_1(k), \ldots, X_n(k) \in Y(k)\}.$$

The corresponding relation on referents g_{BS} is the familiar one we have met long ago in classical logic. It is that function that assigns the value T to an argument consisting of an n-tuple and a relation if the former is a member of the latter, and otherwise assigns them F.

9.2.6 Analytic Truth

A second refinement of intensional logic is the representation within it of analytic truths. These are necessary truths that strictly speaking are not logical truths. The notion of a logically possible world is very generous. It allows any possible assignment of intension and extension to the nonlogical terms of the language as long as these conform to the required generative structure on intensions and extensions. However, in natural languages such as English such assignments of meaning to terms would violate our customary usage. The color terms 'red' and 'green' are always used in English to refer to disjoint sets, and though there is a possible assignment of extensions to them that violates this usage, that assignment represents a 'possible' world only in a very abstract sense. One way to make the point in question is to distinguish between what we may call the logically possible worlds and a narrower set of linguistically possible worlds. In the latter, terms cannot be assigned extensions inconsistent with their regular usage. For example, 'red' could not apply to a set that overlapped the extension of 'green'. Likewise, in every linguistically possible world, though not necessarily in every logically possible world, the sentence 'Bachelors are unmarried' would be true.

In the semantics of intensional logic we have the means to make this distinction very clearly. Each intensional interpretation Int assigns to the nonlogical terms of the language intensions, and to each Int there is a restricted set $[R]_{\mathrm{Int}}$ of the wider set $[R]$ of possible reference relations. Analytic truth may be explained as a variety of necessary truth relative to this restricted set $[R]_{\mathrm{Int}}$, whereas logical or necessary truth in a full sense corresponds to truth in every member of the wider set $[R]$. Thus, each intensional interpretation determines a descriptive language.

DEFINITION: If $L = \langle \text{Syn-IPL}, [\text{Int}], [H] \rangle$ is a Montague intensional language, then by a *descriptive language* permitted by L is meant any $\langle \text{Syn-IPL}, \text{Int}, [R]_{\mathrm{Int}} \rangle$ and a sentence P is said to be *analytic* in this descriptive language if it is assigned T by every R in $[R]_{\mathrm{Int}}$.

Carnap and Montague did not pretend to be able to list all the analytic truths of a language. That is a job for lexicographers. They pointed out, however, that if there really are any analytic truths, then there is a one–one matching between the notion of a descriptive language and the set of its analytic truths. Given some interpretation Int we may define the set X which is T in all R of $[R]_{\mathrm{Int}}$, and conversely, a consistent set of sentences X closed under logical consequence determines some intensional interpretation Int, namely that Int such that X is its set of analytic truths. We shall discuss this topic when we investigate systems.[10]

9.3 THE ALGEBRA OF SYSTEMS AND PROPOSITIONS

9.3.1 Lattice Theory

In this section we develop results that show the close connection between two concepts of proposition. In the first sense a proposition is understood realistically as an intensional entity that determines the referents of sentences, and in the second sense it is understood linguistically as a story or group of sentences that lists the truths of a world. We shall show in some detail how these two ways of speaking capture the same idea. The study is essentially algebraic, and we begin by introducing some concepts from lattice theory. The theorems follow directly from the definitions by elementary logic, and therefore their proofs are left as exercises.

[10] W. V. O. Quine has argued that philosophy would be better served if we abandoned the idea of analytic truth; see 'Two Dogmas of Empiricism' (1953), and *Word and Object* (1960). See also Rudolf Carnap, 'Meaning Postulates' (1956), the papers by Montague previously cited, and Bas C. van Fraassen, 'Meaning Relations among Predicates' (1967).

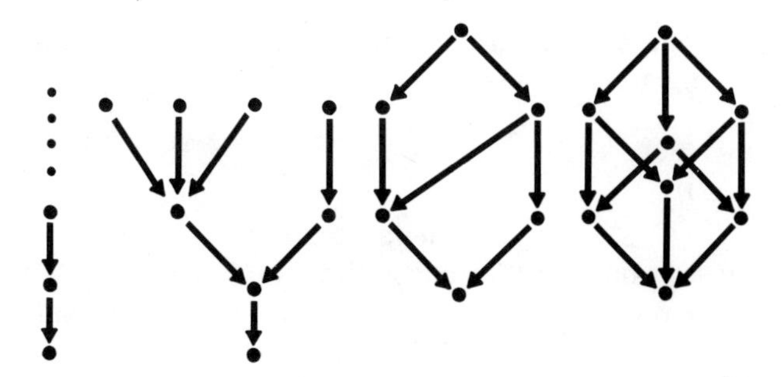

Fig. 9.1

DEFINITION: A partially ordered structure is any pair $\langle C, \leq \rangle$ such that $\leq$ is a binary relation on C, that is

(1) reflexive (for all x in C, $x \leq x$),
(2) transitive (for all x, y, z in C, if $x \leq y$ and $y \leq z$, then $x \leq z$), and
(3) antisymmetric (for all x and y in C, if $x \leq y$ and $y \leq x$, then $x = y$).

EXAMPLES The graphs in Fig. 9.1 determine partial orderings when $x \leq y$ means that there is a continuous route upward from x to y on the graph.

We now introduce names for some important elements above and below the two elements x and y.

DEFINITION: Let $\langle C, \leq \rangle$ be a partially ordered structure, let $A \subseteq C$, and let a, b, and c be members of C. We then define the following ideas:

(1) c is an *upper bound* of A if, and only if, for all x in A, $x \leq c$;
(2) c is a *lower bound* of A if, and only if, for all x in A, $c \leq x$;
(3) c is a *least upper bound* of A if, and only if, c is an upper bound of A, and for any x, if x is an upper bound of A, then $c \leq x$;
(4) c is a *greatest lower bound* of A if, and only if, c is a lower bound of A, and for any x, if x is a lower bound of A, then $x \leq c$;
(5) the *join* of a and b (briefly, $a \vee b$) is the least upper bound of $\{a, b\}$, if one exists;
(6) the *meet* of a and b (briefly, $a \wedge b$) is the greatest lower bound of $\{a, b\}$, if one exists.

Partial orderings that determine joins and meets for arbitrary elements are called lattices.

DEFINITION: Let $\langle C, \leq \rangle$ be a partially ordered structure. Then, we say that the structure is

(1) a *join semilattice* if, and only if, for x and y in C, $x \vee y$ exists,
(2) a *meet semilattice* if, and only if, for x and y in C, $x \wedge y$ exists, and
(3) a *lattice* if, and only if, it is both a join and a meet semilattice.

THEOREM. If $\langle C, \leq \rangle$ is a partially ordered structure and a and b are in C, then the following are equivalent:

(1) $a \leq b$;
(2) $\mathrm{a} \vee \mathrm{b} = \mathrm{a}$;
(3) $\mathrm{a} \wedge \mathrm{b} = \mathrm{b}$.

THEOREM. If $\langle C, \leq \rangle$ is a join semilattice, then

(1) C is closed under $\vee$ (for any x and y in C, $x \vee y$ is in C), and
(2) $\vee$ is idempotent (for any x in C, $x \vee x = x$), commutative, and associative.

THEOREM. If $\langle C, \leq \rangle$ is a meet semilattice, then

(1) C is closed under $\wedge$ (for any x and y in C, $x \wedge y$ is in C), and
(2) $\wedge$ is idempotent (for any x in $C, x \wedge x = x$), commutative, and associative.

Conversely, a partial ordering may be defined in terms of operations that have these properties:

THEOREM. If C is a set closed under a binary operation $\vee$ which is idempotent, commutative, and associative, and if $x \leq y$ is defined to mean $a \vee b = a$, then the structure $\langle C, \leq \rangle$ is a join semilattice.

THEOREM. If C is a set closed under a binary operation $\wedge$ which is idempotent, commutative, and associative, and if $x \leq y$ is defined to mean $a \wedge b = a$, then the structure $\langle C, \leq \rangle$ is a meet semilattice.

9.3.2 Abstract Intensional Languages

We now apply the ideas of lattice theory to two important semantic structures representing different approaches to the idea of proposition. We begin first with a very abstract definition of a language. For our purposes here we need not impose any conditions on the syntax of the language other than that it should possess a set of sentences. How they are constructed does not matter. Semantically we require only that each sentence is assigned an intension called a *proposition.* Intuitively, such propositions possess the features attributed to them by Frege. They determine the referent or truth-value of each sentence in each possible world. We shall use the set theoretic idea of proposition as defined earlier in this chapter. For simplicity instead of identifying a proposition as a function γ from the set of possible worlds K to $\{\mathrm{T}, \mathrm{F}\}$, we identify it rather with the set $\gamma*$ that it characterizes, namely the subset of K of which γ is the characteristic function. Each function γ from K to $\{\mathrm{T}, \mathrm{F}\}$ is the characteristic function of a unique subset of K: $\gamma* = \{k \mid \gamma(k) = \mathrm{T}\}$. Conversely, each subset K' of K has its characteristic function γ defined as that function from K to $\{\mathrm{T}, \mathrm{F}\}$ such that $\gamma(k) = \mathrm{T}$ iff $k \in K'$. Since functions from K to $\{T, F\}$ and subsets of K stand in a 1–1 relationship to one another, talk about one is translatable to talk about the other.

DEFINITION: The set $P(K)$ of *propositions* from the set K of all possible worlds means the set of all subsets of K. An *abstract intensional language* relative to the set K is a structure $\langle \text{Sen}, \text{Int} \rangle$ such that

(1) Sen, the set of *sentences*, is any set of expressions, and
(2) Int is a function from Sen into the set $P(K)$ of propositions from K.

We may use the notion of proposition to define the idea of logical implication. It is quite natural to say that one sentence implies another if the idea of the first is 'contained' in the second, and such formulations have been common in philosophy. In the definition below we abstract somewhat from this idea by allowing one set of sentences to entail another. A set here may be viewed as a kind of generalized conjunction of its members, except that unlike a conjunction a set may be composed of infinitely many sentences.

DEFINITION: Let L be an abstract intensional language $\langle \text{Sen}, \text{Int} \rangle$, and let X and Y be subsets of Sen. Then we say X *logically implies* Y in L (briefly, $X \models Y$) if, and only if, $\text{Int}(X) \subseteq \text{Int}(Y)$.

The standard Leibnizian definition of logical entailment as that relation preserving truth in all possible worlds follows as a special case of the more abstract definition. In the notation for $\models$, if a set of sentences Y contains only a single sentence P, i.e., $Y = \{P\}$, we write P in place of Y. Thus, we write $X \models P$ instead of $X \models \{P\}$ and $P \models X$ instead of $\{P\} \models X$.

THEOREM. $X \models P$ iff (for all k in K, if all Q in X are T in k, then P is T in k).

9.3.3 Tarski's Algebra of Systems

An assertion is represented in language by the sentence used to formulate it. A body of assertions may therefore be represented by sets of sentences. Moreover, if we are rational, we know that when we make an assertion we are also committed to the truth of every sentence that follows logically from what we assert explicitly, even if we do not know what all those consequences are. Thus, it has become the practice in logical theory to identify a *theory* with a set of sentences closed under logical consequences. Tarski, who was one of the first to study these sets, called them *systems*. We now present some of the structural properties of systems as he developed the idea.[11]

[11] Alfred Tarski, 'Foundations of the Calculus of Systems' (1935).

DEFINITION: (1) The set Sys of *systems* is the family of all sets X of sentences such that X is *closed under logical consequence* in the following sense:

$$\text{for any sentence } P, \text{ if } X \models P, \text{ then } P \in X.$$

(2) Let X be a set of sentences. Then the set $\mathrm{Cn}(X)$ of *consequences* of X is $\{P \mid X \models P\}$.

We let the lowercase Greek letters π, σ, τ range over Sys, and X, Y, Z over subsets of Sen.

THEOREM. $\models$ is a *consequence relation* in the following sense:
(1) if $P \in X$, then $X \models P$;
(2) (transitivity) if for all P in Y, $X \models \mathrm{P}$ and also $Y \models Q$, then $X \models \mathrm{Q}$;
(3) if $X \subseteq Y$ and $X \models P$, then $Y \models P$.
THEOREM. Cn is a *closure operation* on $\langle \mathrm{Sen}, \models \rangle$ in the following sense:
(1) (isotonicity) if $X \models Y$, then $\mathrm{Cn}(X) \models \mathrm{Cn}(Y)$;
(2) (extensionality) $\mathrm{Cn}(X) \models X$;
(3) (idempotence) $\mathrm{Cn}(\mathrm{Cn}(X)) = \mathrm{Cn}(X)$.
THEOREM. For all systems π and σ, $\sigma \models \pi$ iff $\pi \subseteq \sigma$.
THEOREM. $\langle \mathrm{Sys}, \models \rangle$ and $\langle \mathrm{Sys}, \subseteq \rangle$ are partially ordered structures.
THEOREM. $\langle \mathrm{Sys}, \models \rangle$ is a lattice such that
(1) the least upper bound $\sigma \vee \pi$ of σ and π is the least τ such that $\sigma \models \tau$ (i.e., $\tau = \sigma \cap \pi$), and
(2) the greatest lower bound $\sigma \wedge \pi$ of σ and π is the greatest τ such that $\tau \models \sigma$ and $\tau \models \pi$ (i.e., $\tau = \mathrm{Cn}(\sigma \cup \pi)$).

[Notice that $\langle \mathrm{Sys}, \subseteq \rangle$ is also a lattice, but its lattice join of $\{\sigma, \pi\}$ is $\mathrm{Cn}(\sigma \cup \pi)$ and its meet of $\{\sigma, \pi\}$ is $\sigma \cap \pi$, the 'duals' of those in $\langle \mathrm{Sys}, \models \rangle$.] In classical logic it is easy to show that $\mathrm{Cn}(P \wedge Q) = \mathrm{Cn}(P) \wedge \mathrm{Cn}(Q)$.

We now introduce a complementation operation on systems. Let L be the subset of Sen containing just the logical truths, i.e., $L = \{P \mid \mathrm{Int}(P) = K\}$.

DEFINITION: $-\sigma$ is the least element π such that $\sigma \vee \pi = L$ (i.e., both $\sigma \vee \pi = L$, and for any τ, if $\sigma \vee \tau = L$, then $\pi \models \tau$).
THEOREM. $\sigma \vee -\sigma = L$.
THEOREM. In general the following are false:
(1) $-(-\sigma) = \sigma$
(2) $\sigma \wedge -\sigma = \mathrm{Sen}$.
(Consider the language in which $L = \varnothing$.) Notice that in classical logic $-\mathrm{Cn}(P) = \mathrm{Cn}(\sim P)$.

9.3.4 Beth's Representation of Systems by Propositions

We now mirror the structure of systems in that of propositions.[12] We draw on three facts already proven:

(1) $X \models Y$ iff $\text{Int}(X) \subseteq \text{Int}(Y)$;

(2) $\langle \text{Sen}, \models \rangle$, $\langle \text{Sys}, \models \rangle$, and $\langle P(K), \subseteq \rangle$ are all partial orderings; and

(3) Int maps $P(\text{Sen})$ into $P(K)$.

We now define the idea of a story corresponding to a proposition. Let α, β, γ range over the set $P(K)$ of propositions.

DEFINITION: T is that function from the set $P(K)$ of propositions to sets of sentences such that $\text{T}(\alpha)$ (called the *truth set* of P) is $\{P \mid \alpha \subseteq \text{Int}(P)\}$.

THEOREM. The following are true (and say the same thing in equivalent ways):

(1) for any α, $\text{T}(\alpha) \in \text{Sys}$;

(2) the range of T is Sys;

(3) T is an 'onto' function.

Propositions, like sets of sentences, need some refinements before they represent rational beliefs. Just as not any set of sentences contains a complete story because it may not be closed under logical consequence, so too not every set of worlds represents a complete story. Merely because a set of worlds agrees on the truth of the same sentences does not mean that some other worlds do not also agree on the truth of these sentences. A set of worlds idealized so as to contain all the worlds they agree with in the assignment of truth is special in just the way systems are special.

DEFINITION: The set $P(K){*}$ *of sensible propositions* is the set of all propositions α such that $\text{Int}(\text{T}(\alpha)) = \alpha$.

THEOREM. $\sigma \in \text{Sys}$ iff $\text{T}(\text{Int}(\sigma)) = \sigma$.

THEOREM. The following are true (and different ways of saying the same thing):

(1) for any X, $\text{Int}(X) \in P(K){*}$;

(2) the range of Int is $P(K){*}$;

(3) Int maps the power set of Sen onto $P(K){*}$.

THEOREM. Int maps Sys 1–1 onto $P(K){*}$ and

(1) $\sigma \subseteq \pi$ iff $\sigma \models \pi$ iff $\text{Int}(\pi) \subseteq \text{Int}(\sigma)$;

(2) $\alpha \subseteq \beta$ iff $\text{T}(\beta) \subseteq \text{T}(\alpha)$;

(3) $\alpha = \text{Int}(\text{T}(\alpha))$ and $\sigma = \text{T}(\text{Int}(\text{Sen}))$.

[12] These results are adapted from E. W. Beth, *The Foundations of Mathematics* (1968).

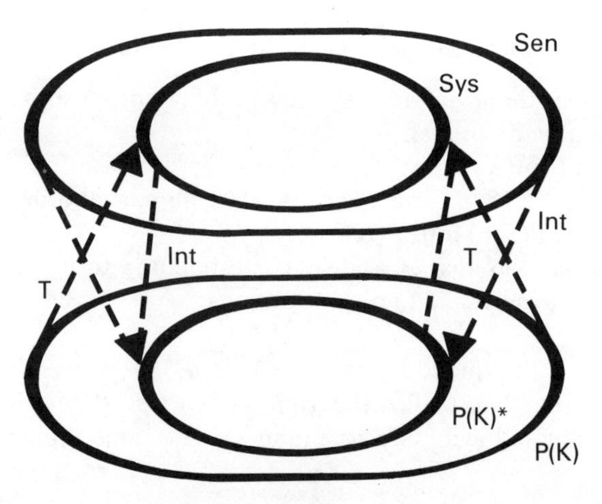

Fig. 9.2

These properties are summarized in the idea of a gallois connection (refer to Fig. 9.2):

THEOREM. Int and T form a *gallois connection* between $\langle \text{Sen}, \subseteq \rangle$ and $\langle P(K), \subseteq \rangle$ in the sense that

(1) both are partial orderings;
(2) Int and T are 'into' mappings from one set to the other;
(3) Int and T are *antitone* mappings in the sense that
  (a) if $\sigma \subseteq \pi$, then $\text{Int}(\pi) \subseteq \text{Int}(\sigma)$, and
  (b) if $\alpha \subseteq \beta$, then $\text{T}(\beta) \subseteq \text{T}(\alpha)$;
(4) $\alpha \subseteq \text{Int}(\text{T}(\alpha))$ and $\sigma \subseteq \text{T}(\text{Int}(\sigma))$.

9.4 SITUATIONAL SEMANTICS

9.4.1 Data: Halfway Extensionality

So far we have encountered two kinds of substitutional contexts, extensional ones in which any coreferential parts may be validly substituted and nonextensional ones in which only logical equivalents may be validly substituted. We found that for purely extensional languages, a compositional semantics need embrace only a theory of reference. The correct substitutional results can be explained as congruence over a homomorphic structure of referents. Nonextensional languages, on the other hand, require a theory of intension as well as a theory of reference. A compositional semantics is achieved by postulating a structure of intensions homomorphic to syntax. Referents form a structure parallel to, but not truly homomorphic to, intensions, and the correct substitutional results follow. Synonyms are validly substitutable because synonymy is a congruence relation determined by the homomorphic mapping from syntax to intensional structure. Coreferential expressions, however, are not validly substitutable because syntax fails to be homomorphic to the structure of referents, and thus coreferentiality is not a congruence relation.

From the point of view of the methods developed in this book, what is interesting in this account is the use of concepts from abstract algebra to explain the logical data within a compositional theory of how language works. There is another kind of data with its own sort of restrictions on valid substitution that invites a similar algebraic analysis. In this case the semantics seems to require that we enrich our concept of the world we refer to by adding to it entities like events, states, and facts. Intuitively, Frege's idea that the referent of a sentence is a truth-value has never been very satisfactory. Its main virtue is simplicity. With this assumption it is possible to state a logically adequate compositional referential semantics for classical propositional logic. The sets of variable assignments, taken as referents of sentences in Tarski's semantics for first-order logic, likewise yield an elegant extensional semantics but at the cost of employing even less intuitive semantic entities. The explanation of nonextensional languages has driven us to complicate the semantics even further by positing major new varieties of entities, and these have been intensional, corresponding to the abstract meanings and senses of traditional theory. So far we have found no need to introduce entities in the real world like events, states, or facts, and considerations like Ockham's razor should lead us to think that we are well off not doing so.[13] But the idea that truth is correspondence to the facts is quite appealing intuitively, and from a philosophical perspective it would be interesting to see the idea precisely analyzed. The following examples motivate just such a theory.

Each of the following sentences contains an italicized part that is either a sentence, an action nominal, a gerund, or an infinitive. Intuitively, these parts describe an event or a fact and the sentence as a whole makes some assertion about the event or fact. Moreover, the italicized phrases are themselves complex expressions made up of nouns and verbs. It is natural to think that the events or facts they describe are likewise complex, made up of the objects and properties picked out, and that the sentence as a whole makes an assertion about this complex entity.

[13] Occasionally in semantic theory events and facts are identified with propositions, but in such cases they are introduced to explain problems in nonextensional languages and are really varieties of intension. What we are discussing is the more common notion in which events and facts are in some sense constitutive of the world we refer to. For examples of intensional notions of event and fact, see Richard Montague, 'On the Nature of Certain Philosophical Entities' (1960), and Enrique Delacruz, 'Factives and Propositional Level Constructions' (1972).

EXAMPLES

Sentences

(1) *Atlantis sank* somewhere west of the pillars of Heracles.

(2) It was before Solon visited Egypt that *Atlantis sank.*

(3) (The fact) that *Atlantis sank* saved Columbus from an awkward detour.

Action nominals

(4) I photographed *the sinking of Atlantis.*

(5) *The sinking of Atlantis* was tumultuous.

(6) *The sinking of Atlantis* frightened the fish.

Gerunds

(7) *Carrying the explosives* wrenched my back.

(8) *Laying the explosives* took two days.

(9) *Blowing up the island* erased it from the face of the earth.

Infinitives

(10) The birds managed *to fly to Egypt.*

(11) The explosion failed *to kill the fish.*

(12) The island was beginning *to sink beneath the sea.*

(13) It took two hours *for the island to disappear under the water.*

The choice of entities used in semantics, however, needs to be guided by careful methodology. If we can explain these expressions without appeal to events or facts, then we ought to. In standard semantics we already have an impressive collection of ontological resources. These include not only the various kinds of references needed in the semantics of extensional languages, but also the various intensions needed for nonextensional languages. Any global metatheory would seem to need at least these resources, and one that did not go beyond them would, all things being equal, be better than one that did. Therefore, we must ask whether the semantic properties of the examples can be explained in terms of the usual resources of extensional and intensional semantics.

The reason for doubting that such a conservative approach will work is that properly speaking the italicized phrases seem to be neither extensional nor intensional. To see why, let us make a simplifying assumption. Let us suppose, as many in linguistics have thought, that all the italicized phrases are disguised sentences. In this view, action nominals, gerunds, and infinitives are at root varieties of sentence disguised in unimportant ways by the vagaries of English syntax. Let us suppose also that these sentences are made up in the usual way out of proper names, predicates, and connectives, and that these parts of speech are all given referents as in classical semantics. Names stand for objects, predicates for sets, and sentences for truth-values. We may now ask whether coreferential parts may be substituted in these examples *salva veritate.*

The answer seems to have two parts. First, coreferential atomic parts do seem to admit valid substitution. If 'Thera' stands for the same thing as 'Atlantis' in Example (1), then it may validly replace it. Likewise suppose all and only the things that sink in a given world are the things that erupt, so that in that world 'to sink' refers to the same extension as 'to erupt'. Then, if (1) is true in that world, so is the result of replacing the one predicate by the other. The other examples are similar; each example consists of a sentence within which coreferential atomic parts seem to be substitutable without altering the truth-value of the entire sentence.

On the other hand, the sentences they make up do not seem to be substitutable as units. Suppose the sentence 'Atlantis sank' has the same truth-value as 'Krakatoa exploded'. These are not substitutable *salva veritate*. Even if Atlantis had sunk somewhere west of Gibraltar, it would not mean Krakatoa exploded there too. In general, if we treat the entire italicized part of each example as standing for a truth-value and substitute it for another grammatically acceptable construction of the same truth-value, we may alter the truth-value of the example as a whole. Let us call *halfway extensional* or *semitransparent* those complex sentences which have coreferential atomic parts that are intuitively substitutable but which have larger materially equivalent sentential parts (i.e., the parts have the same truth-value), in the form of sentence nominals or sentence complements, that are not intuitively substitutable.[14]

What, then, is happening in these sentences? If they were purely extensional, we should find that the entire italicized units were substitutable. On the other hand, if the appropriate semantic structure for interpretation consisted of intensions we should not find that descriptive atomic parts are substitutable. In contrast to the examples above, there are some gerundive and infinitive constructions that are totally nonextensional in the traditional sense. Consider the following example. The premises clearly do not entail the conclusion.

Solon puzzled about *the sinking of Atlantis.*
Atlantis = Thera.
___
Solon puzzled about *the sinking of Thera.*

The premises may be true yet the conclusion false because, for example, Solon had never heard of Thera, or because he knew little about Atlantis but so much about Thera that he did not find it puzzling.

[14] The former term is used by Geach in discussing a set of examples used in teleological explanations. See Peter Geach, 'Teleological Explanation' (1975). For the latter term used to denominate the more general phenomenon, see John N. Martin, 'Facts and the Semantics of Gerunds' (1975). Donald Davidson remarked on a similar property for some causal statements; see Davidson, 'The Logical Form of Action Sentences' (1967) and 'Causal Relations' (1967).

The hypothesis we shall explore is that the earlier examples are really extensional but that the referents of the italicized sentences are not truth-values but events or facts. In this view events or facts should be thought of as constituents of the real world that we genuinely refer to and make assertions about. When we do so we generate contexts in which atomic parts are substitutable but sentential parts are not. A necessary condition for speaking about the same events or facts, in other words, is that the two make use of the same atomic constituents. It is insufficient for the two merely to have the same truth-value. In making assertions about these entities we have a choice of two kinds of predicates to apply to them, extensional and nonextensional. Extensional predicates are like those in the earlier examples. They make some factual claim about the event or fact and are to be evaluated like any other factual claim by determining whether the event or fact has the property in question. We may also apply nonextensional predicates to events or facts. Like the epistemic and attitude verbs of intensional logic, these render any expression in their scope nonextensional. The cognitive and emotional attitudes of such verbs must be explained not in terms of the referents of the associated expressions, but in terms of their intensions. Just as the truth of a belief sentence does not depend on the truth-value of the complement sentence, so a cognitive attitude toward an event or fact will depend not on whether the fact or event obtains but rather on the intension associated with that fact or event.

What we shall concentrate on here is developing the semantics for the more extensional assertions of the earlier examples. The challenge is to define events or facts, and organize them into an abstract structure that we may use to interpret the italicized sentential expressions. Coreferentiality in the new sense should generate a congruence relation that correctly matches our intuitions about substitution.

One simplification we shall make is to speak of events alone in places where it might be more accurate to speak more widely of events, states, and facts. The traditional distinction among these entities in philosophical discussions is that events take place in space and time and have a relatively short or limited duration. States also take place in time but are of long duration. Facts obtain or do not obtain independent of any particular time or place. If issues of time or place are relevant, we shall make them explicit.[15]

[15] On the syntactic distinction among sentences, action nominals, gerundive nominals, and infinitives see R. B. Lees, *The Grammar of English Nominalizations* (1960). Nothing we say here depends on whether these are all basically varieties of sentence. The issue is rather the semantic interpretation of these grammatical types, however they are generated.

Neither do the issues center on whether proper names are properly seen as rigid designators. If so, they may be substituted within nonextensional contexts. Examples of extensional attitudes toward events and facts may then be generated by describing the objects of which they are composed by means of nonrigid designators like definite descriptions.

9.4.2 Davidson's Theory of Events

Donald Davidson has suggested a way of representing action sentences that may be readily generalized to apply to the examples above. His proposal is that the logical form of such sentences should be represented in a first-order language that has a special quantifier that ranges over events. Predications about events are then possible by applying first-order predicates to constants and variables that refer to events. Since coreferential atomic parts of such languages are substitutable *salva veritate*, the representation captures the intuitively acceptable inferences. Moreover, what appear to be simple applications of predicates to sentences that describe events, by Davidson's analysis, turn out to be logically complex sentences that do not have sentential parts standing for events. It follows that since these extensional parts do not really exist, coreferential sentential parts cannot be validly substituted. By this means, he excluded the intuitively invalid substitutions of materially equivalent sentential event nominals. He was therefore able to explain both the valid and invalid substitutions.[16]

To see how the theory works in detail, we postulate a first-order syntax and define within it a new sort of quantifier over events. By $(\exists e)(\ldots e\ldots)$ we mean that there exists something x that is an event and is such that it has the property $\ldots x\ldots$. For this purpose we require that the language have a predicate that in the semantics applies uniquely to the set of events. Within the semantic theory we leave the idea of an event as an undefined primitive term from ontology. Accordingly, we stipulate that there is in the semantics an unanalyzed set E of possible events.

DEFINITION: Let a *Davidson first-order syntax* be any Syn-QL with a special one-place predicate 'event'.

(1) Any expression of the form $(\exists e)P$ we understand to be an abbreviation for the longer expression $(\exists v)(\text{event}(v) \wedge [P]^{x}_{e})$, where x is the first variable in Vb not free in P.

(2) A *Davidson model* is any first-order model such that $R(\text{event}) \subseteq E$.

(3) The *Davidson many-sorted language for events* is $\langle \text{Syn-QL}, [R*] \rangle$ such that Syn-QL is a Davidson syntax and $[R*]$ is the set of referential extensions of its Davidson models.

Because we shall retain some of the English terms from the examples in the symbolic translations, in the first-order translation we separate the predicate from the terms which follow it by putting these terms in parentheses. For example, we write the first-order predication form Fa as $F(a)$ and the

[16] See Donald Davidson, 'Causal Relations' (1967) and 'The Logical Form of Action Sentences' (1967). The analysis here follows that of John N. Martin, 'Facts and Events as Semantic Constructs' (1981).

relational form Rab as $R(a, b)$. Thus, in clause (1) above 'event(v)' is a first-order open atomic sentence saying that v is an event.

We now represent some English sentences in this syntax. Below, (A) is one of the earlier examples stated in English and (B) is an approximation of it in the new syntax. Davidson uses the idea that verbs may represent relations between events and objects. In this case we view a sinking as a relation that events hold to objects.

(A) I photographed the sinking of Atlantis.

(B) $(\exists e)(\text{photographed}(\text{I},e) \wedge \text{sinking}(e,\text{Atlantis}))$

A connotation of the original sentence (A) that is missing in (B) is that the sinking in question was a unique phenomenon. We can explicitly state this uniqueness if we assume Syn-QL contains the identity predicate.

DEFINITION: Let us understand $(\exists! v)P$, read 'there is a unique v such that P', as short for $(\exists v)(P \wedge (\forall v')([P]_v^{v'} \rightarrow v = v'))$. Then we may translate (A) more accurately as

(C) $(\exists! e)(\text{photographed}(\text{I},e) \wedge \text{sinking}(e,\text{Atlantis}))$

If we also wish to make clear the nonprogressive temporal aspect of the assertion, we could also augment the syntax and semantics to contain some vocabulary for locating events at times. We would need to add a quantifier over times, and some special temporal predicates and constants. Though we shall not attempt to do so in a serious way, a more fully explicit version of (A) might look something like

(D) $(\exists! e)(\exists! t)(\text{photograph}(\text{I},e) \wedge \text{sinking}(e,\text{Atlantis}) \wedge \text{occurs-at}(e,t) \wedge \text{before}(t,\text{now}))$

We can show that any of these translations yields the desired logical result. The following argument records an attempt to substitute coreferential proper names, and it is easy to see that it is valid in first-order semantics.

$$\begin{array}{l} (\exists e)(\text{photographed}(\text{I},e) \wedge \text{sinking}(e,\text{Atlantis})) \\ \underline{\text{Atlantis} = \text{Thera}} \\ (\exists e)(\text{photographed}(\text{I},e) \wedge \text{sinking}(e,\text{Thera})) \end{array}$$

Likewise, predicates that are coreferential are validly substitutable. In the following argument, the second premise records in the object language the fact that all and only the sinkings are eruptings, that the predicates 'sinking' and 'erupting' are coextensional.

$$\begin{array}{l} (\exists e)(\text{photographed}(\text{I},e) \wedge \text{sinking}(e,\text{Atlantis})) \\ \underline{(\forall e)(\forall x)(\text{sinking}(e,x) \leftrightarrow \text{erupting}(e,x))} \\ (\exists e)(\text{photographed}(\text{I},e) \wedge \text{erupting}(e,\text{Atlantis})) \end{array}$$

□ **EXERCISE**

Prove the following in a Davidson language.

(a) $\{(\exists e)(\text{photographed}(I,e) \wedge \text{sinking}(e,\text{Atlantis})), \text{Atlantis} = \text{Thera}\} \models (\exists e)(\text{photographed}(I,e) \wedge \text{sinking}(e,\text{Thera}))$

(b) $\{(\exists e)(\text{photographed}(I,e) \wedge \text{sinking}(e,\text{Atlantis})),$
$(\forall e)(\forall x)(\text{sinking}(e,x) \leftrightarrow \text{erupting}(e,x))\} \models$
$(\exists e)(\text{photographed}(I,e) \wedge \text{erupting}(e,\text{Atlantis}))$.

On the other hand, any attempt to substitute what appear to be the sentential parts of (A) will fail. The intuitive candidate for the sentential action nominal of (A) is something like

(i) $(\exists e)(\text{sinking}(e,\text{Atlantis}))$.

But in a strict sense of syntactic part, (i) is not a part of (B), nor of any of the more precise versions of (A). Hence, there is no simple way to validly substitute (i) for one of its material equivalents. Intuitively, the following argument in English is invalid:

I photographed *the sinking of Atlantis.*
The sinking of Atlantis occurred if and only if
the erupting of Krakatoa did too.

I photographed *the erupting of Krakatoa.*

As desired, the translation of the argument into the first-order syntax is demonstrably invalid:

$$\frac{\begin{array}{l}(\exists e)(\text{photographed}(I,e) \wedge \text{sinking}(e,\text{Atlantis}))\\ (\exists e)(\text{sinking}(e,\text{Atlantis})) \leftrightarrow (\exists e')(\text{erupting}(e',\text{Krakatoa}))\end{array}}{(\exists e)(\text{photographed}(I,e) \wedge \text{erupting}(e,\text{Krakatoa}))}$$

□ **EXERCISE**

Define a Davidson model $\langle D, R\rangle$ such that

$R*((\exists e)(\text{photographed}(I,e) \wedge \text{sinking}(e,\text{Atlantis}))) = T$, and
$R*((\exists e)(\text{sinking}(e,\text{Atlantis})) \leftrightarrow (\exists e')(\text{erupting}(e',\text{Krakatoa}))) = T$, but
$R*((\exists e)(\text{photographed}(I,e) \wedge \text{erupting}(e,\text{Krakatoa}))) = F$.

This technique for representing action nominals, gerunds, and infinitives is well known among philosophers of language and widely accepted as adequate. Its main virtue is that it explains the logical intuitions within a logistic language that has a well-developed and relatively uncontroversial semantics. First-order logic both has an elegant compositional semantics and avoids the controversial metaphysical assumptions of intensional logic.

The theory, however, is reminiscent of Russell's theory of descriptions. It may well capture the right inferences, but it posits a major reinterpretation of natural language syntax. Instead of a simple subject–predicate sentence, the full logical form of (A) is something like the following:

(E) $(\exists w)(\exists x)(\text{event}(w) \wedge \text{time}(x) \wedge \text{photograph}(\text{I},w) \wedge$
$\text{sinking}(w,\text{Atlantis}) \wedge \text{occurs}(w,x) \wedge \text{before}(x,\text{now}) \wedge$
$(\forall y)(\forall z)((\text{event}(y) \wedge \text{time}(z) \wedge \text{photograph}(\text{I},y) \wedge$
$\text{sinking}(y,\text{Atlantis}) \wedge \text{occurs}(y,z) \wedge \text{before}(z,\text{now})) \rightarrow$
$(w = y \wedge x = z))$

A theory which matched natural language syntax more closely would be better.

The theory also makes use of a systematic equivalence between objects falling under a relation, on the one hand, and those objects bearing a relation of the same name to an event, on the other. That Atlantis has the property of sinking seems to be in some cases equivalent to Atlantis bearing the sinking relation to an event. Such an equivalence seems to underlie the translation of (A). A simple subject–predicate sentence, however, is not formulated in terms of events. The translation of 'Atlantis is sinking' is usually (ii), not (i).

(i) $(\exists e)(\text{sinking}(e,\text{Atlantis}))$

(ii) Sinking(Atlantis)

What properties of events allow this alternative formulation and why it seems to hold in some cases but not others remain unexplained. Rather than leaving *E* an unanalyzed primitive, its properties should be spelled out in such a way that systematic answers to these questions are forthcoming.

Of course, the weakness of this theory counts for little if there is not an alternative account with which it may be contrasted. We turn to one now that explains the right logical intuitions by probing into the internal nature of events, from which an algebra of events is constructed that provides a truly extensional semantics.

9.4.3 A Structure of Events

One way to ensure that identical individuals and relations may be substituted within an event without altering the event as a whole is to view events as composite entities made up of individuals and relations. As a metaphor, we may use a brick wall. A wall is a composite made up of many individual bricks as parts. The only way to change the wall is to alter the bricks or their arrangement. Evidently, an event is similar. Let $a_1, \ldots, a_n$ be individuals and let R be a relation. From these we construct an event. We want to choose a construct that contains these as parts. One obvious set theoretic candidate for such a composite is a set made up of $a_1, \ldots, a_n$ and R.

Since sets are identical if their parts are, such a construct would ensure the correct substitutional properties. Not just any set containing $a_1, \ldots, a_n$ and R will do. The arrangement matters as well as the components. In atomic sentences the order of the terms is relevant to what event is being described, and this linguistic order is important because it evidently reflects an order in reality. The event of A hitting B is usually quite distinguishable from the event of B hitting A, even if they occur together. Thus a natural candidate for a set theoretic construct for the sort of event referred to by an atomic sentence would be the $(n + 1)$-tuple $\langle R, a_1, \ldots, a_n \rangle$, and we shall call such a construct an *atomic event*. If we wish to make explicit the fact that the event is occurring at a particular time or place, we can think of times and places as numbering among the *relata* of the relation. The sinking of Atlantis at time t and location l would then be represented by using a three-place sinking relation: $\langle$sinking, Atlantis, t, $l\rangle$.[17]

Many things can happen at once and yet it is often natural to think of the totality as a single event. It is natural, for example, to think of the sinking of Atlantis as involving numerous more detailed events. A process is the sort of complex entity that comprises such a series of events because a process is the sort of thing that proceeds through time and space, and is made up of numerous smaller events. Accordingly, we shall group atomic events into sets, and think of each set of atomic events as representing that complex event in which each of the constituent atomic events occurs. Like atomic events, complex events of this sort seem to be completely determined by their component events. If you analyze a process into its component events and

[17] This device for representing the temporal and spatial features of events is used by Jon Barwise and John Perry, *Situations and Attitudes* (1983). Facts, which are atemporal and nonspatial, need have no such additional parameters. The representation of atomic events or facts used here has occurred to many writers. One early use is found in R. M. Martin, 'Facts: What They Are and What They Are Not' (1967). The account here of complex events and the algebra defined on them was first presented in John N. Martin, 'Facts and the Semantics of Gerunds' (1975) and 'Facts and Events as Semantic Constructs' (1981). This algebra is a development of a different structure of events defined by van Fraassen for use in the interpretation of relevance logic; see Bas C. van Fraassen, 'Facts and Tautological Entailment' (1969). In the account here we revert to van Fraassen's sets rather than using matrices as in the author's (1975) paper. We do so because the definitions are somewhat simpler and because sets are now the more common way to represent these complexes. This same algebra of events with only minor differences of style is to be found, for example, in Barwise and Perry (1983), pp. 90–93. In the presentation here we require that events be finite sets. We do so because infinite sets are unnecessary for the applications we make here. An extension to infinite sets in the manner of Barwise and Perry is contained in an exercise. A more abstract approach to essentially the algebra we define is found in Jon Barwise, 'The Situation in Logic—III: Situations, Sets and the Axiom of Foundation' (1986). See Kit Fine, 'First-Order Modal Theories III—Facts' [1982] for a general account of the model theory of facts and events. The account here can be considered as a special case of those studied by Fine.

these contain the relevant information about temporal and spatial order, then there is nothing more to say about the process. Accordingly, we shall represent conjunctive processes by sets of atomic events. Thus if $e_1, \ldots, e_n$ are atomic events we organize them into the conjunctive event $C = \{e_1, \ldots, e_n\}$, which is to be understood as that event in which all of $e_1, \ldots, e_n$ occur.

From the point of view of representing the expressive power of propositional logic, it would be convenient to have complex events containing disjunctive information. If $C_1, \ldots, C_n$ are each conjunctive events, then we represent the event E in which either C_1 or ... or C_n occurs by set theory. Let E be the construct $E = \{C_1, \ldots, C_n\}$. Then, E is that complex event in which at least one of the conjunctive events $C_1, \ldots, C_n$ occurs. Moreover, each C_i is itself a family of atomic events, all of which must occur if C_i does.

Given the structure of a complex event $E = \{C_1, \ldots, C_n\}$, there are straightforward ways to conjoin and disjoin it with other such structures. Let E' be $C'_1, \ldots, C'_n$. Then, the result of conjoining E with E' (briefly, $E \wedge E'$) would be that event in which one of the alternative events in E occurred together with one of those in E'. That is, $E \wedge E'$ is $\{C'' | \text{for some } C \text{ and } C', C \in E \text{ and } C' \in E'$ and $C'' = C \cup C')$. Here, $C \cup C'$ is the set theoretic union of C and C'.

The result of disjoining E with E' (briefly, $E \vee E'$) would be that event in which at least one of the alternatives from either E or E' occurs. That is, $E \vee E'$ is $E \cup E'$. Here $\bar{E} \cup E'$ is the set theoretic union of E and E'.

Complementation on facts and events is a concept that has interested philosophers for some time. Russell discussed it in terms of the idea of a *negative fact* understood as a fact that makes the negation of some atomic sentence true but does not simultaneously make some other nonnegative atomic sentence true.[18] We shall think of complementation rather as an operation on events. As the complement $-\langle R, a_1, \ldots, a_n \rangle$ of an atomic event $\langle R, a_1, \ldots, a_n \rangle$, we shall understand $\langle -R, a_1, \ldots, a_n \rangle$ where $-R$ is the set theoretic complement of the relation R.[19] Let C be a conjunctive event made up of atomic events $e_1, \ldots, e_n$. That is, $C = \{e_1, \ldots, e_n\}$. Then its complement $-C$ would be that event that held if the complement of at least one of the various e_i occurs. We may express this idea in terms of set theoretic notation: $-C$ is $\{\{-e_1\}, \cdots, \{-e_n\}\}$. Then, the complement of a fully complex event $E = \{C_1, \ldots, C_n\}$ would be that event in which the complements of all its conjunctive parts occur. That is, $-E$ is $-C_1 \wedge \cdots \wedge -C_n$.

[18] See Bertrand Russell, 'The Philosophy of Logical Atomism' (1918).

[19] In a nonbivalent account we would have to interpret $-R$ as a kind of restricted complementation. See the author's (1975) paper. Nothing we have said so far has committed us to any particular understanding of what sort of thing R is. If we wish to interpret R as a property, as does Jaegwon Kim then we would need to define a complementation relation on properties by, for example, appeal to a structure of possible world intensions. See Jaegwon Kim, 'Causation, Nomic Subsumption, and the Concept of Event' (1973).

These ideas make a great deal of sense intuitively if viewed as matrix operations. The matrix in Fig. 9.3 represents the complex event $E = \{\{a, b\}, \{c, d\}\}$. Each row of the matrix represents one of the alternative conjunctive events $\{a, b\}$ and $\{c, d\}$ that make up E. The rows themselves are made up of the atomic events a, b, c, and d. We may then represent the three operations as in Figs. 9.4–9.6. We are now ready to define the structure of events more formally.

$$\begin{bmatrix} a & b \\ c & d \end{bmatrix}$$

Fig. 9.3

$$\begin{bmatrix} a & b \\ c & d \end{bmatrix} \vee \begin{bmatrix} e & f \\ g & h \end{bmatrix} = \begin{bmatrix} a & b \\ c & d \\ e & f \\ g & h \end{bmatrix}$$

Fig. 9.4

$$\begin{bmatrix} a & b \\ c & d \end{bmatrix} \wedge \begin{bmatrix} e & f \\ g & h \end{bmatrix} = \begin{bmatrix} a & b & e & f \\ a & b & g & h \\ c & d & e & f \\ c & d & g & h \end{bmatrix}$$

Fig. 9.5

$$-\begin{bmatrix} a & b \\ c & d \end{bmatrix} = -\{a,b\} \wedge -\{c,d\} = \begin{bmatrix} -a \\ -b \end{bmatrix} \wedge \begin{bmatrix} -c \\ -d \end{bmatrix}$$

Fig. 9.6

DEFINITION: The set **AE** of *atomic events* is

$$\{\langle R, a_1, \ldots, a_n\rangle \mid R \subseteq \mathbf{V}^n \ \&\ a_1, \ldots, a_n \in \mathbf{V}\},$$

and the operation $-$ on **AE** is defined as

$$-\langle R, a_1, \ldots, a_n\rangle = \langle -R, a_1, \ldots, a_n\rangle.$$

DEFINITION: The set **CE** of *conjunctive events* is the set of all finite subsets of **AE**, and $-$ is a 1-place operation on **CE** defined as follows:

$$-C = \{\{-e\} \mid e \in C\}.$$

Since we wish to use later the concept of homomorphism on the algebra of events we are about to define and since homomorphisms as we have defined them require the operations in a structure to have a set number of argument places, we make explicit the detail mentioned in Chapter 6 that strictly speaking there is a unique formation rule for each set of n-placed predicates and the atomic sentences formed from them. For each set P^n of predicates of degree n, there is a formation rule f^n_{BS} making up atomic sentences by stringing n terms behind an n-placed predicate. Likewise in the semantic structure of events there will be for each such syntactic function an operation g^n_{BS} on events.

DEFINITION: By the *structure of events* is meant $\langle \mathbf{E}, g^1_{\mathrm{BS}}, \ldots, g^n_{\mathrm{BS}}, \ldots, g_\wedge, g_\vee, g_-\rangle$ such that

(1) **E** is the power set of **CE**,

(2) g^n_{BS} is a binary function defined as follows:

$$g^n_{\mathrm{BS}} = \{\langle x_1, \ldots, x_n, y, E\rangle \mid x_i, \ldots, x_n \in \mathbf{V} \ \&\ y \in \mathbf{V}^n \ \&\ E = \{\{\langle y, x_1, \ldots, x_n\rangle\}\}\},$$

(3) $g_\wedge$ is a binary operation on **E** defined as follows:

$$g_\wedge = \{\langle E, E', E''\rangle \mid E'' = \{C'' \mid \text{for some } C \text{ and } C', C \in E \text{ and } C' \in E' \text{ and } C'' = C \cup C'\}\},$$

(4) $g_\vee$ is a binary operation on **E** defined as the restriction of set theoretic union to the set **E**:

$$g_\vee = \{\langle E, E', E''\rangle \mid E'' = E \cup E'\},$$

(5) g_- is a 1-place operation on **E** defined as follows
$g_- = \{\langle E, E'\rangle \mid \text{for some } C_1, \ldots, C_n,\ E = \{C_1, \ldots, C_n\} \text{ and } E' = -C_1 \wedge \cdots \wedge -C_n\}$.

☐ **EXERCISE**

Of the above operations on **E** only the definition of g_- exploits the fact that E is finite. Generalize the definition of g_- on **E** so that it applies to infinite subsets of **CE**.

The trick is to generalize the operation $\wedge$ so that it is defined on $\{-C|C \in E\}$ even when E is infinite. *Hint*: First define relative to an arbitrary subset E' of **CE** the set of functions f that assign one of the atomic events in C to each C in E'. The ranges of these functions may then be put together to form a generalized $\wedge E'$. Then apply this notion to the special case in which E' is $\{-C|C \in E\}$.

Let us now use this structure to interpret a syntax of expressions standing for events. We can think of these expressions as gerundive nominals formed by first concatenating subjects and predicates to form atomic gerunds and then forming complex gerundive phrases by the usual formation rules for propositional logic.

DEFINITION: Let Syn-G be a *gerundive syntax containing subject–predicate atomic sentences* defined as the inductive system $\langle \text{SNom}, \{\text{PN}, \text{Pd}\}, \{f^1_{\text{BS}}, \ldots, f^n_{\text{BS}}, \ldots, f_\wedge, f_\vee, f_\sim\}\rangle$ on the set of basic elements PN (of *proper names*) and a set $\text{Pd} = P^1 \cup \cdots \cup P^n \cup \cdots$ (of *predicates*), with the formation functions and the set SNom (of *sentential nominals or gerunds*) defined in the standard way: the set BS of *basic sentential nominals* is the union of the ranges of the atomic rules f^i_{BS}, and SNom is the closure of BS under the formation rules for the connectives.

DEFINITION: The set $[R]$ of event interpretations for Syn-G is defined as the set of all homomorphisms from the structure

$$\langle \text{SNom}, f^1_{\text{BS}}, \ldots, f^n_{\text{BS}}, \ldots, f_\wedge, f_\vee, f_\sim\rangle$$

to the event structure

$$\langle \mathbf{E}, g^1_{\text{BS}}, \ldots, g^n_{\text{BS}}, \ldots, g_\wedge, g_\vee, g_-\rangle.$$

Though it is true that each relation in $[R]$ is a homomorphism and thus determines a congruence relation on syntax, this congruence relation is narrower than the more familiar material equivalence (defined as the relation holding between those expressions that determine the same truth-value relative to a reference relation). Exactly how restrictive the new equivalence relation is may be expressed in terms of the notion of the disjunctive normal form of a sentential nominal. Every expression of propositional logic is logically equivalent to some expression in what is called *disjunctive normal form.* Here is an intuitive method for constructing this equivalent. Construct the truth-table for a sentence nominal P. For each line L in which P is assigned T, construct what we may call a *T-conjunction* for L by including as conjuncts in the conjunction the unnegated version of every atomic sentence assigned T in L and the negated version of every sentence assigned F in L. Combine all the T-conjunctions into a long disjunction.

What is interesting about this disjunction is that it records the truth-conditions of a sentence by directly reporting its truth-table. Moreover, two sentences true in exactly the same circumstances will have disjunctions that differ if at all only in the internal order of conjuncts within the conjunctions or that of the disjuncts within the disjunction. So that sentences with the same truth-conditions have the same disjunction associated with them, let us standardize their order. Any unique reordering will do. Let us use a kind of alphabetic order. Assume that BS is indexed and that an atomic expression P_j 'comes after' another P_i in the alphabet if $i \leq j$. If $\sim P_i$ is the negation of an atomic expression, let it come immediately after P_i in the alphabet. Then reorder each conjunction so that alphabetically earlier expressions appear to the left, and reorder the disjunction as a whole so that its disjuncts (the various conjunctions) are in alphabetic order. The result of reordering may be identified for our purposes here with the disjunctive normal form of P. Clearly, any two expressions with the same disjunctive normal form have the same truth-conditions.

☐ **EXERCISE**

It is possible to define the disjunctive normal form of an arbitrary sentence recursively. Atomic sentences and their negations are already in disjunctive normal form. For arbitrary molecular sentences proceed as follows. First move all negations inside to atomic sentences by progressive applications of double negation and DeMorgan's laws. If a disjunction remains, replace each disjunct by its disjunctive normal form. If a conjunction remains, then either it has a disjunction as a part or it does not. If it does not, then that conjunct is in disjunctive normal form. If it does, then distribute one side over the other and replace each resulting disjunct by its disjunctive normal form.

(a) Exhibit the calculation of a disjunctive normal form of $\sim((\sim P \wedge Q) \vee R)$, first by the method of recording the lines of its truth-table and then by the recursive method.

(b) Write out formally a recursive definition for a function dnf that assigns to a sentence P its disjunctive normal form dnf(P).

Notice that 'sameness of truth-conditions' is a notion stronger than sameness of truth-value because two sentences may have the same truth-value yet not have the same truth-conditions. Indeed the following result, which we shall not prove here, shows that having the same truth-conditions is just another name for referring to the same event. Two sentential nominals stand for the same event (are referentially equivalent) if, and only if, they have the same truth-conditions.[20]

[20] For a proof see the author's (1975) paper previously cited.

THEOREM. For any P and Q in SNom and any R in $[R]$, $R(P) = R(Q)$ iff $\mathrm{dnf}(P) = \mathrm{dnf}(Q)$.

The logic of such nominalizations, however, remains classical. We shall say that a complex event 'occurs' if at least one of its conjunctive parts is made up of atomic events in which the subject items stand in the relation predicated.

DEFINITION: By the set D of *designated values* for $\mathbf{E}$ we mean the set of all events E in $\mathbf{E}$ such that E *occurs* in the following sense: E is some $\{C_1, \ldots, C_n\}$ and for at least one C_i every atomic event $\langle R, a_1, \ldots, a_m\rangle$ in C_i is such that $\langle a_1, \ldots, a_m\rangle \in R$.

Logical entailment, then, may be defined as a relation that preserves the property of occurring.

DEFINITION: By the *gerundive event language* LGE we mean $\langle\text{Syn-G}, [R]\rangle$, and for any $X \subseteq$ SNom and any $P \in$ SNom, we say that X *logically entails* P in LGE (briefly, $X \vDash P$) if, and only if, for any R in $[R]$, if for all $Q \in X$, $R(Q) \in D$, then $R(P) \in D$.
THEOREM. $X \vDash P$ iff X entails P in classical logic.

☐ **EXERCISE**

Prove the theorem using the methods of Chapter 7 by showing that there is an 'onto' homomorphism from the structure $\langle \mathbf{E}, D, g_{\wedge}, g_{\vee}, g_{-}\rangle$ to the classical matrix C that preserves designation and nondesignation.

To use these resources to represent fully the earlier examples, we would need to employ the gerundive syntax within a larger language that allows predications that apply to gerundive nominals as subjects. For example, we would need a class of verbs, let us call it GP, that would include verbs like 'discover' and 'photograph' that combine with sentential nominals to yield sentences. For this purpose we would need a formation rule, let us call it f_{GP}, that takes sentential nominals from SNom and predicates from GP as arguments and yields a declarative sentence as value. Syntactically such a function would be much like f_{Att} defined earlier in this chapter: for $P \in$ SNom and $V \in$ GP, $f_{\mathrm{GP}}(V, P) = V^\frown P$. The main difference between attitude constructions and the new sort of gerundive predications would be semantic. While propositional attitude constructions seem to be fully nonextensional, the gerundive predications would be extensional within a semantics of events.[21] To interpret the new expressions generated by f_{GP} we would need to

[21] Barwise and Perry, it may be remarked, believe that even attitude constructions may be construed as extensional if interpreted by an extensional semantics of events of the sort sketched here. The interpretations of gerundive nominals and propositional attitude constructions are just two of the many advantages claimed by these authors for event semantics.

add a semantic operation g_{GP} to the event structure. It would be a rule that takes as arguments the referents of sentential nominals and their predicates and yields as value the referent of a sentence. The nominals, of course, would refer to events, and we might think of their predicates as standing for sets of events, and of the declarative sentence they make up as referring to a truth-value. Then, for any event E and set of events X, $g_{GP}(E, X)$ would be T if $E \in X$, and would be F otherwise.

The resulting theory would both have a fully compositional semantics and validate exactly the right inferences. Moreover, it would do a much better job than Davidson's theory of matching the apparent syntax of natural language.

Bibliography

James C. Abbott, *Sets, Lattices and Boolean Algebras.* Boston: Allyn & Bacon, 1960.

J. L. Ackrill, *Aristotle the Philosopher.* London: Oxford University Press, 1981.

Jon Barwise, 'The Situation in Logic—III: Sets and the Axiom of Foundation' (Stanford: Center for the Study of Language and Information). *In* Alex Wilkie, ed., *Logic Colloquium '84.* Amsterdam: North-Holland Publ., 1985.

Jon Barwise and John Perry, *Situations and Attitudes.* Cambridge, Massachusetts: MIT Press, 1983.

Ermanno Bencivenga, Free Logics. *In* D. Gabby and F. Guenthner, eds., *Handbook of Philosophical Logic, Vol. III: Alternatives to Classical Logic.* Dordrecht: Reidel, 1986.

Merrie Bergmann, Logic and Sortal Incorrectness . *Review of Metaphysics*, 1977, **31**, 61–79.

Merrie Bergmann, Presupposition in Two Dimensions. *Journal of Philosophical Logic*, 1981, **10**, 27–53.

E. W. Beth, *The Foundations of Mathematics.* Amsterdam: North-Holland Publ., 1968.

Philotheus Boehner, *Ockham's Philosophical Writings.* Edinburgh: Nelson, 1957.

I. M. Bocheński, *A History of Formal Logic.* Notre Dame, Indiana: University of Notre Dame Press, 1961.

D. A. Bochvar, On a Three-Valued Logical Calculus and Its Application to the Analysis of the Paradoxes (1937). Merrie Bergmann, trans. *History and Philosophy of Logic*, 1981, **2** 87–112.

Laurence Bonjour, The Coherence Theory of Empirical Knowledge. *Philosophical Studies*, 1976, **30**, 281–312.

James Cargile, *Paradoxes: A Study in Form and Predication.* London: Cambridge University Press, 1979.

Rudolf Carnap, Carnap's Intellectual Autobiography. *In* Paul A. Schilpp, ed., *The Philosophy of Rudolf Carnap.* LaSalle, Illinois: Open Court, 1963.

Rudolf Carnap, *Introduction to Semantics.* Cambridge, Massachusetts: Harvard University Press, 1942.

Rudolf Carnap, *Meaning and Necessity.* Chicago: University of Chicago Press, 1947.

Rudolf Carnap, Meaning Postulates (initially published in 1952). *In Meaning and Necessity.* Chicago: University of Chicago Press, 1956.

Rudolf Carnap, *The Logical Syntax of Language* (initially published in 1934). London: Routledge, 1964.
Noam Chomsky, On Certain Properties of Grammar. *Information and Control*, 1959, **2**, 137–167.
Noam Chomsky, *Aspects of the Theory of Syntax*. Cambridge, Massachusetts: MIT Press, 1965.
Noam Chomsky, Formal Properties of Grammars. *In* R. Duncan Luce *et al.*, eds., *Readings in Mathematical Psychology*, Vol. II. New York: Wiley, 1965.
Alonzo Church, *Introduction to Mathematical Logic*, Vol I. Princeton, New Jersey: Princeton University Press, 1956.
Gregory Currie, *Frege: An Introduction to His Philosophy*. Sussex: Harvester, 1981.
Haskell B. Curry, *Foundations of Mathematical Logic*. New York: McGraw-Hill, 1963.
Donald Davidson, Theories of Meaning and Learnable Languages. *In* Y. Bar-Hillel, ed., *Logic, Methodology, and the Philosophy of Science*. Amsterdam: North-Holland Publ., 1964.
Donald Davidson, Causal Relations. *Journal of Philosophy*, 1967, **64**, 691–703.
Donald Davidson, The Logical Form of Action Sentences. *In* N. Rescher, ed., *The Logic of Decision and Action*. Pittsburgh: Pittsburgh University Press, 1967.
Martin Davis, *Computability and Unsolvability*. New York: McGraw-Hill, 1958.
Enrique Delacruz, Factives and Propositional Level Constructions (initially published in 1972). *In* Barbara Partee, *Montague Grammar*. New York: Academic Press, 1976.
Randall R. Dipert, Set-Theoretic Representations of Ordered Pairs and Their Adequacy for the Logic of Relations. *Canadian Journal of Philosophy*, 1982, **12**, 353–374.
David R. Dowty, Robert E. Wall, and Stanley Peters, *Introduction to Montague Semantics*. Dordrecht: Reidel, 1981.
Michael Dummett, *Elements of Intuitionism*. Oxford: Clarendon, 1977.
Michael Dummett, The Philosophical Basis of Intuitionistic Logic (initially published 1973), The Reality of the Past (1969), Truth (1959). *In Truth and Other Enigmas*. Cambridge, Massachusetts: Harvard University Press, 1978.
George Epstein, ed., *Multiple-Valued Logic*. Dordrecht: Reidel, 1976.
Hartry Field, Logic, Meaning, and Conceptual Role. *Journal of Philosophy*, 1977, **74**, 379–409.
Kit Fine, First-Order Modal Theories III—Facts. *Synthese*, 1982, **53**, 43–122.
Gottlob Frege, *Begriffsschrift* (initially published in 1879). *In* Jean van Heijenoot, *From Frege to Gödel*. Cambridge, Massachusetts: Harvard University Press, 1967.
Gottlob Frege, *Grundgesetze der Arithmetik*. Jena: Verlag Hermann Pohle. Vol. I published in 1893, Vol. II published in 1903.
Gottlob Frege, On Sense and Reference (initially published in 1892). *In* Peter Geach and Max Black, eds., *Translations from the Philosophical Writings of Gottlob Frege*. Oxford: Blackwell, second edition, 1966.
Peter Geach, Teleological Explanation. *In* S. Körner, ed., *Explanation*. Oxford: Blackwell, 1975.
Gerhard Gentzen, Untersuchungen über das logische Schliessen. *Mathematische Zeitschrift*, 1934-1935, **39**, 176–210, 405–431.
L. Goddard and Richard Routley, *The Logic of Significance and Context*. Edinburgh: Scottish Academic Press, 1973.
M. Gross and A. Lentin, *Introduction to Formal Grammar*. London: Allen and Unwin, 1970.
Sorën Halldén, *The Logic of Nonsense*. Uppsala: Universitets Arskrift, 1949.
Paul Halmos, *Naive Set Theory*. Princeton, New Jersey: van Nostrand, 1960.
D. W. Hamlyn, *Metaphysics*. London: Cambridge University Press, 1984.
Leon Henkin, The Completeness of the First-Order Functional Calculus. *Journal of Symbolic Logic*, 1949, **14**, 159–166.
Hans G. Herzberger, Dimensions of Truth. *Journal of Philosophical Logic*, 1973, **2**, 535–556.
Hans G. Herzberger, Canonical Superlanguages. *Journal of Philosophical Logic*, 1975, **4**, 45–65.
Jaakko Hintikka, Semantics for Propositional Attitudes. *In Models for Modality*. Dordrecht: Reidel, 1969.

Jaakko Hintikka, *Time and Necessity*. London: Oxford University Press, 1973.

G. E. Hughes and M. J. Cresswell, *An Introduction to Modal Logic*. London: Methuen, 1968.

Stanisław Jáskowski, Investigations into the System of Intuitionist Logic (initially published in 1936). *In* Storrs McCall, ed., *Polish Logic, 1920–1939*. Oxford: Clarendon, 1967.

R. E. Jennings, A Utilitarian Semantics for Deontic Logic. *Journal of Philosophical Logic*, 1974, **3**, 445–456.

H. W. B. Joseph, *An Introduction to Logic*. Oxford: Clarendon, second edition, 1916.

Donald Kalish, Semantics. *In* Paul Edwards, ed., *Encyclopaedia of Philosophy*. New York: Macmillan, 1967.

Hans Kamp, Two Theories about Adjectives. *In* Edward L. Keenan, ed., *Formal Semantics of Natural Language*. London: Cambridge University Press, 1975.

David Kaplan, Quantifying In. *In* Donald Davidson and Jaakko Hintikka, eds., *Words and Objections*. Dordrecht: Reidel, 1969.

Lauri Karttunen, Some Observations on Factivity. *Papers in Linguistics*, 1971, **4**, 55–69.

Lauri Karttunen, Presuppositions of Compound Sentences. *Linguistic Inquiry*, 1973, **4**, 169–193.

Jaegwon Kim, Causation, Nomic Subsumption, and the Concept of Event. *Journal of Philosophy*, 1973, **70**, 217–236.

C. A. S. Kiparsky and R. P. V. Kiparsky, Fact. *In* M. Bierwisch and K. E. Heidolph, eds., *Progress in Linguistics*. The Hague: Mouton, 1970.

S. C. Kleene, On a Notation for Ordinal Numbers. *Journal of Symbolic Logic*, 1938, **3**, 150–155.

S. C. Kleene, *Introduction to Metamathematics*. Amsterdam: North-Holland Publ., 1959.

William Kneale and Martha Kneale, *The Development of Logic*. Oxford: Clarendon, 1962.

Saul Kripke, Semantical Analysis of Intuitionistic Logic, I. *In* J. N. Crossley and M. Dummett, eds., *Formal Systems and Recursive Functions, II*. Amsterdam: North-Holland Publ., 1965.

Saul Kripke, Is There a Problem with Substitutional Quantification? *In* G. Evans and J. McDowell, eds., *Truth and Meaning*. London: Oxford University Press, 1976.

Hugues Leblanc and Richmond Thomason, Completeness Theorems for Some Presupposition-Free Logics. *Fundamenta Mathematicae*, 1968, **62**, 125–164.

R. B. Lees, The Grammar of English Nominalizations. *International Journal of American Linguistics*, 1960, Part II, 26.

Stephen C. Levinson, *Pragmatics*. London: Cambridge University Press, 1983.

David Lewis, Counterpart Theory and Quantified Modal Logic. *Journal of Philosophy*, 1968, **65**, 113–126.

Seymour Lipschutz, *Schaum's Outline of Theory and Problems of Set Theory and Related Topics*. New York: Schaum, 1964.

Michael J. Loux, The Problem of Universals. *In Universals and Particulars*. Garden City, New York: Doubleday, 1970.

Michael J. Loux, The Ontology of William of Ockham. *In Ockham's Theory of Terms, Part 1 of Ockham's Summa Logicae*. Notre Dame, Indiana: University of Notre Dame Press, 1974.

Jan Łukasiewicz, *Aristotle's Syllogistic* (initially published in 1943). London: Oxford University Press, second edition, 1957.

Jan Łukasiewicz, On 3-Valued Logic (initially published in 1920), On Determinism (1923), Philosophical Remarks on Many-Valued Systems of Propositional Logic (1930). *In* Storrs McCall, ed., *Polish Logic, 1920–1939*. Oxford: Clarendon, 1967.

Jan Łukasiewicz and Alfred Tarski, Untersuchungen über den Aussagenkalkül. *Comptes Rendus des Séances de la Société des Sciences et des Lettres de Varsovie*, 1930, Classe III, **23**, 30–50.

William Lycan, *Logical Form in Natural Language*. Cambridge, Massachusetts: MIT Press, 1984.

John Lyons, Logical Semantics. In *Semantics*, Chapter 6, Vol. I. London: Cambridge University Press, 1977.

John N. Martin, A Many-Valued Semantics for Category Mistakes. *Synthese*, 1975, **31**, 63–83.

John N. Martin, A Syntactic Characterization of Kleene's Strong Connectives. *Zeitschrift für Mathematische Logik und Grundlagen der Mathematik*, 1975, **21**, 181–184.

John N. Martin, Facts and The Semantics of Gerunds. *Journal of Philosophical Logic*, 1975, **4**, 439–454.

John N. Martin, Some Misconceptions in the Critique of Semantic Presupposition. *Theoretical Linguistics*, 1979, **6**, 235–282.

John N. Martin, Facts and Events as Semantic Constructs. *Theoretical Linguistics*, 1981, **8**, 259–285.

John N. Martin, Epistemic Semantics for Classical and Intuitionistic Logic. *Notre Dame Journal of Formal Logic*, 1984, **25**, 105–116.

John N. Martin, The Semantics of Frege's *Grundgesetze*. *History and Philosophy of Logic*, 1984, **5**, 143–176.

John N. Martin, Some Formal Properties of Indirect Semantics. *Theoretical Linguistics*, 1985, **12**, 1–32.

Robert L. Martin, ed., *The Paradox of the Liar*. New Haven; Connecticut: Yale University Press, 1970.

Robert L. Martin, *Recent Essays on Truth and the Liar Paradox*. Oxford: Clarendon, 1984.

R. M. Martin, Facts: What They Are and What They Are Not. *American Philosophical Quarterly*, 1967, **4**, 269–280.

Benson Mates, *Stoic Logic*. Berkeley: University of California Press, 1961; first edition, *The Logic of the Stoa* (1953).

Robert K. Meyer and Karel Lambert, Universally Free Logic and Standard Quantification Theory. *Journal of Symbolic Logic*, 1968, **33**, 8–26.

Richard Montague, On the Nature of Certain Philosophical Entities (initially published in 1960), Pragmatics (1968), Pragmatics and Intensional Logic (1970), Universal Grammar (1970). *In* Richmond Thomason, ed., *Formal Philosophy*. New Haven, Connecticut: Yale University Press, 1974.

Ernest Moody, *Truth and Consequence in Medieval Logic*. Amsterdam: North-Holland Publ., 1953.

Charles Grady Morgan and Francis J. Pelletier, Some Notes Concerning Fuzzy Logics. *Linguistics and Philosophy*, 1977, **1**, 167–177.

Charles W. Morris, Foundations of the Theory of Signs. *In* Otto Neurath, Rudolf Carnap, and Charles Morris, eds., *International Encyclopaedia of Unified Sciences*. Chicago: University of Chicago Press, 1939.

Yiannis N. Moschovakis, *Elementary Induction on Abstract Structures*. Amsterdam: North-Holland Publ., 1974.

Frederick J. Newmeyer, *Linguistics in America*. New York: Academic Press, 1980.

Arthur Pap, *Semantics and Necessary Truth*. New Haven, Connecticut: Yale University Press, 1958.

Günter Patzig, *Aristotle's Theory of the Syllogism*. Dordrecht: Reidel, 1968.

D. Prawitz, *Natural Deduction: A Proof Theoretic Study*. Stockholm: Almqvist and Wiksell, 1965.

Hilary Putnam, The Meaning of 'Meaning'. *In Mind, Language, and Reality*. London: Cambridge University Press, 1975.

W. V. O. Quine, *Mathematical Logic* (initially published in 1940). New York: Harper, revised edition, 1951.

W. V. O. Quine, *Word and Object*. Cambridge, Massachusetts: MIT Press, 1960.

W. V. O. Quine, Notes on the Theory of Reference (1953). In *From a Logical Point of View*. New York: Harper, 1961.

W. V. O. Quine, On What There Is (1948). In *From a Logical Point of View.* Cambridge, Massachusetts: Harvard University Press, second edition, 1961.

W. V. O. Quine, Two Dogmas of Empiricism (1953). In *From a Logical Point of View.* Cambridge, Massachusetts: Harvard University Press, 1961.

W. V. O. Quine, Paradoxes. *Scientific American,* 1962, **206**, 84–95; reprinted in *The Ways of Paradox.* New York: Random House, 1966.

W. V. O. Quine, Russell's Ontological Development. *Journal of Philosophy,* 1966, **63**, 657–666.

W. V. O. Quine, *Set Theory and Its Logic* (initially published in 1963). Cambridge, Massachusetts: Harvard University Press, revised edition, 1969.

W. V. O. Quine, *Philosophy of Logic.* New York: Prentice Hall, 1970.

Nicholas Rescher, *Many-Valued Logic.* New York: McGraw-Hill, 1969.

Nicholas Rescher, *The Coherence Theory of Truth.* Oxford: Clarendon, 1973.

J. B. Rosser and A. R. Turquette, *Many-Valued Logics.* Amsterdam: North-Holland Publ., 1952.

Richard Routley, Some Things Do Not Exist. *Notre Dame Journal of Formal Logic,* 1966, **7**, 251–276.

Bertrand Russell, *A Critical Exposition of the Philosophy of Leibniz.* London: Cambridge University Press, 1900.

Bertrand Russell, Descriptions, Chapter XVI. *Introduction to Mathematical Philosophy.* London: Allen and Unwin, 1919.

Bertrand Russell, *An Inquiry into Meaning and Truth.* London: Allen and Unwin, 1940.

Bertrand Russell, On Denoting. *Mind* (initially published in 1905), 'The Philosophy of Logical Atomism' (1918). *In* Robert C. Marsh, ed., *Logic and Knowledge.* London: Allen and Unwin, 1956.

Bertrand Russell, *Principles of Mathematics* (initially published in 1903). London: Allen and Unwin, second edition, 1956.

Gilbert Ryle, Categories. *In* A. Flew, ed., *Logic and Language* Oxford: Blackwell, 1966.

Kenneth M. Sayre, *Plato's Analytic Method.* Chicago: University of Chicago Press, 1969.

Dana Scott, Advice on Modal Logic. *In* Karel Lambert, ed., *Philosophical Problems in Logic.* Dordrecht: Reidel, 1970.

Dana Scott, Does Many-Valued Logic Have Any Use? *In* S. Körner, ed., *Philosophy of Logic.* Oxford: Blackwell, 1976.

Henry M. Sheffer, A Set of Five Independent Postulates for Boolean Algebras. *Transactions of the American Mathematical Society,* 1913, **14**, 481–488.

T. J. Smiley, Sense without Denotation. *Analysis,* 1960, **20**, 125–135.

Robert C. Stalnaker, Possible Worlds. *Nous,* 1976, **10**, 65–75.

P. F. Strawson, On Referring. *Mind,* 1950, **59**, 320–344.

P. F. Strawson, *Introduction to Logical Theory.* London: Methuen, 1952.

P. F. Strawson, Identifying Reference and Truth-Values. *Theoria,* 1964, **64**, 96–118.

Alfred Tarski, The Semantic Conception of Truth. *Philosophy and Phenomenological Research,* 1944, **4**, 341–375.

Alfred Tarski, Contributions to the Theory of Models. *Indagationes Mathematicae,* 1954, **16**, 572–588.

Alfred Tarski, Foundations of the Calculus of Systems (initially published in 1935), The Concept of Truth in Formalized Languages (1931). In *Logic, Semantics, Metamathematics.* Oxford: Clarendon, 1956.

Alfred Tarski, Truth and Proof. *Scientific American,* 1969, **194**, 63–77.

Neil Tennant, *Natural Logic.* Edinburgh: University of Edinburgh, 1978.

Richmond H. Thomason, Modal Logic and Metaphysics. *In* Karel Lambert, ed., *The Logical Way of Doing Things.* New Haven, Connecticut: Yale University Press, 1969.

Richmond H. Thomason, Indeterminist Time and Truth-Value Gaps. *Theoria*, 1970, **36**, 264–281.

Richmond H. Thomason, A Semantics of Sortal Incorrectness. *Journal of Philosophical Logic*, 1972, **1**, 209–258.

Robert G. Turnbull, Ockham's Nominalistic Logic. *The New Scholasticism*, 1962, **36**, 313–329.

Alasdair Urquhart, Many-Valued Logic, Chapter III.2. *In* D. Gabbay and F. Guenthner, *Handbook of Philosophical Logic*, Vol. III. Dordrecht: Reidel, 1986.

D. van Dalen, *Sets: Naive, Axiomatic, and Applied.* New York: Pergamon, 1978.

Bas C. van Fraassen, Singular Terms, Truth-Value Gaps, and Free Logic. *Journal of Philosophy*, 1966, **63**, 481–495.

Bas C. van Fraassen, Meaning Relations among Predicates. *Nous*, 1967, **1**, 161–179.

Bas C. van Fraassen, Facts and Tautological Entailment. *Journal of Philosophy*, 1969, **66**, 477–487.

Bas C. van Fraassen, *Formal Semantics and Logic.* New York: Macmillan, 1971.

Robert Wall, *Introduction to Mathematical Linguistics.* New York: Prentice-Hall, 1972.

John Roy Wallace, *Philosophical Grammar.* Ph.D. dissertation, Stanford University, 1964.

Julius Weinberg, *Abstraction, Relation, Induction.* Madison: University of Wisconsin Press, 1965.

Richard B. White, Natural Deduction in the Łukasiewicz Logics. *Proceedings of the 10th International Symposium on Multiple-Valued Logic (I.E.E.E.)*, 1980.

Alfred North Whitehead and Bertrand Russell, *Principia Mathematica*, Vol. I (initially published in 1910). London: Cambridge University Press, second edition, 1927.

Raymond L. Wilder, *Introduction to the Foundations of Mathematics* (initially published in 1952). New York: Wiley, second edition, 1965.

Ludwig Wittgenstein, *Tractatus Logico-Philosophicus* (initially published in 1918). *In* D. F. Pears and B. F. McGuiness, eds. London: Routledge and Kegan Paul, 1961.

L. Zadeh, Fuzzy Sets. *Information and Control*, 1965, **8**, 338–353.

Index

B

C

D

E

J

K

L

M

N

Q

T